LOVE DISCONSOLED
Meditations on Christian Charity

Few concepts are more central to ethics than love, but none is more subject to false consolation. This book explores several theological, philosophical, and literary accounts of love, focusing on how it relates to matters such as self-interest and self-sacrifice, and invulnerability and immortality. Timothy Jackson first considers key aspects of what the Bible says about love, then he further examines the meaning of love and sacrifice through a close reading of novels by Fitzgerald and Hemingway. Lastly, he evaluates how love constrains, and is constrained by, other traditional moral concepts.

Throughout, Jackson defends the moral priority of what the Christian tradition calls "*agape*." He argues that a proper understanding of agapic love rejects both moral relativism and the comfort of believing that good people cannot be harmed, or that God causally necessitates every historical action and event. When love is thus disconsoled, it neither fears death nor despises life.

TIMOTHY P. JACKSON is Associate Professor in the Department of Theology at the University of Notre Dame, and he has previously held posts at Yale, Stanford, and Emory Universities. He has published articles in the *Journal of Religious Ethics*, *The Thomist*, *Faith and Philosophy*, *Christianity and Literature*, and the *Journal for Peace and Justice Studies*.

CAMBRIDGE STUDIES IN RELIGION AND
CRITICAL THOUGHT

Edited by
WAYNE PROUDFOOT (*Columbia University*)
JEFFREY L. STOUT (*Princeton University*)
NICHOLAS WOLTERSTORFF (*Yale Univeersity*)

Current events confirm the need to understand religious ideas and institutions
critically, yet radical doubts have been raised about how to proceed and about
the ideal of critical thought itself. Meanwhile, some prominent scholars have
urged that we turn the tables, and view modern society as the object of criticism
and a religious tradition as the basis for critique. Cambridge Studies in Religion
and Critical Thought is a series of books intended to address the interaction of
critical thinking and religious traditions in this context of uncertainty and
conflicting claims. The series takes up questions such as the following, either by
reflecting on them philosophically or by pursuing their ramifications in studies
of specific figures and movements: Is a coherent critical perspective on religion
desirable or even possible? What sort of relationship to religious traditions
ought a critic to have? What, if anything, is worth saving from the Enlightenment legacy or from critics of religion like Hume and Feuerbach? The answers
offered, while varied, uniformly constitute distinguished, philosophically informed, and critical analyses of particular religious topics.

Other titles published in the series

LOVE DISCONSOLED

Meditations on Christian Charity

TIMOTHY P. JACKSON

University of Notre Dame

CAMBRIDGE
UNIVERSITY PRESS

CAMBRIDGE UNIVERSITY PRESS
Cambridge, New York, Melbourne, Madrid, Cape Town, Singapore,
São Paulo, Delhi, Dubai, Tokyo, Mexico City

Cambridge University Press
The Edinburgh Building, Cambridge CB2 8RU, UK

Published in the United States of America by Cambridge University Press, New York

www.cambridge.org
Information on this title: www.cambridge.org/9780521158787

© Cambridge University Press 1999

First published 1999
First paperback edition 2010

A catalogue record for this publication is available from the British Library

Library of Congress Cataloguing in Publication Data

Jackson, Timothy P. (Timothy Patrick)
Love disconsoled: meditations on Christian charity / Timothy P. Jackson.
p   cm. – (Cambridge studies in religion and critical thought; 7)
Includes bibliographical references.
ISBN 0521 55493 4 (hardback)
1. Agape.   I. Title.   II. Series.
BV4639.J33   1999
241'.4–dc21   99–12129   CIP

ISBN 978-0-521-55493-0 Hardback
ISBN 978-0-521-15878-7 Paperback

To Richard Rorty and to the memory of Paul Ramsey

How is one to connect the realism which must involve a clear-eyed contemplation of the misery and evil of the world with a sense of an uncorrupted good without the latter idea becoming the merest consolatory dream?　　　　　　　　　　　　　　　　　Iris Murdoch

Religion in so far as it is a source of consolation is a hindrance to true faith: in this sense atheism is a purification.

Unconsoled affliction is necessary. There must be no consolation – no apparent consolation. Ineffable consolation then comes down.
　　　　　　　　　　　　　　　　　　　　　　　　　Simone Weil

Contents

Figures

Preface

I went from Louisville to Princeton in 1972 to read American literature with Carlos Baker; I stayed to major in philosophy under Richard Rorty. Also taking courses in religion, I was impressed by the work of Paul Ramsey and Gene Outka on Christian love, as well as by Malcolm Diamond on Jewish hope, but this left me with a problem. With a medieval largeness of spirit, Ramsey articulated the transcendental faith that had excited me as a confused highschool senior trying to read Søren Kierkegaard. In Rorty, however, I found a kindly genius who had seen through the dogmatism and false consolation of much philosophy and theology, yet who had managed to fight off misanthropy and despair. His ascetic irony that would worship nothing, not even ourselves, often seemed the best we could hope for in a twentieth century bloodied by unspeakable enthusiasms. And so it was with a rather schizophrenic mindset that I went on to graduate school at Yale in 1976.

As a doctoral student, I had the good fortune to work closely with Rulon Wells in philosophy and with Margaret Farley and Gene Outka, who had migrated northward, in religious studies. These teachers excited me with a sense of how philosophy and theology might make progress in answering contemporary ethical questions. Yet I was simultaneously compelled by Feuerbach, Marx, and Nietzsche as pioneers of a reductive approach in which philosophy and theology come to an end: God and the self are seen as projections of social power and/or powerlessness. My teenage fascination with Kierkegaard lingered as incompatible with such deconstruction, but I occasionally wrote essays speculating on "The Nonexistence of Facts," "The Ubiquity of Language," and "'Deity' as a Bad Idea." I continued to think of *agape* and *askesis* as flatly incompatible – to think of Ramsey and Rorty as two antithetical fathers one of whom had to be slain.

This book is a consequence of a change of heart, a gradual recognition that one test of moral intelligence is, in Fitzgerald's words, "the ability to hold two opposed ideas in the mind at the same time, and still retain the ability to function."[1] What once seemed a primal split in my intellectual and emotional allegiances now seems a constructive conversation. *Agape*, considered on its own terms, actually requires something like the pragmatist's *askesis*, I now believe. Love of the neighbor in time and for her own sake, calls on us to uncouple Christian charity[2] from several notions to which it is traditionally attached: for instance, immortality as a heavenly reward and certainty and invulnerability as earthly ideals (see chapter 5). To be sure, I defend here a view of Christian virtue that is incompatible in basic ways with Rorty's secularity. The "purity of heart" and "passion of the infinite" against which he would "immunize" us in order to avoid cruelty,[3] I take to be what permits us to recognize and appreciate the finite world (including our fallible selves) for what they are. Even so, premodern *agape* and postmodern *askesis*, Ramsey and Rorty, no longer represent for me a pure antagonism, a simple either/or. Instead they stand, together, as a call both to champion and to chasten Christian love. (Seeing God as the righteous Father of both men makes it unnecessary to attempt to slay either.) Hence these pages.

Chapter 1 considers key aspects of what the Bible says about love. I do not attempt to argue from within a dominant exegetical or dogmatic tradition to establish some one position called Christian "orthodoxy." True belief is a basic concern, but moral wisdom is more like a compound produced by chemical reactions than like a pure element gotten by boiling things down or precipitating something out. The Biblical injunction to "make love your aim" (1 Cor. 14:1, RSV) is both my topic and my criterion, yet the character of love is rich, and what precisely it entails can only be worked out *in media res* and *a posteriori*. An excellent way to see the meaning of Christian love is to examine detailed narratives of individual lives. Thus chapter 2 is a close reading of two novels and novelists. F. Scott Fitzgerald's *Tender Is the Night* and Ernest Hemingway's *The Garden of Eden* offer very different conclusions about the value

---

[1] F. Scott Fitzgerald, "The Crack-Up," collected in *The Crack-Up*, ed. by Edmund Wilson (New York: New Directions, 1964), p. 69.

[2] As I make clear below, when "love" refers to *agape*, the self-giving love of God and neighbor, I often use it interchangeably with "charity." The English word "love," rather like the Latin "*amor*," has other meanings, of course, denoting both sexual desire (*Venus*) and friendship (*amicitia*). "Charity" is similarly multivalent, but in these pages it usually refers to a stalwart theological virtue rather than, more narrowly, to supererogatory philanthropy or institutional donation.

[3] Rorty, *Achieving Our Country* (Cambridge and London: Harvard University Press, 1998), pp. 119 and 123.

of desire, health, peace, and especially prudence. Neither author is confessionally religious, but together they and their works represent enduring alternative visions of love and sacrifice. In meditating on charity, I return again and again to the contrasting metaphors they provide.

As important as stories are, we cannot see what love means without also seeing how it constrains, and is constrained by, other traditional moral concepts. Some general conceptual truths must be explored, so I turn in chapter 3 to four notable theorists of the five kinds of love: Saint Augustine and Sigmund Freud, Simone Weil and Edward Vacek. Contemporary accounts of the meaning of *eros* and *agape* still stand in the former pair's shadow, even as the latter pair have penned some of the most challenging recent analyses of self-denial and friendship. In chapter 4, I look at two notions especially important in Biblical ethical discourse: abomination and liberation. By relating these extremes to love, as well as to familiar ethical ideas like freedom and duty, I hope to gesture toward the coherence of the moral life. I aim throughout not at a strict theory of *agape*, a closed system of co-implying principles and propositions, but rather at an eclectic yet captivating gallery of pictures. The pictures will be specific to Western culture for the most part, but the cumulative effect will, I trust, be edifying to Christians and nonChristians alike.

To be fully edifying, an ethic of love must clarify its relation to both traditional theology and secular philosophy. One way to do this is to acknowledge at the outset one's epistemological commitments. As I construe it, *agape* presupposes some form of metaphysical realism: if love is genuinely other-regarding, there must be others who are actually centers of value whom we are bound to recognize and affirm. Love does not merely bestow value on the neighbor, it also recognizes value in the neighbor (a value created by God, not essentially by us) and seeks to serve that value as something real. There are limits on our freedom and invention, most conspicuously other individuals but including groups, traditions, the natural world, and one's own nature. Inspiring and sustaining both the limits and the liberty is the love of God, both God's "*quellende Liebe*" (Luther) for us and our responsive love for God.

Agapic realism holds that humbling oneself, Christlike "in the form of a slave" (Phil. 2:7), requires a self-emptying orientation toward the other, whose reality, need, and otherness count for everything and must therefore not be absorbed into one's own consciousness (in the manner of idealism) or one's own cultural linguistic practices (in the manner of postmodernism). Even in defending realism, however, an ethic of love must be careful to recognize its own finitude and fallibility. Love is most compatible with a self-criticism that subjects key convictions, including the traditional Christian doctrine of immortality, to rigorous questioning. This "scepticism" is not global, as if one could put all allegiances in doubt simultaneously, for *agape* itself is bedrock. But charity, properly conceived, does entail abandonment of "foundationalist" philosophies and theologies that claim incorrigibility. Such certitude is a too easy consolation.[4]

This does not leave us with pure irony or despair (chapter 5), I hasten to add. We may be moved by charity to sacrifice real and important goods, including a cherished self-understanding, as with Abraham (chapter 6). But a steadfast love never falls below justice, never consents to "dirty its hands" by betraying innocent life (chapter 7). Love sometimes rises above justice, especially when the latter is defined exclusively in terms of market contract or achieved merit, but this is an act of faith that transcends all appraisive calculations of reward and punishment. A consistent charity is its own reward, I argue, and when it honestly acknowledges human foible and compassionately addresses human suffering, it can dispense with the support of abstract theodicies and anthropodicies. These are false comforts that tend to blind us to reality. Love disconsoled is willing to bear the cross, then, come what may – even as did the Son of Man. In doing so, however, it may trust that it is not without the ineffable support of a Higher Power.

I dedicate this work to Paul Ramsey (RIP) and Richard Rorty, two very different yet ultimately sympathetic mentors. Several institutional affiliations also helped make this volume possible. During the fall of 1989, I spent two months at The Center of Theological Inquiry in Princeton working on what eventually became chapters 2 and 4. For the whole of the academic year 1992–1993, I was a fellow at The Whitney Humanities Center at Yale, where I began to think through the disconsolation of love in more detail. While teaching at Emory, I have profited immensely from the community of faith and scholarship that is The Candler School of Theology. Finally I would like to thank Wayne Proudfoot, Jeffrey Stout, and Nicholas Wolterstorff, the editors of the

---

[4] Jeffrey Stout has suggested that the idea of *kenosis* better captures the spiritual movement involved in realism, whereas *askesis* better captures the spiritual movement involved in the willingness to forego insistence on immortality (correspondence of August 6, 1998). This paragraph is beholden to his insights.

Religion and Critical Thought series; Kevin Taylor, the religious studies editor, Camilla Erskine and Joanne Hill, all of Cambridge University Press, for invaluable advice on how to improve this manuscript. Jeffrey Stout, in particular, suggested a way of reorganizing my material into a more coherent case for strong *agape*; his help in reconstructing the argument of chapter 7 was the final piece of the puzzle.

Versions of four chapters herein have appeared elsewhere; the prehistory of these pages, now revised and expanded, is as follows. Chapter 2 originally appeared in *Christianity and Literature*, vol. 39, no. 4 (Summer 1990): 423–441; chapter 4 in *Soundings*, vol. 76, no. 4 (Winter 1993): 487–523; chapter 6 in *The Annual of the Society of Christian Ethics*, vol. 17 (1997): 97–119. I am indebted to the editors and publishers involved for agreeing to the republication of this material. Chapter 5 is a revised and expanded version of the article "The Disconsolation of Theology: Irony, Cruelty, and Putting Charity First," which was originally published in the *Journal of Religious Ethics*, vol. 20, no. 1 (Spring 1992): 1–35. Copyright © 1992 by the Journal of Religious Ethics, Inc. Used by permission of the publisher.

I gratefully acknowledge the Metropolitan Museum of Art in New York, the Speed Museum in Louisville, and the Yale Center for British Art in New Haven for permission to reproduce figures 1, 2 and 3, respectively.

June 1999 TIMOTHY P. JACKSON

CHAPTER I

Biblical keys to love

Let all that you do be done in love [*agape*].

i Cor. 16:14[1]

I. LOVE IN HEBREW AND CHRISTIAN SCRIPTURE

What do I mean by "love," and how/by whom is it to be practiced? As a
Christian, I continue to look to the Bible as a touchstone for ethics,
including an account of love, even as the Bible itself looks to the
character and deeds of God. The first of the Ten Commandments,
given by God to Moses and recorded in Hebrew Scripture, reads: "You
shall have no other gods before [or besides] me" (Exod. 20:3). This
categorical insistence on monotheism is elaborated in Deuteronomy
6:4–5: "Hear, O Israel: The Lord is our God, the Lord alone. You shall
love the Lord your God with all your heart, and with all your soul, and
with all your might." Since it deals with humanity's relation to Deity,
this might be called the vertical axis of ethics, and it is further expressed
in such additional commandments as "You shall not make wrongful use
of the name of the Lord your God" (Exod. 20:7). The horizontal axis is
captured in the second table of the Decalogue with such human-to-
human injunctions as "You shall not murder," "You shall not commit
adultery," "You shall not steal," etc. (Exod. 20:13ff.). These injunctions
are expanded on, in turn, in Leviticus 19:18: "You shall not take
vengeance or bear a grudge against any of your people, but you shall
love your neighbor as yourself: I am the Lord." The very heart of
Biblical ethics, then, is the conviction that *the integrity of the one God dictates*

[1] Unless otherwise noted, all Biblical quotations are from *The New Oxford Annotated Bible with the Apocrypha*, New Revised Standard Version (NRSV), ed. by Bruce M. Metzger and Roland E. Murphy (New York: Oxford University Press, 1991). I do occasionally cite the King James (KJ) and the Revised Standard Version (RSV), when these seem preferable for stylistic or other reasons. The KJ translates i Cor. 16:14: "Let all your things be done with charity."

I

a similar integrity in humanity and that this integrity takes the immediate form of love of God and neighbor.[2]

With the giving of the law on Sinai, God called Israel to participate in a special covenant, a covenant mandating that all Israelites reflect God's own holiness (see Lev. 19:1–2).[3] A central facet of that holiness is God's unmerited love for Israel, made palpable in God's delivering the chosen people from exile:

It was not because you were more numerous than any other people that the Lord set his heart on you and chose you – for you were the fewest of all peoples.

[2] The term *"ve-ahabta"* is used in both Leviticus 19 and Deuteronomy 6, my colleague Carol Newsom informs me, *"aheb"* being the common Old Testament verb for "to love," employed indistinguishably for God–Israel and Israel–God relations. *"Ahabah,"* the noun form, appears in contexts of friendship, sexual love, affection, and desire of various sorts, hence it may at times be closer to *"eros"* than to *"agape"* in New Testament Greek. (*"Ahabah"* is additionally used in treaty contexts, however, where it denotes the relationship between kings and their vassals and among vassals.) Referring to the Septuagint, William Klassen writes: "Greek *agapao* predominates as a translation of Heb *aheb* in the Pentateuch and in 1–3 Kingdoms; the Greek noun *agape* similarly serves to represent Heb *ahaba* in the majority of instances . . . The Greek verb *erao*, which can connote sexual love, is avoided altogether in the Pentateuch as a translation of Heb *aheb* (which can have the same connotations)." In the New Testament, "The verb *agapao* in Matt 19:19 and 22:37,39 occurs in citations of LXX." See Klassen, "Love (NT and Early Jewish Literature)," in *The Anchor Bible Dictionary*, (New York: Doubleday, 1992), vol. IV, pp. 381 and 385.

For its part, the Hebrew word *"'hesed"* (a noun with no verbal counterpart) has connotations of loyalty and solidarity, but in late Biblical and post-Biblical contexts it increasingly has connotations of graciousness and generosity. In Qumran Hebrew, it is often paired with a term for "compassionate love" (*"rahamim"*). So, as Newsom notes, *"'hesed"* significantly overlaps *"agape,"* but not entirely. There are secular and theological uses of *"'hesed"* in Hebrew, as well as distinctions between humanity's *"'hesed"* and God's. It is notable, nonetheless, that when Jeremiah has the Lord say to Israel, "I have loved you with an everlasting love; therefore I have continued my faithfulness to you" (31:3), as well as when Hosea has Yahweh say to Ephraim and Judah, "I desire steadfast love and not sacrifice" (6:6), the word translated "love" in both cases is *"'hesed."* The main point I would emphasize is that human love is derivative of the divine. As Karen Sakenfeld has summarized: "Even as God's *'hesed* manifested in forgiveness makes relationship possible at all, so God's *'hesed* manifested as care for the needy undergirds any human caring that makes for a just and peaceable world. From an OT point of view any human loyalty, kindness, love, or mercy (to refer . . . to the translation options for *'hesed*), is rooted ultimately in the loyalty, kindness, love, and mercy of God." See Katharine Doob Sakenfeld, "Love (OT)," in *The Anchor Bible Dictionary*, vol. IV (New York: Doubleday, 1992), p. 380. See also Sakenfeld, *The Meaning of Hesed in the Hebrew Bible* (Missoula: Scholars Press, 1978); and Gordon R. Clark, *The Word* "Hesed" *in the Hebrew Bible* (Sheffield: JSOT Press, 1993).

[3] The Holiness Code (Leviticus 17–26) applies distinctively to Jews and is not synonymous with the Ten Commandments, which are binding on all human beings. But the upshot of the law given on Sinai and of the Hebrew Bible generally is that Jews are to love as God loves and thus be established by God as "his holy people" (Deut. 28:9). Being a chosen people entails being set "high above all the nations of the earth" (Deut. 28:1), but the rigorous demands of this elevation are for purposes of example and more like a burden than a privilege. Israel is to "faithfully bring forth justice" (Isa. 42:3) and thereby be "a light to the nations" (Isa. 42:6), not a tyrant over them. (Cf. Luke 2:32 and John 1:4, 3:19, and 12:35–36, where Jesus is "a light" or "the light"; and Matthew 5:14, where Jesus designates the disciples as "the light of the world." Though the individuals bearing the title differ, the role or mission of "light" remains similar: to embody and teach the righteousness of the Lord.)

It was because the Lord loved you and kept the oath which he swore to your ancestors, that the Lord has brought you out with a mighty hand, and redeemed you from the house of slavery, from the hand of Pharaoh king of Egypt. (Deut. 7:7–8)

God's love provides the foundation, in turn, for the command to love God unreservedly and the command to love the neighbor as oneself:

Know therefore that the Lord your God is God, the faithful God who maintains covenant loyalty with those who love him and keep his commandments, to a thousand generations . . . (Deut. 7:9)

Because "I am the Lord your God, who brought you out of the land of Egypt, out of the house of slavery" (Exod. 20:2), an Israelite is to do two basic things: (1) avoid idolatrous attachments to other goods (including foreign gods), and (2) avoid belligerence, judgmentalism, or neglect toward fellow-Israelites. God's care for Israel is dependable; God sends the prophets to challenge and chastise Israel for its faithlessness, but God does not simply abrogate the original covenant (see, e.g., Jeremiah 30 and 31). The Israelites' obedience to God must be similarly unqualified, therefore, and their relations to one another must be ever-mindful of the mercy and protection God has shown to them as a people. A vital implication of this mindfulness should be practical assistance to the widow, the orphan, and others in special need. "Whoever is kind to the poor lends to the Lord, and will be repaid in full" (Prov. 19:17).

The central Hebrew pronouncements on love are explicitly echoed by Jesus in the Gospels. When asked by the Pharisee lawyer, "Teacher, which commandment in the law is greatest?," Jesus answers (Matt. 22:37–40): "You shall love the Lord your God with all your heart, and with all your soul, and with all your mind. This is the greatest and first commandment. And a second is like it: You shall love your neighbor as yourself. On these two commandments hang all the law and the prophets." It is often claimed that Jesus radicalizes in the New Testament the conception of love in the Old, and this is the case in some respects. Whereas "neighbor" usually means "coreligionist" in Hebrew Scripture, Jesus insists on a more universalist reading. In the parable of the Good Samaritan (Luke 10:29–37), for example, he clearly implies that the neighbor is not just a fellow-Israelite but anyone and everyone, especially someone who helps a stranger. Interestingly, Jesus calls the Samaritan "neighbor" not because he requires assistance but because he extends it unconditionally to an anonymous party in need: someone who has been beaten, robbed, and stripped and thus whose religious

and ethnic identity is uncertain.[4] This suggests that the point of the story
is not merely that *all* persons should *receive* love, as novel as that would
seem to Jesus's listeners (see Matt. 5:43–48, discussed below), but also
that *all* persons should *give* love. Jesus is no sectarian with respect to
either end of neighbor-love.

The debate rages on about the intended scope of Jesus's ministry and
message – Did he live and die for all, or is his a "limited atonement"? Do
believers respond freely in any sense, or is "election" irresistible? – and
each camp can plausibly cite Scripture to its purpose. There are texts on
both sides. For my part, I take a range of representative passages[5] to
imply that Jesus summons (but does not compel) all people to discipleship through the saving power of God's grace.[6] His gospel is both
taxing and inclusive; it relativizes religious, ethnic, racial, national,
familial, age, gender, and socio-economic differences in a general call to
willing service. "Truly I tell you, just as you did it to one of the least of
these who are members of my family, you did it to me" (Matt. 25:40).
Most tellingly, the resurrected Christ commissions his followers: "Go
therefore and make disciples of *all nations* . . . teaching *them* to obey
everything that I have commanded *you* . . . " (Matt. 28:19–20; emphasis
mine). Thus any account of Christian charity that would limit its
normativity to "the elect" or "the church" (in a restrictive sense) misses
the mark. Those outside of the existing community of the faithful will
find it more difficult to hear and appropriate the call to love, but the
vocation applies in principle to all, as both agents and patients. Since
"God is love" (1 John 4:8), charity is the métier of everyone made in
God's Image; this I take to be foundational to Jesus's "good news of the
kingdom of God."

Jesus's departure from traditional Hebrew teachings must not be
overstated. Parts of the Old Testament already suggest an inclusive
construal of neighbor-love, as when Leviticus 19:34 avers: "The alien
who resides with you shall be to you as the citizen among you; you shall
love the alien as yourself, for you were aliens in the land of Egypt: I am

---

[4] Conversations with Steven Kraftchick have helped me to see the significance of this more plainly.
[5] See, *inter alia*, Isaiah 53:4–6, Matthew 23:37 and 24:13–14, Mark 3:35 and 10:26–27, Luke 9:23–24,
John 3:16 and 8:38, Romans 5:18, Galatians 3:27–29, 1 Timothy 2:1–7, and 1 John 4:15–16.
[6] I am a universalist Arminian on matters of grace and free will. Jesus notes the need for a "place"
in the person for his word, but continues to call even his would-be murderers to "do what you
have heard from the Father" (John 8:37–38). For a sampling of the seventeenth-century debate
on these topics, see Jacob Arminius, "A Declaration" [1608], in *The Works of James (Jacob) Arminius*,
trans. by James Nichols, vol. I (London: Longman, Hurst, Rees, Orme, Brown, and Green, 1825),
pp. 516–706; and Christopher Ness, *An Antidote Against Arminianism* [1700] (Edmonton, Alberta:
Still Waters Revival Books, 1988).

the Lord your God." And the idea of the Image of God shared by every human creature (Genesis 1) clearly has universalist and egalitarian implications. Jesus himself says: "Do not think that I have come to abolish the law or the prophets; I have come not to abolish but to fulfill" (Matt. 5:17). If Jesus does not generally annul the Mosaic Law, however, his gospel nevertheless constitutes an appreciably radicalized Torah (cf. Luke 16:16).

Many places in Hebrew Scripture recommend mercy and forbearance; Proverbs 17:9, for instance, states: "He who forgives an offense seeks love, but he who repeats a matter alienates a friend" (RSV). Yet there is nothing in Moses or the prophets quite like Jesus's Sermon on the Mount in Matthew and Sermon on the Plain in Luke. At Matthew 5:38–48, Jesus says:

"You have heard that it was said, 'An eye for an eye and a tooth for a tooth' [cf. Exod. 21:23–24, Lev. 24:19–20, and Deut. 19:21]. But I say to you, Do not resist an evildoer. But if anyone strikes you on the right cheek, turn the other also; and if anyone wants to sue you and take your coat, give your cloak as well; and if anyone forces you to go one mile, go also the second mile. Give to everyone who begs from you, and do not refuse anyone who wants to borrow from you. "You have heard that it was said, 'You shall love your neighbor and hate your enemy.' But I say to you, Love your enemies and pray for those who persecute you, so that you may be children of your Father who is in heaven; for he makes his sun rise on the evil and on the good, and sends rain on the righteous and on the unrighteous. For if you love those who love you, what reward do you have? Do not even the tax collectors do the same? And if you greet only your brothers and sisters, what more are you doing than others? Do not even the Gentiles do the same? Be perfect, therefore, as your heavenly Father is perfect."

These words are not fundamentally at odds with the Hebrew Bible as a totality, but they do override the *lex talionis* and call for an extremely stringent life of charity.[7] The call is still directed at a collective body, but

---

[7] William Klassen, *Love of Enemies: The Way to Peace* (Philadelphia: Fortress Press, 1984), esp. chaps. 2 and 3, argues that even the command to love one's enemies has Jewish roots on which Jesus drew. Even so, Richard Hays rightly notes both continuity and discontinuity between Jesus and traditional Judaism. As Hays observes, "In most of the six antitheses [of the Sermon on the Mount], the teaching of Jesus constitutes an intensification – rather than an abrogation – of the requirements of the Law. The Law prohibits murder, but Jesus forbids even anger; the Law prohibits adultery, but Jesus forbids even lust. In the fifth antithesis (5:38–42), however, Jesus actually overrules the Torah (despite 5:17–18) . . . where Deuteronomy insists, 'Show no pity,' Jesus says, 'Do not resist an evildoer.' The Law's concern for maintaining stability and justice is supplanted by Jesus' concern to encourage nonviolent, long-suffering generosity on the part of those who are wronged. This extraordinary change of emphasis constitutes a paradigm shift that effectually undermines the Torah's teaching about just punishment for offenders." See Hays, *The Moral Vision of the New Testament* (San Francisco: HarperCollins, 1996), pp. 324–325.

now the body is a church that is to be formed out of all those who hear and obey God's Son rather than out of a single, preexisting ethnic group.[8]

In Matthew 5:21–37, Jesus intensifies traditional Hebrew teachings on killing, adultery, divorce, and oath-taking – insisting that inner intention is at least as important as outer behavior – and the degree to which he demands the sharing of possessions and openness to self-sacrifice is particularly striking in Luke. Even so, the most truly novel feature of Jesus's teaching is his assertion that he is the very presence of God with the authority to forgive sins (Luke 5:24). Jesus proclaims to Thomas (John 14:6 and cf. Matt. 11:27): "I am the way, and the truth, and the life. No one comes to the Father except through me." And the final commandment he gives to his disciples in John is not a reiteration of "love your neighbor *as yourself*," but "love one another *as I have loved you*" (John 15:12, emphasis mine; see also John 13:34). This is not a denial of proper self-love, but it does imply that human beings can now love neither God, nor others, nor even themselves rightly without the redemptive assistance of God's Messiah. "As the Father has loved me, so I have loved you; abide in my love" (John 15:9). Men and women tend toward a despairing sinfulness when confronted by the contingencies of life, so a divine corrective is called for.[9] This corrective is epistemic (a normative model for persons to imitate), juridical (an innocent atonement to satisfy God's justice), and ontological (a conveyance of the Holy Spirit to empower a new cooperative community).

In Aristotelian philosophy, the intersection of the two axes of ethics is the self; aspiration for things divine, and justice and friendship toward fellow citizens, find their grounding and inspiration in prudent self-love. There are forms of "bad" self-love, and Aristotle in no way recommends selfishness or even self-sufficiency. Even the happy man needs virtuous friends to help him enact and contemplate worthy deeds. Yet one's own

---

[8] Jesus does attend to individuals as well as to groups, of course; see Luke 5:40, for example, and compare 1 Corinthians 12:27.

[9] Even if sin as such is not gendered, being at root disobedience to God, it may tend to take different typical forms for males (inordinate self-assertion/aggression) and for females (inordinate self-denial/timidity). See Barbara Hilkert Andolsen, "Agape in Feminist Ethics," in *Feminist Theological Ethics*, ed. by Lois K. Daly (Louisville: Westminster John Knox Press, 1994). Sex and gender generalizations must be made with considerable caution, however, since there is much diversity within each group and a host of possible causal factors (biological and cultural) that might explain diversity within and across groups.

essence as a social animal, rightly understood, holds the key to religious wisdom and political order, as well as to personal fulfillment.[10] Ancient Judaism makes love of God the first thing needful, in contrast, but it still looks to (or at least permits) self-love as a guide to how to relate to the neighbor. With the final commandment of the New Testament at John 15:12, the self is still further backgrounded. The axes of ethics now form a cross with Christ at the center, even as the planes of the cross now extend to infinity in both directions – trunk touching God and arms embracing all humanity.

Jesus's Passion wounds us so deeply not merely because we are self-absorbed, but also because we do not really appreciate who we "ourselves" are and what we "ourselves" need. The phrase "love your neighbor as yourself" (or a very close variant) occurs eight times in the New Testament,[11] with Jesus himself frequently endorsing the idea. The life and legacy of Jesus does not gainsay self-love, therefore, but as a symbol of suffering service the cross checks and ultimately displaces self-love as the norm for human relations. We must learn, as Emil Brunner puts it, "to prune self-love" in "self-surrender to the death of Christ."[12] "We know love by this, that he laid down his life for us – and we ought to lay down our lives for one another" (1 John 3:16). Prudence remains a legitimate good, since all creatures of God, including oneself, have sacred worth. And Jesus's affirmation of "the Golden Rule" – "Do to others as you would have them do to you" (Luke 6:31 and Matt. 7:12) – requires imaginative empathy with others based on ready identification with one's own needs and interests. Even this rule is not a principle of reciprocity, however, and in any case the cross represents still another turn of the ethical screw.

The progression from reciprocity to Golden Rule to cross of Christ is one of increasing rigor and historical specificity. The Golden Rule presumes the ability to exchange roles and identify with others, but it need not presuppose tit for tat or mutual benefit. Like the Good Samaritan, I might act to assist an injured stranger along the side of the road, without demanding or even expecting any return. I may simply be moved by the recognition that I would want to be aided myself were I in

---

[10] Aristotle, *The Nicomachean Ethics*, trans. by David Ross, with revisions by J.L. Ackrill and J.O. Urmson (Oxford: Oxford University Press, 1980), bk. IX, esp. chaps. 3–9, [1165b1–1170b19], pp. 225–241.

[11] Matthew 19:19, 22:39; Mark 12:31, 33; Luke 10:27; Romans 12:10; Galatians 5:14; and James 2:8.

[12] Brunner, *The Divine Imperative*, trans. by Olive Wyon (London: Lutterworth Press, 1951), p. 316.

a similar situation. This is a matter of personal consistency,[13] not of relational reciprocity in the usual sense.[14] Some commentators take the Golden Rule of Luke 6:31 to be synonymous with the second love commandment of Matthew 22:39.[15] Even if this is correct, however, neither the rule nor the command is a matter of balancing interests, keeping contracts, or fulfilling shared expectations. More importantly, in relation to both the Golden Rule and self-love, the cross is more tangible and more demanding. The cross is not the only expression of agapic love, and loving your neighbor as yourself is not a minimalist standard.[16] But by specifying a concrete model of action the cross avoids the well-known pitfalls of appealing to pure consistency or even to natural self-interest. The cross escapes, that is, the Golden Rule's problem with those who are uniformly mean-spirited (even to themselves) and the second love commandment's problem with those who love themselves very little (or not at all).[17]

Self-love becomes in the Gospels, first of all and most of the time, a byproduct of true virtue rather than its foundation. Whereas the Golden Rule appeals indirectly to self-referential interests, the New Testament thrust displaces self-realization as a motive and foresees it only as a consequence (a double effect) of discipleship: "If any want to become my followers, let them deny themselves and take up their cross daily and follow me. For those who want to save their life will lose it, and those who lose their life for my sake will save it" (Luke 9:23–24; see also Mark

[13] Cf. Alan Gewirth, *Reason and Morality* (Chicago: University of Chicago Press, 1978), pp. 162–163.

[14] Klassen, "Love," p. 388, describes the Golden Rule as "based on reciprocity," even as Mark B. Greenlee refers to "the idea of reciprocity contained in the Golden Rule." (See Greenlee, "Echoes of the Love Command in the Halls of Justice," in *The Journal of Law and Religion*, vol. 12, no. 1 (1995–1996), p. 264.) What they both have in mind, I believe, is genuine and equal regard for others. This is not the same thing as reciprocity, since, at the extreme, even harmful retaliation in kind is a form of reciprocity.

[15] See, e.g., Victor Paul Furnish, *The Love Command in the New Testament* (Nashville: Abingdon Press, 1972), pp. 56–57.

[16] Oliver O'Donovan, *The Problem of Self-Love in St. Augustine* (New Haven: Yale University Press, 1980), p. 118, notes that "in [Augustine's] language loving one's neighbor as oneself is loving him to the uttermost."

[17] Brunner claims that "there is no sense in commanding men to love themselves, for by nature self-love is already present. The command to love one's neighbour 'as oneself' is not to be understood as an imperative but as an indicative" (*The Divine Imperative*, p. 316). His point is well-taken; rational self-development is a central Greek ideal, rather than a Biblical one. Still, to assume that we naturally know how to love ourselves may be to disguise the fact (underscored by feminists) that proper self-love is often itself a breakthrough (especially for women), however indirectly it must be aimed at. (Cf. ibid., pp. 317–319, on "the duty of self-cultivation" and "self-examination.") One upshot of "pruning" self-love with the cross is, ultimately, healthier growth for the entire Body of Christ.

8:34–35 and Matt. 16:24–25). *Imitatio Christi* here supplants *amor sui* as prior, and not solely in the priory but also in "profane," everyday life.[18] Hence nothing in the classical cardinal virtues fully prepares one for the Gospel vision of *agape*. Aristotle is aware that "it is noble to do well by another without a view to repayment," and he praises the good man who dies for his friends or country.[19] But it is patent to him that "it is nobler to do well by friends than by strangers," and that "not everything can be loved, but only what is good."[20] The Stagirite could only be mystified by an intensely other-regarding ethic that is (1) founded on fidelity to God and God's Son rather than human merit or mutuality, and thus (2) inclusive of strangers, enemies, and sinners. Even Judaism itself had to await its fullest elaboration in a kenotic Word come in the fullness of time.

I have emphasized that Jesus is a Jew who stands recognizably within the traditions of Torah even as he reinterprets or radicalizes them.[21] Jesus is, nonetheless, assigned singular import in the Gospels. John in particular sees him as the Incarnate Word communicating God's love to whomever believes (John 3:16). As the Son of God, Jesus gives believers the ability to receive "eternal life," an ability which they otherwise lack due to sin. Thus, as Søren Kierkegaard reminds us, Jesus is Savior and Redeemer, not merely teacher.[22] He does not just disclose preexisting truths but makes a new reality possible. That new reality is nothing less than full human life, life in accordance with *agape*. Powerlessness and grief, as well as sin, are overcome by the grace of Christ. In the Beatitudes (Matt. 5:3–12), for example, Jesus does not *discover* that the poor in spirit, those who mourn, the meek, *et al.*, are blessed; he *makes* them so by speaking. His words are performative in that they bring

[18] Note that in the sequel to Matthew 19:19, for instance, Jesus says to the rich young man who has "kept the commandments": "If you wish to be perfect, go, sell your possessions, and give the money to the poor, and you will have treasure in heaven; then come, follow me" (Matt. 19:21).
[19] Aristotle, *The Nicomachean Ethics*, bk. VIII, chap. 13, [1162b35], p. 216; and see ibid., bk. IX, chap. 8, [1169a19–20], p. 237. Aristotle is realistic enough to note that "all or most men, while they wish for what is noble, choose what is advantageous." See ibid., bk. VIII, chap. 13, [1162b35], p. 216.
[20] Ibid., bk. IX, chap. 9, [1169b14], p. 238; and ibid., Bk. IX, chap. 3, [1165b14–15], p. 226.
[21] Irving M. Zeitlin, *Jesus and the Judaism of His Time* (Oxford: Polity Press, 1988), p. 76, writes: "Jesus' outlook was highly distinctive [e.g., in comparison to the Pharisees]. For him the chief criterion for the validity of a specific *halakhah* (ordinance) is its compatibility with the love command." Zeitlin goes on, however, to insist: "Jesus was a charismatic religious virtuoso who challenged specific traditions of the elders, but to construe this as 'animus' against the Law is no less than preposterous" (p. 158).
[22] See Kierkegaard (Johannes Climacus), *Philosophical Fragments*, trans. by David Swenson and Howard V. Hong (Princeton: Princeton University Press, 1974), p. 21.

about and/or promise the very reality they declare.[23] If Jesus is Teacher in this sense, he is not simply to be admired but worshipped; he has decisive spiritual significance. He is not simply to be thanked as benefactor but glorified as Messiah.

Jesus's most revolutionary claim, once more, is that he is himself the medium and the message, the means and the end, of God's redemptive love. The divine indicative (who God is and what God has done) remains the touchstone of all human imperatives (who persons should be and what they should do). Yet God's most significant act, most complete self-disclosure, is no longer the election and rescue of Israel but the life, death, and resurrection of Jesus. The history of God's special relation to Israel is now seen as coming to its denouement in the person of Christ (cf. Rom. 11:29). Just as God's previous deliverance of Israel from bondage in Egypt (covenant fidelity) stood as a mandate to the Israelites to reflect God's holiness, so God's deliverance of all creation from bondage to sin (the Atonement of Christ) now stands as a mandate to believers to conform their lives to God's Son. At the center of this process is imitation of Christ's Passion; the cross is now the central revelation of God's nature and an enduring task of Christian ethics (cf. Luke 9:23). Golgotha supersedes, without denying, Sinai. The cross of Christ is the paradoxical proof that true power is "made perfect in weakness" (2 Cor. 12:9), that suffering service is the omnipotent Creator's typical way *with* the world and how that same Creator would have finite creatures live *in* the world. "No one has greater love than this, to lay down one's life for one's friends," says Jesus (John 15:13). "Bear one another's burdens, and in this way you will fulfill the law of Christ," says Paul (Gal. 6:2).

In sum, the story of Jesus Christ provides the key to the Bible as a whole and the content and rationale for Christian charity in particular. As 1 John 4:9–10 puts it, "God's love was revealed among us in this way: God sent his only Son into the world so that we might live through him. In this is love, not that we loved God but that he loved us and sent his Son to be the atoning sacrifice for our sins. Beloved, since God loved us so much, we also ought to love one another." The primacy of love is clear; a concluding word of caution is in order, however. Even Jesus's

---

[23] Though the analogy is inexact, one might say that Jesus teaches the rules of living rather like Abner Doubleday taught the rules of baseball. Doubleday did not discover the game of baseball lying around; he invented it, thereby making a new and joyful human activity possible. Similarly, Jesus did not walk into a thriving church and begin preaching about a distant reality; he embodied the church himself (the *autobasileia*), ushering in God's kingdom on earth with his presence.

obedient death on the cross must not be valorized as the sole legitimate expression of God's charity: Golgotha supersedes, but does not eradicate, the memory of Sinai (or of Moriah[24]); Good Friday is preceded by Palm Sunday and followed by Easter Sunday. More straightforwardly, openness to self-sacrifice is the most distinctive but not the only characteristic of *agape*, even as *agape* itself is the first but not the only virtue commanded in the New Testament.

II. GENERAL FEATURES OF *AGAPE* IN THE THREE NEW TESTAMENT LOVE COMMANDS

"*Agape*" is the New Testament Greek word for the steadfast love God has for human beings, as well as for the neighbor-love humans are to have for one another.[25] (In his epistles, Saint Paul usually identifies humanity's proper attitude toward God with "*pistis*" (faith), but "*agape*" is also used.[26]) Even so, the horizontal axis of love depends on the vertical; the divine form of *agape* precedes and empowers the human. As I have indicated, both Biblical testaments teach that it is God's un-

---

[24] See my comments on Abraham's legacy in chapter 6 below.

[25] William Klassen observes: "*Agapan* describes a life-enhancing action that flows from God to humans (Rom 8:37; 2 Cor 9:7) and vice versa (Matt 22:37). The commandment to love regulates human conduct within the church: 'love one another' (John 13:34; 15:12, 17; 1 Thess 4:9; 1 Pet 1:22; 1 John 3:11; 2 John 5); and husbands are commanded to love their wives (Eph 5:25, 28; Col 3:19). But those outside also are to be loved: the neighbor (Rom 13:9), and enemies (Matt 5:44; Luke 6:28, 35)." See Klassen, "Love," p. 384. For details on the etymology of the noun "*agape*" and of "*agapao*," the verb form, see Ceslas Spicq, O.P., *Theological Lexicon of the New Testament*, vol. I, trans. and ed. by James D. Ernest (Peabody, MA: Hendrickson, 1994), pp. 8–22. See also his *Agape in the New Testament*, vol. I, trans. by Sister Marie Aquinas McNamara, O.P. and Sister Mary Honoria Richter, O.P. (St Louis and London: B. Herder Book Co., 1963). Spicq writes: "[T]he only adequate translation [of *agape*] is 'love in the sense of charity'; in Latin, *caritas* or *dilectio*" (*Theological Lexicon*, vol. I, p. 8). The equation of *agape* and *caritas* is not uncontroversial, however. In his classic work, Anders Nygren argues that "Caritas is not simply another name for Agape"; as interpreted by Saint Augustine, for example, *caritas* is "neither Eros nor Agape, but the *synthesis* of them" – a combination of Greek desire and primitive Christian self-giving – according to Nygren. See Nygren, *Agape and Eros*, trans. by Philip S. Watson (New York: Harper and Row, 1969), pp. 55 and 451–452. John Witte has reminded me that scholastic theology and canon law also did not so easily conflate the terms "*caritas*/charity" and "*agape*/love," the medieval taxonomy of the virtues rendering charity a peculiar form of *caritas* as well as of *conscientia*. For simplicity's sake, I generally ignore these perjinkities, though I discuss Augustine's views at some length in chapter 3, noting where I disagree.

[26] "Only seldom does [Paul] speak explicitly of love for God," Herman Ridderbos observes, "although this is not entirely lacking (Rom. 8:28; 1 Cor. 2:9; 8:3; Eph. 6:24 [love for Christ]) . . . it is remarkable that even when he speaks of love as the fulfilling of the law, he only has love for one's neighbor in view (Rom. 13:8–10; Gal. 5:14), and that 1 Corinthians 13, too, seems to have to be understood specifically of love for one's neighbor." See Ridderbos, *Paul: An Outline of His Theology*, trans. by John Richard DeWitt (Grand Rapids: Eerdmans, 1975), p. 299. A.N. Wilson exaggerates, but only slightly, when he says that *agape* "is love which is one way. It is God's love for his chosen, not the other way round. Paul seldom speaks of human beings loving God." See Wilson, *Paul: The Mind of the Apostle* (New York: W.W. Norton, 1997), p. 84.

merited favor toward the world that enjoins and elicits love between
finite creatures. Creatures are to be loved for their own sakes, as I will
argue in detail in chapter 3, but the impetus for this comes first from the
Deity. Indeed, it is precisely because the love of God (subjective genitive)
is indispensable for proper relations between human beings that the love
of God (objective genitive) has priority among the commandments.
"You shall love the Lord your God with all your heart, and with all your
soul, and with all your mind" is "the greatest and first commandment"
(Matt. 22:37–38) because without such openness and dedication to God,
full human love (including proper self-love) is profoundly threatened.

The first commandment does not reflect God's vanity or authoritarianism, but rather God's graciousness. The second commandment,
"You shall love your neighbor as yourself," depends causally on the first,
even as the first commandment presupposes a prior act of grace (e.g.,
God's election of Israel and/or God's sending of His Son). For the
Christian believer, as much as for the Platonic philosopher, metaphysics
is a guide to morals,[27] but the ethical imperatives of Scripture rest on
theological indicatives narrating the story of a personal Creator and
Lord.[28] Only because God first loves us gratuitously are we commanded
and enabled to love God unreservedly and to love fellow human beings as
(we ought to love) ourselves. But this is not to say that in response to God
one takes the love commands serially, first loving God, then loving
others and oneself in discrete chronological order. One loves God
"first" in the sense of "distinctively," "obediently," and "most fundamentally," but love for others and oneself, indeed for the wide world,
flows spontaneously from this primal fidelity. It is not possible to wait
until one has "mastered" the first commandment before tackling the
second, however incomplete one's love for both God and creatures
remains. "A Christian loves, within limits, what God loves . . . This is not
a matter of God first, after that others, and then perhaps one's self. God
asks our whole heart all the time, and our love for creatures should
increasingly be part of the way we cooperate with God."[29]

This is not to imply, on the other hand, that the two love commandments are simply identical, or that love of neighbor somehow exhausts

---

[27] To use Iris Murdoch's phrase; see Murdoch, *Metaphysics as a Guide to Morals* (New York: The
Penguin Press, 1993).

[28] As Karl Barth clearly saw; see Barth, *Church Dogmatics*, trans. by A.T. Mackay *et al.* (Edinburgh:
T.&T. Clark), III/4, "The Doctrine of Creation," p. 568.

[29] Edward Vacek, *Love, Human and Divine: The Heart of Christian Ethics* (Washington, D.C.: Georgetown University Press, 1994), p. 149. I take up the possible problems with Vacek's understanding
of "cooperation" with God in chapter 3.

or fully determines love of God. One should no more conflate love of God with love of others than one should conflate love of others with love of self.[30] Because God, others, and self are distinct and to be loved for themselves, the vertical and horizontal axes of ethics remain discrete, however closely related. Agapic love directed toward the infinite Creator takes the form of worship and obedience, for instance, which must never be the case in finite creaturely interactions, on pain of idolatry. In prayerful relation to God I need not be constantly thinking of other people, any more than in my caring for others I need always have my self-interest in mind. Though the Incarnation brings God into intimate relation with humanity, not even the final love commandment of Christ fully conflates love of God and love of neighbor.

The mandate from Jesus to "love one another as I have loved you" (John 15:12) is magisterial, at once a reference to and an intensification of the two love commands cited in Matthew 22, precisely because it reveals that God is humanity's neighbor in the person of Jesus Christ. Love of God and love of neighbor meet in the love of Christ in at least eight senses:

(1) Jesus's *giving* of love *to God* is treated as humanity's own gift of love to the Creator; that is, Jesus's obedience to his heavenly "Father" is imputed by God to earthly creatures as though it were their own righteousness.

(2) Jesus's *giving* of love *to his neighbors* is a way God loves the world; that is, Jesus is Immanuel, God with us and for us.

(3) Jesus's *giving* of love *to his neighbors* is a way Jesus loves himself; that is,

---

[30] The first conflation is suggested by Knud Løgstrup in *The Ethical Demand* (Notre Dame: University of Notre Dame Press, 1997), pp. 4–5, while the second can be found in portions of Augustine and Aquinas. Emil Brunner resists the idea that there are "duties towards God" and "duties towards oneself," separable from "duties to our neighbour," noting that: "[T]he characteristic element of a genuine Christian ethic is that it does not start from the idea of duty at all, but from that of Divine grace; this point is constantly emphasized [in the New Testament], and is, indeed, made quite explicit in the doctrine of justification by faith. This doctrine strikes a fatal blow at mysticism and asceticism; it also shows, however, that the threefold division (of God, the self, and the world) is a fundamental error." See Brunner, *The Divine Imperative*, p. 309. Brunner elaborates by maintaining that "[t]he command to love God is not a moral command; it is not on the same level as love of man, but it indicates the root of all morality" (p. 309). These are helpful insistences on the priority of God's grace and the primacy of the first love commandment, but Brunner risks misunderstanding when he writes that "[w]e do not bring anything to God, we simply receive" (p. 310) and that "Good is fully described by the one word: *Love*, and, indeed, in the New Testament sense, as love of our neighbour" (p. 314). These and related passages seem to preclude genuine relation to God by equating all human love with what takes place within earthly community. As Karl Barth observes, "the double command to love points us to two spheres of activity which are relatively – no more, but very clearly so – distinct. Alongside work there is also prayer . . ." See Barth, *Church Dogmatics*, III/4, p. 49.

Jesus's identity as the Lamb of God is realized and expressed in passionate service to others.

(4) Jesus's *giving* of love *to God and his neighbors* provides the model for how human beings are to love God and their fellow human beings; that is, the Imitation of Christ (e.g., his going to the cross) supersedes self-love as a practical criterion.

(5) Jesus's *receiving* of love *from God* is a way God loves the world; that is, God's sustaining and validating the Son in whom God is "well pleased" is also a priceless and redemptive boon to humanity.

(6) Jesus's *receiving* of love *from humanity* is a way humanity loves God; that is, because Jesus is "very God and very man," the presence of Immanuel works both ways, so to speak.

(7) Jesus's *receiving* of love *from humanity* is a way humanity loves itself, and *vice versa*; that is, (a) to follow Christ is to save one's own life (Luke 9:23–24) and (b) to care for the needy neighbor, "one of the least of these," is to love Christ himself (Matt. 25:40).

(8) Jesus's *receiving* of love *from God and humanity* provides the model for how human beings are to receive love from both quarters themselves; that is, the Imitation of Christ (e.g., his patient acceptance of Mary's gift of expensive oil) supersedes anxious consequentialism as a practical criterion.

Jesus is "the way" to the Father (John 14:6); note, however, that loving God is "a way," but not the only way, to love the neighbor, even as loving the neighbor is "a way," but not the only way, to love God. Love is not jealous.

The convergence of love of God and love of neighbor in Christ can be further elaborated with reference to the parable of the Good Samaritan (Luke 10:29–37). This story is often thought to be puzzling because it does not really seem to answer the lawyer's question, "And who is my neighbor?" Instead of focusing on which other people are to be loved, Jesus focuses on what it means to be loving oneself. He illustrates, that is, how to act *as* a neighbor: by showing mercy to a stranger in distress, as the Samaritan did. One way to read Jesus's apparent evasiveness is as a refusal to let the lawyer "justify" himself (see NRSV note). Rather than respond to the explicit point of the lawyer's question, and thereby allow him to congratulate himself on doing his narrowly circumscribed duty, Jesus turns things around to accent the open-ended example of the Samaritan and the need to "[g]o and do likewise." I noted above that, for Jesus, the neighbor is not just a fellow-Israelite but anyone and everyone, especially someone who helps a stranger. And Jesus's intent to foil the lawyer's pride seems clear enough. But there is another dimension to Jesus's response which, when highlighted, helps explain the puzzle of this parable. The key to understanding, I believe, is the realization that Jesus is referring elliptically to himself. In giving himself sacrificially to others, Jesus is the lawyer's neighbor in the same sense that the Good Samaritan is neighbor to the man beaten, robbed, and stripped by the side of the road. When Jesus says, "Go and do likewise" to the inquisitive lawyer in Luke 10:37, he is effectively anticipating his "come, follow me" to the inquisitive ruler in Luke 18:22. In both cases, an interlocutor who expects to be vindicated is left humbled by the dynamic claim of love. Yet even Jesus's equation of himself with the neighbor does not eradicate the distinction between Creator and creature; rather, it lets us see how to love them both.

The Scriptures let us see that, in the context of relations between human beings, *agape* is characterized by three interpersonal features: (1) unconditional commitment to the good of others, (2) equal regard for the well-being of others, and (3) passionate service open to self-sacrifice for the sake of others.[31] The first feature is suggested by the steadfastness of God's covenant with Israel and the graciousness of God's gift of the Messiah; the second feature reflects the inclusiveness and attentiveness of Jesus's practice of neighbor-love; and the third feature follows, at a respectful distance, the example of Golgotha/Calvary. I want to endorse these features, sometimes in tension, but in a way that avoids the abstraction and oversimplification plaguing standard theoretical accounts. For instance, Christians properly associate love with the cross, as I have indicated, but I do not make actual sacrifice essential to every expression of *agape*. Openness to it under the right circumstances, however, I do take to be definitive of the virtue. There is a sublimely indiscriminate, almost imprudent, tenor to this tangibly life-affirming love.

Guido Reni's painting "Charity" (figure 1), *c.* 1630, is emblematic of many of the central themes just adumbrated, both their power and their controversy. In Reni's striking depiction of *agape*, the virtue is personified as a décolletée Madonna holding three nude babies. As I view the work, *agape*'s unconditional willing of the good is symbolized by the

---

[31] On these definitional matters, see Paul Ramsey, *Basic Christian Ethics* (New York: Charles Scribner's Sons, 1950) and Gene Outka, *Agape: An Ethical Analysis* (New Haven and London: Yale University Press, 1972). I use Outka's phrase "equal regard" to refer to but one component of strong *agape*; will and passion (committed action) are also ingredient in the first Christian virtue.

Figure 1. *Charity*, *c.* 1630, by Guido Reni (The Metropolitan Museum of Art, Gift of Mr. and Mrs. Charles Wrightsman, 1974. (1974.348) Photograph © 1983 The Metropolitan Museum of Art.)

woman's relation to the middle child, who sleeps oblivious to the world yet tenderly supported by the woman's right hand. With her left hand, the Madonna supports a second infant, who is nursing from her left breast. This typifies love's passionate disposition to serve, its willingness to give of the self's very substance to nurture another in need. Finally, the Madonna's facing the child on her right is emblematic of equal regard. The infant literally regards her and points to her exposed but unavailable left breast. He wants to be fed. In a stroke of genius, Reni has the woman looking slightly over the baby's head, thus suggesting that "love builds up" (1 Cor. 8:1). In directing her gaze at where the infant will be when he matures, the woman acknowledges him but ignores his immediate plea, schooling him in patience. Indeed, she shows a kind of impartiality in not looking directly into the eyes of any of the children; yet there is a palpable emotional joy on her face. She attends equally to the offspring, although she does not (cannot) treat each exactly the same. They are situated differently, and she relates to them so.

I refer to the Madonna as "the woman" rather than "the mother" because it is unclear to the immediate viewer whether she is the biological parent of these children. Given the genre, we naturally assume that she is, but there is no necessity here. The Madonna cares for the infants, but the possibility that she is not their birth-mother hints at the promiscuity of charity, love's inclination to meet needs whenever and wherever they exist, without reference to consanguinity. The woman's pleasant insouciance and the relaxed chaos of the picture as a whole also suggest a spontaneity that transcends procedural justice and talk of "rights and duties." Such spontaneity must be freely embraced, of course, or else we have plain injustice in the form of servitude. But the fine spirit of Reni's masterpiece is one of freedom and joy.

It will not be unremarked that the giver of love in Reni's masterpiece is female while the receivers appear male.[32] (The vast majority of artistic representations of charity I have run across are feminine; that speaks volumes about the enduring sexism of our culture.) Feminists will rightly object to this as oppressive stereotyping if it is taken to imply that women should be the exclusive (or even primary) caregivers in society. Arguably, we have venerated Mary's nurturing motherhood too much, making it stereotypical; undeniably, Joseph is a forgotten man. We

---

[32] *The Metropolitan Museum of Art Guide*, ed. by Kathleen Howard (New York, 1992), p. 183, refers to "three baby boys," but only two of the infants are indisputably male. Still, for the sake of simplicity, I follow Howard's lead.

desperately need more depictions of the smiling face of fatherly affection in Western art. Moreover, I am troubled by Reni's decision to paint his Madonna rather pallid. In spite of an agreeable facial expression, her ashen complexion makes her seem bloodless, sucked nearly dry by her anthropophagous bambini. I would not confuse love with lassitude, nor endorse the incestuous subtext that some find in Reni's "Charity." Instead, I supplement this look at Reni's work with discussion of a painting I construe as a male "Charity": figure 3 by William Blake (chapter 6). I extol throughout the three features of charity as applicable to both men and women. The three innocent babes, including openness to self-sacrifice, should not be thrown out with the patriarchal bathwater. A willingness to surrender unjust power and privilege is itself part of the disconsolation of love that undercuts gender tyranny.

Hiram Powers's 1870 bust of "Charity" (figure 2), executed together with a "Faith" and "Hope," provides an interesting contrast to Reni's work. Powers also depicts "Charity" as female, but now with a classical Greek, almost impersonal, serenity. She is tranquilly alone yet adorned by a striking tuft of hair rising over her forehead, signifying the flame of a sacred heart. The effect is a lovely introspective tenderness. If Reni's "Charity" is deeply engaged and fleshy, Powers's is kind yet a bit remote; Reni paints an embracing Italian Madonna, Powers abstracts the Platonic Good into an eternally "disarmed" soul. Both pieces are masterful, and in tandem they suggest the complementarity of self-sacrifice and self-possession at the core of virtue. That both are "Charity" points to the elusiveness of agapic love. Still, on balance, Reni's more incarnational and communal scene seems the better representation of a Biblical *agape* that serves neighbors (and God) in time.

My own aim, I emphasize, is not to discredit self-realization – could anyone consistently want to? – but rather to ask how it relates to a nuanced conception of Christian charity. The issue is what constitutes true self-realization and how it relates to the three features of *agape* on which I focus. Are *agape* and self-fulfillment in opposition, or might they be complementary, as Christianity has traditionally taught?[33] How, in

---

[33] Stephen G. Post is wise to be "skeptical of those who would detach love from some degree of self-fulfillment." But one must emphasize that Christlike love is not premised on or centrally motivated by that fulfillment. "Some degree of reciprocity sustains the generous self-giving of love," as Post observes, and the Bible makes it clear that "a suffering God longs for the reciprocation of love." But God's *agape* would build up creatures even when it is not returned, and some measure of kenotic upbuilding is always necessary when one wills the good for others in time. The more one uses the language of "mutuality" and "reciprocity" in describing Christian love, the more it looks like Aristotelian *philia* instead of New Testament *agape*. See Post, *A Theory of Agape: On the Meaning of Christian Love* (London and Toronto: Associated University Presses, 1990), pp. 10–11.

Figure 2. *Charity*, 1870, by Hiram Powers (Speed Museum, Louisville).

particular, do just concern for others and aesthetic cultivation of self relate to the effort to put charity first (cf. 1 Corinthians. 13)? My chief goal in raising these questions is not to exegete, definitively, Biblical teachings but rather to elaborate and probe, suggestively, Biblical motifs. The point is to bring Scripture into dialogue with secular culture. The critical influence will run in both directions, and there will inevitably be tensions between criteria. Nevertheless, the overarching message, gleaned from various sources, is that the integrity of life and of life's Source summons us to agapic love.

III. STRONG *AGAPE*

The governing vision throughout this book I call "strong *agape*." Strong *agape* treats love as the primary human source and end, a "metavalue"[34] that is an indispensable source of moral insight and power. It admits the genuineness of values other than love (e.g., health and happiness, freedom and justice), but it denies that we can have substantive access to these without practicing charity. "Charity is the life of the soul," in Aquinas's words, "even as the soul is the life of the body."[35] This need not mean that villains will literally drop dead of vice, but it does imply that they do not know true *joie de vivre*. As the humanizing passion, the faculty that makes viable persons of us, charity's main worth is not its being instrumental to external rewards. As an expression of one's full humanity and a vehicle to empower love in others, charity is a spontaneous gift. It is a necessary condition for the enjoyment of goods such as happiness, but it is not itself equivalent to or centrally motivated by the desire for those goods. Charity entails willing the good, loving others unconditionally; happiness, in contrast, involves doing well, getting what you want.[36] Thus the two are distinct. This is the case even if, for contingent reasons, one will not in fact do well without being charitable.

In the previous paragraph, I described charity as a "metavalue," a "passion," a "faculty," a "condition," and a specific kind of "willing." This range of reference highlights the many valences of my topic. Charity is both a disposition of agents (a virtue) and a type of action (a value). In some contexts, it is also a normative principle that abbreviates both of these elements and calls for their concrete realization. The realization is both personal and corporate, moreover, in that both good persons and good societies will be loving. Even as the virtue of an

---

[34] I take the term "metavalue," as well as elements of its basic definition, from Gerald Doppelt, "Is Rawls's Kantian Liberalism Coherent and Defensible?," in *Ethics*, vol. 99, no. 4 (July 1989), pp. 823–824.

[35] Thomas Aquinas, *Summa Theologiae* (*ST*) [1256–1272], trans. by the Fathers of the English Dominican Province (New York: Benziger Brothers, 1948), II–II, Q. 23, art. 2, ad 2. My differences with Thomas will emerge across the chapters below, especially with respect to the motive for love of neighbor and the separability of virtue and happiness. Nevertheless, I owe an enormous debt to his version of strong *agape*: "Charity is included in the definition of every virtue," Thomas observes, "not as being essentially every virtue, but because every virtue depends on it . . ." (*ST*, II–II, Q. 23, art. 4, ad 1). For an instructive discussion of Thomas on charity, especially his rejection of equal regard, see Jean Porter, "*De Ordine Caritatis*: Charity, Friendship, and Justice in Thomas Aquinas' *Summa Theologiae*," in *The Thomist*, vol. 53, no. 2 (April 1989): 197–213.

[36] "Happiness" is here defined in modern, more or less Kantian, terms and thus is not synonymous with the Greek word "*eudaimonia*," usually translated as "good living" or "human flourishing." For more on the Greek, see Martha C. Nussbaum, *The Therapy of Desire* (Princeton: Princeton University Press, 1994), pp. 15 and 120–122.

individual depends, in part, on her ability to see and respond to the moral and material needs of others, so the virtue of a society depends, in part, on its ability to foster the well-being of the community as a whole. The attention of individuals will typically focus on immediate family members and friends, even as a society will think first of its citizens and their good. But in neither case is concern exclusively for the proximate or the formally enfranchised, since human needs and values are present and recognizable in the entire species. All are made in God's Image. The injury of the stranger and the starvation of the alien, resident and nonresident, have a claim on us since we too were once strangers to our parents and caregivers, to our cities and countries, even to God. Israel was remembered by God when it was captive in Egypt (Deut. 7:7–8), and creatures were reconciled by God even when they were still God's enemies (Rom. 5:10). Analogously, in the womb before birth, we profited from unearned parental care; and in the family before the age of seniority (whether marked in terms of voting, bearing arms, paying taxes, speaking in temple, etc.), we benefited from unreciprocated social support.

Some persons have been better cared for than others, of course, and nothing I have said is a brief for the idea that parents somehow own their offspring or nations their citizens. But even if I take up the Joycean challenge to "forge in the smithy of my soul the uncreated conscience of my race,"[37] this cannot be an entirely solitary or idiosyncratic affair. The more cultivated my moral sensibilities, the better I can see that my soul itself is forged by others, all races created by a reality larger than themselves. The extent to which the instruments of charity will be public or private, legal or educational, or both, can be left to a balance of individual scruples and community standards. The point, however, is that to conceive of charity as merely a "philanthropic option" that anyone is competent to take or leave is just as dubious as to think of it as a "strict duty" that must be coerced on everyone by an omnicompetent state. In failing to embrace love as a shared responsibility, cutting across all persons and places, both conceptions signify a fundamental lack of gratitude. And joyful gratitude, not fear or greed, is the prime mover in agapic love.

As a (meta-)value, charity provides a (meta-)stability to individuals and groups that goes beyond mere absence of armed conflict.[38] This is just a technical way of saying that both individual integrity and social

---

[37] James Joyce, *A Portrait of the Artist as a Young Man* (New York: Viking Press, 1964), p. 253.
[38] For a discussion of "metastability," see Amitai Etzioni, *The New Golden Rule* (New York: Basic Books, 1996), pp. 23–24.

civility turn on a commitment to care for something larger than oneself or one's tribe. The well-known paradox of virtue is that the person who would be perfectly free and without constraint or obligation becomes the slave to self-destructive whim. And the society that would assert only its own interests or recognize only its own humanity brings a similar devastation on itself as well as others. When the words "pure liberation" or "nonperson" appear in print, in earnest, civilization usually totters. Rather than sustaining a distinctive identity over time, the refusal to uphold others means collapse into banality, or worse. The lives and works of the Marquis de Sade and Albert Speer illustrate, on the personal and corporate levels, that the ultimate "liberation" is an abomination in which autonomy *as* value becomes autonomy *from* value (chapter 4).[39] The only point to add is that The Libertine and The Company Architect live in us all.

Someone might ask: if a person or a community cannot know true flourishing without doing charity, how can we avoid works righteousness?[40] Strong *agape* does not entail works righteousness for two reasons: (1) because love may be the substance of a spiritual conversion that does not *immediately* issue in overt action, and (2) because it is God who infuses this habit into human hearts, with their consent (chapters 5 and 7) but not simply by their own devices. A conversion that did not eventually lead to works of love would be dead (cf. Jas. 2:26), assuming that the agent lives long enough to act. Active participation in God's life is ingredient in the *Summum Bonum*, however, not a means to it; and Christian faith has held from the beginning that God is the giver of this good gift, not we ourselves. God is the strong*est* agapist, Love itself. Creatures made in God's Image can resonate with Yahweh's steadfast love, but like tuning forks they must be struck by another.[41]

How does strong *agape* differ from weaker versions? Whereas a weak agapist sees charity as a moral suzerain, the first virtue/value among

---

[39] In the bedroom and in the Third Reich, "efficiency" and absence of fellow feeling mean the death of conscience. See Speer, *Inside the Third Reich*, trans. by Richard and Clara Winston (New York: Macmillan, 1970), p. 10. See also Hannah Arendt's analysis in *Eichmann in Jerusalem: A Report on the Banality of Evil* (New York: Viking Press, 1964). And cf. Sade's "To Libertines," in *Philosophy in the Bedroom*, trans. by Richard Seaver and Austryn Wainhouse (New York: Grove Weidenfeld, 1965), p. 185.

[40] As my Calvinist colleague John Witte has asked, how do we account for the thief on the cross being assured cohabitation with Christ in Paradise (the highest good) based only on his recognition of Christ (the thief having been the opposite of charitable all his life)?

[41] I have addressed elsewhere the question of whether virtue, including agapic love, is best explained in naturalist or supernaturalist terms; see my "Naturalism, Formalism, and Supernaturalism: Moral Epistemology and Comparative Ethics," forthcoming in *Journal of Religious Ethics* (Fall 1999).

equals with which it competes, the strong agapist sees charity as the moral sovereign, possessing unique authority. The weak agapist treats love as a great (even the greatest) good, that is, but a good still qualitatively similar to other worthwhile ends (e.g., courage and temperance). Strong *agape*, on the other hand, finds in love a singular source of religious and moral motivation; indeed, strong *agape* is a direct upshot of Biblical monotheism. God's own nature is agapic love (1 John 4:8), and the strong priority of this love is indicated in three basic ways: (1) metaphysically, by the fact that nothing finite would exist without God's gracious will to create and sustain a reality other than Deity, (2) Christologically, by the fact that human sins would not be forgiven without the atoning sacrifice of Jesus on the cross, and (3) interpersonally, by the fact that human persons, made in God's Image and redeemed by God's Son, would still not develop without an unearned care extended to them by others similarly made and redeemed. As Paul writes in 2 Corinthians 5:14–21, "the love of Christ urges us on, because we are convinced that one has died for all; therefore all have died . . . All this is from God, who reconciled us to himself through Christ, and has given us the ministry of reconciliation . . . so that in him we might become the righteousness of God."

As important as other goods are, including erotic love and friendship, these are dependent on *agape* for their genesis and ordered continuance. If we are not loved agapically first, and if we do not, in turn, first love others agapically, then our efforts to love erotically or philially will either never emerge or degenerate once they do. Without a foundation in *agape*, *eros* tends to become possessive or even homicidal, as the stories of so many spurned lovers attest. And one who lacks charity will also lack the trust to venture friendship or to prevent friendship from becoming cliquish and self-serving. Preferential attraction to what is excellent and beneficial, in sum, as well as solidarity based on shared interest and commitment, require a prior allegiance that is without calculation and reciprocity.[42] "God proves his love for us in that while we still were sinners Christ died for us" (Rom. 5:8).

This does not translate into a "love monism" in which *agape* is the only good thing – again, there are other genuine virtues and values – but it does imply that there is finally no competition between *agape* and these others. Or, what amounts to the same thing, the outcome of any conflict is preordained. One may have to surrender things of real worth in order

---

[42] Søren Kierkegaard's *Works of Love*, trans. by Howard and Edna Hong (New York: Harper and Row, 1962) remains one of the most profound Christian analyses of the various loves.

to love God (e.g., peace and happiness); one may have to rise above already demanding principles (e.g., justice) in order to love the neighbor; one may even have to lose oneself (i.e., suspend prudence) in order to find oneself. But it is never appropriate to foresake *agape* for anything else. The reason has already been indicated: *agape* is participation in the very holiness of God, and one will have little or no meaningful access to the supposedly rival good in the absence of *agape*. Charity sustains other values and schools other virtues, then, but this does not mean that they have no impact on or significance for charity. Even as God interacts with and is influenced by the world, so *agape* is not detached from other human emotions and enterprises.

Parental affection can teach one about self-sacrifice, for instance; friendship can help show one the meaning of steadfastness; and sexual pleasure can yield a joy akin to divine ecstasy. Yet *agape* remains sovereign, in that its unconditional commitment to the good undergirds all appraisive and exclusive loyalties, including *eros* and *philia* (chapter 3),[43] even as the Creator and Redeemer precedes the creation and creatures. Pursuing any other good without agapic love will leave one but "a noisy gong or a clanging cymbal" (1 Cor. 13:1–3). "Without love nothing can please God," maintains "Clement's First Letter" (*ca.* 96 C.E.); and Thomas Aquinas allows in the *Summa Theologiae* (1266–1273) that "no true virtue is possible without charity."[44]

Does this mean that atheists are incapable of charity for the neighbor? Obviously, if *agape* is defined as self-conscious love of God and neighbor inclusively, then atheists are no more capable of it than flat-earthers are capable of intending to sail around the world. One need not define *agape* in this way, however. Strong *agape* maintains (a) that charity is a necess-

---

[43] For more on the interrelation of *agape* and other forms of love, see Colin Grant, "For the Love of God: Agape"; Carter Heyward, "Lamenting the Loss of Love: A Response to Colin Grant"; Edward Collins Vacek, S.J., "Love, Christian and Diverse: A Response to Colin Grant"; Gene Outka, "Theocentric Agape and the Self: An Asymmetrical Affirmation in Response to Colin Grant's Either/Or"; and Colin Grant, "A Reply to My Critics" – all five pieces in *Journal of Religious Ethics*, vol. 24, no. 1 (Spring 1996). Grant is critical of recent efforts to supplant *agape* with *eros*, *philia*, or self-love. For an attempt to give aspects of *eros*, especially sexual pleasure, more autonomy, see Christine E. Gudorf, *Body, Sex, and Pleasure* (Cleveland: The Pilgrim Press, 1994). Cf. also Mary Daly on the "double-sidedness" of terms for passion and craving in *Pure Lust: Elemental Feminist Philosophy* (San Francisco: HarperCollins, 1984).

[44] "Clement's First Letter," in J. Philip Wogaman and Douglas M. Strong, eds., *Readings in Christian Ethics* (Louisville: Westminster John Knox Press, 1996), p. 7; and Thomas Aquinas, *ST*, II–II, Q. 23, art. 7. Thus the English mystic Richard Rolle simply extends a long line when he writes: "Every virtue to be true virtue must be rooted in charity. A man can possess no virtue that has not been planted in this love of God. He who multiplies virtues or good works apart from the love of God might as well throw precious stones down a bottomless pit!" See Rolle, *The Fire of Love* [1343], trans. by Clifton Wolters (Harmondsworth: Penguin, 1972), p. 102.

ary condition for the enjoyment of other human goods, and a Christian account of strong *agape* will also hold (b) that charity is not causally possible without the grace of God mediated by the Son and the Spirit. It is still another matter to insist (c) that explicit belief in the Biblical God or the historical Christ is a necessary condition for embodiment of charity. The dynamics of caring relations (motives, means, consequences) will differ depending on the presence or absence of religious faith. More forcefully, a Biblical perspective will always consider "pagan virtue" alienated from gratitude and obedience to the true God to be impoverished and unstable, if only because it fails to give credit where due and tends to see itself as dependent on contingencies of birth or luck.[45] But *all* human aspirations to *agape* are partial and flawed, inside or outside any particular church or creed, and an inclusive tenderness is extolled in several nonBiblical and even in some nontheistic moral visions.

I discuss in chapter 2 F. Scott Fitzgerald's efforts to embody a suffering love, and the examples could be multiplied to include considerably more political figures. Albert Camus, shaped by Nazi-occupied France; Mahatma Gandhi, shaped by British-occupied India; and Tenzin Gyatso, shaped by communist-occupied Tibet, are capable of extraordinary compassion without Judeo-Christian piety. So is Black Elk in the Wasichu-occupied Northern Plains of America. This is not to say that they are all "saying the same thing," but rather that a defense of Christian charity must not, of all things, fall victim to the sin of pride. Unity of vision and integrity of character are hard-won virtues, but syncretism too has its place. Rigoberta Menchú combines indigenous Quiché religion with Biblical narratives and revolutionary socialism for a compelling witness to love and justice in war-torn, "Spanish-occupied" Guatemala.[46]

[45] John Casey writes, "'[P]aganism' has always seen the good life as being to a significant extent under the sway of fortune. That there should be a good for man independent of circumstance is asserted again and again in the Christian texts." See Casey, *Pagan Virtue: An Essay in Ethics* (Oxford: Oxford University Press, 1990), p. 208. Casey believes that there is an "irreconcilable conflict within our moral inheritance" (p. 212) between worldly accents on honor and destiny and otherworldly accents on equality and humility, between the "pagan" virtues (courage, temperance, practical wisdom, and justice) and the Christian virtues (faith, hope, and love). I share Casey's sense that the classical cardinal virtues can often be competitors with the theological ones, but I disagree with the despairing lesson he draws from this fact. Whereas Casey considers the attempt to unify the West's "confused system of values" both inevitable and "impossible" (p. 226), "the priority of love" encapsulates one such ongoing attempt.

[46] See Camus's *The Plague*, trans. by Stuart Gilbert (New York: Knopf, 1964); Gandhi's *All Men Are Brothers* (New York: Continuum, 1998); the Dalai Lama's *Kindness, Clarity, and Insight*, trans. by Jeffrey Hopkins (Ithaca: Snow Lion, 1984); Black Elk's *Black Elk Speaks*, as told through John G.

That said, it must be granted that the claim to be able to love the neighbor without knowing or loving God is as suspect, from a Biblical point of view, as the claim to be able to know or love God without loving the neighbor. 1 John 4:7 insists that "love is from God; everyone who loves is born of God and knows God," while 1 John 4:20 equally emphatically claims that "those who do not love a brother or sister whom they have seen, cannot love God whom they have not seen." In Paul, moreover, "just as love for one's neighbor springs altogether from the new relationship of love between God and believers in Christ and cannot for a moment be considered as an independent 'love of neighbor' or 'philanthropy,' so also, conversely, love for God shows itself in particular in love for one's neighbor."[47] Love for God and love for the neighbor are not identical, but the latter naturally grows out of the former, and *vice versa*. "[I]f we love one another, God lives in us, and his love is perfected in us" (1 John 4:12). The challenge is not to reduce this broadly spiritual point to a narrowly catechetical one.

A Biblical agapist considers all charity to flow from the Holy Spirit, but this does not mean that it must flow from a single historical ideology. Christian love is premised on truth claims about divine agency and human nature. Because the truth or falsity of belief matters and can be tested existentially – "you will know them by their fruits" (Matt. 7:20, and cf. Gal. 5:22) – we are not left with relativism. Putting charity first should not dictate dogmatism, however, since that would itself be untrue to our experience of the beauty and insight of other cultures, not to mention faith in the ubiquity of God. It has been tempting to some Western theologians to argue that if faith without works is dead (Jas. 2:17), works (of love) without overt Christian belief are stillborn. But this is highly dubious, as the examples of Camus, Gandhi, the Dalai Lama, Black Elk, and many others attest.

Just as a pitcher may regularly throw a wicked curve-ball without being able to rehearse the theoretical laws of physics, so a person might embody the virtue of charity without knowing the name of the One who makes it possible. Training in Scriptural truth will surely improve one's chances of hitting the mark, and a Christian ethicist may be forgiven for thinking that the strong*est agape* awaits deliberate union with the person

Neihardt (Lincoln: University of Nebraska Press, 1961); and Menchú's *I, Rigoberta Menchú: An Indian Woman in Guatemala*, trans. by Ann Wright (London and New York: Verso, 1984). William Klassen, "Love," p. 383, notes that "Epictetus speaks of something very close to enemy love when he says that the true Cynic must 'while he is being flogged . . . love (*phileo*) the men who flog him, as though he were the father or brother of them all' (*Disc.* 3.22.54–55)." Epictetus believed in a God, to be sure, but not the Biblical God.   [47] Ridderbos, *Paul*, p. 299.

of Christ. But anyone who truly cares for others is touched and upheld by God's grace, according to Jewish and Christian Scripture (e.g., Ps. 41:1 and Matt. 5:7–9), whether that someone knows it or not. Such blessedness requires a modicum of "faith," if only the "mustard seed" that escapes despair or cynicism about life (cf. Luke 13:18–19), and in the New Testament Jesus has a decisive role in disclosing and enacting God's will. Practical love is his concern, however, not orthodox theology. A *public denial* of Jesus will lead to being denied by him before God (Matt. 10:33), but Jesus seldom if ever directly ties salvation to the presence or absence of a *conscious, public confession of doctrine*. (Paul, Peter, and the early church are a different matter; cf. Acts 4:12.) "Not everyone who says to me, 'Lord, Lord,' will enter the kingdom of heaven, but only the one who does the will of my Father in heaven," Jesus declares in Matthew 7:21; and he adds, "I tell you many will come from east and west and will eat with Abraham and Isaac and Jacob in the kingdom of heaven" (Matt. 8:11). There is no contradiction, then, in affirming both that Jesus is "the way, the truth, and the life" and that nonChristians can be loving. Whoever has seen Jesus has seen the Father (John 14:9); whoever loves Jesus is loved by the Father (John 14:23); but the Son is sometimes like a magnifying glass through which the Father is seen and loved without attending to the glass itself. These observations are simply the application of Biblical charity to sociological data and Biblical exegesis itself.[48] And the New Testament thesis remains that the more deeply one opens to God's Messiah, a painful process, the more widely one loves the world.

Given this strong reading, does the New Testament injunction to love (*agapan*) amount to a strict duty, a kind of categorical imperative, at least for Christians? In *Agape in the New Testament*, Ceslaus Spicq suggests the complexity of any satisfactory answer here. He maintains, seemingly unambiguously, that "[t]o love one's neighbor is not just a lofty ideal or a work of supererogation, but a true commandment. Its observance is required for eternal life (Mt. 19:16–21)." But on the very same page, he contends that "[t]he act of charity is a gift, and the more elevated this 'virtue,' the more complete the gift. Love of neighbor follows the same rhythm and can reach the same heroism as love of God."[49] This is the

---

[48] Cf. Karl Rahner on "anonymous Christians" in *Theological Investigations*, trans. by Karl-H. and Boniface Kruger (New York: Seabury, 1977), vol. VI, pp. 390–398.

[49] Spicq, *Agape in the New Testament*, vol. I, p. 54. Cf. also Pope John Paul II, *The Splendor of Truth* ("*Veritatis Splendor*") (Washington, D.C.: U.S. Catholic Conference, 1993), p. 31: "[V]ocation to perfect love is not restricted to a small group of individuals."

paradox *in nuce*. Charity is definitely required for Christians, but it is also
a "gift" that savors finally of "heroism." How can this be? The answer
lies, I think, in the fact that *agape* is the root of all virtue, the foundation
of obligation itself. *Agape* is both a commandment and a gift, both
required and heroic, because, as noted above, it is the metavalue
without which a moral life is impossible.

On the one hand, *agape* is duty-like in that it is not merely an optional
good deed; it is certainly not the apodosis of a hypothetical imperative
like "If you want to prosper in life, then you must love God and
neighbor." On the other hand, *agape* is more-than-dutiful in that it is not
merely one obligation among others; it is not on a par with "You shall
not commit adultery" or "You shall not steal," as important as these are.
Rather, *agape* is *primal* goodness, the impetus behind all ethical actions
and principles.[50] In as much as it involves forgiveness and openness to
self-sacrifice, *agape* outstrips modern definitions of justice referring to
contract or merit and therefore cannot readily be captured in the
language of "rights" and "duties." Rights and duties are usually thought
to be based on rational interests and claims, and as such they have an
important place in political contexts. So defined, however, rights and
duties are parasitic on charity as the uncalculating care that nurtures
rights-bearers into existence. Charity focuses on needs that must be met
and potentials that must be cultivated for rational persons to grow and
survive. Scripture addresses believers with a "You *shall* love," but there
is an ineliminably spontaneous element here. The divine command is
also a divine permission,[51] and to define charity in terms of owed
reciprocity is to forget that it is a free offering modelled on God's grace.

Shall we say then that charity gives more to others than is their due,
that it goes "above and beyond the call of duty"? Yes and no. *Agape* as
adoration is due the Holy Other as a matter of strict justice, since God is
utterly lovable; but as passionate service to other creatures *agape* is
ultimately an unmerited gift, since creatures are fallen and continuously
sinful. If *agape* is to be genuinely *for* neighbors, it is crucial to insist that
they are loved for their own sakes – that each finite individual is loved as
such, not merely in or for God.[52] It is equally crucial, however, to
distinguish between the recipient of and the rationale for *agape*. Agapic

---

[50] As Spicq concludes, "Charity, sum of the moral law, is more than law." See ibid., p. 66.
[51] Karl Barth, *Church Dogmatics*, III/4, p. 14, quoting Dietrich Bonhoeffer.
[52] As we will see in chapter 3, much (but by no means all) of the Western Catholic tradition has
   inclined to see charity as primarily, if not exclusively, directed toward God, with the neighbor
   being loved "for God's sake." See, for example, Aquinas, *ST*, II–II, Q. 23, art. 5, ad 1. This pious
   inclination risks making other human beings and neighbor-love itself instrumental values only.

love builds fellow sinners up, but it is not (primarily) motivated by their evolved worth or past performance. Caring for the needy might be called a "duty of charity,"[53] thus making clear the force of the divine command; but this kind of obligation is to be contrasted with a standard "duty of justice," which presumes some sort of historical merit or achievement.

Charity attends to the human essence, the common need and potential to give and receive care, that is prior to any temporal accomplishment. So calling charity a "duty" to other human beings is a category mistake if we do not make clear that something can be required as a duty (a commandment) yet be gratuitous (not based on merit, exchange, or other elements of a calculating justice). As the benevolence that nurtures finite persons into being, charity precedes and makes possible duties of justice to such persons.[54] (Heeding the divine call of *agape* allows one to hear, and others to issue, the human call of *eros*.) The rationale behind an agapic existence is fidelity to God and service to the neighbor in need, to repeat, not recognition of human excellence or winning of personal reward. A life of charity may not contribute to one's earthly happiness; on this point, strong *agape* breaks decisively with all Greek eudaimonism. As Anders Nygren pointed out in the 1930s, spontaneous service to the weak and needy (*agape*) is distinct from self-interested desire for the beautiful and satisfying (*eros*).[55] The obedient Christian will unfailingly love the neighbor, not as a muscular grab for heaven or a masochistic denial of self, but out of gratitude to God and concern for the creature's well-being.

For the strong agapist, benevolent motivation can be uncoupled from

---

[53] I take this expression from Allen Buchanan, "Justice and Charity," *Ethics*, vol. 97, no. 3 (April 1987): 558–575. I give it a slightly different meaning and application from Buchanan, however. Where I refer to "a duty of charity," the legal profession would speak of "a duty of reasonable care" or even "jural love – a legal manifestation of the call to put ourselves in the place of our neighbor"; see Mark B. Greenlee, "Echoes of the Love Command," p. 269.

[54] Spicq refers to *agape* toward God as "a duty" and to fraternal charity toward the neighbor as "the first of all duties." (See *Agape in the New Testament*, vol. I, pp. 64 and 74.) Again, this usage is understandable, but it must be carefully nuanced. It risks blurring the distinctively meta character of Christian love, making *agape* dependent on distributive justice, rather than the other way round. We may plausibly say that we have a duty to God to love the excellence of God, but a duty to love all human beings is usually a duty owed to God as Creator and to creatures as made in the Image of God (i.e., as in need of and capable of charity). Otherwise, we entangle charity in the web of social exchange, claim and counter-claim, calculation and reward. We may acquire duties of justice to others by the actions we or they take (think of spouses), but some duties of charity (e.g., to our parents) may simply be a function of who others innately are and what they need, and thus come to us (as to the Good Samaritan) unbidden.

[55] Nygren, *Agape and Eros, passim*. As I make clear in chapter 3, I do not oppose *agape* and *eros*, unlike Nygren, though I do distinguish them.

a host of things, in addition to the self's happiness and the neighbor's merit, to which it is traditionally tied. *Agape* is separable, for instance, from both insistence on immortality (interpreted as endless life) and longing for death (at times associated with unfettered *eros*). Love's priority, its being "strong as death" (Song of Solomon 8:6), implies the moral irrelevance of an afterlife as well as the moral acceptability of this one, I argue in chapter 5.[56] We need neither cling to, nor flee from, temporal existence; were an endless or superhuman existence our chief motive for action, we would crassly despise our finite selves. We may innocently hope for immortality, but just as there may be no final convergence of virtue and happiness (*pace* Kant), so there may be no heavenly resurrection for the faithful (*pace* Paul). To insist on resurrection as something owed the life of love smacks of trying to strike a lawlike bargain with God. The strong agapist holds that love and the goods it makes possible, now, will be enough even if death is the end of everything for individuals. Practical reason does not require one to postulate, or prove, an afterlife.[57]

Where for the strong agapist is belief in divine providence? She will likely hope for an afterlife, again, but the truly strong agapist is willing to find in the giving and receiving of charity Immanuel enough. To claim that everything that happens in time is directly willed by God or even that it works together for good would be an absurd denial of human evil and suffering, a false consolation. Some individuals are deeply harmed, perhaps even undone (chapters 4 and 5), by abuse and misfortune. But neither my strong agapist nor Saint Paul himself claims universal harmony. Paul's assertion is that "all things work together for good *for those who love God*, who are called according to his purpose" (Rom. 8:28). This line is subject to misunderstanding – it may tempt us, like snakehandlers,

---

[56] A succinct statement of what I argue against can be found in Peter Kreeft's *Love Is Stronger than Death* (San Francisco: Ignatius Press, 1992), p. xvi: ". . . if death is not meaningful, then life, in the final analysis, is not meaning-full. For death is the final analysis. If there is nothing at the end of the road, then the road leads nowhere, points to nothing, means nothing." If charity is its own reward, this quotation is less than persuasive. I maintain in chapter 5, echoing the Song of Solomon, that it is sufficient that love be "*strong* as death"; it need not be strong*er*.

[57] The question of whether Kant held, in his *Critique of Practical Reason*, that one must postulate the *existence* of God or merely the *possibility* of God, is a moot point. Many commentators, including Lewis White Beck, suggest that Kant's concern to safeguard the Highest Good (where happiness and virtue coincide) led him to postulate the reality of God and immortality as a requirement of moral rationality. M. Jamie Ferreira has argued, however, that Kant in fact postulates only the possibility of God and immortality. See Ferreira, "Kant's Postulate: The Possibility *or* the Existence of God?," *Kant Studien*, vol. 74 (1983): 75–80. Ferreira's reading of Kant leaves room for seeing immortality as a "blessed hope" rather than a theological certitude, in the ways I outline in chapter 5.

to affirm a literal invulnerability or present perfection for Christians – but it remains a glorious affirmation of *agape*'s primacy. "The maelstrom has us all,"[58] but God can bring good out of admitted evil. Where there is love for God, and *a fortiori* from God, there is abundant life (cf. John 10:10), though not possession of all good things nor avoidance of all bad.[59]

When interpreted most broadly, strong *agape* between human beings involves all three dimensions of the moral life: traits of character, forms of action, and concrete social consequences. No end of mischief has been caused by trying to reduce ethics to just one of these dimensions, as though good intentions or deontic rules or maximal utility alone were enough. When we look only at how we are behaving, we neglect who we are becoming; even as when we ask only about what we are achieving, we inevitably treat others as mere means. Thus a disconsoled charity recognizes that it must balance a range of goods and principles according to context, even as it insists that the call to *agape* is fundamental. Emotions play a crucial role in such practical wisdom, moreover. Far from being enemies of reason and the good life, emotions cannot be divorced from sound moral judgment; they have cognitive content and can either disclose or conceal salient truths about ourselves, other people, and the world.[60] To think that morality is chiefly an intellectual problem, subject to a single (even a quantifiable) decision procedure, is yet another soporific comfort that keeps us from feeling the real pains (and pleasures) of life with others. The Bible, in contrast, is chock-full of stories in which encounter with God requires a passionate response from the whole person.

Fine literature and art are among the most supple means of depicting and eliciting the complex emotions (such as compassion) partially constitutive of virtue, and to two especially provocative novels I now turn.

---

[58] Conrad Aiken, *Preludes for Memnon* (New York: Charles Scribner's Sons, 1931), Prelude XIX, p. 35.

[59] On the meaning of Romans 8:28, see Joni Eareckson, *Joni* (New York: Bantam Books, 1978).

[60] As Martha Nussbaum observes, emotions are "ways of perceiving" that are "ineliminable" from rationality; and this "means that in order to represent certain sorts of truths one must represent emotions. It also means that to communicate certain truths to one's readers one will have to write so as to arouse the reader's emotions." See Nussbaum, "Emotions as Judgments of Value," in *The Yale Journal of Criticism*, vol. 5, no. 2 (Spring 1992), pp. 205, 201, and 210. Similar points are made in her *The Fragility of Goodness: Luck and ethics in Greek tragedy and philosophy* (Cambridge: Cambridge University Press, 1986), *Love's Knowledge: Essays on Philosophy and Literature* (Oxford: Oxford University Press, 1990), and *The Therapy of Desire*. See also Alison M. Jaggar, "Love and Knowledge: Emotion in Feminist Epistemology," in *Gender/Body/Knowledge: Feminist Reconstructions of Being and Knowing*, ed. by Alison M. Jaggar and Susan R. Bordo (New Brunswick and London: Rutgers University Press, 1989).

CHAPTER 2

Back to the garden or into the night

You must live through the time when everything hurts.

Stephen Spender[1]

It is . . . good to love: because love is difficult.

Rainer Maria Rilke[2]

INTRODUCTION

Spender's exhortation to "live through the time" could stand as the motto for Ernest Hemingway's *The Garden of Eden*.[3] Like the Genesis creation story from which it takes its name, Hemingway's posthumously published novel is about innocence and surviving the loss of it. In the modern version, an all too human Adam and Eve double in the roles of God and the devil, respectively. But the focus remains the relation between moral freedom and limitation, breaking rules and being personally broken. What interests me in particular, however, are matters on which Spender's famous line is silent but about which Hemingway speaks volumes: by what *means* and with what *motives* are we to "live through"? And why is there so much hurting in human life to begin with? If Hemingway's evocation of fall is notably Biblical, his vision of the hows and whys of redemption is considerably less so. The shape and adequacy of that vision, and of a perennial alternative, are my main concerns.

In his *Garden* Hemingway is evidently attempting to rewrite both Scripture and F. Scott Fitzgerald's *Tender Is the Night*, as well as to reframe his own and Fitzgerald's marriages. Yet he does not manage to displace the originals: one must still choose between a tenderness that

---

[1] Spender, "Double Shame," in *Selected Poems* (New York: Random House, 1964), p. 50.
[2] Rilke, *Letters to a Young Poet*, trans. by Stephen Mitchell (New York: Vintage Books, 1986), p. 68.
[3] Hemingway, *The Garden of Eden* (New York: Charles Scribner's Sons, 1986).

accepts suffering and sacrifice as parts of love and an ecstasy that seeks to escape them as incompatible with prudence.

I. BACK TO THE GARDEN

The *Garden*'s David Bourne, an American writer on his honeymoon in France, is unspeakably happy. In addition to being deeply in love with his rich and beautiful wife of three weeks, Catherine, he is soon to discover that his second novel received the sort of rave reviews Adam might have hoped for after naming the animals. All seems Edenic for "the young man" and "the girl" infatuated with each other. But in the midst of their obliviousness there is a foreboding. From the beginning, the couple are ravenous. "They were always hungry but they ate very well." "They were always so hungry for breakfast that the girl often had a headache until the coffee came." "Then they were so hungry that they did not think they would live until breakfast . . ." (p.5) Frequent eating is punctuated by frequent lovemaking, as one expects from newlyweds, but again there are troubling associations. Hemingway lightly sounds the note of perversity, with just a hint of cannibalism. "Do you always get so hungry when you make love?" she asks, noting later: "I'm getting hungry already and we haven't finished breakfast" (p.5).

Having proclaimed that she is "the destructive type," Catherine returns from town one day with her hair "cropped as short as a boy's," and this seemingly trivial occasion suggests the ambiguity of her new freedom and the risks run by anyone committed to her:

"You see," she said. "That's the surprise. I'm a girl. But now I'm a boy too and I can do anything and anything and anything." "Sit here by me," he said. "What do you want, brother?" "Oh thank you," she said. "I'll take what you're having. You see why it's dangerous, don't you?" "Yes. I see." "But wasn't I good to do it?" "Maybe." "Not maybe. No. I thought about it. I've thought all about it. Why do we have to go by everyone else's rules? We're us." "We were having a good time and I didn't feel any rules." (p. 15)

In this temptation scene, like the one in Genesis, woman plays the antinomian force disturbing her husband's tranquility. And this time she needs no silver-tongued serpent to cajole her: she "thinks all about it" herself. The violated "rules" are chiefly society's rather than God's, but Catherine (like Eve) aims to stretch the couple's knowledge of good and evil by acting independently and asserting their identity ("We're us"). David (like Adam) is rather ambivalent, having not felt the need to take the initiative himself ("I didn't feel any rules"). Hemingway stays close to the Augustinian interpretation of the original Hebrew story by capping the preceding dialogue with Catherine's saying, "[W]e must be proud . . . I love to be proud," and David's responding, "So do I . . . We'll start being proud now" (p.16). With this, the "Fall" is nearly complete. That evening, we surmise, Catherine manually sodomizes David, with his acquiescence and partial (if stunned) help. In the aftermath, they both feel "dead and empty" (p.17).

This is a story of perversity but not merely or even mainly the sexual kind. Catherine takes a female lover, Marita, only then to encourage a *menage à trois*, and she more than once effectively sodomizes David. But these actions are symptoms. Hemingway's concern is with sexuality gone wrong, to be sure, but more palpably with the difficulties of trying to love and understand someone who is not capable of loving or understanding herself. Catherine's radical changes of hair style and obsession with getting the darkest tan, drinking the most potent liquor, etc. are transparent efforts to be unlike other people. Her bisexuality as well may have been for Hemingway an incidental sign of spiritual gluttony, a manic self-centeredness, but she could just as well have been compulsively heterosexual. Catherine ends up quite mad, hence beyond wickedness; but her deep discomfort with finitude (her being "panicked by time" [p.231]) is acted out gradually and, at least initially, by choice. She hates her husband's creativity as a jealous suitor hates a rival, as Satan hates the privileged place of Adam and Eve; so she burns David's most beautiful and most personal stories to "help" (p.222) him. To be wedded to someone like Catherine inevitably involves even more than the usual marital torment.

If Catherine, an erstwhile Eve, also plays the devil in this piece – being called such by her husband – it may appear that David is cast as both Adam and Christ. If Christ experienced anguish for his "bride's" sake, so too does David Bourne. He suffers for and from Catherine's limitless desire. Yet the troubling question concerns how innocent or redemptive this suffering is. David's passive self-denial, though partially motivated by commitment to his wife, actually contributes to her collapse. In accepting so unquestioningly her frantic iconoclasm, he seems not merely victim of, but collaborator in, the destructiveness that ensues. Here the Christlikeness ends.

Hemingway skillfully portrays the dangers of prideful unrestraint, the ambiguities of being free to do "anything and anything and anything" suggested, for example, by the newlyweds' car needing its brakes fixed.

But his fictional creation, Bourne, appreciates the fine line between liberation and abomination too late to save Catherine and nearly too late to save himself.[4] This is the novel's central drama but also its signal limitation. The novel asks, is recovery possible when a loved one (a chosen person, if not people) falters? Can there be a resurrection? But the reader wonders whether Bourne's "crucifixion" has not been the result, however well-intentioned, of his own capitulation to wantonness. His eventual "resurrection" as a writer seems more like a resuscitation, due more to animal vitality than to moral vindication. Has he served anyone, including himself, or only survived – *merely* "lived through" a painful period?

II. OR INTO THE NIGHT

It is instructive to compare Hemingway's *The Garden of Eden* with F. Scott Fitzgerald's *Tender Is the Night*,[5] both of which deal with American marriages breaking down on French beaches and what it would take to save them. Fitzgerald once observed that he wrote with the authority of failure, Hemingway with that of success, and this rings both true and false when we contrast the two novels. The plot of *Tender* does not unfold chronologically and is more complex than that of *Garden*, at least in its final edition, but the essential facts are straightforward.

Dick Diver, M.D. (whose name connotes a leap into a breathless world) "cures" a woman of dementia at the cost of his own talent and integrity. Sexually violated by her father while a girl, Nicole Warren is rich and beautiful and hungry and unbalanced. Though at the beginning of a promising psychiatric career, which includes (as with Bourne) the writing of a third book, Dick loses his clinical distance and chooses against the advice of his older colleague to marry her. With time, Nicole acquires enough ego-independence to divorce Dick and remarry, while he, depleted by years of struggling to cope with her madness and not be possessed by her money, becomes a hack doctor wandering somewhere in upstate New York. Dick's book and his promise are never realized.

In contrast, Hemingway's David Bourne (whose name is equivocal between having borne and having been born) *fails* to save Catherine, although in moving to forgive and forget her he is *himself* born again aesthetically. He is his own second Adam and even gets a second Eve, Marita, whose personality he has shaped in his own image and likeness.

---

[4] I examine the meaning of "liberation" and "abomination" in detail in chapter 4.
[5] F. Scott Fitzgerald, *Tender Is the Night* (New York: Charles Scribner's Sons, 1962).

Fitzgerald's book is a successful tragedy, the tale of an Orphean descent without subsequent ascent[6]; Hemingway's book is a successful epic, the log of an odyssey come full circle. Yet Fitzgerald's is the more touching literature. Dick Diver's collapse is more complete than David Bourne's but also more redemptive. Both men are debilitated by the infirmity of wealthy wives who eventually leave them, and both compromise themselves in adulterous relations (Bourne with Marita and Diver with Rosemary Hoyt). Yet whereas only Bourne regains equilibrium, describing himself as "not a tragic character" (p.148), only Diver suffers without also aggravating his wife's psychosis. Indeed, he actively engineers his wife's "completeness," her ability to "stand alone without him" (p.288), only to become heartsick when she denies him for another man.

Diver's loss of integrity is the effect of a too burdensome self-sacrifice – a "wild submergence of soul" (p.217) – that has made him bitter and brooding (a kind of moral *kenosis*); Bourne's recovery is tied to a capacity to "not think" (p.18; see also pp. 31, 56, 151, 193, 211, 238) (a kind of amoral prudence). Bourne is often described as imaginatively distancing himself from reality, for instance, while a striking feature of Diver is that he is "all complete there" (p.19). Immediately after cutting Dick off, Nicole wept; but "[l]ater in the garden she was happy" (p.276). For Dick there is no earthly *eudaimonia*, no retreat to the garden. Dick's self-sacrifice is more compelling than David's self-preservation, but we must not underestimate the latter's power and even beauty. No character in these books is a pure archetype of good or evil.

It would be worse than oversimplification to aver that David is self-serving, Dick self-giving; Catherine egotistical, Nicole egoless; David blind, Dick visionary; Catherine always violating, Nicole only violated. Both David and Dick love and wish to help their wives, and at times both are acutely aware how much this kindness will cost them. Catherine is often more desperate and confused than malicious, and Nicole is quite capable of jealousy and hardness of heart, as well as adultery (with Tommy Barban). Still, there are basic dissimilarities. Whereas Catherine's dementia is a function of her intentional crossing of boundaries (corporeal, psychological, and moral), Nicole's paranoia is initially the result of someone else's transgression. The women's diverse fates are also reflected in, and partially determined by, the

---

[6] The analogy to Orpheus was made by Mabel Dodge Luhan in a letter to the *New York Tribune* that Fitzgerald saved in his scrapbooks. The scrapbooks were published posthumously as *The Romantic Egoists*, edited by Matthew J. Bruccoli, Scottie Fitzgerald Smith, and Joan P. Kerr (New York: Charles Scribner's Sons, 1974); see p. 202.

differences between their husbands. Whereas Catherine's condition rapidly declines after marriage, Nicole's gradually improves. Bourne stoically accepts yet, through his art, seeks to transcend Catherine's corruption; Diver schools and in the end heals Nicole yet, having exhausted his art, himself spiritually dies when she turns from him.

Fitzgerald's hero drinks fully the cup of self-immolation and consciously embraces a form of death for Nicole's sake. Bourne recognizes his "changing of allegiance" to Marita as "a grave and violent thing" (p.238), but the last word of the novel has him and his writing still apparently "intact" (p.247). Dick's efforts to wean Nicole from him so they *both* might live are as doomed as Christ's attempts to educate his disciples without the exigency of the cross.

> Many times he had tried unsuccessfully to let go his hold on her . . . but always when he turned away from her into himself he left her holding Nothing in her hands and staring at it, calling it many names, but knowing that it was only the hope that he would come back soon. (p.180)

Fitzgerald has informed us that in relation to Nicole "Dick was paying some tribute to things unforgotten, unshriven, unexpurgated" (p.91). Only a crucifixion will liberate here; we watch for stigmata.

Beyond their relations to their wives, both Bourne and Diver initiate impressionable young women into moral and sexual sensibility, but Dick finds no consolation (no second Eve) in his affair with Rosemary. *In limine*, she is described as wanting "to hold him and devour him" (p.66); *post lectum*, she proves not to love him, nor he her. Ultimately, Dick judges his time with Rosemary a "self-indulgence" (p.213). His flirtation is a brief and futile attempt to deaden his pain, for it is Dick's permanent lot vicariously to expiate another's guilt. The guilt is more Nicole's father's (his sexual perversity) than Nicole's (her cuckolding and divorcing of Dick). But Nicole herself says at one point, "When I get well I want to be a fine person like you, Dick . . . You'll help me, Dick, so I won't feel so guilty" (p.161). By contrast to Diver's kind of crucifixion, in which comparative innocence redeems corruption by assuming its full weight, Bourne's enlightenment seems a bit facile. His experiences have been filtered through an extraordinarily observant sensibility, but has he really *learned* anything? About two thirds of the way through the story, "he began to realize what a completely stupid thing he had permitted" (p.178), but do we have concrete reason to believe that a disastrous plot will not soon unfold involving David and Marita?

The conclusion to *The Garden of Eden* is a peculiar hybrid of self-abnegation and self-rediscovery, a kind of Platonized Buddhism in which personal identity is *lost* via withdrawal into recollection. Buddhist and Christian wisdom equally affirm that the course from abomination to liberation runs through a "loss of self"; but at least in some popular versions of the former individual agency is extinguished, while in the latter it is annealed.[7] This difference marks David Bourne and Dick Diver as treading fundamentally divergent moral paths: a return to innocence that transcends time and self versus an acceptance of guilt that transforms them.

Bourne cultivates "his father's ability to forget . . . and not dread anything that was coming" (p.147). He does reflect, at times, but in a decidedly resigned and amoral fashion:

[H]e thought of [Catherine and Marita], not critically, not as any problem of love or fondness, nor of obligation nor of what had happened or would happen, nor of any problem of conduct now or to come, but simply of how he missed them. (p.132)

Diver also takes his father as "guide" (p.203), but he exhorts an hysteri-cal Nicole with "Control yourself" (p.112), wrestles with the "ethics" (p.65) of his relation with Rosemary, tells a patient "We must all try to be good" (p.185), wishes "he had always been as good as he had intended to be" (p.204), and repeatedly struggles to "think" (pp. 188, 202, 207), especially about his "responsibility" (p.105) to others. We can picture David and Marita on their honeymoon again tanning on the Riviera, while the final scene in which Dick figures has him making the sign of the cross from the terrace overlooking that "bright tan prayer rug of a beach" (p.3) before Gausse's *Hôtel des Etrangers*. His being a Good Samaritan to his strange(r) and estranged wife has cost him dearly. "The case was finished" (p.302), the narrator has notified us, thus echoing

---

[7] The "Buddhism" I describe is but one strand of a complex set of teachings. Particularly in the Mahayana tradition, emphasis is seldom on flight from individuality as such but rather on overcoming those desires that make for suffering and/or retard true self-understanding. Such a process requires moral effort and is aimed at compassionate healing of others as well as oneself. In *A Flash of Lightning in the Dark of Night*, His Holiness The Fourteenth Dalai Lama also recommends tenderness: "Let us stop being stubborn and thinking only of ourselves . . . However, if beings have no real existence, who is in pain? Why try to dispel suffering? Although the "I" does not truly exist, in relative truth everyone wants to avoid suffering. This is sufficient reason for dispelling the suffering of others as well as our own. What is the use in discriminating?" See Tenzin Gyatso, *A Flash of Lightning in the Dark of Night: A Guide to the Bodhisattva's Way of Life*, trans. by The Padmakara Translation Group (Boston and London: Shambhala, 1994), pp. 102–103. See also Guy Newland, *Compassion: A Tibetan Analysis* (London: Wisdom Publications, 1984). Western mysticism too is highly variegated, but my point is that a panlogism (whether Oriental or Occidental) that fully reduces temporal agency and personal identity to illusion remains outside of the Christian theological mainstream.

Christ's last words (John 19:30). And though Dick will forgive Nicole, he will not forget her; he will not come again to the Mediterranean in this life.

Diver's course is more of an *Imitatio* than Bourne's, but his Christlikeness also extends only so far. However admirable his gift of self and selfhood to Nicole, Dick ends tragically. He becomes a drunk and a boor, used and used up, even suicidal. His final act of kindness is to not take Nicole with him into this dark night, but his finish remains one of moral bankruptcy; in a letter to Edmund Wilson, Fitzgerald himself describes Dick as a combination of an *"homme épuisé"* and an *"homme manqué."*[8] Such a fate has no parallel in the Biblical Jesus's case, though trying to say exactly why and how is a puzzlement. Christ experiences the abandonment of God on the cross (*"Eloi, Eloi, lema sabachthani?"* – Mark 15:34), but he neither flees from time nor is he corrupted by events within it.

Both Bourne and Diver fall morally, losing themselves in the process, but Christ is nowhere so much himself nor so virtuous as when he dies. Hans Frei overstates the case when he contends that Jesus is never enriched by human contact, in no way receptive to or needful of good from others;[9] but Jesus is never impoverished by such contact, in no way ethically compromised. The Synoptic Gospels depict a Christ who is tempted during his life but does not sin, who knows dread before the prospect of his death but responds with obedience ("not my will but yours be done" – Luke 22:42). During the Last Supper, he commands others to feed off his body and blood, thereby undoing the original disobedient eating in Eden, but he himself does not consume (others).

Martin Luther contended that during his Passion Jesus became sinful: he did not simply *receive* the punishment for human iniquity, he actually *became* guilty, "the greatest transgressor, murderer, adulterer, thief, rebel, blasphemer, &c. that ever was or could be in all the world."[10] (Saint Paul may also seem to suggest this in 2 Corinthians 5:21: "For our sake [God] made him to be sin who knew no sin . . .") If such a soteriology is adopted without qualification, then Dick Diver is even

---

8 See Fitzgerald, *The Crack-Up*, p. 278.
9 Hans Frei, *The Identity of Jesus Christ* (Philadelphia: Fortress Press, 1975), p. 81. Consider as possible counter-examples: John's baptizing Jesus, Mary of Bethany's anointing him with nard, even Peter's confession of faith in him as the Christ. Each of these acts seems, commonsensically, to have enriched Jesus's life. He did weep, after all, over the death of Lazarus.
10 Luther, "A Commentary on Saint Paul's Epistle to the Galatians" [1531], in *Martin Luther: Selections from His Writings*, ed. by John Dillenberger (Garden City: Anchor Books, 1961), p. 135; see also pp. 136–138.

more Christlike in one respect than I have allowed. For, again, Dick becomes guilty, although partially as a result of empathy for another: "He could not watch [Nicole's] disintegrations without participating in them" (pp. 90–191). Many detect a dark profundity in Luther's view of the cross – Does not divine love sacrifice its own integrity, "dirty its hands," to make satisfaction for others' sins? Must not good embrace (even *cause*) evil to redeem those possessed by it? – but such an understanding of Christ's death sets a bad precedent for imitation. In addition to endorsing the principle of doing evil that good might come, it risks making nonsense out of the Passion narratives. Sin for Luther entails broken relation with and consequent alienation from God, and Christ undeniably feels forsaken by God on the cross. But should we literally see Christ as "a sinner"[11] during his final days?

The Suffering Servant Song of Isaiah 53, taken by Luther and the Christian tradition generally to refer to Christ, describes him as "numbered with the transgressors" (Isa. 53:12). But the pathos of this proleptic account of Christ's suffering is that he preserves his innocence throughout.[12] To be counted as a trangressor is not the same as actually becoming one (cf. Luke 22:37), and while "the Lord has laid on him the iniquity of us all" (Isa. 53:6), the servant "had done no violence, and there was no deceit in his mouth" (53:9). Indeed, the servant is called "the righteous one" (Isa. 53:11), and one thinks of 1 John 3:5's comment on Jesus: "[I]n him there is no sin." The heart of the Song in Isaiah drives home the limit of Diver's Christlikeness:

Surely he has borne our infirmities and carried our diseases; yet we accounted him stricken, struck down by God, and afflicted. But he was wounded for *our* transgressions, crushed for *our* iniquities; upon him was the punishment that made us whole, and by his bruises we are healed. (Isa. 53:4–5; emphases mine)

Dick courageously accepts suffering for Nicole's sake, but he is wounded

---

[11] Cf. Luther, "A Commentary on Galatians," p. 135.

[12] Frei makes a similar point in *The Identity of Jesus Christ*, p. 58. Insisting on the innocence of Christ also has its problems, however. As Nietzsche suggested, if the crucifixion of a guiltless Christ is positively willed by God and actively imposed by God – as opposed to willed by creatures and merely accepted by Christ – then God seems "gruesome." See Friedrich Nietzsche, "The AntiChrist," in *The Portable Nietzsche*, ed. and trans. by Walter Kaufmann (New York: The Viking Press, 1974), section 41, p. 616. Wouldn't it be "cosmic child abuse," to use the contemporary phrase, for God to scapegoat the Son in this way? This difficulty is avoided if one thinks of the Passion as an expression of God's consequent will, designed to meet the needs of sinful creatures rather than antecedently ordained by God for its own sake. Christ's saying, "Father, forgive them; for they do not know what they are doing" (Luke 23:34), makes no sense unless his execution is unjust, something anticipated and turned by God to good purposes rather than something positively commanded.

in part for *his own* transgressions.)

In spite of the Christian overtones of Dick Diver's vicarious suffering, *Tender Is the Night* is much more classically tragic than the Gospels. For even though God allows the punishment for sin to fall on Christ, a punishment that would properly be visited on human beings, Christ's own sinlessness is contrasted with the guilt of Barabbas (Luke 23:13–25) and is vindicated in his Resurrection. That resurrection suggests that Christianity cannot be an utterly tragic religion. Christ was not faced with a moral dilemma in Gethsemane in which he was fated to choose between alternatives all of which entailed becoming guilty; rather, he was offered the cup of obedience to God unto death or the temptation of self-preservation. His acceptance of death was a remedy for human sin, but it was not itself a sinful act; Christ surrendered life to reveal God's grace, but he did not surrender integrity. Doctor Diver, on the other hand, while noble, is also fatally flawed. He does in fact become an adulterer; more venially, he is forever being seized by "[a]n overwhelming desire to help, *or to be admired*" (p.206, emphasis mine). Near the end of *Tender*, the prideful and adulterous Dick tries to show off for Rosemary by doing tricks on a ski-board being pulled by a speed boat. He attempts to lift another man on his shoulders, but they both plunge awkwardly into the sea. "He could not rise" (p.284), we are told, not above gravity much less the grave. Dick is tangibly Christlike, but he is not the Second Coming.

There is a point of diminishing returns in seeking general labels for the work of idiosyncratic authors, but Hans Frei's discussion of gnosticism can be helpful in my attempt to contrast Hemingway's and Fitzgerald's novels. Frei argues that in a gnostic myth "alienation and redemption . . . finally come to be one and the same thing. In effect, this unity of opposites means that one's identity and the acceptance of his nonidentity are one; presence and nonbeing or lack of presence are one . . . true identity is equivalent to having none."[13] This passage comes close to describing the creed implicit in *The Garden of Eden* (and in much of its author's biography), although Bourne (like Hemingway) also embodies elements of what Frei calls "orgiastic" or "mystery" religion.[14] Simultaneous fear and love of nothingness – at least cheerful acquiescence in it – is quite explicit in that segment of "A Clean Well-lighted Place" that includes Hemingway's version of the Lord's Prayer:

What did he fear? It was not fear or dread. It was nothing that he knew too well.

---

[13] Frei, *The Identity of Jesus Christ*, p. 61. [14] Ibid., p. 54.

It was all a nothing and a man was nothing too. It was only that and light was all it needed and a certain cleanness and order. Some lived in it and never felt it but he knew it all was *nada y pues nada y nada y pues nada*. Our *nada* who art in *nada*, *nada* be thy name thy kingdom *nada* thy will be *nada* in *nada* as it is in *nada* . . . Hail nothing full of nothing, nothing is with thee. He smiled and stood before a bar with a shining steam pressure coffee machine.[15]

In opposition to Hemingway's anti-hero-as-Cheshire-Cat, who disappears against a well-lighted background with only his smile reflected in a shining machine, Fitzgerald's hero does not go gentle into his good night. An obvious clue to Fitzgerald's counter-sensibility is the epigraph to *Tender* from "Ode to a Nightingale":

> Already with thee! tender is the night . . .
> . . . But here there is no light,
> Save what from heaven is with the breezes blown
> Through verdurous glooms and winding mossy ways.

Like Keats, Fitzgerald and his fictional creations are aware of the lure of nonentity but do not merely recede into the natural, much less the mechanical. In the "Ode," the song of the nightingale reminds Keats of the powerful connection between ecstasy and nonbeing, natural beauty and physical death:

> Now more than ever seems it rich to die,
> To cease upon the midnight with no pain,
> While thou art pouring forth thy soul abroad
> In such an ecstasy!

But thoughts of human suffering – "hungry generations," "the sad heart of Ruth," and "faery lands forlorn" – pull Keats out of imaginative absorption in the nightingale and back to himself:

> Forlorn! the very word is like a bell
> To toll me back from thee to my sole self!
> Adieu! the fancy cannot cheat so well
> As she is famed to do, deceiving elf.

It is the sad heart of Nicole that serves this purpose for Diver, that calls him out of ecstasy and back to tenderness in a world where there is no light (and one thinks, of course, of Zelda and Scott). Imagination is not enough; unchecked, it seduces one out of attention to reality, especially human pain.

---

[15] *The Complete Short Stories of Ernest Hemingway* (New York: Charles Scribner's Sons, 1987), p. 291.

III. HEMINGWAY AND FITZGERALD AS ICONS OF PRUDENCE
AND SELF-SACRIFICE

It is hard not to conclude that *The Garden of Eden* and *Tender Is the Night* rehearse their authors' histories, or at least reflect their dispositions. In a letter to Fitzgerald dated July 1, 1925, some three months after the publication of *The Great Gatsby*, Hemingway wrote:

I wonder what your idea of heaven would be – A beautiful vacuum filled with wealthy monogamists, all powerful and members of the best families all drinking themselves to death. And hell would probably [be] an ugly vacuum full of poor polygamists unable to obtain booze or with chronic stomach disorders that they called secret sorrows. To me heaven would be a big bull ring with me holding two barrera seats and a trout stream outside that no one else was allowed to fish in and two lovely houses in the town; one where I would have my wife and children and be monogamous and love them truly and well and the other where I would have my nine beautiful mistresses on 9 different floors . . . Then there would be a fine church like in Pamplona where I could go and be confessed on the way from one house to the other and I would get on my horse and ride out with my son to my bull ranch named Hacienda Hadley and toss coins to all my illegitimate children that lived [along] the road.[16]

Though humorous, these lines are revealing. Hemingway was reluctant to accept tragedy (if not responsibility) in his life as well as in his writing. Metaphorically, he locates *both* his "houses," his moral and libidinal selves, in heaven. His first full-length novel, *The Sun Also Rises*, though like *Garden* a portrait of "how people go to hell,"[17] nevertheless managed to find a semi-optimistic title in Ecclesiastes. The sun both sets and rises; darkness is not permanent, though the cycles of nature are impersonal and irresistible. This vision is finally very different, however, from faith in a providential God who "makes his sun rise on the evil and on the good" (Matt. 5:45), for there is no moral dimension.

Even Papa's suicide appears to have been more a resigned than a self-indicting act, albeit undeniably tinged with desperation. Kenneth S. Lynn has argued that at its close Hemingway's life approached tragedy,[18] but this is not how the novelist saw it. There was a sense of decay and doom, even bouts of paranoia, but these played themselves out in largely nonmoral terms. Lynn is correct that Hemingway's killing him-

---

[16] *Ernest Hemingway: Selected Letters, 1917–1961*, ed. by Carlos Baker (New York: Charles Scribner's Sons, 1981), pp. 165–166.

[17] This is Hemingway's description of his book to Fitzgerald in a letter of May 1926. See *Selected Letters*, p. 204.

[18] Lynn, *Hemingway* (New York: Fawcett Columbine, 1987), pp. 106 and 575. Lynn does document in detail the paranoia and longing for death that gripped Hemingway after his Muse had flown, or been drowned in an ocean of alcohol and pills.

self was neither unambiguously "an act of courage" nor "the ultimate proof that he had always lived a lie,"[19] but the death *was* consistent with the sometimes poignant, always flamboyant, quest for release that typified his life. When Hemingway wept towards the end, it was over his lost vigor: his growing inability to recuperate (physically and artistically) from life's blows.[20] Fitzgerald's end-of-life lament, on the other hand, was chiefly over his lost *virtue*. Decline in health was symptom rather than disease, in his case, with shame and self-loathing rather than corporal and aesthetic desiccation being the main woes.

Early in *The Sun Also Rises* (1926), Robert Cohn says to Jake Barnes, Hemingway's neutered alter ego: "Do you know that in about thirty-five years more we'll be dead?" "What the hell, Robert," Jake says, "What the hell. . . . I've had plenty to worry about one time or other. I'm through worrying."[21] With *The Sun*, Hemingway began his literary career on the far side of a fall (World War I being one aspect) and strove thereafter to get back to innocence, or at least unconcern. Fitzgerald began his authorship with *This Side of Paradise* (1920) but ended up "revisiting" not Eden but Babylon. Four years before his death, Fitzgerald published three essays describing with painful candor his ongoing mental and moral "crack-up." He had lost his Catholic faith but not his Catholic sensibilities across a lifetime of "too much anger and too many tears."[22] He described his decline partially in terms of waning physical and emotional stamina. The same sort of "lesion of enthusiasm and vitality" described in *Tender* (pp. 208 and 222) reappeared in "The Crack-Up" as "the leak through which, unknown to myself, my enthusiasm and my vitality had been steadily and prematurely trickling away."[23] Unlike Hemingway, however, Fitzgerald struggled to uncover the *moral* causes and effects here. At age thirty-nine he had found himself with "a sad attitude toward sadness, a melancholy attitude toward melancholy and a tragic attitude toward tragedy," tending to identify himself "with the objects of my horror or compassion."[24] Yet he further

---

[19] Ibid., p. 10.

[20] James R. Mellow speculates that Hemingway's five concussions over the course of his lifetime may have had more to do with his final psychiatric problems than has been recognized. See Mellow, *Hemingway: A Life Without Consequences* (Menlo Park, CA: Addison-Wesley, 1992), p. 596. The fractured skull sustained in a 1954 plane crash seems to have been especially devastating to his overall health and stability.

[21] Hemingway, *The Sun Also Rises* (New York: Charles Scribner's Sons, 1954), p. 11. Cohn was remarkably prophetic, after a fashion: Hemingway took his own life in 1961, exactly thirty-five years after the first typesetting of *The Sun*. Could the author have even been thinking of the quoted passage when he pulled the trigger? Doubtful.   [22] Fitzgerald, *The Crack-Up*, p. 71.

[23] Fitzgerald, "Handle With Care," in ibid., p. 80.

[24] Ibid., pp. 80–81. Though she is never mentioned by name, one of the "objects" with whose extinction Fitzgerald identified was his afflicted wife Zelda.

characterized his breakdown as "a deflation of all my values,"[25] not merely as a collapse of his natural abilities.

There are several themes in the "Crack-Up" collection that are direct echoes of *Tender*: "being impelled to think," not recovering from a jolt but rather making a "clean break" and "becoming a different person,"[26] etc. Where Diver feels "a vast criminal irresponsibility" (p. 233), Fitzgerald experiences "a vast irresponsibility toward every obligation."[27] Without multiplying references, the point is clear: the Fitzgeralds' turbulent life had left Scott bitter and (ostensibly) unloving and unlovable. He no longer believed in himself as a moral agent, a person with an identity. Yet to his relative credit, he did not become involved with Beatrice Dance and then Sheilah Graham until Zelda had badly broken down and been more or less permanently institutionalized. He never divorced her.[28]

Hemingway's reaction to Fitzgerald's sorrow and its public revelation is notorious. Whereas in the late 1920s and early 30s, Hemingway's letters had been extremely warm and admiring, even deferential, to Scott – encouraging him to write and solicitous of Zelda and her health problems – by the middle of 1934 his tone has changed markedly. Hemingway had written to Maxwell Perkins in 1934 that "much of [*Tender Is the Night*] was so good it was frightening" and "How I wish [Scott] would have kept on writing."[29] Especially with the publication of "The Crack-Up" two years later, however, the patient prodding of earlier days has given way to a bullying of Fitzgerald with all the subtlety of General Patton slapping his shell-shocked private.[30] This had a disheartening effect on Scott, though he was still able to write of Hemingway: "Somehow I love that man, no matter what he says or does, but just one more crack . . ."[31] Indeed, despite protests of nihilism, in naming his cracked attitude a "heady villainous feeling,"[32] Fitzgerald recognized it as something to be worked (not merely lived) through. He could be amazingly childish and self-destructive, especially when drunk, but he would not dub his wantonness "wisdom." Fitzgerald labored on

---

[25] Ibid., p. 78.   [26] Ibid., pp. 78, 81, 76.   [27] Ibid., p. 78.

[28] In breaking off his brief 1935 affair with Dance, Fitzgerald informed her that he would never leave Zelda, "my invalid," adding in a subsequent letter that "[t]here are emotions just as important as ours running concurrently with them – and there is literally no standard in life other than a sense of duty." Quoted by Matthew J. Bruccoli in *Some Sort of Epic Grandeur: The Life of F. Scott Fitzgerald* (New York and London: Harcourt Brace Jovanovich, 1981), p. 398.

[29] *The Romantic Egoists*, p. 201.

[30] In the original version of "The Snows of Kilimanjaro," for example, Hemingway wrote of "poor Scott Fitzgerald and his romantic awe of [the rich] . . . He thought they were a special glamorous race and when he found they weren't it wrecked him just as much as any other thing that wrecked him." See ibid., p. 212.

[31] In a letter to Maxwell Perkins of September 19, 1936, several months after "The Crack-Up"; see *The Romantic Egoists*, p. 212.   [32] Fitzgerald, *The Crack-Up*, p. 82.

without finishing *The Last Tycoon*, but he did manage to forgive Hemingway for a number of humiliating unkindnesses.

In a May 1934 letter discussing *Tender*, Hemingway tells Scott: "[Y]ou cheated too damned much in this one . . . a long time ago you stopped listening except to the answers to your own questions."[33] These comments are soon followed by an oft quoted bit of advice:

> Forget your personal tragedy. We are all bitched from the start and you especially have to be hurt like hell before you can write seriously. But when you get the damned hurt use it – don't cheat with it. Be as faithful to it as a scientist – but don't think anything is of any importance because it happens to you or anyone belonging to you.[34]

Hemingway's emphasis on impersonal detachment versus Fitzgerald's sometimes morbid fixation on personal suffering is fully apparent. Detachment is also the theme in a letter from Hemingway discussing insomnia, by which both authors were plagued:

> [S]ince I have stopped giving a good goddamn about anything in the past it doesn't bother much and I just lie there and keep perfectly still and rest through it and you seem to get almost as much repose as though you slept . . . If you can lie still and take it easy and just consider your life and everything else as an outsider and *not give a damn* – it is a hell of a help.[35]

The attitude of oblivion recommended here is quite reminiscent of the way David Bourne reacts to Catherine's erotic permutations. "Let's lie very still and quiet . . . and not think at all," David Bourne says to his wife (p.18); "just lie there and keep perfectly still and rest," Bourne's creator advises Fitzgerald.

Against this background, Hemingway's *Garden* seems a self-conscious attempt to rewrite Fitzgerald's marriage with Zelda – the saga of a talented friend whom he considered ruined by a crazy wife – giving it (and therefore both *Tender* and Genesis) what he took to be a more satisfactory conclusion.[36] The new conclusion reflects a masculinity that pities but is not undone by "feminine" weakness. Women are to be loved but not permitted to become sabotagers of male prowess.[37] Again, there are parallels in Hemingway's own life.

[33] Hemingway, *Selected Letters*, p. 407. [34] Ibid., p. 408.

[35] Ibid., p. 428; emphasis in original.

[36] Kenneth Lynn discusses Zelda's madness and sexual history, as well as Hemingway's reaction to it, in *Hemingway*, esp. pp. 283–288.

[37] This is a recurrent theme in Hemingway; as Bill enjoins Nick in "The Three Day Blow" (1925): "Fall for them [women] but don't let them ruin you." See *In Our Time* (New York: Collier Books, 1986), p. 46. Mellow has observed that, throughout his life, Hemingway wanted "an Eden without an Eve"; see his *Hemingway: A Life Without Consequences*, p. 162.

In *A Moveable Feast*, on which Hemingway worked concurrently with *Garden* and which was also published posthumously, he recounts the famous incident in which his first wife Hadley let a suitcase containing the only copies of several of his stories be lost or stolen. He writes, retrospectively, that he was not angry and that "it was probably good for me to lose early work."[38] When David Bourne is initially unable to remember his burned stories, this is akin to a sentence of death, a militant angel barring the return to Paradise. For Hemingway too, capacity for literary work is the key to appreciation of the world and other people, a sense of life's meaning. Alienated from his own imagination, he suffers disintegration, as at the end of his life. In touch with this power, he achieves, paradoxically, a kind of impersonal ecstasy. It is an ecstasy, however, without the check of truthful memory or personal responsibility. All of this is tied up, for both Bourne and Hemingway, with over-indulgence in alcohol and sex – those notoriously ambivalent sources of creativity and loss of control, heightened sense of pleasure and a little death.[39] (Of the two times Bourne feels "empty and hollow" [pp.13 and 164], one is after making love and the other is after writing.) Also like Bourne, in any case, the Hemingway who loses his early manuscripts is soon able to write again and soon possessed of a second wife, Pauline, with whom he has had an affair while still married to the first.

Three years after Scott's death (and two years before beginning *Garden*), Hemingway wrote to Maxwell Perkins:

A woman ruined Scott. It wasn't just Scott ruining himself. But why couldn't he have told her to go to hell? Because she was sick. It's being sick makes them act so bloody awful usually and it's because they're sick you can't treat them as you should. The first great gift for a man is to be healthy and the second, maybe greater, is to fall [in] with healthy women. You can always trade one healthy woman in on another. But start with a sick woman and see where you get.[40]

To Hemingway, Fitzgerald must have seemed as fated to marry Zelda as Oedipus was to marry his mother; a single woman to sacrifice for was the "unnatural" destiny of both. I know of no better statement of Hemingway's opposing, cyclical philosophy (as embodied in his four marriages) than: "The first great gift for a man is to be healthy." Nor

---

[38] Hemingway, *A Moveable Feast* (New York: Collier Books, 1987), p. 74.

[39] Hemingway's friend, Buck Lanham, provides a striking picture of the link between the novelist's dynamism and creativity, on the one hand, and his self-forgetfulness and self-destructiveness, on the other: Hemingway usually wrote "standing up, with a pencil in one hand and a drink in the other." Quoted in Lynn, *Hemingway*, p. 527.

[40] Hemingway, *Selected Letters*, p. 553.

can I think of any better gloss on *Garden* than: ". . . start with a sick woman and see where you get."

Hemingway's fourth wife, née Mary Welsh, wrote a 1961 piece for *Look Magazine* that strongly echoes her husband's sentiments on these matters. Published just two months after his suicide, it is entitled "Hemingway: A personal story by the great writer's wife." Nominally an account of their life together, particularly their safaris and fishing trips, its every line shouts: "See how the good wife admired and protected her husband's genius." I end this section by stringing together telling passages, with little comment:

I sparred and fenced and tried to fend off intruders when Papa was working at the bookcase in his bedroom in Cuba, knowing that if they jerked him . . . far back from the places and people he was making inside his head and on the paper, he might not that day manage to make the return journey to his private places and secret people. But . . . he liked me when I came up to the house from the gardens carrying woven-reed trays of our fresh vegetables for lunch or baskets of roses . . .

[Safari living] has the sense of freedom that comes from living in miles and miles of unencumbered space. It has totally fresh air, no telephones, no brackets of time chopping the days into dull, dutiful segments. The responsibilities are few . . .

After we had fished [off Peru] more than a month without a break, I reached a new conclusion and said to Papa, "The most important asset any woman of yours needs, lamb, is durability."

Whatever kind of day the Gulf Stream gave us, we welcomed it. We were proud and happy about our close, smooth teamwork. We felt not merely male and female, but friends and brothers. Papa was my only brother and the best friend I ever had.[41]

The themes I have highlighted fairly jump off the page: writing as a "return journey," the good wife as carrying reminders of "the garden(s)," freedom as coming from living "unencumbered" and with "few responsibilities," "durability" as "the most important asset," spouses

[41] Mary Hemingway, "Hemingway," *Look Magazine*, September 12, 1961, pp. 19–20, 20, 22, and 23. This article contains several color photographs, including a 1¼ page spread of Mary with her left hand holding a rifle and her right hand being held by Ernest. They are gazing into one another's eyes, "lovingly," as they stand beside a kudu that Mary has just shot. Only their black African companion (presumably a guide or gun-bearer) is looking at the dying animal, kneeling to support its head with both his hands as blood drips from its mouth. The Hemingways' shared ecstasy could be exceptionally cruel at times.

who are "proud and happy," "not merely male and female, but friends and brothers." Who had been feeding lines to whom?[42]

CONCLUSION

Whatever the (auto)biographical correlations, when taken together Hemingway's and Fitzgerald's novels present an old alternative: either back to the garden or into the night. In the aftermath of a fall, one may flee from time in search of one's lost repose; or one may accept temporal affliction (if not guilt) for the sake of others' redemption (if not one's own). The options are a repristinating recollection, common to some forms of idealism and Hemingway's naturalism,[43] or an atonement closer to what Søren Kierkegaard calls "repetition."[44] The first path deemphasizes individual identity and the decisiveness of moral choice, the key to tranquility being (in the extreme) the acceptance of one's own nothingness and the utter ineffability of its origin and end. The second path accents personal identity and moral choice as crucial – as irreducible parts of lived reality and of whatever reality by which one's life may be judged – and thus sees the flight to nonentity as a temptation and an avoidance of responsibility.

The way of ecstatic recollection assumes an enduring continuity between one's present reality and ideal humanity, such that (in its naturalistic form) cultivating good habits, finding a healthy wife, maintaining imaginative detachment, relying on instincts, trying not to think too much, and generally giving oneself over to the rhythms of the

---

[42] In *Hemingway: A Life Without Consequences*, p. 382, Mellow remarks that Hemingway often perceived "love and sex as a merger of sexual identities." Kenneth Lynn cites an entry written by Ernest into Mary's diary to establish that Hemingway actually lived out a version of sexual transposition with his last wife – an "embrace . . . quite new and outside all tribal law" (quoted in *Hemingway*, p. 533).

[43] Hemingway eschews any "higher" virtue or knowledge in favor of the wisdom of the body. At his best, he approaches the no-nonsense courage and endurance taught by Epicurus at "the Garden" in Athens; at his worst, he embodies the selfish pursuit of physical pleasure mistakenly associated with "Epicureanism." Epicurus's Garden was a moral destination rather than an amoral retreat.

[44] Repetition is, roughly, self-realization brought about by ethical choice, what Kierkegaard describes as "the earnestness of existence" or "acquired originality." The great obstacles to repetition are guilt and the general impossibility of achieving personal transparency (unmixed motives leading to nondubious acts) in time. Human effort is necessary but not sufficient; ultimately, only a suffering divinity ("the eternal") can save fallen humanity, according to Kierkegaard. Quotations are from Kierkegaard's *Repetition*, ed. and trans. by Howard V. and Edna H. Hong (Princeton: Princeton University Press, 1983), p. 133; *Journals and Papers*, vol. III, ed. and trans. by the Hongs, assisted by Gregor Malantschuk (Bloomington: Indiana University Press, 1975), no. 3795, p. 764; and the "Supplement" to *Repetition*, p. 324.

universe are the means to recovering peace. To recur to an earlier image, Hemingway's sacred and profane "houses" can both be situated in heaven, with an unbroken road running between them. In this case, the Spenderian ideal of "living through the time" ultimately entails *escaping from time itself* into un-self-consciousness, the blissful absence of all moral ideals.

Hemingway's drive to "redo," to flee from consequences and limitations, to "take life over," is a tendency characteristic of him and us. But Hemingway came to sense, however inconsistently, that the quest to deny or escape outer effects is the result of an original accent on them. If utility must be maximized, say, or world historical significance won, the task proves far too daunting for a finite individual, at least one who feels and thinks. The guilty past and the boundless demands of the future shall not be denied. Nobody can permanently tame fate, if only because nobody can fully cheat death. Even a "successful" life of martial glory or literary fame or public service will end up longing for release from endless effort with unpredictable outcome. In the short story "Soldier's Home," Hemingway says of Harold Krebs, whose name suggests the mindless natural cycle by which food is converted to energy: "He did not want any consequences. He did not want any consequences ever again. He wanted to live along without consequences."[45] Better to "live through the time" with no moral ideals at all, no regrets and no lasting effects or affects.[46]

Putting these points more technically, Hemingway's longing to return to the innocence and oblivion of the Garden is the upshot of initially accepting the consequentialist gambit. Consequentialism self-destructs when pursued single-mindedly; the burden of producing objective results, unconstrained by principle, can only be relieved by a pervasive irony in which past actions and present relationships do not define us – we can cut them loose at a moment's notice, as a stud gambols away from a breeding mare, simply by not caring. (Call this the Nietzschean paradox: the will to power and dominion ends in a rather passive *amor fati*, if not insanity.) Hemingway's gift was one part an inexhaustible bravado that sought to dominate reality, to rely on instinct and industry for lasting achievement, and one part an impersonal detachment that saw the impossibility of finally pulling this off. What he failed to appreciate, I believe, is that the consequentialist gambit itself is to be declined in

---

[45] Hemingway, *In Our Time*, p. 71.
[46] Mellow takes the passage from "Soldier's Home" as summing up its author's emerging philosophy of life; it also suggests the subtitle of Mellow's biography. See *Hemingway: A Life Without Consequences*, p. 125.

favor of inner accountability to love, with all its liabilities. Hemingway is not unaware of finer truths about love and kindness, but he is ashamed of them and struggles prudently to forget or ignore them.[47]

The way of tenderness and atonement, in contrast to Hemingway's innocent ecstasy, acknowledges a decisive break between what is and what ought to be, such that an extraordinary heroism, rather than prudence or hygiene, is now required as corrective. Atonement carries an acute awareness of the ruptures due to moral failure (a.k.a. original sin) and hence of the fact that continued commitment to ideals and relations will be accompanied by tenderness, ambiguity, and pain – some species of descent into hell or wandering "through verdurous glooms and winding mossy ways." This is not to suggest that no human life is good or that no historical achievement is meaningful, but rather that we admire most those figures who are aware of the contingency of their achievement, the range but also the limits of their will and ability. Even an eventual resurrection after a fall (unlike a resuscitation) would presuppose a death, not a longed-for extinction but an accepted crucifixion. This insight was definitive of Fitzgerald's genius.

Both Innocence and Experience may be spiritually profound paths – just as both *The Garden of Eden* and *Tender Is the Night* are moving literature – but the difference between them makes all the difference in the world. Hemingway's example displays, at its best, the liberating power and impersonal love of beauty associated with ecstatic religion; whereas Fitzgerald's choice of tenderness accepts, even at its worst, the vulnerability that full openness to the pain of others brings.[48] (Ecstasy can decay into narcissism, of course, and tenderness fall into masochism.) Yet I find in Fitzgerald's art (and life) the greater virtue;[49] he leads us, not back to a morning in Eden, but forward into the night in a very different garden, Gethsemane. What happens beyond that night is the weightiest question raised by *Tender*. Here the key contrast is not between Ernest and Scott but between Scott and Matthew, Mark, Luke, and John. Is Dick Diver, in not relying on *any* power (natural or supernatural) for his

---

[47] Mellow is very good on the theme, originally struck by Ezra Pound, of Hemingway's hidden sensitivity. See *Hemingway: A Life Without Consequences*, p. 377.

[48] For a perceptive discussion of the choice between tenderness and ecstasy in the works of Vladimir Nabokov, see Richard Rorty, *Contingency, Irony, and Solidarity* (Cambridge: Cambridge University Press, 1989), chap. 7, esp. pp. 158, 161, and 168.

[49] Toward the end of his life, Hemingway punctuated his "Second Poem to Mary" with the moral: ". . . no contrition, no bloody fucking contrition, only love and compassion." In context, I find these among the most powerful words he ever composed, something of a breakthrough in his understanding of virtue. During most of his career, though, accent was on "no contrition" rather than "love and compassion." For a recording of this piece by the author, hear "Ernest Hemingway Reads" (New York: HarperCollins, 1965 & 1992).

deliverance (pre- or postmortem), morally superior to Jesus of Nazareth? Is pure tragedy a truer or nobler appraisal of human existence than Christian faith and hope?

In "Sleeping and Waking" (1934), Fitzgerald describes how in his late thirties he became beset by insomnia. Even when exhausted, he could no longer lull himself to sleep by rehearsing youthful fantasies (e.g., of quarterbacking the Princeton football team to victory over Yale). As he lay awake in the dark, romantic dreams of recreating his past would give way to a sense of "horror and waste," recollection of unnecessary cruelties and lost opportunities. Then would come the question:

> . . . what if this night prefigured the night after death – what if all thereafter was an eternal quivering on the edge of an abyss, with everything base and vicious in oneself urging one forward and the baseness and viciousness of the world just ahead. No choice, no road, no hope – only the endless repetition of the sordid and the semi-tragic. Or to stand forever, perhaps, on the threshold of life unable to pass it and return to it.[50]

Christianity maintains that, although sin is a reality, there is a way out of hell, that such tragic and semi-tragic visions need not be the final word. There is a third alternative to oblivion (utter self-forgetfulness) and the mere repetition of the sordid (not the "repetition" envisioned by Kierkegaard). That alternative is long-suffering love (*agape*), understood as a curative gift of God.

Christian orthodoxy holds that so long as one does not circumvent the cross, personal rebirth is possible. Jesus of Nazareth walks the Via Dolorosa, but the Risen Christ prefigures the final *convergence* of tenderness and ecstasy, sacrifice and liberation. The choice between the night and the garden is real and fundamental in time – one must go forward rather than backward – but the end of time will see the dawning of a new day. A foretaste of this consummation may be possible, but only in eternity will wholeness flow from a fully restored relation to God. This is the Christian hope, as I understand it, though I must delay until later considering how such hope relates to belief in an afterlife (chapter 5). Fitzgerald, for his part, concluded his second "Crack-Up" article tantalizingly: "I have the feeling that someone, I'm not sure who, is sound asleep – someone who could have helped me to keep my shop open. It wasn't Lenin, and it wasn't God."[51]

A saving incarnation who is both man and God no doubt seemed a

---

[50] Fitzgerald, *The Crack-Up*, p. 67. Compare the ending of "Ode to a Nightingale": "Was it a vision, or a waking dream? / Fled is that music: – do I wake or sleep?"

[51] Fitzgerald, "Pasting It Together," in ibid., pp. 79–80.

metaphysical impossibility (if not a moral delusion) to both Fitzgerald and Hemingway. Thus they leave us with irony and tragedy, at the edge of repetition in Kierkegaard's fullest sense. Whether a passion and sacrificial death can in fact be followed by a resurrection and healing ascension is an issue which literary criticism as such is not equipped to address. But literature can raise the question, and poetry in particular may gesture toward a night that is not permanent and a love that is not futile:

> 1
> This night there are no limits to what may be given.
> This is not a night but a marriage,
> a couple whispering in bed in unison the same words.
> Darkness simply lets down a curtain for that.

> 2
> A night full of talking that hurts,
> my worst held-back secrets: Everything
> has to do with loving and not loving.
> This night will pass.
> Then we have work to do.

> 3
> Night comes so people can sleep like fish
> in black water. Then day.
>
> Some people pick up their tools.
> Others become the making itself.

> 4
> Inside water, a waterwheel turns.
> A star circulates with the moon.
>
> We live in the night ocean wondering,
> *What are these lights?*[52]

---

[52] These lines are by the Sufi mystic Rumi (Jalal ad-din Rumi, 1207–1273), "Four Poems on the Night," trans. by John Moyne and Coleman Barks, in *World Poetry*, ed. by Katharine Washburn, John S. Major, and Clifton Fadiman (New York: W.W. Norton, 1998), p. 478. Karen Armstrong writes: "Like other Sufis, Rumi saw the universe as a theophany of God's myriad Names. Some of these revealed God's wrath or severity, while others expressed those qualities of mercy which were intrinsic to the divine nature. The mystic was engaged in a ceaseless struggle (*jihad*) to distinguish the compassion, love and beauty of God in all things and to strip away everything else." See Armstrong, *A History of God: The 4000–Year Quest of Judaism, Christianity and Islam* (New York: Knopf, 1994), p. 241.

CHAPTER 3

The five loves

How do I love thee? Let me count the ways.

Elizabeth Barrett Browning[1]

[L]ove covers a multitude of sins.

1 Peter 4:8

INTRODUCTION

Poets seldom count anything, but in the case of love, they make an exception. It is standard practice even for eloquent theologians to distinguish types of love, the three most prominent being: *agape* (steadfast love of God and neighbor), *eros* (preferential desire), and *philia* (friendship). Sometimes a fourth and fifth are identified as distinct types: *storge* (affection for the less than fully personal) and *amor sui* (self-love).[2] The meaning and even the tenability of these standard distinctions are not universally agreed on, however. When Anders Nygren argued in the 1930s that *agape* and *eros* are "different attitudes to life, different tendencies, which are in actual conflict with one another,"[3] for example, he touched off a debate that is still with us today. Much literature on love has sought either to uphold Nygren's position or to reconcile love of neighbor with preferential loves and/or love of self.[4] For my part, I want

---

[1] Barrett Browning, *Sonnets from the Portuguese and Other Love Poems* (New York: Doubleday, 1990), sonnet XLII, p. 53.

[2] See, for example, Anders Nygren, *Agape and Eros*; C.S. Lewis, *The Four Loves* (New York and London: Harcourt Brace Jovanovich, 1960); and Ceslas Spicq, O.P., *Theological Lexicon of the New Testament*, vol. I, and *Agape in the New Testament*, vol. I. With reference to love-of-God and love-of-neighbor, Oliver O'Donovan prefers "to speak of 'aspects' of love rather than of 'kinds' . . ." See O'Donovan, *The Problem of Self-love in St. Augustine*, p. 13.

[3] Nygren, *Agape and Eros*, p. 56.

[4] See, for instance, the exchange between Colin Grant, Carter Heyward, Edward Collins Vacek, S.J., and Gene Outka in *Journal of Religious Ethics* (Spring 1996). Grant defends the uniqueness and indispensability of *agape*; for a defense of the sufficiency of "the eros tradition," see Alan Soble's *The Structure of Love* (New Haven and London: Yale University Press, 1990).

to defend a vigorous contrast between *agape, eros, philia,* and self-love, affirming the priority of *agape* in several senses, yet I stop short of pitting the loves against one another. I mention *storge* along the way, but it concerns me least as a type since it seems so closely allied with, if not part of, *agape.*

To hold that agapic love is antithetical to neither erotic desire nor reasoned justice for oneself or one's friends is comparatively (though not entirely) uncontroversial.[5] What remains less clear, however, is what it means to affirm the primacy of *agape* as first Christian virtue. One thing I believe it means is that *agape* is not to be conflated with, derived from, or put on the same plane as *eros, philia,* or prudent self-love.[6] Understood properly, *agape* "covers a multitude of sins," in the sense of forgiving and healing them. Understood improperly, *agape* "covers" sins in the quite different sense of leading us to ignore or even commit them. I support these contentions in section I by contrasting the supreme fifth-century advocate of *caritas* (Saint Augustine) with the ablest twentieth-century defender of *eros* (Sigmund Freud). Having done that, I turn in section II to discuss love of neighbor as it relates specifically to self-love and friendship. Here I examine two contemporary champions of love (Simone Weil and Edward Vacek), appreciating both but fully endorsing neither. My partial counter-thesis is the Protestant claim that the first (human) task of Christian ethics is neither to love others nor to love oneself, but *to accept being loved by God.* A love that would sustain a relation to others or oneself, in other words, is second to a love that would produce the possibility of relation itself. In section III, I discuss briefly Jesus's final commandment in the Gospel of John as the necessary inspiration for any Christian understanding of love.

I. *AGAPE* AND *EROS*: NEITHER AUGUSTINE NOR FREUD

Saint Augustine and Freud form a natural pair for my purposes because both sought to rationalize Platonic *eros,* the wrinkle being that Augustine would school *eros* toward a distinctively Christian charity,

---

[5] On the compatibility of *agape* with other forms of love, see, for instance, Edward Collins Vacek, S.J., *Love, Human and Divine,* chap. 5; and Robert M. Adams, *The Virtue of Faith* (Oxford: Oxford University Press, 1987), chap. 12. Interestingly, Vacek associates desire for relationship with another with *philia* (see his pp. 157–158), while Adams equates the same desire with *eros* (see his p. 190).

[6] As Paul Ramsey notes, "it should be affirmed, first of all, that 'prudence' has rightly to be understood to be in the service of some prior principle." See Ramsey, *War and the Christian Conscience* (Durham, N.C.: Duke University Press, 1961), p. 4.

Freud away from it. Augustine did not invent the "reign of charity,"[7] but
he did help solidify it in Latin theology; similarly, Freud did not depose
charity, but he did diagnose and prescribe its decline in Western culture.
Both Augustine and Freud have been dismissed by many as hopelessly
mythic and misogynist, but any current defense of Christian charity still
falls under the shadow of these two Titans. How do their visions
compare, and how might an alternative understanding of agapic and
erotic love bear on related ethical norms, especially justice?

To anticipate, my thesis is that Christian charity is neither aim-
inhibited *eros* (*pace* Freud), nor aim-enhanced *eros* (*pace* Augustine). *Agape*
has singular priority to all other forms of love; it both precedes them
causally and governs them epistemically. Unlike Nygren, however, I see
eros, *philia*, *storge*, and even self-love as growing out of *agape* as its proper
fruits, rather than being entirely discontinuous with (or even contradictory to) *agape* as its implacable rivals. The loves are distinct, but they are
not antithetical. To be sure, Christian theists hold that all of reality
stems causally from God. But a unified field theory of loves, in which all
are fully reducible to one, denies the complexity of human experience;
even as a chaos theory, in which various loves are fully contradictory,
denies life's coherence. These conclusions are pressed on us, I believe,
when we allow Freud and Augustine to come into mutually corrective
dialogue.

A. Freud on agape and eros

Freud explicitly rejects faith, hope, and agapic love as ideals; but he does
not immediately dismiss them as based on propositional falsehoods.
Religious faith performs real sociological and psychological functions,
he grants, and these give it the continuing power "to overwhelm Reason
and Science."[8] Because there are latent truths or at least accustomed
satisfactions in religious "illusions," a purely intellectual critique cannot
displace traditional piety; one must attend to the social and psychic
benefits that have allowed theological virtues to endure for so long, even
if in attenuated form. Only then can religion be overcome in favor of a
more rational and scientific worldview that better serves social harmony

---

[7] Augustine, *On Christian Doctrine* [397, with a fourth book added in 426], trans. by D.W. Robertson
(New York: Macmillan, 1958), bk. three, chap. XV, p. 93.

[8] Freud, *Moses and Monotheism*, trans. by Katherine Jones (New York: Vintage Books, 1967), p. 157,
quoted in J. Samuel Preus, *Explaining Religion: Criticism and Theory from Bodin to Freud* (New Haven
and London: Yale University Press, 1987), p. 161.

and psychic stability.[9] For all his recognition of the tenacity of religious faith, hope, and love, however, Freud holds that they must ultimately be unmasked as personally unhealthy (repressive of instincts), socially unjust (disrespectful to friends and family), politically intolerant (disutilitarian), as well as basically deluded (false).[10]

Freud's critique takes particular aim at several interrelated features of *agape*,[11] but for my summary purpose here two are primary: its universality and its unconditionedness. In calling for equal regard for all other human beings, *agape* is not psychologically possible, Freud believes: we simply cannot love more than a few people with genuine concern and intimacy. If we hold ourselves to a standard of universal love, therefore, the self-criticisms levelled by conscience will inevitably make us petulant and/or neurotic.[12] In being unconditional, moreover, *agape* is unjust: it fails to honor those who are truly excellent or to whom we have special obligations (friends and relatives), and it wrongly upholds those who are hostile or offensive. As Freud candidly puts it, "not all men are worthy of love," so any standard of behavior that requires us to treat them as such is misguided.[13] If we would build an ethic on love, we must begin with *eros* instead of *agape*, or rather we must recognize that *agape* is but an

---

[9] Freud, *The Future of an Illusion*, trans. by W.D. Robson-Scott, revised and ed. by James Strachey (Garden City, NY: Anchor Books, 1964), pp. 76–82.

[10] On religion (especially *agape*) as unhealthy, see *Civilization and Its Discontents* trans. and ed. by James Strachey (New York: W.W. Norton, 1961), pp. 108–109. On religion as unjust, see ibid., pp. 57 and 66. On religion as intolerant, see *Group Psychology and the Analysis of the Ego*, trans. and ed. by James Strachey (New York: W.W. Norton, 1959), p. 39; and *Civilization and Its Discontents*, pp. 72–73. On religion as deluded, see *The Future of an Illusion*, p. 86; and *Civilization and Its Discontents*, pp. 31–32 and 36.

In *The Future of an Illusion*, Freud claims that religions are "illusions," i.e., wish-fulfillments, but he protests that "[i]llusions need not necessarily be false" (p. 49) and that "[t]o assess the truth-value of religious doctrines does not lie within the scope of the present enquiry" (p. 52). The protests are disingenuous, however. When he goes on to suggest that religion is "the universal obsessional neurosis of humanity" (p. 71) and to write of "the absurdities that religious doctrines put before [a man]" (p. 78), the veneer of agnosticism falls away. It is clear that Freud thinks of religion as imposing on believers "psychical infantilism" and "mass-delusion," as he puts it in *Civilization and Its Discontents* (p. 36), something "so patently infantile" and "so foreign to reality" (p. 22) as to be pitiful. Peter Gay notes that Freud "visualized the confrontation of religion and science as one of pure and permanent animosity," and that "it was as an atheist that Freud developed psychoanalysis." See Gay, *A Godless Jew: Freud, Atheism, and the Making of Psychoanalysis* (New Haven and London: Yale University Press, 1987), pp. 4–5 and 37.

[11] Ernest Wallwork specifies "five major lines" along which Freud, in *Civilization and Its Discontents*, criticizes the Christian love commandment: "(1) it cannot be kept, (2) its call for treating 'neighbors' with equal love is unjust to those to whom we are tied by special relations, (3) it ignores the evidence that not all persons are equally worthy of love, (4) it handles aggression so poorly that it actually encourages hostility toward outsiders, and (5) it is a source of considerable unhappiness." See Wallwork, "Thou Shalt Love Thy Neighbor as Thyself: The Freudian Critique," in *Journal of Religious Ethics*, vol. 10, no. 2 (Fall 1982), p. 267.

[12] Freud, *Civilization and Its Discontents*, p. 109.

[13] Ibid., pp. 36, 56–58, 66–67; the quotation is from p. 57.

"aim-inhibited" form of *eros* that calls for too radical a suspension of prudence and reciprocity.

Eros is the Freudian touchstone, the instinct of love and life that stands opposed to the instinct of hatred and death.[14] It is important to emphasize, nonetheless, that for Freud *eros* also involves an "overvaluation" of the loved object, an "idealization" that is often delusional and destructive.[15] The erotic lover projects onto his loved one perfections that he cannot realize himself, in a vicarious attempt to find happiness and fulfillment. In its widest Freudian sense, *eros* does not exclude tenderness for and unity with others,[16] but whatever altruism or self-sacrifice may be possible for a person will itself flow from (deflected) erotic energies and will require that she receive basic ego gratifications in return.[17] The idealization of the other may lead to "selfless" action on the lover's part, but there is an ineliminably narcissistic and self-serving cast to Freudian *eros*. The problem is that in unilaterally serving the idealized other the erotic lover jeopardizes his own self-esteem and ego strength; he may become morbidly dependent on, and/or possessive of, the object of his inflated attention.

Freud's therapy in light of *agape*'s liabilities and *eros*'s own tendency to be maladaptive is to bind instinct with justice. "The first requisite of civilization . . . is that of justice – that is, the assurance that a law once made will not be broken in favor of an individual."[18] Freud's accent on justice is not simply political. On the individual level, he recommends a reciprocity in which the emotional energy one gives in loving another is roughly balanced by the ego enhancement one receives in being loved

[14] "What are commonly called the sexual instincts are looked upon by us as the part of Eros which is directed toward objects. Our speculations have suggested that Eros operates from the beginning of life and appears as a 'life instinct' in opposition to the 'death instinct' which was brought into being by the coming to life of inorganic substance. These speculations seek to solve the riddle of life by supposing that these two instincts were struggling with each other from the very first." See Freud, *Beyond the Pleasure Principle*, trans. and ed. by James Strachey (New York: W.W. Norton, 1961), p. 73, ftnt. 21.

[15] Freud, "On Narcissism: An Introduction," in *The Standard Edition of the Complete Psychological Works of Sigmund Freud*, vol. XIV, trans. and ed. by James Strachey (London: The Hogarth Press, 1957), p. 94; and *Group Psychology*, pp. 56–57.

[16] See, for example, Freud, "The Most Prevalent Form of Degradation in Erotic Life," in *Sexuality and the Psychology of Love* (New York: Collier Books, 1963), pp. 59–60; *Group Psychology*, pp. 44 and 57; and *Civilization and Its Discontents*, p. 105.

[17] As Ernest Wallwork puts it: " 'Reciprocity,' not universal love, is the key to Freud's own ethic." "Freud's psychological position is not finally destructive of an other-regarding ethic," Wallwork declares, but he also acknowledges that "continuing altruism, in the absence of self-gratification, is simply not possible from the perspective of classical psychoanalytic theory." For Freud, "in loving another, we expect egoistic rewards in return, and the relationship will not last if these rewards are not forthcoming." See Wallwork, "The Freudian Critique," pp. 266, 268, 274, and 276.   [18] Freud, *Civilization and Its Discontents*, p. 49.

by another. To avoid love relations altogether would be pathological,[19] but one must insist on a reliable mutuality in which basic needs and expectations are met on both sides. On the social level, Freud recommends checking one's instinctual drives in order to give others (including strangers) those basic considerations that preserve public peace. One tailors sexual gratification, for example, according to the proper time, place, and person; similarly, one limits aggressive competition to the extent that others do the same, to the benefit of all. This reining in of natural tendencies can be consensual and even creative, but it is finally a rather Hobbesian *modus vivendi* rather than the respect and sacrificial service required by traditional *agape*.[20] The *modus vivendi* comes at a psychic cost, moreover; a certain discontent is inevitable for the civilized person, who "has exchanged a portion of his possibilities of happiness for a portion of security."[21] A tense but livable union between erotic and aggressive impulses and the demands of civilization, rather than the irrational beliefs and crippling guilts associated with *agape*, is the best we can hope for.[22]

Freud is not recommending an instinctual egoism that is merely hedonistic or somehow "beyond good and evil."[23] He does not reject outright the category of moral guilt, for instance; as the fruit of an internalized sense of right and wrong, it is inevitable and even desirable within a rational social system. "It seems . . . that every civilization must be built up on coercion and renunciation of instinct";[24] and within limits, the guilt associated with conscience helps us to control instincts that, if given their head, would be destructive.[25] But, again, Freud

---

[19] "A strong egoism is a protection against falling ill, but in the last resort we must begin to love in order not to fall ill, and we are bound to fall ill if, in consequence of frustration, we are unable to love." See Freud, "On Narcissism," p. 85.

[20] On the genesis of social justice out of initial hostility and envy, via group identification with an exceptional leader, see Freud, *Group Psychology*, pp. 66–68.

[21] Freud, *Civilization and Its Discontents*, p. 73.   [22] Ibid., p. 74.

[23] This fact keeps Freud a recognizably ethical thinker, unlike Nietzsche, who sought to replace ethical notions like love and justice, good and evil, with purely aesthetic values like health and power, joy and *amor fati*. See Nietzsche, *Beyond Good and Evil* and *On the Genealogy of Morals*, both in *Basic Writings of Nietzsche*, ed. and trans. by Walter Kaufmann (New York: Modern Library, 1968). On Freud's rejection of "egoistic hedonism," see Wallwork, "The Freudian Critique," pp. 265–266.   [24] Freud, *The Future of an Illusion*, p. 5.

[25] Freud contrasts "the normal, conscious sense of guilt" with "maladies" like obsessional neurosis and melancholia, in which "the sense of guilt is over-strongly conscious." See *The Ego and the Id*, trans. by Joan Riviere, revised and ed. by James Strachey (New York: W.W. Norton, 1960), pp. 51–52. Freud goes on to note that "even ordinary normal morality has a harshly restraining, cruelly prohibiting quality" (p. 56), but he clearly sees the superego and conscience as indispensable in the ego's "progressive conquest of the id" (p. 58). See also *Civilization and Its Discontents*, pp. 84–86 and 95–96.

disdains theological virtues like *agape* as setting "overstrict" standards and thus producing unreasonable or surplus guilt.[26] *Agape* is nothing but aim-inhibited *eros*, but a more realistic *eros* tempered by justice, rather than an idealized *agape* transcending justice, is the primary Freudian norm.

How might a Christian theologian respond to Freud? One of the enduring problems with Freud's view is its reductionism. He affirms that religious commitments are responses to something real, but he does not take the first-person accounts of believers to be accurate explanations of their experiences.[27] The issue is how far one can depart from the lived experience of theological virtues, especially charity, without falsifying them. Freud is notorious for writing:

> The nucleus of what we mean by love naturally consists (and this is what is commonly called love, and what the poets sing of) in sexual love with sexual union as its aim. But we do not separate from this – what in any case has a share in the name "love" – on the one hand, self-love, and on the other, love for parents and children, friendship and love for humanity in general, and also devotion to concrete objects and to abstract ideas. Our justification lies in the fact that psycho-analytic research has taught us that all these tendencies are an expression of the same instinctual impulses; in relations between the sexes these impulses force their way towards sexual union, but in other circumstances they are diverted from this aim or are prevented from reaching it . . .

Freud does not flinch from the primacy of the erotic, going on to observe that:

> In its origin, function, and relation to sexual love, the "Eros" of the philosopher Plato coincides exactly with the love-force, the libido of psycho-analysis . . .
> Psycho-analysis, then, gives these love instincts the name of sexual instincts, *a priori* and by reason of their origin.[28]

Freud is aware that many reject such a position as perverse "pansexualism," but he thinks the main motivation is a "faintheartedness" that finds sex "mortifying and humiliating."[29] Such prudery is not my agenda. One need not be obsessive or puritanical about matters venereal to ask: is it really plausible to reduce love of neighbor to a

---

[26] Freud, *Civilization and Its Discontents*, pp. 88 and 108–109.

[27] Preus notes that both Durkheim and Freud "began by honoring the conviction of the religious that their ideas and actions are responses to something real – some generative system of forces quite exceeding the critical power of reason either to reproduce or to eradicate . . . Despite their concession, however, Durkheim and Freud agreed that believers do not understand the real grounds of their convictions." See *Explaining Religion*, p. 162. Durkheim located the genesis of religion in the social collective, while Freud offered a more psychoanalytic approach. But Preus states the undeniable: "[F]or Freud, religion is obsolete and to be superseded in the name of the inexorable progress of reason and truth" (p. 164).   [28] Freud, *Group Psychology*, pp. 29–30.

[29] Ibid., p. 30.

deficient or deluded or deflected form of sexual love (Freudian *eros*)? I defend below a negative answer to this question, but some views held by Christian theologians tend to support Freud's suspicion.

B. *A comparison with Augustine on* eros *and* caritas

Consider, for instance, Saint Augustine. Augustine depicts moral education in terms of schooling *eros* into *caritas*, thus suggesting to some that the drive or energy which passes through God and is directed toward the neighbor is basically sexual (or at least preferential) in origin. Where Freud speaks of "aim-inhibited" libido or *eros*,[30] Augustine alludes, as it were, to aim-enhanced *amor* or *eros*. Augustine thinks of the schooling of *eros* – the outward-inward, inward-upward path of Plato – as a process of liberation and enlightenment. By turning one's psychic attention from mutable physical objects to the morally responsible soul, and then from the still sinful soul to the transcendent and perfect God, one is empowered to know the truth and to love others as God loves. One comes to appreciate God as the excellent and unchanging (the incorporeal *Summum Bonum*), and this restores human freedom and community (*libertas et communitas*), at least to a degree.[31] Freud, on the other hand, sees the turn to God and unconditional love of neighbor as a process of repression and falsification. One's personal energies and social skills are retarded by an erroneous vision of the world; we end up sick or unhappy because *agape* requires too large a sacrifice of natural instinct. Better, thinks Freud, to remain with the temporal objects of *eros*. Both Augustine and Freud imply, however, that a displacement of the natural object of *eros* is the initiating step in the ascent or descent to *agape*.

Augustine wishes ultimately to reconcile *eros* and *agape* by referring them both as *caritas* to God: *eros* as appraisive desire climbs upward to God, while *agape* as gracious creativity flows downward from God, thus a human–divine circuit is described. Freud, in contrast, wishes to reform *eros* and reject *agape* by denying that either refers to God: human love of finite things is all there is, and this must be reined in by the civil disciplines of delayed or foregone gratification. Freud's reductionism remains, nevertheless, the mirror image of Augustine's expansionism. We are left with endless disputes, with Augustinians insisting that Freudians have not sublimated *eros* enough and Freudians insisting that

---

[30] See, e.g., Freud, *Civilization and Its Discontents*, p. 65; see also *Group Psychology*, pp. 56 and 91.
[31] See Augustine, *Confessions* [397–400], trans. by R.S. Pine-Coffin (New York: Penguin Books, 1961), bk. VII, chap. 17, pp. 151–152, and bk. X, chap. 40, pp. 248–249. See also *On Christian Doctrine*, bk. two, chap. VII, pp. 38–40, for an outline of the seven steps to "wisdom."

Augustinians have repressed *eros* too much. Moreover, we wrestle with the nagging sense in Augustine that one is not loving the neighbor for her own sake (genuine *agape*), but rather "using" her as a means to ascend to God; even as we wrestle with the explicit insistence in Freud that one should not love the neighbor for his own sake, but rather accommodate him in order to descend into self-knowledge. The key motif in Freud is achieving depth: "Where id was, there ego shall be";[32] in Augustine the dominant metaphor is scaling height: "Where *cupiditas* was," to paraphrase, "there *caritas* shall be." (Freud would drain the Zuider Zee,[33] while Augustine would irrigate Plato's cave.) But the problem in both cases is beginning with a form of *eros*. To start with *eros*, natural desire guided by appraisive rationality, is to fail to see the unmerited bestowal of worth (*agape*) by which we all live. The Father in heaven "sends rain on the righteous and on the unrighteous" (Matt. 5:45).

I begin where I take the New Testament to begin: with the experience of *being loved uncritically* rather than with the effort to love self and others justly. I start, most fundamentally, with the kenotic love of God, a love made manifest in the free creation of the world *ex nihilo*. (Neither life nor ethics can begin with self-sufficiency.) This anti-Copernican revolution makes possible two important departures from both Freud and Augustine: (1) acknowledging a plurality of *kinds* (not merely objects) of love, with *eros* and *agape* being related but distinct;[34] and (2) putting charity first (what I earlier called strong *agape*), with *agape* seen as a gift of grace that transforms natural instinct. *Agape* is the inbreaking of the Sacred, the very power that created us, according to the New Testament, yet having such charity is a necessary condition for full human flourishing. It is this paradox of finding ultimate meaning in a love that surrenders personal advantage that Freud cannot account for and that Augustine struggles, with only partial success, to free from neo-Platonic fetters.

---

[32] Freud, *New Introductory Lectures on Psychoanalysis*, trans. and ed. by James Strachey (New York: W.W. Norton, 1965), p. 80.   [33] Ibid.

[34] My view partially parallels that of Nygren, who writes: "Eros and Agape belong originally to two entirely separate spiritual worlds, between which no direct communication is possible . . . we cannot count on any *direct* correspondence and commensurability between Eros and Agape." See Nygren, *Agape and Eros*, p. 31. Nygren is surely right to distinguish the two loves, but he overstates his case in construing *agape* as opposed to *eros*, neighbor-love as excluding self-love, Christian love as at odds with retributive justice, and so on. I take the first term in each of these three pairs to hold the key to a proper version of the second term; putting charity first makes possible the valid expression of erotic desires, commitment to the neighbor clarifies and deepens one's own personality, forgiveness grounds justice, etc. *Eros* unsubordinated and justice alone can become the enemies of *agape*, even as can a self-love that is idolatrous, but the remedy is emphasis on the *priority* of *agape* rather than on its exclusive validity (as I explain more fully below).

Freud surmised that there are two fundamental, and *sui generis*, human instincts: (1) *eros*, the drive to preserve life and create greater unity, and (2) *thanatos*, the drive to destroy life and collapse into utter nonentity. Both instincts are a function of the empirical "fact" that organic beings evolved out of inorganic matter, according to Freud, and both instincts are essentially conservative and repetitive. (Like Hemingway's David Bourne, Freudian instincts "tend toward the restoration of an earlier state of things."[35]) *Eros* is the desire to sustain life processes already achieved, that is, while *thanatos* is the desire to return to inanimate beginnings.[36] According to strong agapists, however, instinctual *eros* is not enough in humanity's struggle with destruction and death. Freud's own cogent account of (1) "the feebleness of our own bodies," (2) the "powerful share of aggressiveness" among human instincts, and (3) "the fatal inevitability of the sense of guilt"[37] suggests the normative necessity of *agape*. If we were left with the erotic energies that Freud specifies, civilization would be faced with insufficient resources to cope with its "discontents." Freud insists, for instance: "If I love someone, he must deserve it in some way . . . He deserves it if he is so like me in important ways that I can love myself in him; and he deserves it if he is so much more perfect than myself that I can love my ideal of my own self in him."[38] Because we usually see little merit in others and have a limited capacity for empathy with those different from ourselves, however, this insistence excludes from consideration the greater part of humanity.

Even the maternal instinct that Freud so valorizes is called into question by sadly familiar headlines: a young mother drowns her two infant sons in a lake, then claims they have been abducted by a stranger, evidently in order to be more attractive to an ambivalent lover; a second young woman gives birth in a bathroom stall, then leaves her newborn son strangled in a trash bin and returns to drink and dance at her high-school prom. These women need exactly the kind of compassion and support that they declined to give their offspring and that Freud declines to give civilization. Indeed, without a source of benevolence that is unconditional and forgiving, an intolerable guilt would seize us all. Need I say, fatherly love is at least as precarious as and perhaps even more liable to perversion than motherly; for instance, "fathers [are] the second largest group of incest perpetrators after uncles."[39]

Freud concedes that "if this grandiose commandment ['Thou shalt

---

[35] Freud, *Beyond the Pleasure Principle*, p. 44.
[36] See Ibid., chaps. 5 and 6, pp. 40–74; and *Civilization and Its Discontents*, pp. 77–82.
[37] See Freud, *Civilization and Its Discontents*, pp. 37, 68, and 95.   [38] Ibid., pp. 66–67.
[39] Diana E.H. Russell, *The Secret Trauma: Incest in the Lives of Girls and Women* (New York: Basic Books, 1986), p. 230.

love thy neighbor as thyself'] had run 'Love thy neighbor as thy neighbor loves thee,' I should not take exception to it."[40] But with this he falls below the Golden Rule, as well as Biblical *agape*, and thereby gives the game away. For we all live by the service and mercy of strangers whose love outstrips anything explicable in terms of reciprocity or desert or natural impulse. To repeat, a just and rational eroticism is not enough to keep physical vulnerability and moral culpability within livable bounds. Freud himself refers to "the contradiction – probably an irreconcilable one – between the primal instincts of Eros and death";[41] and though he ultimately rejects the simplistic hypothesis explored in *Beyond the Pleasure Principle* that "*the aim of all life is death*,"[42] he remains pessimistic about the long-term prospects of *eros*. Freud's view is dualistic, even agonistic: the life and death instincts are forever at odds, with no "instinct toward perfection" that might vanquish *thanatos* or otherwise impel human beings steadily to evolve.[43] He is well aware, of course, that Christians consider agapic love (e.g., the atoning sacrifice of Christ on the cross) to be both necessary and sufficient to redeem humanity's aesthetic and ethical shortcomings.[44] But for Freud the burden of charity (love of neighbor) is too demanding, and the promise of charity (eternal life) is falsely consoling; however much individuals may strive against it, their beginning in inanimate matter seems to dictate their end in same. This, then, is the bedrock issue: how tragic or futile is human existence, and what means do we have for coping with it?

The strong agapist holds that there are several means, but that *agape* has pride of place. There is at most a family resemblance between *agape*, *eros*, *philia*, *storge*, and self-love – each involves an intense caring about a life – but even when *agape* has priority, the five loves need not be reduced to a single type. Augustine and Freud notwithstanding, *agape* need be neither an enhanced nor an inhibited form of *eros*, because it is primarily a matter of bestowal rather than appraisal[45] – the subjective extension of value to another rather than an objective calculation of another's intrinsic merit. *Agape* is neither the undervaluation nor the overvaluation of someone's or something's worthiness, since it is self-consciously indiscriminate and other-enhancing. Love of the neighbor need not be irrational, in short, though it requires suprarational resources. Chris-

---

[40] Freud, *Civilization and Its Discontents*, p. 67.   [41] Ibid., p. 106.
[42] Freud, *Beyond the Pleasure Principle*, p. 46; emphasis in original.
[43] Ibid., pp. 50–51 and 63–64.   [44] See Freud, *Civilization and Its Discontents*, p. 99.
[45] See Irving Singer, *The Nature of Love*, vols. I–III (Chicago: University of Chicago Press, 1984–1987).

tians judge, at any rate, that God's gracious bestowal of value on individuals makes possible their bestowal of value on others. Human beings love because they are first loved by others and the Holy Other; and, as Kierkegaard, following Saint Paul, notes, "love builds up" even as it presupposes an innate capacity for growth.

Friendship may be the highest human relation when a rational ethic is the highest human capacity, but Christianity puts charity first, higher even than friendship. In fact, Christianity sees love of all neighbors to ground the preferential affections of *eros* and *philia*. *Eros* is purely appraisive, a discriminating attraction to what is considered intrinsically valuable, especially when this value is to the direct benefit of the lover. When brought to heel by reason, *eros* aims at evaluative justice, at appreciating persons and things for who and what they are or can do. In Augustine, this intimate connection between love and justice is explicit: "you [God] have commanded us not only to be continent, but also to be just; that is, to withhold our love from certain things and to bestow it on others."[46] Justifying love means schooling natural desire (*"amor"*) away from investment in material things (*"cupiditas"*) and toward communion with God (*"caritas"*). This is done by recognizing that the immutable Deity alone is truly excellent and able to satisfy the human longing for rest: ". . . you [God] made us for yourself and our hearts find no peace until they rest in you."[47] The unconditional willing of the good that I have associated with *agape*, on the other hand, entails a bestowal of worth that outstrips pure appraisal. *Agape* may be said to have a *limited* appraisive dimension, in as much as certain basic capacities must be judged to be in place for a caring relation to get off the ground. *Agape* must be able to perceive another's situation, for example, in order to move constructively to improve that situation. But *agape* most typically extends value to the loved one, helping him to realize dormant or distant potentials, regardless of any merit perceived in the beloved or any utility produced for the lover. *Agape* wants relationship with others, but it does not insist on personal advantage. Such charity is not founded on a just estimation of its object, to repeat, and it is not the result of schooling of one's natural erotic desires to be more generous and inclusive. It is, instead, a wondrous birth of the impulse to care without qualification.

The enigma is familiar: *eros*, which would look appraisively at its beloved object, is often deluded and self-absorbed, while *agape*, which would bestow value, sees others more clearly and reaches out to them as they are. Nearly a century before Freud, Stendahl observed that "the

---

[46] Augustine, *Confessions*, bk. X, chap. 37, p. 246.   [47] Ibid., bk. I, chap. 1, p. 21.

moment he is in love, the steadiest man sees no object such as it is," noting as well that those who are romantically infatuated "think they are enjoying such and such an object, while, under cover of that object, they are enjoying themselves."[48] Kierkegaard points out that agapic love, in contrast, "believes all things – and yet is never deceived" (cf. 1 Cor. 13:7).[49] *Agape* is never deceived because its faith corresponds to an action, a task; it *wills* the neighbor's good in trust, and by accepting the consequences of this it remains true to itself and aware of the world.

Perverted forms of *agape* can be self-beguiling, of course, as when "compassion" is really manipulation. And one must take care not to slander *eros* by identifying it exclusively with error or egotism. A Christian Platonist might maintain that by directing our *eros* toward what is truly worthwhile, culminating in God as the *Summum Bonum*, we become empowered to (re)turn to the world and to love others as God loves them: unconditionally and for their own sakes. She might distinguish, that is, between the upward path of a moral dialectic (governed by *eros*) and the downward path (governed by *agape*). On the upward path, when one is still a spiritual tyro, persons and things are to be "used" for the sake of coming into relation with God; otherwise, one might be distracted by friendship or distressed by sin and mortality. On the downward path, however, after one has been converted by God's grace, persons and things are to be served and appreciated more directly, for their own sakes.

Alas, in spite of his sensitivity to the Biblical demand to love the neighbor, Augustine himself never quite allows a disinterested appreciation of finite creatures. "If the things of this world delight you, praise God for them but turn your love away from them and give it to their Maker," he advises in the *Confessions*.[50] Like Plato and most neo-Platonists, he has enormous difficulty making sense of any obligation to invest himself in the mutable world of temporal beings, especially after he has seen the pure and unchanging light of eternity. Why should the philosopher reenter the cave of *The Republic*, bk. VII, when this would seem to mean again being mired in the world of mutable persons and things? Why should Augustine weep over the death of his own mother Monica?

As Augustine says, notoriously, in *On Christian Doctrine*:

. . . there is a profound question as to whether men should enjoy themselves, use themselves, or do both. For it is commanded to us that we should love one

---

[48] Stendahl, *On Love* [1822], trans. by Philip Sidney Woolf and Cecil N. Sidney Woolf (Mount Vernon: The Peter Pauper Press, n.d.), pp. 31 and 46.

[49] Kierkegaard, *Works of Love*, pp. 213 ff.　　[50] Augustine, *Confessions*, bk. IV, chap. 12, p. 82.

another, but it is to be asked whether man is to be loved by man for his own sake or for the sake of something else. If for his own sake, we enjoy him; if for the sake of something else, we use him. But I think that man is to be loved for the sake of something else.[51]

This is not, of course, a prescription for manipulation or abuse of others; it is, rather, a caution against idolatrous attachments. We are to love all human beings equally and to assist them in enjoying God, their proper end. But the "immutable" Trinity is "the highest good" and the only thing in which we may rest with satisfaction for its own sake; "nothing should hold us on the road"[52] to that destination. Augustine insists that "no one ought to enjoy himself either . . . because he should not love himself on account of himself but on account of Him who is to be enjoyed."[53] So here is no simple psychological egoism. Yet, as with Freud, there is an undeniable instrumentalism in Augustine's account of neighbor-love, especially in *On Christian Doctrine*: "[E]very man should be loved for the sake of God, and God should be loved for His own sake."[54] And, similarly: "When you enjoy a man in God, it is God rather than the man whom you enjoy; for you take joy in Him who will make you blessed."[55]

That said, Augustine does sometimes downplay ulterior motives and uphold love of neighbor more independently. In the *Confessions*, he says straightforwardly: "You [God] want us not only to love you, but also to love our neighbor."[56] In *The City of God*, he avers: "Now God, our master, teaches two chief precepts, love of God and love of neighbor; and in them man finds three objects for his love: God, himself, and his neighbor; and a man who loves God is not wrong in loving himself."[57] Finally, in *The Enchiridion* we find a marvelous statement of the priority of love:

[T]he end of every commandment is charity, that is, every commandment has

[51] Augustine, *On Christian Doctrine*, bk. one, chap. XXII, p. 18. This sentiment is alive and well, some 950 years later, in Richard Rolle's *De Incendio Amoris*: "All love which is not God-directed is bad love, and makes its possessors bad too . . . Love for God and love for the world cannot coexist in the same soul: the stronger drives out the weaker, and it soon appears who loves the world, and who follows Christ." "For if it is for God's sake that we love everything, we love God in it rather than the thing itself. And so we rejoice, not in it but in God . . ." See Rolle, *The Fire of Love*, pp. 48–49 and 55.

[52] Augustine, *On Christian Doctrine*, bk. one, chap. XXXIII, p. 29; and bk. one, chap. XXXIV, p. 30.   [53] Ibid., bk. one, chap. XXII, p. 18.   [54] Ibid., bk. one, chap. XXVII, p. 23.

[55] Ibid., bk. one, chap. XXXIII, p. 28. Even God "does not enjoy us but uses us," referring "His use of us to His own good" (see ibid., bk. one, chaps. XXXI–XXXII, p. 27). See also Augustine, *The City of God* [413–425/6], trans. by Henry Bettenson (New York: Penguin Books, 1984), bk. XI, chap. 25, pp. 458–459.   [56] Augustine, *Confessions*, bk. X, chap. 37, p. 246.

[57] Augustine, *The City of God*, bk. XIX, chap. 14, p. 873.

love for its aim. But whatever is done either through fear of punishment or from some other carnal motive, and has not for its principle that love which the Spirit of God sheds abroad in the heart, is not done as it ought to be done, however it may appear to men. For this love embraces both the love of God and the love of our neighbor.[58]

If seeing other people as a means to God is not charitable, not loving of *them*, why does Augustine prove so ambivalent concerning the second love command? There are perhaps two related reasons.

The more general reason, already touched on, is that he nowhere sufficiently breaks free of his Platonic starting point in *eros* to explain how such love can eventuate in Christian *agape*. He recognizes the limits of "the Platonists' books": they neglect the need for confession and sacrifice, overlook the perversity of the human will, nowhere permit a suffering Incarnation of God, etc.[59] He even asks, "[H]ow could I expect that the Platonist books would ever teach me charity?"[60] In *The Trinity*, in particular, he is acutely aware of the futility of beginning with natural knowledge or inclination, including self-love, and trying to educate it into beatitude.[61] But he still habitually conceives of love as a craving (*appetitus*) for what will make one permanently happy, and even as Plato denies that one can have true knowledge (*episteme*) of the changeable world, so Augustine denies that one can have true love (*caritas*) for it. The enlightened soul turns away from *cupiditas*, but *caritas* and *cupiditas* are both appetitive motions of the soul. The only difference is that the former aims at what will really provide stable contentment (the eternal), while the latter aims at what is bound to decay and thus disappoint (the temporal).[62]

I call "charity" the motion of the soul toward the enjoyment of God for His own sake, and the enjoyment of one's self and one's neighbor for the sake of God; but "cupidity" is a motion of the soul toward the enjoyment of one's self,

---

[58] Augustine, *The Enchiridion on Faith, Hope, and Love* [421], trans. by J.F. Shaw (Washington, D.C.: Regnery, 1961), CXXI, p. 139. And compare: "The greatest reward is that we enjoy [God] and that all of us who enjoy Him *may enjoy one another in Him*" (*On Christian Doctrine*, bk. one, chap. XXXII, p. 28, emphasis added).

[59] Augustine, *Confessions*, bk. VII, chaps. 9 and 20–21, pp. 144–145 and 154–156.

[60] Ibid., bk. VII, chap. 20, p. 154.

[61] See Augustine, *The Trinity* [400–c.420], trans. Edmund Hill, O. P., ed. John E. Rotelle, O.S.A. (Brooklyn, New York: New City Press, 1991), esp. the Prologue to book IV and all of book XV. For the case against directly equating self-love with the desire for happiness, see O'Donovan, *The Problem of Self-love in St. Augustine*, pp. 56–59.

[62] Hannah Arendt writes: "Love understood as craving desire (*appetitus*), and desire understood in terms of the Greek tradition from Aristotle to Plotinus, constitutes the root of both *caritas* and *cupiditas*. They are distinguished by their objects, but they are not different kinds of emotion . . ." See Arendt, *Love and Saint Augustine* (Chicago: University of Chicago Press, 1996), p. 18.

one's neighbor, or any corporeal thing for the sake of something other than God.[63]

As Nygren shows, a tension abides, therefore, between desire for the excellent that ascends and concern for the needy that descends. It is a mystery how one can love the finite and fallen neighbor when God alone is perfect. Unless charity is seen as distinct from and prior to *eros* (a.k.a. *amor*), that is, it is never attained.

A second, more specific reason for Augustine's ambivalence is his tendency to what I would call "ontological and chronological telescoping." On the one hand, he grants that "every being, so far as it is a being, is good," since it is created by a supremely good God.[64] Evil is not quite an illusion, but it is not a metaphysical substance but rather a privation of goodness, absence of or a wrong relation to what is intrinsically valuable. On the other hand, Augustine inclines to see "the *Highest* Good" of relation to God as "the *Final* Good" for which everything else is sought, even as he inclines to see "the *Highest* Evil" of damnation or "second death" as "the *Final* Evil" for which everything else is to be avoided.[65] The ordered hierarchy of reality, the *ordo amoris*, is thus telescoped and the plurality of goods that might be embraced by charity is effectively reduced to one (God), even as the plurality of evils that might be shunned is effectively reduced to one (alienation from God). Thus the tendency in Augustine for the *Summum Bonum* to become the *Solum Bonum*, and for the *Summum Malum* to become the *Solum Malum*.

Something analogous occurs with reference to the neighbor. On the one hand, as noted, Augustine acknowledges the Scriptural command to love the finite person before him, in addition to God above. The fellow human being has a genuine claim on him, and it is "not wrong" even to love himself. On the other hand, he is so struck by the frailty and sinfulness of others, as well as himself, that he effectively turns away from real persons existing in the present and looks to ideal persons as they will be perfected by God in the future (or rather in eternity). The providential unfolding of history, what might be called the "*tempo amoris*," is thus telescoped and the concrete neighbors who might be loved for their own sakes here and now are reduced to spectres "in God," even as the self who is to be loved becomes "a problem to myself."[66] Despite protests, in sum, the wondrous affirmation that "love

---

[63] Augustine, *On Christian Doctrine*, bk. three, chap. X, p. 88.
[64] Augustine, *The Enchiridion*, XII–XIII, pp. 12–13.
[65] Augustine, *The City of God*, bk. XIX, chap. 1, p. 843, emphases added.
[66] Cf. Augustine, *Confessions*, bk. IV, chap. 12, p. 82, and bk. X, chap. 16, p. 223.

is the weight (*pondus*) by which I act" is not squared with the miracle that "we are raised by love."[67]

C. An ancient complexity and some tentative conclusions

My all too brief account of *agape* and *eros* would be remiss if I did not note an ancient complexity. I have treated *eros* as the natural desire for possession of what is perceived to be excellent. *Eros* is not to be equated without remainder with *Venus*, sexual passion, but I have construed it as a preferential and needful longing. This is the sense the word usually has in Plato and neo-Platonism, and it is the force that drives the Augustinian ascent to perfection as well as the Freudian descent to illusion. John M. Rist is not alone in pointing out, however, that there are hints in Plato, as well as in Plotinus and Origen, of a "non-appetitive *eros*" – indeed, of a "tradition of descending *eros*" in which erotic love is self-sacrificial and creative rather than desirous and grasping.[68] Along these lines, Allan Bloom correlates Socratic/Platonic "eroticism" with pregnancy rather than hunger: "[I]t gives rather than takes. Its oppressive character comes from fullness and the need to release the tension constituted by that overflowing presence."[69] Such *eros*, as Rist notes, is considerably closer to Christian *agape* than commentators like Anders Nygren allow.[70] But the question then becomes: at what point does "down-flowing" or "overflowing"[71] *eros* cease to be recognizable as erotic? When do we have a second mode of being and acting with a discrete causal explanation? However one answers this question, my previous point remains that when defined as preferential desire, *eros* is distinct from *agape*. Agapists love God obediently and their neighbors as themselves, not first because God is perceived to be excellent and

---

[67] Ibid., bk. XIII, chap. 9, p. 317. Post Nygren, two of the best book-length studies of Augustine on the forms of love, in English, are John Burnaby's *Amor Dei: A Study of the Religion of St. Augustine* (London: Hodder & Stoughton, 1938) and Oliver O'Donovan's *The Problem of Self-Love in St. Augustine*. For a recent article defending Augustine against the charge of seeing the neighbor "as a tool in one's personal project of salvation," see Helmut David Baer, "The Fruit of Charity: Using the Neighbor in *De doctrina christiana*," in *Journal of Religious Ethics*, vol. 24, no. 1 (Spring 1996): 47–64.

[68] Rist, *Eros and Psyche: Studies in Plato, Plotinus, and Origen* (Toronto: University of Toronto Press, 1964), esp. pp. 206 and 216. See also Rist's *Augustine: Ancient Thought Baptized* (Cambridge: Cambridge University Press, 1994), chap. 5.

[69] Bloom, *Love and Friendship* (New York: Simon & Schuster, 1993), p. 511. These words are an elaboration of Diotima's comments to Socrates in *The Symposium*.

[70] Rist, *Eros and Psyche*, pp. 205–206. Nygren emphasizes that neo-Platonists distinguish between "heavenly *eros*," directed at permanent spiritual realities, and "vulgar *eros*," which lusts after mutable material goods. But he does not allow for an utterly spontaneous version of *eros* that loves others unconditionally.   [71] Ibid., pp. 34–39.

humans innately perfectable, but because God loved humanity stead-fastly through the person of Christ (John 17:25–26; 1 John 4:10, 19) and thus empowered it to turn from self-absorption.

Augustine attempted to combine elements of Greek eudaimonism with Biblical faith, while Freud tried to uncouple the former from the latter. Yet together they suggest the limits of the traditional erotic quest. Augustine was well aware that the things we naturally pursue as condu-cive to happiness (e.g., material goods) do not prove satisfying, and he departed from Plato's and Aristotle's intellectualist equation of virtue with knowledge by locating vice primarily in the will. With the famous story of his youthful theft of some pears "to do wrong for no purpose," Augustine gave voice to a distinctively Christian doctrine of sin as perversity rather than mere ignorance or weakness of will. He confessed, in most unGreek fashion: "The evil in me was foul, but I loved it. I loved my own perdition and my own faults, not the things for which I committed wrong, but the wrong itself."[72] Nonetheless, Augustine con-tinued to hold two eudaimonistic premises that were fundamental to his ascent to God: (1) that "[w]e all certainly desire to live happily,"[73] i.e., "no one hates himself";[74] and (2) that "when I look for you, who are my God, I am looking for a life of blessed happiness,"[75] i.e., I can *find* a worthy object of love only in God, "because you made us for yourself and our hearts find no peace until they rest in you."[76]

For his part, Freud finds "the most universal endeavor of all living substance" to be "to return to the quiescence of the inorganic world,"[77] rather than to ascend to the quiescence of the timeless God. For Freud, "postponement of satisfaction" based on a rational perception of reality carries the ego "beyond the pleasure principle";[78] even as, for Augustine, reason helps translate *cupiditas* for material things into *caritas* for God. But because Freud rules out any supernatural origin or end for human nature,[79] he can allow only a perpetual contest between the two basic instincts of (biological) life and death. Freud is no crude hedonist; he equates *eros*, the life instinct, with "tendencies more primitive than [the pursuit of pleasure] and independent of it."[80] But the struggle between

---

[72] Augustine, *Confessions*, bk. II, chap. 4, p. 47.

[73] Augustine, *On the Morals of the Catholic Church* [388], trans. by R. Stothert, chap. III, in *Basic Writings of Saint Augustine*, ed. by Whitney J. Oates, vol. I (New York: Random House, 1948), p. 320.

[74] Augustine, *On Christian Doctrine*, bk. one, chap. XXIV, p. 20.

[75] Augustine, *Confessions*, bk. X, chap. 20, p. 226.   [76] Ibid., bk. I, chap. 1, p. 21.

[77] Freud, *Beyond the Pleasure Principle*, p. 76.   [78] Ibid., p. 7.

[79] In *Beyond the Pleasure Principle*, Freud attributes the origin of life to "the action of a force of whose nature we can form no conception" (p. 46).   [80] Ibid., p. 17.

eros and *thanatos* lies at the root of the human quest for happiness, and this struggle is played out entirely within the physical world. The endless drama of civilization it provides is without reference to the divine.[81]

Freud reverses the outward–inward, inward–upward model of Platonism, telescoping being and time backward into the primordial rather than forward into the eschatological. His calling *agape* "aim-inhibited *eros*" gives priority to sexual instinct and its preferential desire. When this is done, we can only "love" the extant qualities of others and try to give them their due, thus justice is the highest virtue. The appraisive moment of *eros* prevails, even in friendship, and the challenge of ethics is to check "overvaluation" of the erotic object with rational judgment. *Eros* is capable of genuine concern for the other, but it tends to be narcissistic in being motivated by ego-gratification and the demand for reciprocity. Ego-gratification becomes for Freud what the service of God is for Augustine, and for related reasons; starting with *eros*, however wise it becomes, each author must refer all love back instrumentally to his *Summum Bonum*. This is the imperfect biological self in Freud's case, the perfect theological Other in Augustine's. Freud does not worship the ego, but his starting point in *eros* prevents him from regressing human origins back far enough to find a self-giving love prior to a self-seeking one, not to say a Creator prior to creation. For Freud, there is no internal "instinct towards perfection" and no prior power that (even ideally) overcomes the conflicted "dualism" of life instincts and death instincts, love and hate.[82]

II. SELF-LOVE AND FRIENDSHIP: NEITHER WEIL NOR VACEK

Thus far, I have primarily considered how *agape* compares to *eros*, but more needs to be said of its relation to self-love and friendship. The latter two loves are making a decided comeback these days. Self-love is increasingly celebrated in popular literature and song. And some have thought *philia* to combine the other-regard of *agape* with the passionate connectedness of *eros*, without promoting either self-destructiveness or selfishness. Here I find the work of Simone Weil and Edward Vacek providing a useful contrast, with Weil offering an extraordinary brief for impersonal sanctity and Vacek standing up for personal dignity.

---

[81] See Freud, *Civilization and Its Discontents*, p. 82.

[82] Freud, *Beyond the Pleasure Principle*, pp. 50 and 63–64. As Jacques Lacan says, "Freud is a humanitarian but not a progressive," someone "literally horrified by the idea of love for one's neighbor" and for whom "*jouissance* is evil." See Lacan, *The Ethics of Psychoanalysis, 1959–1960: The Seminar of Jacques Lacan, Book VII*, ed. by Jacques-Alain Miller and trans. by Dennis Porter (New York: W.W. Norton, 1992), pp. 184–186.

A. Simone Weil on the love of God and self-decreation

Augustine nowhere explores his intriguing suggestion that some things are to be both enjoyed and used,[83] but this prospect might be applied to human beings. Simone Weil, another Christian Platonist, comes close to doing just this, delineating love of God and love of neighbor in terms of an upward and a downward path. Several remarks in her *Waiting for God* move in this direction, even giving priority to *agape*'s unmotivated descent over *eros*'s critical ascent:

Christ has bidden us to attain to the perfection of our heavenly Father by imitating his indiscriminate bestowal of light. Our intelligence too should have the same complete impartiality . . . Such a love does not love beings and things in God, but from the abode of God.[84]

The love of our neighbor is the love which comes down from God to man. It precedes that which rises from men to God.[85]

That is why expressions such as to love our neighbor in God, or for God, are misleading and equivocal . . . Just as there are times when we must think of God and forget all creatures without exception, there are times when, as we look at creatures, we do not have to think explicitly of God.[86]

Let us love the country of here below [the material universe]. It is real; it offers resistance to love. It is this country that God has given us to love.[87]

In these and similar passages, Weil advances the usual discussion of Christian charity. She often does a better job than Augustine of allowing for a spontaneous love of neighbor, one that is attentive to others' real wants and needs on their own terms. Whereas Augustine tends to justify love of neighbor with reference either to God or to the perfected creature that the neighbor may eventually become, Weil writes: "The love of neighbor in all its fullness simply means being able to say to him: 'What are you going through?'"[88]

   Weil does less well than Augustine, however, in finding room for proper *self*-love. Having eloquently described "supernatural justice" as the extension of equality and respect to those in an unequal or vulnerable position,[89] she seems to undercut herself by avowing a circular conception of divine love. For Weil, at least at her most neo-Platonic, human love is ultimately but a means for God to love Himself. All temporal love – including love for fellow creatures, but especially love

---

[83] Augustine, *On Christian Doctrine*, bk. one, chap. III, p. 9; but cf. ibid., bk. one, chap. XXXII, p. 28, quoted in ftnt. 51 above.
[84] Weil, *Waiting for God*, trans. by Emma Craufurd (New York: Harper and Row, 1951), p. 97.
[85] Ibid., p. 150.   [86] Ibid., p. 151.   [87] Ibid., p. 178.   [88] Ibid., p. 115.   [89] Ibid., p. 143.

for ourselves – is at best part of the circuit of eternal self-love. As she says in *Gravity and Grace*:

At each moment our existence is God's love for us. But God can only love himself. His love for us is love for himself through us.[90]

Love is a sign of our wretchedness. God can only love himself. We can only love something else.[91]

Here Weil attributes to God the same sort of Augustinian dichotomy between enjoyment (*frui*) and use (*uti*) that she refuses to attribute to horizontal human loves. God, it seems, can only use us to love God. The upshot of this conception of divine love is that we must "decreate" ourselves and allow God's love to flow back to God alone:

May God grant me to become nothing.   In so far as I become nothing, God loves himself through me.[92]

Behind these words is Weil's complex association of the good and the beautiful with the *im*personal. This is not world-hatred – love of the neighbor and of the beauty of the world are forms of the "implicit love of God"[93] – but rather a critique of the "Personalism" that has so seized the modern age. Weil writes:

There is something sacred in every man, but it is not his person. Nor yet is it the human personality. It is this man; no more and no less. I see a passer-by in the street. He has long arms, blue eyes, and a mind whose thoughts I do not know, but perhaps they are commonplace. It is neither his person, nor the human personality in him, which is sacred to me. It is he. The whole of him. The arms, the eyes, the thoughts, everything. Not without infinite scruple would I touch anything of this . . . So far from its being his person, what is sacred in a human being is the impersonal in him. Everything which is impersonal in man is sacred, and nothing else.[94]

The *other*-regarding implication of this view of sanctity, as I have indicated, is that we should love others just as we find them. The *self*-regarding implication, in turn, Weil takes to be an emphatic auto-abnegation. "I do not in the least wish that this created world should fade from my view, but that it should no longer be to me personally that it shows itself."[95] Reminiscent of those mystics who favor metaphors of personal extinction over transubstantiation, she makes a virtue of ex-

---

[90] Simone Weil, *Gravity and Grace*, trans. by Emma Craufurd (London and New York: Ark Paperbacks, 1987), p. 28.
[91] Ibid., p. 55.   [92] Ibid., p. 30.   [93] Weil, *Waiting for God*, p. 137.
[94] Weil, "Human Personality," in *The Simone Weil Reader*, ed. by George A. Panichas (Mt. Kisco, NY: Moyer Bell Limited, 1977), p. 314.   [95] Weil, *Gravity and Grace*, p. 37.

treme self-effacement. For her, the highest thing a human person can do is to consent to returning to, or being used by, an impersonal God. God "loves," and humanity is in the loop of this love in some sense, but our loftiest and freest achievement is to "decreate" ourselves and not let our distinctive needs, desires, and imaginings interrupt the divine circuit.[96] "God gave me being in order that I should give it back to him."[97]

It would be a mistake to write Weil off as simply masochistic or anorexic, but there is admittedly a fine line between the pious and the pathological in her.[98] She knows the indispensable power of self-sacrifice at the heart of Christianity. "In denying oneself," she writes, "one becomes capable under God of establishing someone else by a creative affirmation. One gives oneself in ransom for the other. It is a redemptive act."[99] Yet she pines for a horrific mortification of the flesh in the so-called "terrible prayer":

Father, in the name of Christ grant me this. That I may be unable to will any bodily movement, or even any attempt at movement, like a total paralytic. That I may be incapable of receiving any sensation, like someone who is completely blind, deaf and deprived of all the senses. That I may be unable to make the slightest connection between two thoughts, even the simplest, like one of those total idiots who not only cannot count or read but have never even learnt to speak. That I may be insensible to every kind of grief and joy, and incapable of any love for any being or thing, and not even for myself, like old people in the last stage of decrepitude . . . Father, since thou art the Good, and I am mediocrity, rend this body and soul away from me to make them do things for your use, and let nothing remain of me, forever, except this rending itself, or else nothingness.[100]

Weil recorded this prayer in her notebooks the year before her death, a death at least partially due to her refusal of food out of sympathy with the victims of Nazism. She does go on to note: "Words like these are not efficacious unless they are dictated by the spirit. One does not voluntarily ask for such things."[101] But one cannot doubt that here the vocation of waiting reaches absurd proportions. Late in her life Weil was fascinated

---

[96] Ibid., pp. 28 ff.   [97] Ibid., p. 35.

[98] In an exceptionally balanced appraisal of Weil, George Steiner has lamented that "[u]ncritical reverence on the one hand, exasperation and distaste on the other, mark the debates around her 'works and days.' " See Steiner, "Sainte Simone–Simone Weil," in *No Passion Spent: Essays 1978–1995* (New Haven and London: Yale University Press, 1996), p. 172. Steiner appreciates that Weil reflected on love "at often compelling and originating depths," yet he also finds in her "the traits of a classical Jewish self-loathing . . . carried to fever pitch" (pp. 173, 177). This piece originally appeared in *The Times Literary Supplement* (June 4, 1993).

[99] Weil, *Waiting for God*, pp. 147–148.

[100] Quoted by Robert Coles in *Simone Weil: A Modern Pilgrimage* (Reading, MA: Addison-Wesley, 1987), pp. 131–132.   [101] Quoted by Coles, p. 132.

by the gnostic Cathars, and her own end may have been tied to the Cathar *endura* ritual of self-starvation by the elite. Still, one cannot read her without feeling oneself in the presence of a remarkable spiritual power. Though only thirty-four when she died, her insights into human sympathy and cruelty have a maturity that astonishes. There has seldom been a less anthropomorphic, a more disconsoling, soul.

Weil's charisma stemmed from a very real affliction (migraines coupled with a sense of unworthiness before God) that refused to stop loving. Though frail, she did not spare herself the pain of attention to others. Her history and psychology made her an outsider, from the Catholic Church and even from her own self, yet she consented to "wait" for God and to try to be patient with her condition. She had, undeniably, a morbid imagination the equal of any of her countrymen from Sade to Foucault, as when she envies Christ on the cross.[102] Her *amor fati* was not nihilistic fatalism, however, but closer to an acceptance of life, freely embraced, that is true liberation. She did distinguish between "destruction" (coercive imposition of death for its own sake) and "decreation" (the consensual giving of self in service to others).[103] And whether one counts her a saint herself, Weil marked unforgettably the difference between sainthood (which changes violence into redemptive suffering) and idolatry (which changes suffering into limitless violence).[104] She highlighted the charisma of goodness precisely by being so sensitive to "the contagion of sin."[105]

The beauty of Weil's moral vision can be greatly enhanced by untying two pairs of broad theses that she tended to conflate:

(1) "Only God can love God."
(2) "God can only love himself."

and

(3) "Everything which is impersonal in man is sacred."
(4) "Only the impersonal in a human being is sacred."

Claim (1) can be seen as an orthodox assertion of the human need for grace in order to be transformed by and for *agape*. The finite cannot directly aspire to the infinite, and if human beings must acquire charity on their own, they will fail. Claim (2) is distinct from the first, and very

---

[102] Weil, *Waiting for God*, p. 83.
[103] See, e.g., Weil, *Gravity and Grace*, p. 28; but cf. *Waiting for God*, p. 147, which speaks of "the destruction of oneself." [104] Weil, *Gravity and Grace*, p. 65.
[105] Ibid., p. 64. George Steiner, "Sainte Simone," p. 3, points out, however, that for all her sensitivity to the cruelty of political collectives, Weil was curiously silent on the Holocaust that ravaged European Jewry in her own lifetime.

questionable. If the second proposition is interpreted to mean "God can love only himself," as Weil's French implies,[106] then she gives us a narcissistic Deity. A God who can love only Himself is one whose creation of "otherness" is finally either utterly opaque (a futzing around) or self-serving (a kind of divine autoeroticism). When she writes, "In so far as I become nothing, God loves himself through me," Weil departs from the Judeo-Christian tradition of a personal God and shows her deep affinities with the impersonalism of the ancient Greeks, notably Pythagoras.[107]

Claim (3) offers a potent remedy for the individualism and hypercognitivism that many associate with Western culture since the eighteenth century. Enlightenment bashing is of limited value, and Weil does not typically indulge in this. But her highlighting of the impersonal dimensions of existence shared by us all can provide clues to a better handling of moral issues ranging from abortion to senile dementia. Weilan impersonalism can help us realize, for instance, that fetuses have needs and potentials to be respected before the dawn of personal consciousness, and that Alzheimer patients are capable of a "noncognitive well-being" to be sustained even after the dusk of rational self-awareness.[108] As Weil notes, the entirety of someone capable of undergoing good and evil, help and harm, is sacred and commands our attention.[109] Her claim (4), however, seems an unnecessary and implausible denial of the worth of personhood altogether. If the hairs on our heads are numbered by God and the exercise of our temporal freedom is not overridden by God, then individual identity also matters. If God revels in the particular as well as the universal – as Scripture attests, calling all of creation "good" (Genesis 1) – there is every reason to affirm both the personal and the impersonal.[110]

---

[106] In *La Pesanteur et La Grâce* (Paris: Librairie Plon, 1948), Weil writes:

> *A chaque instant notre existence est amour de Dieu pour nous. Mais Dieu ne peut aimer que soi-même. Son amour pour nous est amour pour soi a travers nous.* (p. 36)

> *L'amour est un signe de notre misère. Dieu ne peut aimer que soi. Nous ne pouvons aimer qu'autre chose.* (p. 71)

The English translation (*Gravity and Grace*) by Emma Craufurd has the second sentence of each of these quotes declare that "God can only love himself," but the French clearly should be rendered "God can love only himself" – i.e., God is the only possible object of God's own love.

[107] See Weil, *Intimations of Christianity Among the Ancient Greeks* (London and New York: Ark Paperbacks, 1987). The quotation is from Weil, *Gravity and Grace*, p. 30.

[108] I take the phrase "noncognitive well-being" from Stephen G. Post, *The Moral Challenge of Alzheimer Disease* (Baltimore: Johns Hopkins University Press, 1995), p. 9. Post's excellent book, together with David Keck's equally impressive *Forgetting Whose We Are: Alzheimer's Disease and the Love of God* (Nashville: Abingdon Press, 1996), helps us to escape the stranglehold that "personhood" has on medical ethics. See my review in *Studies in Christian Ethics*, vol. 11, no. 1 (1998): 94–99. [109] Weil, "Human Personality," p. 315.

Where, then, does this leave us in evaluating this woman of genius and her views on love? *Contra* Augustine, strong agapists hold that love of neighbor does not merely facilitate love of God or love of self. This instrumentalism offends against the individuality of other created beings, making them a means to one's own happiness. *Contra* Weil, however, strong agapists also believe that neither love of self nor love of neighbor should be submerged into God's self-love. This makes God self-absorbed and manipulative, using creatures for extraneous purposes rather than loving them for themselves. Many Western theologians hold that the self is sinful and that its (highest) capacities must be activated by God, but in effectively denying her distinctive self-worth, even *in potentia*, Weil neglects Genesis and the Christian doctrine of the goodness of individual creation. Her Stoic patience seems cold and disembodied.

Weil's longing to be "like a total paralytic" in obedience to God recalls the austere beauty of Hiram Powers's statue of "Charity" (figure 2). The purity of this sculpted woman is manifest, but she is alone and literally disarmed. The tuft of hair above her forehead connotes a sacred heart, aflame with love, but she supports no infants on her lap, clutches no lover to her breast, wields no weapon in a just war. She has no feet on which to dance, even with God. Guido Reni's "Charity" (figure 1) is more human. Weil sought to lead a loving life, but love of neighbor came much more readily to her than self-love. Although the desire for benevolent action was lived out dramatically, practical self-regard seems to have been lacking. She fought with the anti-Franco forces in Spain, for instance, but she had to be sent home after stepping into a pot of boiling soup. Though she was evidently capable of deep friendship, the venereal was conspicuously absent. *Pace* Weil, I would suggest both *agape* and *eros* clarify finite personalities and redound to their individual good, though of course they do not guarantee happiness.

If the preservation of both idiosyncratic identity and other-affirming relationship are so crucial to love, why not find in friendship the first virtue? (Weil herself says that friendship is "the one legitimate exception

---

[110] The enthusiastic personalism of Martin Luther King, Jr., stands in stark contrast to Weil on goodness. Indeed, in *Stride Toward Freedom* (San Francisco: Harper and Row, 1958), p. 100, King goes to the opposite extreme: "Personalism's insistence that only personality – finite and infinite – is ultimately real strengthened in me two convictions: it gave me metaphysical and philosophical grounding for the idea of a personal God, and it gave me a metaphysical basis for the dignity and worth of all human personality." Weil's impersonalism and King's personalism are ultimately not reconcilable, but read together these twentieth-century saints help us balance love of God and love of neighbor, as well as *agape* and social justice. Weil's patient "waiting for God" complements King's (im)patient "not waiting" for humanity. See King, *Why We Can't Wait* (New York: Mentor, 1964).

to the duty of only loving universally."[111]) I have noted that Freud holds up friendship and justice as the highest rational ideals, but Edward Vacek has recently argued for a *Christian* elevation of *philia* above both *agape* and *eros*. Let me respond now to his superbly textured work.

B. *Edward Vacek on cooperative friendship with God*

Edward Vacek stands at the other end of the spectrum to Simone Weil on self-love and personal freedom in relation to God. Weil represents an advancement on Augustine on love of others, to repeat, yet she falls down in treating her self as inherently unlovable (both by God and by herself), and thus as in need of "decreation." Vacek, on the other hand, wisely escapes a narcissistic God and an extinguished self, but his elevation of self-love and friendship suggests too complete a swing of the pendulum in the other direction, I believe. His vision of creatures becoming "partners" with God, not so much commanded to do God's will as called to "cooperate" with God's hopes, is a truly noble eschatological ideal. But, as he predicts, agapists fear that it makes us forgetful of human finitude and sin.

Vacek does not simply elevate *philia* as mutuality to the status of the one true Christian love; he advocates "a pluralistic approach" in which *agape* and *eros* also have their place. He is well aware that "[w]e can love those who do not love us," but he gives priority to friendship. "The central thesis" of his book, Vacek writes,

is that communion or *philia* is the foundation and goal of Christian life. This love is a "power that creates unity and forms the human community ever more extensively and intensively" [quoting Max Scheler]. Indeed, all human love finds its culmination and ultimate goal in a community of solidarity with and in God.[112]

This dethroning of *agape* is ill-advised. It may be that philial communion is the *goal* of love, in some sense, but the *foundation* of love is the unconditional willing of the good, equal regard, and passionate service of *agape*.[113] For friendship with God and other human beings is impossible without unmerited favor. Both giving and receiving love with joy and in solidarity is Godlike, but the giving comes first and is even called "more blessed" by Jesus (Acts 20:35).

---

[111] Weil, *Waiting for God*, p. 98.

[112] All quotations in this paragraph are from Vacek, *Love, Human and Divine*, p. 280.

[113] Thomas Aquinas goes so far as to say that "charity *is* the friendship of man for God," a virtue that is "imperfect here, but will be perfected in heaven" (*ST*, II–II, Q. 23, art. 1; emphasis added). Vacek generally shies away from such a direct equation.

There appear to be significant Biblical warrants for Vacek's position, of course, especially these famous words from Jesus:

No one has greater love than this, to lay down one's life for one's friends. You are my friends if you do what I command you. I do not call you servants any longer, because the servant does not know what the master is doing; but I have called you friends, because I have made known to you everything that I have heard from my Father. (John 15:13–15)

Note, however, that Jesus does not *identify* the unsurpassable love with friendship. Friends (*"philoi"*) are the *beneficiaries* of this love, but the self-giving love itself is called *"agape"* in the Greek and seems prior even to friendship. Vacek rightly foregrounds love, looking to God and the Bible for the definition of this supreme good, and he provides a very helpful corrective to natural law emphases that neglect love altogether and predestinarian emphases that make God the sole causal (much less loving) agent. Nonetheless, for all his insight, I ultimately find Vacek nearly as vexing a genius as "Saint Simone."

Vacek repeatedly translates 1 Corinthians 3:9 as "we are God's cooperators," but this is controversial. The NRSV translates the relevant passage as "we are God's servants, working together," whereas the King James reads "we are laborers together with God." The Greek word in question is *"sunergoi,"* which is perhaps best rendered in English as "fellow-workers." When the larger passage is put in context, however, it is clear that it is *Paul and Apollos* who are described as "working together" or "laborers together," not these two (or us) and God. The two men are doing God's bidding, to be sure, but the "togetherness" is chiefly theirs, even as the primacy is God's. In response to growing factionalism in the Corinthian church around the leadership of Apollos, Paul writes:

What then is Apollos? What is Paul? Servants through whom you came to believe, as the Lord assigned to each. I planted, Apollos watered, but God gave the growth. So neither the one who plants nor the one who waters is anything, but only God who gives the growth. The one who plants and the one who waters have a common purpose, and each will receive wages according to the labor of each. For we are God's servants, working together; you are God's field, God's building. (1 Cor. 3:5–9)[114]

A fairly typical Pauline "self-denial" is apparent in these lines, but however important one thinks human agents may be in providential

---

[114] In Jesus's "I do not call you servants any longer" (John 15:15), the Greek word translated "servants" is *"douloi,"* which implies a much more distinctive subservience than *"ergoi"* or *"sunergoi."* *"Douloi"* could equally well be translated "slaves."

history, it is Paul and Apollos who "have a common purpose" in the 1 Corinthian verses. *They* are the ones cooperating, in God's work and under God's authority, with the Corinthian congregation being their joint venue. Vacek's powerful insistence on divine–human cooperation, while plausible in some settings as an antidote to hard determinism, risks blinding us to the Pauline sense of God's priority: "only God gives the growth."[115]

I have no quarrel with Vacek's language of "a cooperative friendship with God" as the ideal *consummation* of love. Such a partnership may indeed be the experience of some saints in this life and the eventual lot of all believers graced with an afterlife. But to describe friendship, either with God or with creatures, as the *first* virtue is to put the cart before the horse. As Jesus reminds the twelve, "You did not choose me but I chose you" (John 15:16). What we first know and depend on in *this* life, what nurtures us into persons, is not *philia* but *agape*. God meets creatures initially as a righteous Lord before whom they are dependent and sinful and who must indict and forgive them before they can be sanctified. What we are called on to reflect in our own lives here and now, furthermore, is first of all *agape* for God and second *agape* for the neighbor. Vacek writes eloquently of the *terminus ad quem* of love, if you will, but the Biblical accent falls on the *terminus a quo*. The basic problem with Vacek's view, then, is not that friendship is no virtue but that it cannot claim *primacy* among loves.

Genuine friendship suggests mature individuals, or at least individuals at roughly the same maturational level, meeting as equals and joyfully cooperating in common enterprises. The shared activities may range from conversation, to card games, to peace-making, to warfighting. But the stress is on mutuality and respect for one another's freedom in carrying out pursuits "side by side."[116] According to Aristotle, friends "must be mutually recognized as bearing good will and wishing well to each other."[117] He grants that "bad men" may love one another fitfully, or "be friends for the sake of pleasure or of utility," and he allows that some lesser friendships involve "an inequality between the parties."[118] Nonetheless, Aristotle judges that "equality and likeness are friendship [in the fullest sense], and especially the likeness of those who are like in virtue."[119] The stress of *agape*, in

---

[115] See Richard Hays's analysis of 3:9 in *First Corinthians: Interpretation* (Louisville: John Knox Press, 1997), pp. 52–53.   [116] C.S. Lewis, *The Four Loves*, p. 91.

[117] Aristotle, *The Nicomachean Ethics*, bk. VIII, chap. 2, [1156a5], p. 194.

[118] Ibid., bk. VIII, chap. 4, [1157a35–b1], p. 199; and bk. VIII, chap. 7, [1158b11], p. 203.

contrast, is on *in*equality, a more powerful figure assisting a less power-ful one. Rather than being based on the *shared virtue* of one's fellow, much less on his *instrumental value*, agape reaches out to the *idiosyncratic need* of one's neighbor. The need may be material (food or shelter), political (liberty or public membership), and/or moral (forgiveness or encouragement). There is equal regard for all others' well-being, as I have noted, but reciprocity is not a prerequisite and unilateral or unrecognized giving is often the norm.[120] The other's personhood, most basically a gift of God, is to be passionately built up rather than assumed. *Agape* wants communion, to be sure, but it first promotes the other as such.

On most definitions, friendship implies a preferential and exclusive affinity between a small group of extant persons,[121] while *agape* is an unlimited and steadfast willing of the good for potential as well as actual persons. This does not imply that the strong agapist barely tolerates or even vilifies friendship as a human phenomenon.[122] The joy and sym-pathy that accompany friendly ventures, the simple animal high spirits, help make life worth living and (within limits) are justifiable on their own terms. In addition, friendship too is creative. We must not reduce friendship (especially Aristotelian *philia*) to a minimalist or degenerate form in which two or three self-interested individuals work together only for selfish benefit, or pursue shared interests forever settled at the outset. The parties to a friendship often grow aesthetically and morally in and through the relation, sparking one another to unexpected discoveries

---

[119] Ibid., bk. VIII, chap. 8, [1159b1–4], p. 206.

[120] Gene Outka, *Agape: An Ethical Analysis*, pp. 280–281, makes clear that while equal regard is not premised on reciprocity, it need not reject or be entirely disinterested in it. *Agape* may desire (even pine for) mutual relation, that is, without insisting on it. Stephen Post has criticized Outka's analysis of equal regard as tending to reduce *agape* to an abstraction, a "universal love of humanity" that is more akin to Kantian respect for persons than to storied Christian love. See Post, *A Theory of Agape*, pp. 12–13, 30–32, and *passim*. Post's defense of the narrative and communal character of love is admirable, but he tends to overstate the "disinterestedness" of Outka's picture of *agape* as well as to understate the ways in which such "special relations" as family and church must themselves be governed by *agape*. The family can be a school of virtue, a model of care and sacrifice for a couple and the wider community, but Reinhold Niebuhr touches on a perennial problem when he writes: "The family is still essentially selfish, and many a man is beguiled from ideal ventures by a false sense of obligation to his family." See his *Leaves from the Notebook of a Tamed Cynic* (Hamden, CT, The Shoe String Press, 1956), p. 158.

[121] See Aristotle, *The Nicomachean Ethics*, bk. IX, chap. 10, [1171a1–12], pp. 243–244.

[122] Søren Kierkegaard is often criticized for denying the goodness of "spontaneous" loves such as friendship, for at times seeing them as incompatible with charity. See, for instance, Gene Outka, *Agape*, esp. pp. 13–24; Lawrence A. Blum, *Friendship, Altruism and Morality* (London: Routledge & Kegan Paul, 1980), pp. 77 and 81; and Knud Ejler Løgstrup, *The Ethical Demand*, chap. 13. I defend Kierkegaard against Løgstrup's more extreme charges in a review for *Modern Theology*, vol. 14, no. 3 (July 1998): 459–461.

about themselves and the world. As Aristotle puts it, "the friendship of good men is good, being augmented by their companionship."[123] So there is no question of dismissing *philia* as insignificant or of attacking it as inherently wrong.

Christian charity is no more intrinsically antithetical to *philia* than to *eros*; the experience of solidarity and sacrifice common to the best friendships can even help sustain Christians in the theological virtues of faith, hope, and agapic love. Nevertheless, the strong agapist's point is twofold: (1) that God does not *first* meet us as a friend in the usual sense, any more than our parents do,[124] and (2) that even *virtuous* friendships become stunted and unstable when detached from an appreciation of wider humanity. Even though friendship ideally produces novelty and value for individuals and their society, rather than merely protecting vested interests, the friends themselves are *originally* brought into personhood by something prior.[125] In addition, the dangers of making unwarranted exceptions for those close to us must be checked by a fundamental commitment to equal regard for all others. Especially when (as in Aristotle) "true" friendship is linked to enduring virtue,[126] the capacity for *philia* presupposes both the experience of *agape* and an ongoing regulation by *agape*. As Gene Outka observes, "the presence of agape is a necessary but not a sufficient condition for philia, and . . . the presence of philia is a sufficient but not a necessary condition for agape."[127] If even faith is "working through [literally, activated by] love

---

[123] Aristotle, *The Nicomachean Ethics*, bk. IX, chap. 12, [1172a11], p. 247.

[124] Aristotle denies that there can be any friendship at all with God, due to God's remoteness; see ibid., bk. VIII, chap. 7, [1159a5], p. 204. Aristotle does speak of an "unequal" friendship between parents and children, but he makes two observations: (i) "parents love their children as soon as these are born, but children love their parents only after time has elapsed and they have acquired understanding or the power of discrimination by the senses," and (ii) "no one could ever return to them [gods or parents] the equivalent of what he gets." See ibid., bk. VIII, chaps. 12 and 14, [1161b25–27] and [1163b17], pp. 213 and 219.

[125] Stanley Hauerwas and Charles Pinches observe that "*philia* in the Christian church forms Christians to embody the love theologians have described as *agape*." See their *Christians Among the Virtues: Theological Conversations with Ancient and Modern Ethics* (Notre Dame: University of Notre Dame Press, 1997), p. 82. There can indeed be a mutually supportive relation between charity and other loves – having good and faithful friends usually makes us better neighbors to strangers (cf. p. 83) – but this must not blind us to the priority of *agape*. The *receipt* of unconditional love from God and other creatures comes before any preferential personal attachment, so, most fundamentally, *agape* makes possible *philia*, rather than the other way round. Hauerwas and Pinches themselves allow that "[i]n an important way the church never is a *friend* to the world, and so there is good reason to keep alive both the terms *agape* and *philia* in our vocabulary" (p. 82).

[126] Aristotle, *The Nicomachean Ethics.*, bk. VIII, chap. 4, [1157a23], p. 198. In *Friendship, Altruism and Morality*, p. 82, Lawrence Blum warns against the "overmoralized view of friendship" that he finds in Aristotle. [127] Outka, *Agape*, p. 283.

(*agape*)," as Paul maintains in Galatians 5:6, how much more is friend-ship?[128]

The centrality of equality and of getting and giving the same marks the standard cases of Aristotelian *philia* as significantly different from and posterior to Christian *agape*. But Aristotle is still further from charity when he writes of nonstandard cases: "In all friendships implying inequality [e.g., between father and son, husband and wife, ruler and subject] the love also should be proportional, i.e. the better should be more loved than he loves, and so should the more useful . . ."[129] Here the superior and funded figure loves *less not more* than the subordinate and destitute, the obverse of divine *kenosis*. Elsewhere, Aristotle maintains that "friendship depends more on loving" than on being loved, but in every instance perceived "merit" is at the root of the relation.[130] Why then does Vacek look to friendship for his ethical paradigm?

Vacek takes his most fundamental cues on love from Christian Scripture and theology rather than Greek politics and philosophy, of course. His perspective is "outside of" or "posterior to" history, in the sense that he focuses on the Trinity and on our consummating friend-ship with God in heaven. I attempt instead to see love from a vantage-point "within" or (in one sense) "prior to" history, thus I focus on God's saving *agape* in the Incarnation of Christ as well as on God's originating *agape* in the creation of the world. "Friendship" between the Persons of the Trinity in some sense "precedes" time itself, but theological talk about this is like cosmological speculation on the moment of or "before" the Big Bang: dicey.[131] Agapic love must precede any *human* friendship, in any case, because until God gratuitously creates human lives they do not exist, and until God mercifully redeems human beings, they do not

---

[128] Stephen Post writes: "The tension between *philia* and *agape* is, I think, a false one. God's love is *philia* or communion that takes on the form of self-sacrifice out of necessity rather than preference due to the tolerance of human freedom that God must exhibit." See Post, *A Theory of Agape*, p. 33. The problem with this, however, is that it suggests that costly service could be avoided if people were morally better, when in fact the need for openness to self-sacrifice is a function not only of contingent human sin but of essential human need and vulnerability – human finitude as such. *Agape* grounds *philia* because the need to receive care precedes both virtue and vice, even as *agape* governs *philia* because the desire to give care both outstrips justice and guards against injustice. Post's criticisms (p. 33) notwithstanding, Gilbert Meilaender is right to highlight the goodness but also the penultimacy of friendship; see Meilaender, *Friend-ship: A Study in Theological Ethics* (Notre Dame: University of Notre Dame Press, 1981).

[129] Aristotle, *The Nicomachean Ethics*, bk. VIII, chap. 7, [1158b24–26], pp. 203–204.

[130] Ibid., bk. VIII, chap. 8, [1159a33–34], p. 205; and see ibid., bk. VIII, chap. 11, [1161a20–21], p. 211. Even "goodwill," which for Aristotle is a kind of prelude to or inactive form of friendship, "arises on account of some excellence and worth." See ibid., bk. IX, chap. 5, [1167a18], p. 231.

[131] We have Genesis and John 1 for clues about "the beginning," but we look first to Jesus's life and death for a guide to the middle and the end.

love. Similarly, in earthly circles only individuals who have been freely nurtured into personhood can enter into lasting friendships as equals. Our parents are not first our friends but our caregivers, if we are lucky, even if they eventually become our friends in some meaningful way. And memory of and gratitude for their (or their surrogates') unearned care, an echo of God's own, are indispensable for subsequent trusting relations. As Linda Mayes and Sally Provence, professors of child development at Yale, write:

Continuity of affectionate care by one or a small number of caregivers who can give of themselves emotionally, as well as in other ways, originates the development of the child's love relationships . . . Having repeated experiences of being comforted when distressed, [for instance,] is a part of developing one's own capacity for self-comfort and self-regulation, and later, the capacity to provide the same for others.[132]

In this sense, *agape* is the conatus for all finite conscience.[133]

Vacek himself warns that we must not imagine that God is literally our or the world's equal:[134] God remains Creator, and we God's creatures, even in the most cooperative of love relations. Yet, in spite of his careful qualifications, the choice of "friendship with God" as the central image for Christian ethics cannot help but blur important distinctions. God does respect human freedom, in the sense that God's grace is not irresistible and does not destroy the creaturely integrity of finite individuals. But God's love first must school us into holiness by convicting us of sin and directing us away from selfish preoccupations.[135] Similarly, God does affirm human worth – Jesus even praises Peter as a "rock" (Matt.

---

[132] These lines are quoted by Margaret Talbot, in "Attachment Theory: The Ultimate Experiment," *The New York Times Magazine* (May 24, 1998), p. 27. Talbot adds that "although attachment theorists generally assume that the person with whom a baby is figuring all this out will be her mother, nothing in the theory excludes a loving father from filling the same role" (p. 28).

[133] C.S. Lewis calls the love with which parents rear their offspring "affection," translated from the Greek "*storge*." The first image that comes to his mind here is that of a mother nursing a baby, and he associates this with a "Gift-love" that takes pleasure in giving but also "needs to be needed." See Lewis, *The Four Loves*, pp. 53–54 and 88. I have emphasized the charitable or agapic elements in parental nurturence to highlight its steadfastness even when warm and comfortable feelings are absent. This is not to say that *agape* is without emotion or is somehow opposed to *storge*. Indeed, William Klassen writes: "The range of meaning expressed by *agapao* in Greek of the classical period and later includes affection, fondness, and simple contentedness." See Klassen, "Love," p. 381. My point is that parental love, like *agape* generally, involves both affection and willing the good even when comfort fails. For more on *agape* and parental (especially maternal) love, see Sally B. Purvis, "Mothers, Neighbors, and Strangers: Another Look at Agape," in *Journal of Feminist Studies in Religion*, vol. 7 (Spring 1991): 19–34.

[134] Vacek, *Love, Human and Divine*, p. 163.

[135] See Martin Luther on "the theological use of the law," in his "Commentary on Galatians," p. 140.

16:18) – and Vacek is surely correct to fault Nygren for seeing absolutely no goodness in sinful human beings.[136] But I would walk more of an Anglican *via media* between Vacek's Catholicism and Nygren's Lutheranism by stressing the primacy of God's *agape* as what creates, expands, and sustains finite worth. Vacek beautifully describes the creative aspect of God's love. With respect to neighbor-love, moreover, he rightly notes that "our love is directed not simply to generic human beings, but to individual persons" with unique identities "which God and they (along with many outside influences) have brought and are bringing into being."[137] Because God loves us far more that we might *become* valuable and cooperative, than because we already are so, however, the language of "friendship" must remain subsidiary to that of "charity."

The *Imago Dei* as the capacity to receive, and secondarily to act on, God's love remains even amid depravity. (If this were not so, then creatures could utterly destroy God's good creation.) But the *Imago* is a *passive* potential for loving relations with God and other creatures that must be activated by divine grace. And this potential is recalcitrant in the extreme. Often, as Vacek knows, we must be brought kicking and screaming into responsible agency, liberated to loyalties and commitments that we do not even remotely aim at on our own. There must be a moment of consent to God's will on some level, lest we have fatalism, but the One who is our Judge and Savior is not first of all our friend. God *commands* us to love, and we love not because we chose God but because God first chose us. God's commandments to creatures *are themselves* divine love, but we can only recognize ourselves as covenant partners after this *agape* has done its work on us. As Barth puts it, "the Law is obviously the form of the Gospel; the judgment declared by the Law is the shape taken by the grace of God."[138]

Not surprisingly, Vacek wants to distance any form of divine command ethics. "Mutual affirmation not one-sided obedience"[139] is to characterize our relation to God, on his view. And "God's love for us affirms our freedom," even as "our love for God should expand that freedom."[140] The strong agapist does not so much disagree with these claims as find them out of sequence. Fidelity aims at concordance between the infinite and the finite, as Vacek illustrates, but first God must *create* our genuine freedom, break us out of our bondage to false

---

[136] Vacek, *Love, Human and Divine*, pp. 167–168.   [137] Ibid., pp. 171 and 170.
[138] Karl Barth, *Church Dogmatics*, trans. by G.W. Bromiley *et al.* (Edinburgh: T.&T. Clark, 1957), II/2, "The Doctrine of God," p. 618.   [139] Vacek, *Love, Human and Divine*, p. 136.
[140] Ibid.

gods. Again, even this is done with our consent (cf. Matt. 23:37), but it is not first and foremost a cooperative enterprise; we have to be graciously lifted by the Holy Spirit to a new self. I myself explore in chapter 6 the possible limits of "absolute duty" to God, but Vacek seems overly bold when he writes: "Our cooperative actions . . . will not be a blind willing of whatever God wills, but rather an intelligent and loving willing of what *we* see to be objectively good."[141] The question is how we come to such enlightenment. When the rich young man in the Gospel of Matthew asks Jesus what he must do to have eternal life, Jesus tells him to "keep the commandments," referring him in particular to the second table of the Decalogue: "You shall not murder," "You shall not commit adultery," etc., and ending with "You shall love your neighbor as yourself" (Matt. 19:17–19). The young man announces that he has kept all these yet still wonders what he lacks. In the Marcan version of the story, interestingly, we are told at this point that "Jesus, looking at him, loved him" (Mark 10:21). The Greek root used is "*agapao*," not "*phileo*," and as Barth remarks, "the form of the love of Jesus is the command" to the young man to sell his possessions, give the money to the poor, and follow him.[142]

The truth of human faith is typically somewhere between blind obedience and the precocious wisdom to which Vacek refers. We must, above all, avoid the false dichotomy of thinking that obligation comes to us as either an alien, heteronomous imposition or a self-legislated, autonomous choice. The New Testament depicts a God who is a loving Lord rather than an abusive martinet, but divine commands have authority precisely because God is both sovereign Creator and faithful Redeemer. A human being is called to be a covenant partner with God, but this involves a theonomy in which each individual's entire being is known and claimed by a fulfillment beyond her immediate ken.[143] "Man's highest achievement is to let God be able to help him,"[144]

---

[141] Ibid., pp. 139–140.   [142] Barth, *Church Dogmatics*, II/2, p. 618.

[143] Ibid., p. 655. Barth's answer to the Euthyphro question stands in stark contrast to Vacek's, as well as to Kant's: "If there is an *ought*, it must not be the product of my own will, but touch from outside the whole area of what I can will of myself. It must lay upon me the obligation of unconditioned truth – truth which is not conditioned by myself. Its authority and power to do so must be intrinsic and objective, and not something which I lend to it. Its validity must consist in the fact that the very question of its validity is quite outside the sphere of my own thinking and feeling; that I can no longer entertain the idea of making sure of its authority and power by seeking its basis in what I myself have understood or seen or felt or experienced . . . The essence of the idea of obligation is not that I demand something from myself but that, with all that I can demand of myself, I am myself demanded" (ibid., p. 651).

[144] Søren Kierkegaard, *Journals and Papers*, vol. I, ed. and trans. by Howard V. and Edna H. Hong, assisted by Gregor Malantschuk (Bloomington: Indiana University Press, 1967), no. 54, p. 22.

Kierkegaard reminds us, but the help is initially one-sided. We must trust it without fully understanding it. Indeed, "[t]he fact of the matter is that man prefers to be free from the kind of liberation which God and Christianity have in mind."[145] Thus friendship, which implies equal liberty and common preference, cannot be the first love theologically. A divine command simultaneously implies "the invitation, permission and liberation for fidelity,"[146] but it is a real command, with authority, not a democratic referendum. Jesus himself says, "You are my friends if you do what I command you" (John 15:14).

III. THE NEW COMMANDMENT: SELF-LOVE AND CHRISTLIKE LOVE

Few injunctions could be better calculated to offend our modern sense of personhood than John 13:34: "I give you a new commandment, that you love one another. Just as I have loved you, you also should love one another." Love, it seems, can be commanded on the model of a master with authority. Could any notion be more alien to our assumptions about the essential privacy and autonomy of our most powerful emotions and commitments? For Jesus, elective affinities – erotic and friendly – were trumped by intrepid obedience to God and sacrificial service to neighbors. Neither sectarian loyalties nor even family ties were the chief object of loyalty or main source of personal fulfillment (see Luke 14:26). The very idea of directly questing after individual fulfillment, though not entirely anachronistic in New Testament contexts, is subordinated to a vision of a new Church faithful to God and one another unto death.

Jesus's summary of the law in Matthew 22:37–40 commands love of God and neighbor, but the new commandment replaces the self-referential norm of "as yourself" with reference to Jesus's own practice. Jesus instructs the disciples to love one another "even as I have loved you." There is genuine novelty here, yet not a simple contradiction of the second love commandment in Matthew. As his teachings on love of enemies, dietary laws, keeping the Sabbath, marriage and divorce, and the stoning of sinners, make clear, Jesus is not averse to infringing (or even directly violating) traditional religious rules when this seems mandated by charity. However, we do not have in John 13 the pattern of:

---

[145] Ibid., vol. II, no. 1277, p. 77.
[146] Barth, *Church Dogmatics*, III/4, p. 198. Barth is here referring specifically to fidelity within marriage, but the point can be generalized to other forms of fidelity to God and neighbor.

"You have heard it said . . . , but I say . . ." Matthew is notoriously ambivalent as to whether Jesus is best seen as fulfilling the old Torah or as supplanting it with a new one, but in John 13:34 Jesus is not just contrasting Mosaic Law with his own gospel. For Jesus has himself repeatedly endorsed the two love commandments of the Pentateuch. If he were straightforwardly overturning the decree to love your neighbor as yourself, he would be undermining his own explicit teaching rather than reforming ancient mores (see Matt. 19:19, 22:39; Mark 12:31,33; Luke 10:27; Rom. 12:10; Gal. 5:14; and Jas. 2:8).

It is better to read John 13 as an elaboration of Matthew 22 rather than a denial. The new commandment cannot but seem to the disciples a radicalization of what has come before, and so it is in some respects. Self-love is a more stringent norm than reciprocal justice, since to love neighbors "as yourself" means treating them as you would *want* to be treated, not as one actually *is* treated. In John 13, however, self-love is itself displaced for something still more demanding: the example of Christ. Even so, the reader can still see the novelty as a deeper explanation of what *true* self-love amounts to. Shrewd psychologist that he is, Jesus knows that after his death the disciples will feel betrayed and lost. "Those who eat my flesh and drink my blood abide in me, and I in them," Jesus says in the synagogue at Capernaum (John 6:56), thereby allowing the twelve and others (proleptically) to vent some of their resentment toward a Messiah who apparently abandons them. "As the Father has loved me, so I have loved you; abide in my love," Jesus says in the context of the Last Commandment, thereby showing the disciples concretely how to care for themselves as well as others. Eating him and imitating him, both give bread for life beyond what everyday prudence could imagine.

Christianity preaches patient self-abnegation, then, but this is paradoxically Good News for both individuals and groups. "Then Jesus told his disciples, 'If any want to become my followers, let them deny themselves and take up their cross and follow me. For those who want to save their life will lose it, and those who lose their life for my sake will find it'" (Matt. 16:24–25). Don't resist evildoers; turn the other cheek; go the extra mile; don't let the right hand know what the left hand is doing. Attention to others rather than assertion of self is the manifest rule of faith, yet precisely by so "losing" the self, one "finds" it. However painful or costly obedience to God and service to neighbor may be – and they will be both – there is no final contradiction between them and genuine love of self. "Impersonal" virtue goes hand in hand with

"personal" fulfillment, though not necessarily with worldly prosperity or
private happiness.

CONCLUSION: *AGAPE* BEFORE *EROS*, AND SANCTITY BEFORE DIGNITY

In contrast to both Augustine and Freud, strong agapists break altogether with Greek eudaimonism, taking Christ's final injunction to "love
one another as I have loved you" (John 15:12) to regulate even the
commandment to "love your neighbor as yourself" (Matt. 22:39). The
Imitatio Christi takes priority over the *anamnesis* of Greek philosophy, the
amor sui of Latin theology, and the sublimated *libido* of German
psychoanalysis. This is so not because self-knowledge, self-love, and self-
integration are illegitimate ends, but because they are impossible beginnings. We do not finally know ourselves and can make no practical
progress in loving ourselves or harmonizing our psyches without the
empowerment of God's grace. The willing forgiveness of sins and
pathos-filled service of neighbor characteristic of Christian ethics are not
natural aspirations – as Aristotle says, "nature seems above all to avoid
the painful and to aim at the pleasant"[147] – but rather echoes of the
kenotic and unconditional love of God. On purely human terms, this
love is impossible, "but for God all things are possible" (Matt. 19:26).

For strong agapists, openness to the sacrifice of life itself based on
faithful imitation of Christ carries the soul "beyond the reciprocity
principle." Better, *agape* opens one to a divine reality that comes *before*
reciprocity or any instinctual drive as its foundation. Christianity
equates *agape* with uplifting others to their supernatural origin and end,
in ways more primitive than *eros* and more profound than either justice
or friendship. Without an unconditional affirmation by others, individuals cannot emerge with erotic impulses and desires, corporate goals
and interest-based rights, that a rational justice regulates or a personal
friendship respects. *Human sanctity precedes personal dignity*, in the sense that
creatures' impersonal needs and passive potentials, engaged by *agape*,
come before their meritorious actions and mutual enjoyments.

Agape passionately wills the good for others for their own sakes (*pace*
Augustine), but willing that good may mean sacrifices that outstrip the
demands of strict justice and natural preference. If *agape* is a supernatural virtue that makes natural aptitudes possible, in short, then neither

---

[147] Aristotle, *The Nicomachean Ethics*, bk. VIII, chap. 5, [1157b16], p. 200.

fair erotic praxis (Freud) nor free friendly partnership (Vacek) is the highest good. The call to sacrifice can be overdrawn (cf. Weil), but *agape* grounds both *eros* and *philia* and renders self-love a good far more found than made.[148]

[148] For a contrasting discussion of how various loves relate to morality, see Martha C. Nussbaum, *Love's Knowledge*, esp. chaps. 13 and 14. See also Allan Bloom, *Love and Friendship*, esp. part three.

CHAPTER 4

Love, abomination, and liberation

Yes, what we should seek for is indeed – is it not? – an exaltation and not an emancipation of the mind. The latter goes only with an abominable pride. Our ambition should not lie in revolt but in service.

André Gide[1]

MORE: And what would you do with a water spaniel that was afraid of water! You'd hang it! Well, as a spaniel is to water, so is a man to his own self . . . Is there no single sinew in the midst of this that serves no appetite of Norfolk's but is just Norfolk? There is! Give *that* some exercise, my lord.

Robert Bolt[2]

INTRODUCTION: GOING TO EXTREMES

People have traditionally tried to put their deepest hopes and fears into words, thereby defining themselves. As we look back on the twentieth century, a century that has seen extremes of brutality as well as humanity, the apposite words don't come easily. We in the West still speak in ethical terms, of course. But in the wake of Stalin's purges, Mao's Cultural Revolution, the Killing Fields of Cambodia, the mass suicides/ murders of Jonestown/Waco, and above all else the Nazi Holocaust, we are wary of the ideologue's eloquence. Strong moral condemnation seems to invite fanaticism – Voltaire's *"Ecrasez l'infame"* symbolizing the excesses of 1789 and beyond – while comparable praise seems either to entail hopelessly subjective judgments or to ossify inevitably into mind-numbing rules of right behavior. Individuals have their heroes, from Gandhi to Gorbachev, and their private lives proceed apace; but Spirit,

---

[1] Gide, *Strait is the Gate*, trans. by Dorothy Bussy (New York: Vintage Books, 1952), p. 76.
[2] Bolt, "A Man for All Seasons" (New York: Vintage Books, 1988), act 2, pp. 123–124.

in Edith Wyschogrod's phrase,[3] is in ashes. The dominant mood is not despair, but rather an uneasy reticence about vice coupled with a too easy loquaciousness about virtue. The upshot is a paradoxical inarticulacy about human height and depth amid a welter of talk about breadth; pluralism gets more intelligent play than either profundity or perversity. There are perhaps two reasons for this.

On the one hand, we want a vocabulary for opposing evil that will not incite what it condemns, a means of resisting oppression that won't itself encourage a spirit of intolerance. On the other hand, we want a diction of praise that will not endorse inflexible standards, a mode of appreciation that won't repress personal innovation. The upshot of these two desiderata is a tendency either to abridge the moral lexicon or to multiply neologisms without end. Oddly, we tend in the name of prudence and open-mindedness thus to blind ourselves to the very extremes of human life and death that make ethical self-understanding both possible and necessary. Lest we offend, academics in particular often deny radical vice and trivialize profound virtue by evacuating robust ethical terms of distinctive meaning by underuse or overindulgence.

I focus in this chapter on the fortunes of two such robust terms: *"abomination"* and *"liberation."* Though the first word carries very negative connotations and the second very positive – we sense that brutality and humanity are at issue – a cursory check of recent usage suggests that there is little agreement on precisely what these words mean, or at least on how they are to be applied. A professor at Louisville's Presbyterian Theological Seminary argues for "gay/lesbian liberation as a specific case of liberation theology."[4] Four years later, the Southern Baptist Convention, which also has a seminary in Louisville, condemns homosexuality as an "abomination in the eyes of God."[5] Pope Paul VI and the Second Vatican Council label abortion an "abominable" and "unspeakable" crime, respectively.[6] Twenty years later, a professor of sociology at the University of California, San Diego, notes that women's liberation groups "made the 'unspeakable' speakable" when "they

---

[3] Edith Wyschogrod, *Spirit in Ashes: Hegel, Heidegger, and Man-made Mass Death* (New Haven and London: Yale University Press, 1985).

[4] George R. Edwards, *Gay/Lesbian Liberation: A Biblical Perspective* (New York: Pilgrim Press, 1984), p. 9.

[5] At their annual meeting in San Antonio, as reported in *The New York Times* on June 17, 1988.

[6] Pope Paul VI, "Respect for Life in the Womb: Address to the Medical Association of Western Flanders" (April 23, 1977), reprinted in *On Moral Medicine*, edited by Steven Lammars and Allen Verhey (Grand Rapids: Eerdmans, 1987), pp. 396–397; and *"Gaudium Et Spes,"* in *The Documents of Vatican II*, ed. by Walter M. Abbott, S.J. (Chicago: Follett Publishing Co., 1966), p. 256.

began to use the language of *rights* in talking about women and abortion."[7] Why such radical diversity?

"Abomination" and "liberation," with all their present vagaries, roughly encapsulate two distinct worldviews. Those comparatively few professional ethicists now likely, in earnest, to call something an "abomination" tend to identify themselves as conservative: upholding duty, family, natural law, and religious tradition. Here accent falls on the recognition and courageous acceptance of the *limits* of human life, the biological, sociological, and theological "givens": birth, death, gender, physical frailty, intellectual fallibility,[8] moral culpability, and finally spiritual dependency on God. These things precede personal choice and constrain any choice that would be sensitive to the demands of living with others. The moral glance of those concerned with the abominable is cast backward; the task is to remember who we are and have been and thereby to arrive at definite evaluative judgments within a more or less closed moral system. As a first approximation, then, an abomination might be defined as what radically undercuts or transgresses those bounds (material and cultural) that have made and continue to make an ordered human existence possible.

Those many ethicists with "liberation" on their lips, in contrast, are generally liberal: emphasizing autonomy, creativity, individual rights, and progressive politics. In this case, accent falls on the *freedom* of individuals to transcend what has been bequeathed to them by nature, history, or providence and to remake themselves and their communities into something new and better. Those preoccupied with the liberating look forward, imagining as-yet-unrealized human possibilities. Rather than venerating place, they celebrate movement. Against such a background, a liberation may initially be construed as what delivers us from the dead hand of the past for a future that is indeterminate yet largely subject to human control. Rather than accenting *terms of responsiveness* ("discernment," "acceptance," "patience," "conformity-to-reality"), liberationists give currency to *terms of initiation* ("construction," "resistance," "exuberance," "transformation-of-reality"). While abominators

---

[7] Kristin Luker, *Abortion and the Politics of Motherhood* (Berkeley and Los Angeles: University of California Press, 1984), pp. 96–97.

[8] Religious believers in abominations are often thought of as dogmatic and self-righteous, so the reference here to "intellectual fallibility" may seem inapt. It is important to realize, however, that appeals to Scriptural inerrancy are, at their best, intended as expressions of humility. We are to trust not variable human "knowledge" but God's "revealed truth," the argument goes. Once the principle of fallibility is applied to Scripture itself, of course, one is in a quite different moral universe.

would preserve honored traditions, including the vision of the world as a substantially fixed chain of being, liberators would promote innovative change. Whereas abominators embrace "natural hierarchies" and the awe and obedience that go along with them (e.g., between God–humanity, priest–laity, parent–child), liberators advocate egalitarian social experiments and a spirit of uncoerced cooperation (as in open-door churches and social contract theories). The school of abomination commends "sacrificial service" where that of liberation hails "revolutionary solidarity," but the key contrast concerns their perceptions of the nature and relative import of moral limitation and freedom. This leads to corresponding differences of emphasis on memory and imagination among agents and on closure and openness among the (con)texts they produce.[9]

Even as the conservatives sing the praises of memory while the liberals extol the virtues of imagination, so they differ on which private and public *vices* are most threatening. The conservatives worry about pride, solipsism, blasphemy, and anarchy, while the liberals vilify sloth, unoriginality, timorousness, and tyranny. (Call the former the fear of flying and the latter the anxiety of influence.) The original sin for abominators is to forget one's finitude and to lust after limitless power to the neglect or corruption of other people; the comparable fall for liberators is to accept false restraints of mind or heart and to impose them on others thereby stunting their liberty. This basic disagreement is nicely captured by the fact that for conservatives "self-love" is often the very paradigm of transgression, while for liberals it is the *sine qua non* for moral maturity. A careful unpacking of the meaning of the phrase "self-love" (chapter 3) may reveal some of this divergence to be merely verbal, but not all.

Juxtaposing "conservative" and "liberal" outlooks in this broad way helps draw a rough distinction between "abomination" and "liberation," but it also carries a danger. It may suggest that the latter two terms (and the theories they abbreviate) represent a simple either/or. One must just decide, it might seem, between the conservative and liberal schools as but one more version of a law/gospel or, alternatively, a responsibility/license dichotomy. I contend, however, that a proper reading of the quoted terms reveals their codependence and, in one

---

[9] For more on conservatism, liberalism, and the acceptance/rejection of limitation, see Christopher Lasch, "Conservatism Against Itself," in *First Things*, no. 2 (April 1990): 17–23. For a discussion of openness and closure in literary works, see Wayne C. Booth, *The Company We Keep: An Ethics of Fiction* (Berkeley: University of California Press, 1988), pp. 60–70.

sense, complementarity. (We are not faced here with Alasdair MacIntyre's choice between Aristotle or Nietzsche,[10] much less one between Moses and Christ.) Though basic opposites, the most plausible definitions of "abomination" and "liberation" actually share assumptions about human limitation and freedom, and any account of morality which does not leave room for both will do justice to neither. Language games come and go, but to recommend forgetfulness of "abomination" as obsolete, for example, in order to usher in new forms of "liberation," is to indulge in double-talk. For the abominable, I ultimately suggest, is whatever fundamentally thwarts the distinctively human capacity for love (of both oneself and others), while the liberating is whatever fundamentally expands it. If there is no moral subject who is vulnerable to the "abominable," then there is none to be "liberated" or "liberating" either. The terms stand or fall together, however much they may differ in surface grammar and political appeal; Gide notwithstanding, we need not associate liberation/emancipation with "an abominable pride," leaving us with an ideal of exaltation alone. One can no more lament abomination and ignore liberation, or celebrate liberation and neglect abomination, than one can map the globe without attending to both poles.

By treating "abomination" and "liberation" (and their referents) as polar opposites explicable in terms of love as personal care, we can do for ethics what Parry and Byrd did for geography: orient and enrich our common life by charting its extremities. Because the moral lexicon shapes the contours of our self-understanding, to define the limits of that lexicon in terms of "abomination" and "liberation" is to begin to comprehend the worst and best we are or may be. It helps to clarify everyday life within ethics, even as the study of disease and its therapy helps to clarify health within medicine. This does not settle all substantive ethical disputes – we may still disagree on the application of our terms – but it is a helpful first step toward moral articulacy.[11] The point of my inquiry is not to deny real differences of opinion between cultural conservatives and liberals but to look for underlying commonalities that mitigate the basic dispute. I find the primal commonality, humanity's "True North" as it were, in the need and capacity for agapic love.

Part of the moral of my story is as old as that of Greek tragedy: the Dionysian longing for ecstasy requires the Apollonian respect for boundaries. *There can be no true freedom without limitation, no human consumma-*

---

[10] MacIntyre, *After Virtue* (Notre Dame: University of Notre Dame Press, 1981), chap. 18.
[11] See Charles Taylor, *Sources of the Self: The Making of the Modern Identity* (Cambridge: Harvard University Press, 1989), esp. chap. 3.

tion without the possibility of perversity, no liberation without the threat of abom-ination. To hope for inspiration and escape from the encumbrance of distinctions without ordered judgment and self-control is to invite calamity – murder being the final Bacchic license.[12] "Happiness is appeased horror," in Alain's words,[13] and liberation is evaded abomination. For all its savoring of Greek balance, however, my treatment of abomination and liberation is distinctive in grounding them both in the priority of agapic love. The abominable is a fundamental "No" to love's respect for the actual integrity of human beings, their "otherness" as independent centers of value, even as the liberating is a fundamental "Yes" to love's enhancement of the ideal potential of human beings, their capacity for growth and drive to fulfillment.

I. ABOMINATION

A. Etymologies and extensions

The term "abomination," if used at all these days, is typically reserved for the most heinous, the least forgivable, of offenses; levelling the charge gives proof of one's ongoing capacity for righteous indignation. How precisely to understand the term is often far from clear, however. One may suspect, in fact, that at present it serves usually as "rhetorical flourish."[14] Still, a basic meaning of the word is indicated by its etymology, which the Oxford English Dictionary notes is either *"absit"* + *"omen"* or *"ab"* + *"homine."* The former possibility, which I will call the theological reading, is the older of the two and construes the abominable as what is without good omen or God's blessing, what offends the Deity or incurs God's wrath. The latter, anthropological reading entered the English language through John Wycliffe's translation of the Bible – he followed the French medievals in spelling "abomination" with an "h"[15] – and sees the abominable as what departs from or

---

[12] As Jan Kott, *The Eating of the Gods: An Interpretation of Greek Tragedy* (New York: Random House, 1973), p. 228, has observed, "Dionysus promises liberation from alienation and freedom from all ties, but he grants only one ultimate freedom: the freedom to kill." The relation between "the 'Dionysiac' state of mind" and violence is explored in depth by René Girard in *Violence and the Sacred*, trans. by Patrick Gregory (Baltimore: Johns Hopkins University Press, 1977).

[13] Alain, *The Gods*, trans. by Richard Pevear (New York: New Directions, 1974), p. 109.

[14] See Jeffrey Stout, "Moral Abominations," in *Ethics After Babel: The Languages of Morals and Their Discontents* (Boston: Beacon Press, 1988), p. 146. This essay initially appeared in *Soundings*, vol. LXVI, no. 1 (Spring 1983): 5–23.

[15] "Ab*h*omination," as in his translation of Titus 1:16, and as later shared in places by Shakespeare. See *The Compact Oxford English Dictionary*, vol. I (Oxford: Oxford University Press, 1984), p. 7; *The New Testament*, [1380], trans. by John Wycliffe (London: Pickering, 1848); and *Love's Labor's Lost*, act V, scene i, line 24.

destroys the essentially human. Just what (if anything) is the essentially human is much debated, but before taking up this issue let me make a few remarks on moral reasoning in order to expand on the two readings of "abomination."

We tend to think in three moral dimensions: the aretaic, the deontic, and the consequentialist (or telic). What I will call "aretology" (from "*arete*," the Greek word for excellence or virtue) is concerned with the *character of agents* acting; deontology (from "*deon*," meaning duty) examines the *form or quality of actions* performed; and consequentialism focuses on the *kind or quantity of effects* produced. Christian believers will integrate all three dimensions with reference to a fourth, overarching one: God's redemptive relation to the world. But, in any case, how one understands the abominable, in both theological and anthropological forms, will depend on which dimension is paramount. This is partly a reflection of the fact that aretology, deontology, and consequentialism carry with them different models of truth and justification.

The theological interpretation of "abomination," as typified by the Bible and the early medievals, often connotes the disorder that follows from disobedience to God or transgression of natural limits. The motive for disobedience or transgression (e.g., pride) may be quite important, but labelling something "abominable" frequently points also (if not chiefly) at effects. It implies a hazardous impairment to social harmony or a personal regression to animality *after* the fact of sin: a *corruption* that is shunned by God and therefore to be shunned by creatures. A good example of this telic dimension is Isaiah 1:11–13:

> What to me is the multitude of your sacrifices? says the Lord; I have had enough of burnt offerings of rams and the fat of fed beasts; I do not delight in the blood of bulls, or of lambs, or of goats. When you came to appear before me, who asked this from your hand? Trample my courts no more; bringing offerings is futile; incense is an abomination [*to'eba*] to me. New moon and sabbath and calling of convocation – I cannot endure solemn assemblies with iniquity.

Note it is both false piety and empty ritual that is abominable to Yahweh. It is "solemn assemblies *with* iniquity," not merely iniquity, that God "cannot endure" (see also Prov. 15:8 and cf. Amos 5:21–24).

I hasten to emphasize that the moral accent is by no means exclusively on consequences in Judeo-Christian Scripture, not generally and not even with reference to abominations. Good actor, good action, and good end are inextricably tied. God often highlights bad acts or disordered effects in order to shift humanity's moral focus to an inner motivation founded on right relation to God, which in turn is to be effectively acted on. The Lord says to Judah, for instance, "I desire steadfast love and not sacrifice, the knowledge of God rather than burnt offerings" (Hos. 6:6); and Jesus echoes these words with: "Go and learn what this means, 'I desire mercy, not sacrifice'" (Matt. 9:13).

There are four Hebrew words in the Old Testament translated as "abomination" ("*piggul*," "*siqqus*," "*seqes*," and "*to'eba*"), and these display a broad range of meanings.[16] The first is applied to sacrificial flesh which has been left too long and turned foul; the second refers to pagan gods or to objects connected with idolatry; while the third is a technical term extending to food prohibited for Israelites as ritually unclean. The fourth term (*to'eba*) "[i]n almost all cases . . . has reference to objects and practices abhorrent to Y'", and opposed to the moral requirements and ritual of his religion," including "the worship of heathen deities and of the heavenly bodies (Deu. 13:14, 17:4 and oft), the practice of witchcraft and kindred arts (Deu. 18:12), gross acts of immorality (Lev. 18:22, 26ff), falsification of weights and measures (Pro. 11:1), and 'evil devices' generally (Pro. 15:26)."[17] The New Testament Greek word translated "abomination" ("*bdelygma*") appears six times in the Gospels and Revelation and means, generally, what elicits the disgust and/or the wrath of God.[18] In addition, the epistles of Saint Paul illustrate that premodern Christian usage involves aretaic, deontic, as well as consequentialist elements, even in elaborating the significance of the "unnatural" or "perverse" (Rom. 1:26–32, KJ and RSV).

The anthropological reading of the "abominable" also ranges over aretaic, deontic, and telic concerns. It is possible to interpret the "inhumanity" of abominations in terms of debilitating consequences – Shakespeare associates abomination with drunkenness, for example[19] – but when seen deontologically, being abominable is not the effect of improper actions but their cause, not an atavistic breakdown after immorality but a violation of the moral law. In fact, a deontological

---

[16] L.L. Morris, "Abomination," *The New Bible Dictionary*, ed. by J.D. Douglas (Grand Rapids: Eerdmans, 1967), p. 4. Different authorities give various transliterations of the four terms. Compare, for example, *Dictionary of the Bible*, ed. by James Hastings and revised by Frederick C. Grant and H.H. Rowley (New York: Charles Scribner's Sons, 1963), p. 5.

[17] *Dictionary of the Bible*, p. 5.

[18] M.H. Lovelace, "Abomination," *The Interpreter's Dictionary of the Bible*, ed. by G.A. Buttrick, vol. I (Nashville: Abingdon Press, 1962), pp. 12–13; and *A Greek-English Lexicon of the New Testament* (Chicago: University of Chicago Press, 1957), p. 137.

[19] See William Shakespeare, *The Tempest*, act II, scene ii, lines 160–161. All quotations from Shakespeare are from *The Complete Signet Classic Shakespeare*, ed. by Sylvan Barnet (New York and London: Harcourt Brace Jovanovich, 1972).

abomination is most distinctively a conscious rejection of the moral law itself and with it practical standards for human conduct. Finally, when seen aretologically the abominable is a mode of existence that is so intrinsically vicious as to undermine the normativity of any state of character. As extraordinary vice or brutality, the abominable subverts the very idea of personal integrity. In both deontic and aretaic contexts, therefore, an anthropological abomination is an extreme *inhumanity* that is both shocking and condemnable.

B. *Personal care and anthropological abomination*

Let me sketch a strictly anthropological approach to abominations more fully. My account begins with the proposition that a human being is capable of personal care and in need of personal care;[20] correlatively, it recognizes that a human being often fails to show such care and/or has the need for such care often go unmet. All these permutations involve either the presence or absence of autonomy and sympathy, the key capacities for responsible action attentive to self and others. Autonomy is that virtue most closely identified with individuality, while sympathy correlates with community. But both are essential for human flourishing, on this view. Neither the privatization nor the abstraction of morality is responsible living. (Ethics is an art, but not a specialty.)

The generic capacity to care may be thought of as the ability to guide one's actions consciously toward a goal, minimally the ability to feel and the desire to avoid pain. Whether animals, human fetuses, or even certain artifacts "care" in this sense is an interesting question but one finally irrelevant to my present concerns. For in referring to "*personal* care," I have something more specific in mind than general purposiveness. To be capable of personal care is to be capable of furthering human beings themselves as of intrinsic worth, while to be in need of personal care is to need valuing by others. To care for human beings as

---

[20] A number of recent authors have emphasized the primacy of care: *inter alia*, Martin Heidegger, Martin Buber, Milton Meyeroff, Paul Ramsey, Carol Gilligan, Nel Noddings, Michael Ignatieff, Sara Ruddick, and Jeffrey Blustein. I have been most influenced by Heidegger's *Being and Time*, trans. by John Macquarrie and Edward Robinson (New York: Harper and Row, 1962); Ramsey's *The Patient as Person* (New Haven: Yale University Press, 1970); Gilligan's *In a Different Voice* (Cambridge: Harvard University Press, 1982); and Noddings's *Caring: A Feminine Approach to Ethics and Moral Education* (Berkeley: University of California Press, 1984). Influence is not always agreement, of course. On the Gilligan–Kohlberg debate, I have found *An Ethic of Care: Feminist and Interdisciplinary Perspectives*, ed. by Mary Jeanne Larrabee (New York: Routledge, 1993), very helpful.

such is to value their status as (real or potential) valuers, and to need care from other human beings is to require their valuation in order to acquire moral ends of one's own. Personal care is, in other words, self-conscious and other-regarding. Developing personhood, becoming ourselves, re- quires that others extend to us gratuitous attention. Once personal care is actualized, however, our lives matter to us, and it matters that they matter: we value ourselves as valuers. Hence the possibility of an abominable thwarting of this process.

Personhood cannot be equated with a single faculty (such as reason), and "impersonal" attributes (such as shared human nature) are insepar- able from moral value (cf. Weil). But it makes sense, especially in secular moral contexts, to speak of the need and capacity for personal care as basic. (In medical contexts, some other facet of human nature may be key, such as brain function.) Commonsense evidence for this thesis abounds, but I limit myself to two vignettes. I believe it was Louis XIV who wanted to know what tongue was primitive, so he instructed the attendants in his Royal Nursery not to speak to the babies in their charge but simply to feed and clothe them. The thought was that the infants would eventually begin speaking the natural human language (presumably French). Of course, not being humanly addressed, all the babies died. Their physical needs were met but not their spiritual. More recently, there is the case of Genie, the so-called "Wild Child" reported on by *NOVA*.[21] Genie's parents evidently kept her chained to a potty-seat for weeks at a time and seldom spoke to her or let her out of the house. The neglect was appalling. The result was that Genie never learned to speak, never acquired a sense of herself as a moral agent. Even after she had become a physically mature woman, she had the mental and emotional age of a two-year-old.

As these two stories suggest, personal care is first virtue because without it there is no virtue at all. Some form of the virtue is our deepest need as moral patients and our greatest achievement as moral agents. In showing personal care, we strive most fundamentally to enlarge human- ity, not primarily in a numerical sense (though this may be involved) but in the sense of fostering human beings who are themselves caring and cared for. This account assumes – on anthropological, sociological, and philosophical evidences – that the need and capacity for personal care is a universal human trait, as ubiquitous as language competence among

---

[21] "Secret of a Wild Child," a *NOVA* Production by the WGBH/Boston Science Unit in associ- ation with BBC-TV (1994).

undamaged individuals.[22] The relevant ability is what the scholastics called a "passive potential,"[23] however. If it is not cultivated by other caring human beings, it atrophies and is never actualized. There is this performative aspect to personal care; it does not merely acknowledge but also generates moral worth in others. In fact, the root issue in an ethics of personal care is not so much how to distribute interpersonal sympathies assumed to exist, much less physical commodities, as how to *produce* these sympathies to begin with. Thus any philosophy that would ground ethics by assuming free and purposive agents neglects the prior question of how to bring them into being. In denying personal care, we not only deprive others of care here and now but also render them (and us) unable to care or to be cared for in the future. The loss is ultimately of the potential for dignity, if not for sanctity.[24]

An interesting example of use of the word "abominable" to refer to what undermines dignity can be found in Joseph Conrad's *Lord Jim* (1900). Jim is on trial for having deserted his post as officer of the (apparently) sinking ship *Patna*, leaving the hundreds of Islamic pilgrims on board to drown. Though physically handsome, the very flower of English youth, Jim seems morally uncultivated. He seems not to care about the charges brought against him and declines to defend or even explain his evident cowardice. Upon leaving the courtroom, Captain

---

[22] See, e.g., Melford Spiro, *Culture and Human Nature* (Chicago: University of Chicago Press, 1989); Barry Schwartz, *The Battle for Human Nature: Science, Morality, and Modern Life* (New York: W.W. Norton, 1986); and several of the essays in Martha C. Nussbaum and Amartya Sen, eds., *The Quality of Life* (Oxford: Clarendon Press, 1993), esp. Nussbaum's "Non-Relative Virtues: An Aristotelian Approach."

[23] I am indebted to Lee Yearley for calling this concept in Saint Thomas to my attention.

[24] Someone might object that my construal of the relation between human nature and ethics commits the naturalistic fallacy of reasoning from "is" to "ought." It must be admitted that if one allows that prescriptions and admonitions must be unrelated to descriptions and interpretations, then an anthropological account of abominations is indeed impossible. For a moral realist like myself, however, this allowance is dubious dogma.

Why should the dogma have gained currency? One reason, I believe, is that the term "naturalism" is systematically ambiguous. For some, it implies not just generally reasoning from "is" to "ought" but drawing moral conclusions from narrowly biological or physiological facts alone. It is indeed unclear how the latter could be done. If we rule out references to such distinctively human (but "nonnatural") activities as suffering, hoping, regretting, exulting, intending, loving, hating, and promising, then in fact no description of humanity will have any normative significance. But such omissions make for an indefensibly reductionist account. For others, the term "naturalism" is associated with a naive and inflexible natural law theory, with the contention that all societies reflect a narrow set of anthropological categories which is fixed and may be known exhaustively. Such foundationalist essentialism is also dubious, given the variability across cultures of both mores and morals, including conceptions of the person.

My analysis of personal care attempts to be neither reductionist nor foundationalist. It refers to capacities which are, in all likelihood, beyond the pale of a physicalist translation, and it does not claim that all societies have actually shared its conception of humanity. I have offered a brief outline of one particular view of human nature, considered ethically; but any account of the abominable and the liberating will, by definition, require *some* substantive view.

Brierly, the paradigmatic British seaman impressed with his own sense of "honor," says:

"This infernal publicity is too shocking: there he sits while all these confounded natives, serangs, lascars, quartermasters, are giving evidence that's enough to burn a man to ashes with shame. This is abominable. Why, Marlow, don't you think, don't you feel, that this is abominable; don't you now – come – as a seaman?" . . . "The worst of it," he said, "is that all you fellows have no sense of dignity; you don't think enough of what you are supposed to be."[25]

This passage conveys, in an understated way, the basic meaning of an anthropological abomination – "not thinking enough" of one's own or others' humanity – but the sequel to it illustrates the pitfalls of such a notion. Brierly is so undone by Jim's failures (including the failure to be ashamed) and the reminders they afford of Brierly's own past indiscretions (as well as of human frailty generally) that he commits suicide. The risk of buying in on terms like "abominable," "shameful," "dignified," and "honorable" is that this may either overwhelm one with a guilty conscience or puff one up with an insufferable (and possibly racist or sexist) self-righteousness. The thrust of postmodernism is to deny that this risk is worth running, but the most straightforward defense of the language of "abomination" is that it captures an undeniable (if somewhat opaque) extremity of the moral life.

Why should the abominable be opaque? Our judgment of "ordinary vices" (Shklar) assumes several shared moral categories and experiences. We find greed, dishonesty, cruelty, and unchastity intelligible (however objectionable) because we recognize in ourselves the capacity for such lapses. Inordinate love of money, deceit, callousness, cupidity, and the like remain within what might be called "normal" sinfulness precisely because most of us see in them both turpitude and temptation. Remove the immediate plausibility of ourselves as actors, in contrast, while preserving or enhancing the sense of culpability, and you begin to approach the abominable. Mary Douglas and Jeffrey Stout have pointed out that abominations threaten or even directly assault our basic (moral) distinctions,[26] hence they fall under what might be called "revolutionary" or "unnatural" vice. When the question of motive is brought to the fore, this unnaturalness helps to explain why the agents of abomination are sometimes perceived as almost superhumanly wicked, self-consciously evil. The thought is that nobody could really want to do

---

[25] Conrad, *Lord Jim* (New York: Penguin Books, 1986), p. 92.
[26] Mary Douglas, *Purity and Danger* (London: Routledge & Kegan Paul, 1966), esp. pp. 41–57; and Stout, "Moral Abominations," pp. 149–150. My original interest in this topic was stimulated by Stout's reading of his article, in manuscript, at a Yale Ethics Colloquium in April 1982.

that for its own sake, nobody could really mistake *that* for the good or the right.

At its most distinctive, an anthropological abomination is too big a lapse to count as ignorance or weakness of will; no other category seems to fit but the vaguely troubling one of "perversity." As Augustine says in his *Confessions*, writing of his pre-conversion theft of the pears, "The evil in me was foul, but I loved it. I loved my own perdition and my own faults, not the things for which I committed wrong, but the wrong itself."[27] It is as if one wants evil to triumph in oneself and in the world. Such a prospect is normally repellent, even ineffable, so uncanniness is often a prominent feature of the abominable. What one finds uncanny will depend on basic moral perspective, however, and this varies across time and personalities.[28]

C. *Strong* agape *and theological abomination*

Theological commitments make a difference to what one judges abominable and why, of course. Pope Paul VI considers abortion an "abominable crime," as noted, while others of a more recent sensibility see it as a "right" or "contraception of last resort"; the prophet Jeremiah labels the child-sacrifice of ancient Israel an "abomination" (Jer. 7:30–31), while at least one contemporary utilitarian philosopher finds that "the cultures that practiced infanticide were on solid ground";[29] the author of Leviticus sees incest as an "abomination" (*to'eba*), while some today see it as "the last taboo." And so on. One does not have to be religious to be against abortion, child-sacrifice, and/or incest, but one's opposition will have a distinctive shape and inspiration.

The theological reading of "abominable" suggested by the Greek and Hebrew words cited reflects the classical unity of the true, the good, and the beautiful. Biblical "abominations" range from what is false (lying) to what is malicious (injustice) to what is putrid (tainted meat) not because use of the term is unprincipled but because its principle is premodern. It is not that no distinction has yet been drawn between empirical, moral, and aesthetic judgments – in the Hebrew Bible, the Ten Commandments are clearly demarcated from the Holiness Code – but that these judgments are still related systematically in terms of the will of God or

---

[27] Augustine, *Confessions*, bk. II, chap. 4, p. 47.
[28] See Stout, "Moral Abominations," pp. 156–157.
[29] Peter Singer, *Rethinking Life and Death: The Collapse of Our Traditional Ethics* (Oxford: Oxford University Press, 1995), p. 215. See also Singer's *Practical Ethics* (Cambridge: Cambridge University Press, 1993).

the created order of the universe. Error, evil, and ugliness are not quite synonymous, but they are equally contrary to divine purposes and thus "off omens" symptomatic of one another. They put one in wrong relation to God and to the created order. The purely anthropological reading of "abominable," on the other hand, emerged in the context of the breakdown of this theological unity.

The course from Wycliffe through Shakespeare to Kant is, despite their intentions, one of the progressive disintegration of (accounts of) human faculties even as humanity more and more takes theoretical center stage. The disintegration is by no means complete by the end of the eighteenth century, but the effort to hold together scientific, ethical, and artistic reasoning has become Herculean – as is apparent in Kant's three *Critiques*. By the end of the nineteenth century (Nietzsche's death in 1900), it appeared to many that neither God, truth, goodness, beauty, nor even "Man" himself could survive the corrosive effects of the (anti-)Copernican turn to the subject. If this were so, then with the exception of some Thomists and Southern Baptists (on the side of religion) and some neo-Platonists and Straussians (on the side of philosophy), the "abominable" could no longer mean *anything* distinctive to Western intellectuals. Strong agapists believe otherwise, however.

The distinctive feature of a theologically based account of abomination is that it begins not with human care but with divine grace. The need to give and to receive personal care is recognized, but God's loving will grounds this dialectic rather than creaturely autonomy and sympathy alone. The anthropocentric understanding of "abomination" is not denied, then, but the theocentric has primacy. For Christian agapists, more specifically, the love of God revealed in Jesus Christ makes caring relations possible, even as it unmasks the debasing of these relations. I will return to this point below.

II. LIBERATION

A. Etymologies and extensions

As with "abomination," two general readings of "liberation" are possible. The Latin root of the word (*liber*) means "free"; but there are at least two possible elaborations of this freedom, elaborations as old as Augustine: mere freedom of choice (*liberum arbitrium*) or the more holistic notion of good disposition, candor, and personal integrity (*libertas*). Freedom of choice (liberty of indifference) refers exclusively to the will and says nothing about the ends to which free choice is put, while *libertas* is a more normative notion in which the whole person (rather than just the will) flourishes. Liberation in the sense associated with *libertas*, it should be clear, entails more than having an external encumbrance removed. We do speak of "liberating" a town, say, when we mean delivering it from foreign occupation; but the most robust sense of "liberation" involves internal empowerment, a revolution in the self rather than in its circumstances, a fundamental heightening of the capacity for personal care.

External, telic liberation is *from* something rather than *for* something. Such liberation is often a very great good, crucial for autonomous individuals as well as for democratic polities, but it clearly does not exhaust the meaning of the word and is not the most positive sense of liberty. As Northrop Frye notes in his study of Blake: "Rousseau says, on a basis of nature and reason, that man is born free, and is everywhere in chains. The imagination says that man is not chain-bound but muscle-bound; that he is born alive, and is everywhere dying in sleep . . ."[30] To describe the problem of unfreedom as "muscle-boundedness" is to locate it as fundamentally internal to the human mind and heart, but this does not imply that the solution is purely a matter of personal transformation. The personal and the political are inseparable; an individual's options for action as well as for self-understanding will depend on the economic, educational, and legislative institutions in which he or she is embedded. Even so, there are limits to the external liberation often associated in liberal societies with politics – for example, with the removal of governmental tyranny or the extension of govern-mental assistance. For if the end of oppression and the offer of aid do not fundamentally empower individuals to care for and about themselves – if, that is, the liberation is merely outward and material – then it is at best incomplete and at worst paternalistic. Negative political freedom, defined roughly as unobstructed choice, presupposes a richer concep-tion of liberation in which the object is cultivation according to ideals that outstrip present wants and physical needs. Purely negative or value-neutral "liberation" is inadequate even for a liberal state, since the inevitable conflicts of negative liberty must be adjudicated on the basis of a positive conception of human well-being.[31] Even as a broad reading

---

[30] Frye, *Fearful Symmetry: A Study of William Blake* (Princeton: Princeton University Press, 1969), p. 259.

[31] Cf. William Galston, *Liberal Purposes: Goods, Virtues, and Diversity in the Liberal State* (Cambridge: Cambridge University Press, 1991), chap. 4, esp. pp. 83–84. Here I depart from Isaiah Berlin's famous discussion of positive vs. negative liberty in *Four Essays on Liberty* (Oxford: Oxford University Press, 1982), particularly the Introduction and chap. III. Berlin holds that "the

of "abomination" is not limited to the sense of ritual impurity, so attention to the deontic and aretaic connotations of "liberation" directs us to those features of human nature that used to be called "inwardness" or "spirituality."[32]

When seen deontologically or aretologically, it is not the number or usefulness of external goods created that is important, but the character of the creations or creators. Paramount is the quality of the action or character of the agents involved. A deontic liberation may be defined as an action that conforms to duty so as to facilitate the performance of duty itself. Those exercises of autonomy that overcome personal inclinations and/or psychological limitations are most morally significant here because most conducive to (future) right action. An aretaic liberation, in turn, cultivates a trait (e.g., *phronesis*/practical wisdom) that itself enhances the potential for virtuous states of character. Quite generally, just as abominations contract humanity's capacity to care and be cared for, thus making for bondage to bondage, so liberations expand that capacity, thus making for "freedom to be free" (in Arturo Paoli's phrase, echoing Galatians 5:1).[33]

I would not sanitize the many actions and traits called "liberating" by various moral and religious traditions. There is often an antinomian impulse at work, as when normal prohibitions against certain forms of sex and violence (e.g., incest and war) are violated on special occasions or by extraordinary individuals. Much ritual (like humor) is iconoclastic in the short run, temporarily freeing persons from the burdens of civilization, even if the long-term result is to reinforce standing mores. But my point is that, appearances notwithstanding, ritual "violations" must finally heighten the aptitude for care if they are to be true liberations; otherwise, they are mere ecstatic excesses or even abominations. A festival that degenerates into sheer chaos, for example, no

---

fundamental sense of freedom is freedom from chains, from imprisonment, from enslavement by others" (p. lvi) and that "the rhetoric of 'positive' liberty" is often (though not always) but "a cloak for despotism" (pp. xlvi–xlvii). I allow a much more substantive role to positive liberty. Berlin would be sceptical of my appeal to personal care as a metaprinciple that helps settle normative conflicts, but a "prophetic" liberalism based on Christian love would lower the wall between the two freedoms.

32 Though they are often accused of being too political, many liberation theologians include (even accent) inwardness as an ingredient of liberation. It is frequently, in fact, the substance of their holism and universalism. Leonardo Boff, for example, notes that "[a] theology – any theology – not based on spiritual experience is mere panting" and that liberative practices are "concerned with the promotion and advancement of 'the whole human being and all human beings.'" See Leonardo and Clodovis Boff, *Salvation and Liberation: In Search of a Balance Between Faith and Politics* (Maryknoll and Melbourne: Orbis/Dove, 1985), pp. 2 and 4.

33 Arturo Paoli, *Freedom to Be Free*, trans. by Charles Quinn (Maryknoll: Orbis, 1973).

longer engenders the spontaneity and catharsis that make it worth celebrating. In addition, even in the most productive contexts, where the boundary-crossings associated with liberation are most fertile, the emphasis is not usually teleological but aretological.[34]

Even as abomination is a key theme in the Hebrew Bible, so too is liberation. The importance to Judaism of the Exodus event, in which God delivers the Israelites out of slavery in Egypt, can hardly be overestimated. And neither is this merely an external liberation. The Exodus is emblematic of a host of other deliverances, including those from sin (Ps. 51) and from ignorance (Isa. 42:6–7), which were to shape the life and thought of exilic and post-exilic Israel. An emphasis on the essential inwardness of liberation (however communally enjoyed) is not restricted to the Old Testament, of course, being (if anything) even more pronounced in the New. And in addition to the Gospel of John and Paul's epistles, Seneca makes a similar point:

. . . not to put up with anything is not liberty (*libertas*); we deceive ourselves. Liberty is having a mind that rises superior to injury, that makes itself the only source from which its pleasures spring, that separates itself from all external things in order that man may not have to live his life in disquietude . . .[35]

Epictetus echoes this sentiment in identifying "serenity" as "the work of virtue."[36]

Given that the Stoic ideal is self-sufficiency and a placid acceptance of whatever lot Fortune deals one, it may seem odd to quote Seneca and Epictetus as concerned to expand our capacity for personal care. Don't they seek rather to dispense with personal care in a state of utter indifference? It is not that simple. They do aim at unperturbability in the face of natural and social disaster (bodily affliction, the death of a loved one, loss of reputation, political betrayal, and so on), but such

---

[34] Georges Bataille, *Erotism: Death & Sensuality*, trans. by Mary Dalwood (San Francisco: City Lights, 1986), p. 115, notes that "only secondarily is transgression an action undertaken because of its usefulness." It remains possible, however, that a transgression may be *avoided* by others mainly because of its destructiveness. Bataille is quite right to compare an extreme like war to "a convulsive explosion" (p. 115) rather than a nicely calculated effect, noting that: "War is not a political enterprise in origin, nor sacrifice a piece of magic. Similarly the orgy did not originate in the desire for abundant crops. The origins of war, sacrifice and orgy are identical; they spring from the existence of taboos set up to counter liberty in murder or sexual violence" (pp. 115–116). Both the strength and the weakness of Bataille (and of his admirer Foucault) is that he repeatedly blurs the distinction between peace and war, *eros* and *thanatos*, creative and destructive transgression. See ibid., pp. 145, 242, 267, etc.

[35] Seneca, "*De Constantia*," XIX. 2, in *Seneca: Moral Essays*, vol. I, trans. by John W. Basore (Cambridge: Harvard University Press, 1985), p. 103.

[36] Epictetus, *Discourses*, bk. I. IV. 6, trans. by W.A. Oldfather (Cambridge: Harvard University Press, 1979), p. 29.

tranquility is accomplished only through a revolution of consciousness. Genuine peace of mind is attained when one appreciates the nature and extent of personal freedom, but the proper understanding of this freedom requires utmost effort and is of supreme moral urgency. Seneca remarks that "Disaster is Virtue's opportunity,"[37] while Epictetus observes that "a bull does not become a bull all at once, any more than a man becomes noble, but a man must undergo a winter training . . . "[38] Despite inclinations, one ought not to care about such things as material prosperity or political success, because these are finally not in one's control. Only virtue and vice constitute true profit and loss, and these are entirely subject to rational decision. If Stoicism accents invulnerability from without, it simultaneously accents inward accountability; we may aim at a form of indifference (*ataraxia*) because we are essentially self-governing and self-sufficient (autarkic). Epictetus, for one, commends a "moral purpose" that is "harmonious with nature, elevated, free, unhindered, untrammelled, faithful, and honourable."[39]

Closer to home, Elaine Scarry's recent analysis of pain, in acknowledging much more personal vulnerability and displaying decidedly more communitarian ideals than the Stoics, gives us a still fuller perspective on the inwardness of liberation. In discussing torture, Scarry points out that the infliction of pain is often a means of making a victim's body and voice absent by making them acutely present.[40] Through the aches and screams, pain cuts the individual off from body and soul until finally pain itself no longer registers; but rather than being the limit of the torturer's abuse, such insensibility is precisely the point, the culmination of a process of "unmaking" the other's humanity. Insensibility of this

[37] Seneca, "*De Providentia*," IV. 6, in *Seneca: Moral Essays*, vol. I, p. 27.

[38] Epictetus, *Discourses*, bk. I. II. 32, p. 23.

[39] Ibid., bk. I. IV. 18–22, p. 33. An emphasis on liberation is not universal in ancient Greek philosophy. According to Stuart Hampshire, *Morality and Conflict* (Cambridge: Harvard University Press, 1983), p. 44: "The notions of freedom and of liberation are not [to] be found at the centre of Aristotle's ethics and philosophy of mind . . . The exercise of the crucial powers of mind, of real intelligence and imaginative feeling, is not represented as a liberation from a natural state in which these faculties are blocked and not available. Nature and freedom are not in opposition. In a reasonably favourable social environment a character and moral temperament of the right kind will develop naturally by habituation . . . His philosophy is, as it were, pre-lapsarian; neither in his philosophy of mind nor in his ethics is there some imagined redemption, or salvation, following upon a fallen state, a state of bondage." Judeo-Christian philosophy, on the other hand, is distinctly postlapsarian. It holds that human beings must be schooled into steadfast love of neighbor in spite of themselves and their fallen natures. The liberation that is love is a supernatural virtue now at odds with many of humanity's deepest inclinations. It must be commanded, even if its performance is chiefly a gift of grace.

[40] Elaine Scarry, *The Body in Pain: The Making and Unmaking of the World* (Oxford: Oxford University Press, 1985), chap. 1.

kind is the farthest thing imaginable from Stoic *ataraxia*. When pain communicates its impact to the moral vocabulary of the soul the result is abomination not liberation. The conscience is rendered inarticulate by degradation, and to experience such degradation across time is to perceive oneself as a means only. This is bondage raised to the second power. Stopping the pain (though important) does not itself restore the person, does not liberate the victim from the power of the victimizer. It is only in restoring a sense of personal dignity and responsibility that this bondage is broken, that true liberation is effected.

The freedom to be free requires (re-)constructing a meaningful language through which proper self-understanding and self-expression can emerge. Physical pleasure may play a role in this process, but it too is but the occasion for something else. The remedy for suffering is joy, which is autonomy and sympathy synthesized. As the distinctive end of liberation, joy enables people again to see themselves and be seen by others as ends, worthy of respect. From a theological perspective, it is joy which allows persons to communicate most directly with themselves and God, and thus to love their neighbors as themselves.

Just as one may show sympathetic antipathy toward abominations, however, so one may show antipathetic sympathy toward liberations. One may be attracted to admitted abominations and repelled by admitted liberations, i.e., attracted to what is destructive and repelled by what is creative. This is because a liberation also blurs or undoes socially significant categories. Dread and ambivalence always accompany such revolutionary activity, whether theoretical or practical, because our very selves are at stake. To be liberated is not first of all to change our circumstances but to be changed ourselves. Unlike abominations, however, liberations undermine our prevailing categories in highly beneficial ways – ways which allow for new and exponentially better forms of being and acting. Liberations make for a broader expanse of humanity both personally and politically as well as, for believers, a deeper communion with divinity. This empowerment is a megavirtue, since it augments moral identity; and in leading to partly unpredictable consequences, it requires a leap of faith. Speaking anthropocentrically, liberation prompts persons to care about the broadest, highest, and deepest realization of personal care itself. We want to integrate as many people as completely into the moral community as possible. "Liberation leads to liberation."[41]

If reference to "abomination" can degenerate into a repressive conservatism, reference to "liberation" can become mere fascination with

---

[41] G.I. Gurdjieff, "Inner Slavery: An Early Talk of G.I. Gurdjieff," in *Parabola*, vol. 15, no. 3 (August 1990), p. 16.

the novel. Advocacy of liberation, when uncritical, dissolves into a crude relativism; just as avoidance of abomination, when undialectical, decays into fatalism. Talk of a "new human" and "permanent revolution," rather than expanding humanity, can threaten the very idea of a normative human identity. Change advocated for its own sake loses its moral point, and cultural critique can seldom be purely negative or open-ended. Exodus out of Egypt is liberating only if you are headed somewhere; haphazard flight or itinerancy is indistinguishable from lostness. One must know both what one is against and what one is for. Without a positive vision of abiding ends, one is unable to place limits on the means employed in overthrowing the old, oppressive ones. Thus one is likely to get something still worse, even to lose that humanity one hopes to expand. In short, not all uses of "liberation" are liberating; some are actually abominable, as when the "North American Man–Boy Love Association" (NAMBLA) advocates pederasty as part of the sexual liberation of children.

Promoting liberation no more requires relativistic moral assumptions than does avoiding abomination. Ethical relativism stifles liberation. If feminism and liberation theology were to embrace as liberating a "no nature" view of the self, for instance, such a departure from moral realism would cut completely ties to the tradition it seeks to reform. Moreover, it would deny the very subjects it holds dear. For the upshot would be that women and the poor were not victimized in the past because there were no moral claims or claimants with an integrity independent of the prevailing political power relations. Someone may object that at times it is exactly our conceptions of gender or poverty or human nature that must be overcome, that need to be essentially reshaped. In these cases there is no reliable criterion to appeal to, no truth recognizable as such under the present paradigm, on the basis of which to challenge the status quo. We must become the sort of people who embody radically new values, the objection runs, thus revolution not reformation is necessary. There is considerable force to these re-marks, but the absence of a sure test for truth, antecedently specifiable, is not the same as there being no moral truth of the matter. Far from compelling on us some form of moral relativism or subjectivism, the history of feminism and liberation theology tells us something significant about personal integrity and the dynamics of liberation. It tells us that empathy has constantly to be schooled; talk of power may make us fearful about ourselves, but it is not enough to make us care for each other.

B. *Liberation and liberal society*

"Liberation" only becomes a term of approbation if it is possible to evaluate some motives as higher or better than others. We are after a particular kind of inwardness, one which lends our lives elevation and substance beyond mere freedom from external constraint. What Charles Taylor calls "the aspiration to fullness"[42] lies behind the kind of self-evaluation that gives "liberation" a distinctive moral meaning. But, again, liberal society often flinches at this point. The aspiration to fullness vies, especially in a democratic culture, with what might be called "the aspiration to emptiness." Any thick reading of "liberation" is here (as with "abomination") dismissed as quaint or deluded. The very overuse of the word "liberation," some would contend, is evidence of its vacuity; megavirtue like megavice is, at best, too highfalutin an idea to be taken seriously and, at worst, a hazardous form of propaganda. All we need is the external liberty associated with a secular liberal society. We have no inwardness other than dispositions that are more or less conditioned and motives that are but means to narrowly prudential ends. Hence we must be liberated from "liberation" in any textured sense.

This is a major challenge to my central theses, but there are two possible responses. The first response is suggested by Taylor:

> The sense that human beings are capable of some kind of higher life forms part of the background for our belief that they are fit objects of respect, that their life and integrity is sacred or enjoys immunity, and is not to be attacked . . . The rejection of the higher can be presented as a liberation, as a recovery of the true value of human life. Of course, the moral value attaching to this liberating move itself presupposes another context of strong good. But with that curious blindness to the assumptions behind their own moral attitudes, utilitarians and modern naturalists in general can just focus on the negation of the older distinctions and see themselves as freeing themselves altogether from distinctions as such.[43]

The first response is, in sum, an appeal to consistency. The very critics who explicitly refuse to identify "liberation" with human fulfillment often end up implicitly making this refusal itself their paradigm of flourishing, of "the higher."

The second response, more substantive, is to flesh out a positive doctrine of liberation that explains its unique meaning in relation to other ethical values, especially love. In this context, a defining question

---

[42] Taylor, *Sources of the Self*, p. 43.   [43] Ibid., pp. 25 and 81.

is whether liberation is to be construed in anthropological or theological terms, or both. Even a secular philosophy of liberation will need to identify "some kind of higher life" beyond mere *liberum arbitrium*, I have argued, but the issue of whether *libertas* is an exclusively human capacity or requires divine assistance is unavoidable. What might a positive doctrine of both abomination and liberation look like?

III. A SCALE OF MORAL MOTIVES, ACTIONS, AND EFFECTS

Combining the analysis of abomination and liberation with a common understanding of more conventional terms, we get the following typological scale. The list ascends from worst to best and does not claim to be exhaustive. The categories are not always mutually exclusive, moreover, and though I offer precising definitions that elaborate everyday usage, my remarks contain no pure neologisms. I aim for verbal insight without idiosyncrasy. The object is to depict the moral universe as an intelligible whole, with liberation and abomination as opposing poles. What makes the universe one world, so to speak, is that each of the categories can be explained in terms of the priority of love, the human need to receive care and the human capacity, if only with divine grace, to give it.

> *LIBERATION*: What fundamentally and often intentionally enhances the capacity to give and receive love-as-personal-care of an individual, class, or community: megavirtue, *bonitas*, freedom to be free, holiness, radical good, redemption that redefines the right, abundant life, Truth – from *"liber"* / *"libertas"*

> *SUPEREROGATION*: Virtue above and beyond the call of duties of justice, yet perhaps fairly localized in effect: beneficence, heroism, mercy, etc. – from *"super"* + *"erogare"*

> *OBLIGATION*: The morally required, right if done and wrong if not done: strict duty, prescription, the categorical imperative

> *[NONARISTOTELIAN PRUDENCE, SELF-INTEREST]*: What is provident or tasteful: e.g., exercising regularly, cultivating a palate for fine wines, etc. – an aesthetic category?

MERE PERMISSION: The morally indifferent, neutral either way

[INFRAVETATION, FOLLY]:   The foolish or tasteless but literally "less than prohibited": e.g., getting out of shape, eating junk food, bungee-jumping, etc. – aesthetic?

PROHIBITION: What is morally forbidden, wrong if done and right if not done: proscription, "You shall not . . ."

PERVERSION: A self-conscious turning away from the good, yet perhaps in a limited or isolated way: taboo, corruption, unnatural vice, etc. – from *"per"* + *"vertere"*

ABOMINATION: What fundamentally and often intentionally thwarts the capacity to give and receive love-as-personal-care of an individual, class, or community: megavice, *malitas*, bondage to decay, the demonic, radical evil, a fall that blinds to the wrong, everlasting death, Error – from either *"absit"* + *"omen"* or *"ab"* + *"homine"*

Let me first briefly define the middle seven terms, then return to "liberation" and "abomination" against this backdrop. An act of supererogation is an act above and beyond the usual call of duty, a virtuous performance that is not obligatory but that literally "pays out" more than is required. The action may accrue an abundance of merit and have far-reaching consequences (as in the standard example of a heroic soldier falling on a hand-grenade to save his or her fellows), or it may be far less spectacular and entail quite limited and local consequences (as in pausing on your way to work to help an elderly person, not in distress, across the street). Failure to perform an act of supererogation is not wrong, and arguably not vicious. An obligation, in contrast, is an action that it is culpable to forego, that must be performed on pain of vice and guilt. Some ethicists have argued that meeting one's obligations does not accrue merit and thus is not due praise, that *only* supererogatory actions are due moral praise. This seems unduly harsh, however. Because doing one's duty can occasionally be extraordinarily difficult (e.g., due to external threats or internal weaknesses), it does seem proper at times to praise actions required by the moral law, even if one says that (technically speaking) they are without substantive merit.[44] We rightly

---

[44] On the possible distinction between praise and merit, see David Heyd, *Supererogation: Its Status in Ethical Theory* (Cambridge: Cambridge University Press, 1982), p. 145.

admire a penurious judge's refusal to take a bribe, for instance, though this is only just.

What *never* deserves either praise or blame, in contrast, is the merely permissible. Such an action (say, scratching my ear under normal circumstances) is morally neutral; it may be performed or not indifferently. The morally prohibited is, of course, an action that it would be wrong to perform, right not to perform. A prohibition takes the form "You shall not . . ." and, unless merely *prima facie*, does not admit of exceptions. A perversion, on the other hand, is not just wrong but radically corrupt, so far below the call of duty that it is not merely prohibited but taboo. A perversion threatens basic moral distinctions in literally "turning away" from the proper end of an important activity, though this may take a fairly self-contained form (as in shoe fetishism) that does not necessarily undermine an entire personality or society.

There are two especially problematic notions within my scale: self-interest and infravetation. A self-interested or narrowly prudential action is one that is good or tasteful but not quite morally obligatory. I have in mind things like staying in shape, eating right, cultivating various talents (e.g., for chess). An infravetatory action, by contrast, is one that is foolish or tasteless but not quite culpable – literally, "less than prohibited" or "below the forbidden" – as is, perhaps, letting yourself get flabby, eating junk food, watching grade-B movies late at night. So defined, self-interest and infravetation are arguably aesthetic rather than ethical ideas, but I include them provisionally in my typology for the sake of roundedness. Partially to summarize, then, the self-interested or provident is morally desirable but less than required; the infravetatory is morally dubious but less than prohibited; the perverse is morally bad but more than prohibited; the supererogatory is morally good but more than obligatory.[45]

It now becomes clearer what it means to call liberation "megavirtue" and abomination "megavice." A liberation is at the extreme of supererogation, a radical good freely given that (more or less) self-consciously empowers a whole person, class, or community for love-as-personal-care; an abomination is at the extreme of perversion, a radical evil freely undertaken that (more or less) self-consciously destroys the potential for that same fundamental, holistic good. Locating liberation at the limit of supererogation highlights its prophetic capacity to transcend standing obligations and to redefine moral rightness in new and unexpected

---

[45] In chapter 7, I argue against including "the dilemmatic" as an additional ethical category.

ways. This reorienting of commitments may make liberation seem like either a miracle of deliverance or a fall out of innocence; but if the former it is not an abrogation but a fulfillment of human nature, and if the latter it is a *felix culpa* in as much as it generates a truer freedom. Thus far, I have accented the enhanced powers of the liberat*ed*, but a truer freedom also redounds, through love, to the liberat*or*. As Edward Vacek writes,

When we freely love, we also experience liberation because we let the beloved's real and ideal goodness displace our egocentricity or everyday world. Our fascination with our own goodness is broken; our fearful preoccupation with self-protection is overcome; our fixation with some particular object is loosened. In a word, we are freed from our narrowness. That is, we freely consent to allowing our self to be partially defined by the beloved and its needs or fulfillments.[46]

Liberation is not beyond all good and evil, nor does it violate genuine duties, since this would be mere wantonness rather than mega*virtue*. There must, in short, be some continuity between the old dispensation and the new if the latter is to qualify as progress. But liberation may revolutionize our conception of good and evil or even "teleologically suspend" erstwhile moral rules in order to achieve something higher and better (as when benevolence and forgiveness supersede strict contractual or punitive justice). Similarly, situating abomination at the limit of perversion captures its frequently diabolical character in blinding individuals to the true nature of right and wrong.[47]

The abominable is not just bad but an assault on the very idea of badness (and thus goodness). If liberation may teleologically suspend everyday ethics, abomination would permanently and pointlessly destroy it. The relevant contrast here is between constructive iconoclasm

---

[46] Vacek, *Love, Human and Divine*, p. 64.

[47] My repeated characterization of "liberation" as the antonym of "abomination" may seem odd, especially in theological contexts. Am I showing too many Kantian colors here, even in a volume that purports to see Kantianism as a threat to Christian charity? Am I preoccupied with Enlightenment concerns over freedom? In the spirit of these questions, Stanley Hauerwas, *After Christendom?* (Nashville: Abingdon Press, 1991) writes: "I would suggest that to make the metaphor of liberation central or overriding as a description of the nature of Christian existence, as is done in much of liberation theology, is a mistake . . ." (p. 55). "As Christians we do not seek to be free but rather to be of use, for it is only by serving that we discover the freedom offered by God. We have learned that freedom cannot be had by becoming 'autonomous' – free from all claims except those we voluntarily accept – but rather freedom literally comes by having our self-absorption challenged by the needs of others" (pp. 53–54). I take Hauerwas's point, but why let the Enlightenment have the final word on "liberation," any more than on "love"? Why not retrieve it for theological purposes by again tying it, as I do, first to "*libertas*" rather than "*liberum arbitrium*"? It is *libertas* that is at the root of the "glorious liberty" lauded by Paul (Rom. 8:21). "For freedom Christ has set us free" (Gal. 5:1).

and destructive narcissism. It is an irony of the moral life, an indication of the import but also the limit of freedom, that the height of human fulfillment (liberation) cannot simply be obligated and the depth of human depravity (abomination) must be more than just prohibited. From a Biblical perspective, a charity outstripping natural justice is crucial to individuals and communities, but the Biblical "love commandments" are holy oxymorons that can only be taken to heart by persons who have been touched by grace and thus already long to love God, neighbors, and self. If self-sacrificial love is seen as a straightforward duty of justice, it loses its distinctive generosity; and if genocidal misanthropy is treated as one more moral mistake, it loses its unique horror.

The fact that virtue can be raised to the second power is suggested (however crudely) by the medieval Catholic teaching that supererogatory actions generate a treasury of merit that can aid oneself and others in the expiation of sin. The Protestant Reformers objected, of course, to the selling of that merit in the form of indulgences and to the very idea that one can do more than God commands or duty requires. I myself would not hypostatize saintliness into a magical substance that can improve moral character impersonally and *ab extra*, like an ethical elixir that one just drinks down, but the inspirational effect of extraordinary goodness seems undeniable. Protestant and Kantian attacks on supererogation that would reduce all actions to three categories only – obligation, mere permission, and prohibition – fail to do justice to moral heroism, as well as to radical evil. Heroic individuals do seem able to cultivate personal care in others by treating them with a kindliness that is above and beyond the call of duty. Again, this kindliness cannot directly and irresistibly induce virtue in others, but it can augment those spiritual resources already in place if individuals are open to this. Goodness has a charisma. The Good Samaritan gave the victimized stranger moral as well as material help, we imagine, and that help (call it a sense of sanctity) has been communicated to anyone who reads about him across the generations. For Christians, the doctrine of Christ's Atonement itself points to the broadly liberating power of self-sacrificial *agape*.[48] Christian charity is based in the Personal Care of God.

If supererogatory actions generate (in a suitably muted sense) a treasury of merit, perverse actions have the opposite effect. At the extreme, abominations produce a repository of *de*merit, a kind of moral

---

[48] See Heyd, *Supererogation*, chaps. 1 and 3.

bankruptcy, that makes virtue qualitatively harder to attain for a person, class, or entire moral community. This is vice raised to the second power and follows from the depth of the assault on the good – from a perverse denial, for instance, of the very idea of moral uprightness that makes vice all but invisible as such. Someone's doing an abominable deed cannot be explained in terms of *akrasia* (weakness of will), as I have noted; it is too big an error for that. Rather, a positive malevolence seems at work, so we often speak of a "demonic personality" when accounting for an abomination, even as we often speak of a "saintly vocation" when explaining a liberation. (The Holocaust is a paradigmatic abomination because the Nazis did not merely wish to kill millions of Jews, they wanted physically to break and spiritually to humiliate them – cruelly to unmake their humanity by distorting or destroying all memory of them, both their own and other people's.) Instead of the redemption associated with liberation, then, abomination represents a radical fall; and the legacy of this fall is very like that traditionally associated by theologians with original sin: bondage to decay. One thinks here of Satan's lines from book IV of *Paradise Lost*:

> So farewell Hope, and with Hope farewell Fear,
> Farewell Remorse: all Good to me is lost;
> Evil be thou my Good . . . [49]

We are all vulnerable to this kind of abominable unmaking, even by our own hand. Whether one gives "abomination" a solely humanistic or a distinctively theistic reading, a nuanced conception of the spectrum of moral traits, actions, and results can neglect neither radical good nor radical evil, neither liberation nor abomination.

I locate liberation, again, at the extreme of supererogation and abomination at the extreme of perversion, but there are at least two interesting features of these ideas that may seem to call my typology into question. First, we sometimes enjoin "liberation" not as an optional, meritorious act but as a requirement of justice to which someone has a right. We often think of women's liberation, for example, as involving obligatory rather than supererogatory performances and correctives. My response here is twofold: (1) It may be required that *someone* (or society at large) do some action X (e.g., promote the welfare of women) and yet be optional for a *particular* person S voluntarily to do X. Reform of sex discrimination laws, say, may be generally mandatory for the legislature but a specific individual's decision to dedicate his life to

---

[49] I thank Kevis Goodman for reminding me of this passage.

that cause may be heroic and praiseworthy. In this case his liberating intention and effects are supererogatory. (2) Even in a liberal state, negative duty and justice do not exhaust the meaning of and need for liberation. Beyond this, however, I acknowledge that "liberation" is indeed sometimes used in a rectificatory sense in which a past injustice must be righted by the party or parties guilty of the wrongdoing. In these corrective instances, liberation is not technically supererogatory. In this respect the word "liberation" is similar to the words "pardon" and "forgiveness," which also have both supererogatory and rectificatory uses. To pardon someone who has sinned against you is usually an act of supererogatory forgiveness, but the state is *obliged* to "pardon" a convict if he is subsequently shown to be innocent of the charge against him.[50]

The second problematic feature of my scale is posed by the saint and his/her self-understanding. A saint is someone who is consistently supererogatory, a liberated and liberating personality, who empowers others to love. Yet such an individual often feels that an extraordinary benevolence is her *obligation* rather than merely an admirable *option*. She frequently thinks of charity and self-sacrifice as her unshirkable calling, instead of as something above and beyond the duty of justice (cf. Mother Teresa). Similarly, sociopaths like Raskolnikov (from fiction) and Charles Manson (from real life) seem paradigms of the abominable and abominated, yet they often see themselves as having special *license* to ignore or violate even the most basic obligations that hold for other people, rather than as being criminally *demonic*. The saint, in other words, is often a first-person rigorist rather than a self-described supererogationist, while the devil is typically a first-person wanton or perhaps a Nietzschean *Übermensch* rather than a self-described pervert. It makes sense to place liberation at the extreme of supererogation and abomination at the extreme of perversion, nevertheless, because these actions are to be judged from the third-person perspective. An ideal observer, possessed of limitless knowledge and empathy, would identify liberation as a virtue that outstrips and even undergirds obligation, even as she would identify abomination with a vice that falls well below the exceptional as well as the wrong.

The saint and the sociopath are simply mistaken if they think of themselves as merely dutiful or as altogether beyond duty, respectively. Let me dwell for a moment on the saint. The saint may charitably

---

[50] Heyd, *Supererogation*, pp. 154–164.

sacrifice his legitimate interests, but there is a difference between com-
mending such action and prescribing it as a strict duty. It is only when
one thinks that ideals of virtue must be obligatory as a matter of justice
for all, as in unnuanced versions of utilitarianism, that moral heroism
collapses into duty[51] – and "duty," in turn, prompts an oppressive
statism. But there is more to morality than maximizing consequences,
and the extreme costliness of some personal sacrifices (whether or not
they are made for the sake of general utility) renders them admirable but
not to be imposed by any other. This follows from the nature of finite
agency. Because we are embodied persons with irreducibly individual
problems and prospects, our actions may (and indeed must) have a
properly self-referential component. Even the Christian call to Christlike love must acknowledge that our cares remain our own even when
shared with others, just as our actions remain our own even when
undertaken in concert with or for the sake of others. *Pace* Simone Weil,
even as the Body of Christ we do not utterly disappear into the Love of
God; *pace* pure utilitarians, no one is a dispensable vehicle for the
production of maximal social benefits. The second of these points has
two key implications: (1) not everything that would be good were it to
happen is permitted to be done, and (2) not everything that would be
good were we to do it is obligatory to do.[52] We may not do evil that good
might come (Rom. 3:8), nor need we do good solely that guilt might go.
The saint's strenuous virtue is undeniably good, but nonetheless supererogatory; it is not simply optional, but rather a duty of charity rather
than of justice.[53] This is so precisely because the saint remains a finite
agent with a distinct set of needs and interests that may be freely
sacrificed. One can only sacrifice what is antecedently one's own, if not
by natural right then as a gift of God.

There are limits to admirable self-sacrifice, in addition. Self-abnegation that stems from stupidity, indecision, prodigality, or masochism is
manifestly vicious. Coercion and compulsion are also ruled out. One
must aim voluntarily at others' happiness, not directly at one's own
suffering. There are limits even to *epistemic* self-sacrifice. The saint is not
saintly because he underrates his own merit; that would make virtue a
function of ignorance, if not mendacity. Still, the saint may be radically
good *in spite of* her self-misapprehension. (The sociopath is radically evil

---

[51] Ibid., pp. 79–80; and see also pp. 138–139, on why thinking that one is doing one's duty does not
disqualify one's action from being in fact supererogatory.
[52] On these issues, see Thomas Nagel, *The View From Nowhere* (Oxford: Oxford University Press,
1986).   [53] See the discussion of these terms in chapter 1.

partially *because of* willful benightedness.) Part of the beauty of saintliness surely consists in its *not dwelling on* its virtues, but some of those virtues are in fact supererogatory. If they weren't, they wouldn't be nearly so lovely or liberating.[54]

IV. AGAINST MINIMALISM

Given its emphasis on personal care, human and divine, this chapter is at odds with the minimalist character of much ethical discourse today. One strand of this discourse aims at radicalizing conventionalist emphases and thus being thoroughly postmodern. Postmodern minimalism encompasses those forms of thinking, speaking, writing, and acting that seek to dispense, not only with the four great premodern ideas of God, Providence, Nature, and Reason, but also with such modern successors as essential humanity, teleological history, objective reality, and universal truth. The latter, lower-case ideas are still too wedded to the notion of fixed moral limits to be acceptable to postmodern iconoclasm. In the light of all this, can we in fact restore the moral lexicon?

It is possible that a century from now such postmodernist authors as Jacques Derrida, Michel Foucault, and Richard Rorty will be seen as analogous to Luther, Calvin, and Zwingli in their liberating effects. (I am waiting for some disciple to title a piece "The Freedom of a

---

[54] David Little has argued, persuasively, that benevolent acts are purely or properly supererogatory only when the benefactor's sacrifice is high. Some acts, though "barely permissive" in not being strict duties, nevertheless "ought" to be done – as when one can save a stranger's child from drowning with minimal effort and risk. Little, "The Law of Supererogation," in Santurri and Werpehowski, eds., *The Love Commandments: Essays in Christian Ethics and Moral Philosophy* (Washington, D.C.: Georgetown University Press, 1992), p. 174, writes: "Insofar as the concept 'charity' denotes benevolent concern for the welfare of others, it presupposes the quality of permissiveness that . . . is associated with all beneficent, or 'gift-giving' acts. On the other hand, as Locke states, in extreme circumstances charity is required ('gives every Man a Title'). In those circumstances, one is, so to speak, bound to give gifts, bound to be benevolent, a condition that puts an obvious strain on the normal conceptual boundaries between justice and charity." I would only add that my references to "saintly" acts (and, by extension, saintly dispositions) are intended to denote instances of charity that are highly sacrificial, in the relevant sense, and thus clearly beyond what is required by justice.

I am unsure what to make of Little's further claim that the saint's works of supererogation should be associated with a "subjective duty" (p. 179). A "subjective duty" may sound like a contradiction in terms, thus I prefer to speak of "the call of *agape*" or "a duty of charity." Overall, it seems better to attribute "moral modesty" to the saint than to privilege her first-person rigorism as a matter of *justice*, since the latter threatens the very idea of supererogation. A saint may find it personally unthinkable, even physically impossible, not to act heroically; but, as Bernard Williams notes, "practical necessity, even when grounded in ethical considerations, does not necessarily signal an obligation [of justice]." See *Ethics and the Limits of Philosophy* (Cambridge: Harvard University Press, 1985), p. 188, cited in Jeffrey Blustein, *Care and Commitment: Taking the Personal Point of View* (Oxford: Oxford University Press, 1991), p. 120.

Postmodern" or "The Athenian Captivity of the University.") In this
event, postmodernism will continue to harken back to Nietzsche as its
Wycliffe-figure, even as it continues to call up "Counter-Reformers"
like Saul Kripke, Stanley Rosen, Alan Gewirth, and Thomas Nagel; but
the intellectual landscape of the Western world will have been permanently altered. And this for the better in thousands of minds. The
likelihood of this happening depends on how successful postmodernists
are in appearing martyrs for the cause of freedom. It depends, to push
the historical metaphor still further back, on how well they cast their
conservative critics in the role of Pharisees and themselves in the role of
misunderstood and perhaps victimized Children of Light. Though
prophecy on these matters courts regret, I don't believe that postmodernists have yet posted Ninety-five (or even two) Theses, much less
communicated a New (or Final) Testament. We have a postcard from
Derrida, but to look for material that aspires to permanence or perhaps
even to being emancipatory is quite probably to misunderstand most
postmodern minds.

The minimalist temper is ultimately hostile to defining "abomination" and "liberation" with any recognizable sense. Foucault is a
good example of someone so concerned to see history in terms of
contingent but ubiquitous relations of power and domination that he is
suspicious of all talk of "human nature" and "personal care." He wants,
in effect, liberation from liberation itself as just one more political
snare,[55] even as Derrida effectively abominates abomination as one
more philosophical ruse. Yet both men thereby erode the moral urgency and intellectual honesty that animate their best work. Theirs is
not the Bodhisattva's renunciation of nirvana to teach the unenlight-
ened or the Guardian's altruistic return to Plato's cave, but rather flight
into moral vacuity. Liberation from liberation displays what Kenneth
Burke calls "the paradox of 'pure escape': "in freeing oneself *perpetually*,
one would in a sense remain perpetually a prisoner, since one would

---

[55] Says Foucault, *The Order of Things: An Archaeology of the Human Sciences*, trans. by Alan Sheridan
(New York: Random House, 1973), pp. 342–343: "To all those who still wish to talk about man,
about his reign or his liberation, to all those who still ask themselves questions about what man is
in his essence, to all those who wish to take him as their starting-point in their attempt to reach
the truth, to all those who, on the other hand, refer all knowledge back to the truths of man
himself, to all those who refuse to formalize without anthropologizing, who refuse to
mythologize without demystifying, who refuse to think without immediately thinking that it is
man who is thinking, to all these warped and twisted forms of reflection we can answer with a
philosophical laugh – which means, to a certain extent, a silent one." By what measure,
however, can a Nietzschean archaeologist/genealogist call something "warped and twisted"?
He allows no standard . . . usually.

never have definitively escaped."[56] Liberation thus becomes indistinguishable from abomination, dissipating the charisma of goodness.

As limits, abomination and liberation have structural similarities, already described. It is even possible to pass through one pole on the way to the other, the moral world being round. Hate may be turned to love (via forgiveness), and love may lapse into hate (via cruelty). Quite generally, some forms of insight and growth only come with pain. Yet, for all that, here is no *coincidentia oppositorum*. Liberation and abomination are not identical but obverse; as what purifies (vs. annihilates) the self, charity remains life's magnetic north. Coalescing the poles renders ethical orientation impossible; trying to use unbounded license as a direct means to good is a blunder as old as Dionysus, as blasphemous as Carpocrates, and as destructive as Sade. Foucault's equation of "limit experiences," of self-realization with self-effacement, for example, flirts with torture-fascination, if not longing for violent death. This is not a failure of intelligence – there is no denying Foucault's genius any more than Weil's – but an intentional "No" to virtue, whether spoken in the name of "freedom" or "*amor fati*."[57]

The minimalist tendency is not limited to France, though it finds its most flamboyant recent expression there. Among American academics (who are not to be confused with American society) terms such as "decadence" and "perversion" have long had an air of quaintness about them. "Philology leads to calamity," says the prescient maid in Ionesco's *The Lesson*; and etymology documents the extent to which Americans too have lost faith in those vocabularies that make a unified system of evaluation possible. The once substantial terms of intellectual and moral condemnation associated with classical theories of virtue almost uni-

---

[56] Burke, *A Grammar of Motives* (Berkeley: University of California Press, 1969), p. 36. Burke thinks that "the element of 'pure escape' . . . lies at the roots of liberalism" (ibid.).

[57] See James Miller, *The Passion of Michel Foucault* (New York: Simon and Schuster, 1993). Miller maintains (pp. 278, 296–298, 314–318) that Foucault recognized the danger of his own rhetoric and, after 1975–1976, partially reversed himself on the usefulness of violence and the impossibility of self-transcendence. He even embraced "liberalism" (p. 314), though of a highly idiosyncratic sort. Miller's kind and insightful biography leaves open the question, however, of how seriously to take the philosopher's recurring sado-masochistic prescriptions, as well as his indications that the self is created *ex nihilo*. For suggestive criticisms of Foucault along the lines I pursue, see Jeffrey Stout, "Modernity Without Essence," in *Soundings*, vol. 74, nos. 3–4 (Fall/Winter 1991), pp. 531–532. For hints on how to read Foucault and other poststructuralists as humorous and hyperbolic, see Allan Megill, *Prophets of Extremity: Nietzsche, Heidegger, Foucault, and Derrida* (Berkeley: University of California Press, 1985). For the later Foucault's more moderate ethical views, including an acknowledgment that not all truth is reducible to power and that not all power is to be equated with domination, see Foucault, *Ethics: Subjectivity and Truth*, vol. I of *The Essential Works of Foucault 1954–1984*, ed. Paul Rabinow (New York: The New Press, 19997), esp. pp. 296–301.

formly incorporate the view that man[58] has an essence, life has a purpose, and reason (or the Church) speaks with one authoritative voice. Again, "perversion" is literally what has turned, or been turned, from the true path of life (from *per* + *vertere*); "decadence" is a falling down from excellence or vitality (from *de* + *cadere*); and "heresy" is what one has chosen for oneself alone in opposition to catholic truth. Similar sentiments lie behind such epithets as "fallacy," "equivocation," and "vice." This is our linguistic heritage, but the first three words just quoted are now frequently considered either quaint, dangerous, or meaningless (by intellectuals); and even the second three are suspect to influential postmodernists.[59]

The upshot is that contemporary philosophers and theologians tend to remain preoccupied with consistency within a given discipline or cultural matrix rather than with substantive questions of anthropology and doctrine of God; concern for truth itself is sometimes repressed as pointless or too provocative. Richard Rorty, that American with the most Keatsian negative capability, writes: "[T]he moral world does not divide into the intrinsically decent and the intrinsically abominable, but rather into the goods of different groups and different epochs"; thus we must acknowledge that "something traditionally regarded as a moral abomination can become an object of general satisfaction," and that because "humanity has no nature" there is no enduring reality to which to appeal to evaluate such moral change.[60]

The retreat from substantial or defensible conviction about human excellence is often motivated by a commitment to pluralism. This frequently amounts to an attempt to purchase tolerance at the expense of nihilism, but there are understandable reasons behind it. The story behind "the silence on the abominable in contemporary ethical theory,"[61] in particular, is a mixed tale of profit and loss. The displacement of psychological, social, and metaphysical hierarchies that once

---

[58] I use the word "man" here because classical theories of virtue typically took the male of the species as the paradigm, which bias it is best to acknowledge at the outset. Inclusive language is important, and I embrace it myself, but if used prematurely it can retard our understanding (and reform) of key moral terms by blurring their etiology. At various times in the past, only men were deemed capable of real liberation and only women deemed capable of real abomination; at present, one sometimes sees the reverse proposition intimated. Both judgments are manifestly false.

[59] See Richard Gilman, *Decadence: The Strange Life of an Epithet* (New York: Farrar, Straus and Giroux, 1979); and compare Michel Foucault, *The History of Sexuality*, vol. I, trans. by Robert Hurley (New York: Vintage Books, 1980), esp. pp. 36–49, and *The Archaeology of Knowledge*, trans. by A.M. Sheridan Smith (New York: Pantheon Books, 1982).

[60] Quotations in this paragaraph are from Rorty, "Feminism and Pragmatism," *The Michigan Quarterly Review* (Spring 1991), pp. 235 and 233.   [61] Stout, "Moral Abominations," p. 146.

gave sense to talk of "decadence," "dishonor," "perversion," and "abomination" has helped accomplish the liberalization of culture. A frequent corollary, however, is that no longer sure of her own identity as teacher (much less practitioner) of virtue, the average university professor now finds any common human identity dubious. Having lost a sense of the human, she finds it all but impossible to speak of the *in*human; in turn, judgments of what is "shameful" or "despicable" or "corrupt" go by the boards, even as do meaningful claims about what is liberating. One cannot call a motive "unworthy" if one has no sense of what various human personalities are worth. The most one can do is to stick with what Charles Taylor calls "weak evaluation" and assay what outcomes of actions are useful given one's antecedent preferences.[62]

I do not belittle the liberal sensibilities that are wary of any attempt to recapture robust moral notions like "abomination." The dogmatism and intolerance, the sheer smugness, that can attend the use of such terms – what Henry James calls "the brutality of a good conscience"[63] – is almost enough to make one long for the modesty that accents what Judith Shklar (following Montaigne) calls the "ordinary vices": treachery, disloyalty, cruelty, and the like. It is debatable which has caused the more mischief and outright tragedy: supposedly lax moral standards or the righteous indignation that leads to remorseless attempts to remedy them, the unpretentiousness of pragmatism or the zealotry of those intent on stamping out "radical evil" and "extraordinary vice."[64] There is no doubting that the word "abomination" itself can be put to abominable uses, as when a reactionary church or state or business accuses innocent but marginal groups of "unspeakable" crimes in order to justify persecuting them.[65] The (usually implicit) argument is simple:

---

[62] Taylor, "What Is Human Agency?," in *Human Agency and Language: Philosophical Papers*, vol. I (Cambridge: Cambridge University Press, 1985), p. 16.

[63] See James, "The Middle Years," collected in *The Figure in the Carpet and Other Stories*, ed. by Frank Kermode (New York: Penguin, 1986), p. 254.

[64] An excellent example of zealous illiberalism is Max Nordau's 1896 tome *Degeneration* (New York: D. Appleton and Co., 1896). Nordau includes under the rubric of "degeneration" such phenomena as "the *fin-de-siècle* mood," "mysticism," "ego-mania," and "realism." He links the idea of "degeneration" to that of false "liberation" (p. 5). It might be possible to laugh off Nordau as anal were it not for his increasingly ominous tone. Beneath Nordau's claim that "the graphomaniacs and their critical body-guard dominate nearly the entire press" (p. ix) simmers a violent resentment. It is chilling to see how readily his talk of "protecting and saving" the "diseased" slides into the prescription to "crush" them (pp. 556–557).

[65] On the tendency of (formerly) persecuted groups to charge fringe elements with the same crimes for which the groups themselves were once (wrongly) condemned, see Carlo Ginzburg, *Ecstasies: Deciphering the Witches' Sabbath* (New York: Pantheon, 1991).

"They're inhuman, so why not treat them inhumanly; they're an offense to God, so why not exterminate them; they're abominations, so why not treat them abominably?"[66] Thus words like "savagery" and "abomination" become an excuse for – indeed, an instrument of – torture and genocide. Under certain conditions, that is, "abomination" becomes a performative: denoting someone with the term helps to make (or unmake) her into what the term connotes. By stripping her of her social identity, the dominant culture renders the idiosyncratic individual brutish, beyond liberation.

If employing the vocabulary of "perversity," "dishonor," "degeneration," and "abomination" inevitably leads us to objectify others, then my project is indefensible. But, in fact, there is no necessary connection between adopting these normative terms and perpetrating the abuses described. Just the opposite. The irony of intolerance and parochialism is that in giving words like "abomination" a bad name, they have made it difficult to condemn (even to describe) the profoundly evil practices that so blight this century. Without the nuanced capacity to judge radical evil, the full gravity of the Holocaust must go unrecognized; and when not recognized, a practice is more likely to be repeated. In this way, even as the Inquisitorial language of "paganism," "heresy," and "anathema" served not to defend but to discredit Christianity, so the inept deployment of "degeneration," "perversity," and "abomination" contributes to the rise rather than the fall of inhumanity. Thus our fondest moral hope – for purity of heart, true liberation – subverts itself. We can no longer name our worst and best selves because belief in our own moral identity has proven too painful or dangerous. This is regrettable and unnecessary; abominable uses of "abomination" are possible,[67] but so are liberating ones. Naming radical evil may prompt us to throw off

---

[66] As Kurtz says to the "International Society for the Suppression of Savage Customs," "Exterminate all the brutes!" See Joseph Conrad, *Heart of Darkness* (Englewood Cliffs, N.J.: Prentice-Hall, 1960), p. 42.

[67] Four hundred years before Nordau there was the *Malleus Maleficarum* ("Witch Hammer"), originally published in 1486, two years after Pope Innocent VIII's Bull "*Summis desiderantes affectibus*" establishing the Holy Office of the Inquisition. The *Malleus* was the work of two German Dominicans, Heinrich Kramer and James Sprenger, and became the accepted wisdom on witches and their prosecution for centuries. My favorite line is: "There is . . . concerning witches who copulate with devils, much difficulty in considering the methods by which such abominations are consummated." On a more serious note, Kramer and Sprenger inform us that "the natural reason [that superstition is chiefly found in woman] is that she is more carnal than a man, as is clear from her many carnal abominations." See *Malleus Maleficarum*, trans. by Montague Summers (Tiptree, Essex: Arrow Books Ltd., 1971), pp. 111 and 117. The misogyny of this book is staggering; that, need one say, is the real abomination.

its yoke,[68] just as naming radical good gives us a particular alternative to strive for.

CONCLUSION: COMING TO OURSELVES, AND GOD

By going to extremes we have come to ourselves. In contrast to postmodernism, that is, the moral scheme I have defended both assumes and supports the view that there are shared features of human nature with profound ethical significance. There is such a thing as human height and depth – inwardness. The need and capacity for personal care is the singular feature that helps to make sense of "abomination" and "liberation" as complementary terms. Being liberated for love promotes those basic human goods the destruction of which is abominable. To treat personal care as synonymous with love is not to valorize "personhood" as the sole good, for, as I have argued, it is only because we support the *im*personal that we can be persons. It is only as we address the shared needs of others (including the infant, the stranger, the enemy), as well as have our own impersonal needs met by others (while we are ourselves infants, strangers, and enemies) that anything like human personhood can emerge and endure. Abominators want to defend what potential for personal and personal*izing* care we have, while liberators want us to have more. If we cannot make sense of personal care as a defining human good, however, then *a fortiori* we must fail to make sense of abomination and liberation as what enhances and thwarts it. Such a failure is a catastrophic impoverishment of our moral self-understanding.

Christians in particular have no excuse for such an impoverishment, for they believe that the Incarnation of Christ provides the key to both abomination and liberation – avoiding the one and realizing the other. All human beings are made in the Image of God, so what I have called the "theological" and the "anthropological" readings of "abomination" are linked, even as are the commands to love God and neighbor. What elicits God's wrath is also what thwarts human personality, though we need the example of Christ to show us both God's will and human

[68] No less an aesthetic curmudgeon than Ezra Pound can be quoted in support here: "The whole of great art is a struggle for communication . . . this communication is not a leveling, it is not an elimination of differences. It is a recognition of differences, of the right of differences to exist, of interest in finding things different. Kulture is an abomination; philology is an abomination, all repressive uniforming education is an evil." See Pound, "A Brief Note," in *Henry James: A Collection of Critical Essays*, ed. by Leon Edel (Englewood Cliffs, N.J.: Prentice-Hall, 1963), p. 30. The cited words were penned in 1918, well prior to Pound's seduction by fascism.

flourishing in their fullness. Similarly, the two senses of freedom behind "liberation" meet in Jesus. As Michael Ignatieff has reminded us, in our individualist culture "[w]e have Augustine's first freedom, and because we have it, we cannot have his second."[69] But the theonomy of Jesus is for believers a reconciliation of *liberum arbitrium* and *libertas*: an uncoerced love of God that empowers us to serve others and realize ourselves. Christlike love both "fulfills the law" (Rom. 13:10) and bestows "the glorious liberty of the children of God" (Rom. 8:21).

Relation to God holds the key, for Christians, to the "three dimensions" of ethics. Ethically we normally think of ourselves as moving "autonomously" in the three realms of character, action, and effect, even as physically we move more or less "freely" in the three dimensions of space. But there is a fourth dimension in both cases, and our awareness or unawareness of it makes a difference. Just as the fourth metaphysical dimension of time is a continuum with space yet at present allows motion in only one direction, so the fourth ethical dimension of eternity interpenetrates our selves and situations yet originally descends from above. Trying to meet someone at a particular place, without attention to the date, is as liable to disappointment as trying to love someone agapically, without openess to the Deity. God's providence does not meet us as a fate, however; with Jesus, eternity "entered" time creating, so to speak, a "worm hole" for the faithful. That voluntary alteration of the moral past known as forgiveness is now possible, for instance, both horizontally between creatures and vertically between creatures and their Creator.[70]

The Imitation of Christ will revolutionize the theory and practice of personal care and self-fulfillment, even to the point of seeming, paradoxically, to replace liberation with abomination. Jesus's "eat my flesh and drink my blood" (John 6:54) and Paul's "through love become slaves to one another" (Gal. 5:13) are undeniably hard sayings. But such reversals clarify and restore the moral lexicon, and the moral life, rather than destroy them. The hard sayings drive home to Christians that they are not self-created or self-sustaining but rather dependent on God and one another. The aspiration to unbridled autonomy is not liberating but abominable, not Christlike freedom but sin and alienation. In contrast, "If the Son makes you free, you will be free indeed" (John 8:36).

---

[69] Ignatieff, *The Needs of Strangers* (New York: Penguin, 1984), p. 78.

[70] For a highly creative (if outrageously yet ironically classist, sexist, and racist) meditation on dimensional perspectives, see Edwin A. Abbott's little classic, *Flatland: A Romance of Many Dimensions* [1882] (New York: Dover, 1952), including the Introduction by Banesh Hoffmann.

CHAPTER 5

The disconsolation of love

There is nothing alive more agonized than man of all that breathe
and crawl across the earth.   *The Iliad*, bk. 17, 515–516[1]

[H]uman beings are born to trouble just as sparks fly upward.

Job 5:7

Humanis concedere rebus [yield to human life].   Lucretius

INTRODUCTION: THE FACILITY OF GOODNESS

In *The Consolation of Philosophy*, Lady Philosophy informs us that, because
of God's Providence, "all fortune is good." "Since all fortune, whether
sweet or bitter, has as its purpose the reward or trial of good men or the
correction and punishment of the wicked, it must be good because it is
clearly either just or useful."[2] "Nothing in the realm of Providence is left
to chance," moreover, and "the evil which is thought to abound in the
world is really non-existent."[3] Virtue is its own reward and wickedness
its own punishment,[4] and "the reward of good men . . . time cannot
lessen, nor power diminish, nor the wickedness of any man tarnish."[5]
Such supposed attractions as honor, power, and material riches, in
contrast, are transitory and "not good in themselves": to pursue them as
true ends is to cease to be human, to become "worse than the beasts."[6]
Hence, in Boethius's theodicy, moral goodness is proof from Fate, both
invulnerable and self-sufficient: no external factors can detract from
virtue and no external factors need be added to it. Indeed, no external
factors *could* be added to it, since "nonmoral goods" are ultimately base

---

[1] Homer, *The Iliad*, trans. by Robert Fagles (London: Penguin Books, 1990), p. 457.
[2] Boethius, *The Consolation of Philosophy* [524], trans. by Richard Green (Indianapolis: Bobbs-Merrill,
1962), pp. 97–98.   [3] Ibid., p. 96.   [4] Ibid., pp. 81–82.   [5] Ibid., p. 82.
[6] Ibid., pp. 33–35.

or illusory. Boethian Reason, it seems, is capable of an imperturbable certainty about the nature of the good.

This consoling doctrine or network of doctrines I call (playing off of Martha Nussbaum) "the facility of goodness," implying thereby not that Boethian virtue is easy (far from it) but rather that it is supremely dextrous and splendidly prosperous. I intend the term "facility" to refer to three facets of the good: (1) its certainty, (2) its self-sufficiency, and (3) its invulnerability. The outlines of the doctrine are at least as old as Plato. For Boethius, as for Plato, an assertion of the facility of goodness goes hand-in-hand with a championing of Reason and Philosophy and a vilifying of Fortune and Poetry. Reason is that human faculty which alone is capable of apprehending God and permanent moral truth, and when functioning properly reason recognizes that the contingent realities praised by the poets are "vile."[7] To subscribe to the facility of goodness is not merely to hold that some things, especially states of character, are intrinsically valuable or disvaluable regardless of personal preferences or external consequences; it amounts also to a cherishing of valuation itself. Virtue's habit of judging desires inherently good or bad, noble or base, is sublimely worthwhile, regardless of whether it serves other human interests.[8] In a Boethian world, the individual's moral life trumps everything in time and leads in turn to surety about eternal beatitude.

I want in this chapter to examine how Christianity's putting charity first among the theological virtues – "the greatest of these is love" (1 Cor. 13:13) – compares to a consoling, Boethian view of ethics.[9] By construing

---

[7] Ibid., p. 30.

[8] The facility of goodness involves what Charles Taylor would call a "strong evaluation" of strong evaluation itself. See Taylor, *Human Agency and Language*, p. 16; *Philosophy and the Human Sciences*: *Philosophical Papers*, vol. II (Cambridge: Cambridge University Press, 1985), p. 220; and *Sources of the Self*, p. 4.

[9] In *The Evils of Theodicy* (Washington, D.C.: Georgetown University Press, 1991), Terrence Tilley argues that neither Boethius nor Lady Philosophy offers a theodicy in the *Consolation*. The work is instead "a dialogue of repression" in which Lady Philosophy does not convey "moral truths" but rather "silences the prisoner's voice," thereby forcing him to diagnose and heal himself. The text is "a prescription for healing," "a way to overcome one's own voice of passion with one's own voice of reason," according to Tilley (pp. 150–151). As such it does not call for identifying oneself-as-reader or Boethius-as-author exclusively with either the miserable prisoner or the perfect philosopher.

This is a novel interpretation of real power, but to the extent that it depends on finding in the text a distinction between "the goods of fortune" (which are "superfluous") and "basic needs" (which are "part of human nature") (p. 155), I find it strained. Such a contrast is, at best, only implicit, and it is overwhelmed by what remains a paean to virtue's self-sufficiency and passionlessness. (The prisoner's silence seems to give Boethius's consent to Lady Philosophy's Platonism, or else why call the book a "consolation"?) Tilley himself grants that "*Consolation* is poison for those whose basic needs are not fulfilled. It is not medicine for those who have no food, clothing,

agape as superlatively valuable as well as divinely inspired, is Christianity committed to the self-sufficiency and invulnerability of love? By construing love, together with faith and hope, as in some sense beyond doubt (i.e., as remedies for scepticism), is Christianity committed to the dogmatic certainty of its view of love? And what, finally, is the relation between love, justice, and eternal rewards? Christianity's high estimation of charity and related intellectual and moral virtues has had many detractors over the years: Nietzsche and Freud, to mention but two. But I shall focus on two more recent critics: Richard Rorty and Judith Shklar. Rorty, unlike Shklar, does not suggest the abandonment of Christian love as tending to be cruel, but he does recommend love's radical privatization. He does not think, moreover, that there can be an overarching theory about how to combine love as a personal commitment and our various social hopes and responsibilities, since he rejects moral realism as well as religious faith.[10] (We can appeal to neither human nature nor God to ground our moral reflections.) Both Rorty and Shklar suggest putting the avoidance of cruelty first[11] rather than extolling such a positive virtue as universal love; both relish literature, including poetry, and are suspect of any elevation of reason; both have a lively sense of the inescapable contingency and fragility of human fortune, thus a suspicion of all attempts to "fend off thoughts of mortality";[12] and both identify the good life more with prudence and an aesthetic self-cultivation sensitive to the pain and humiliation of others than with traditional ethics referring to inviolable rules, a transcendent God, or an afterlife.

Rorty and Shklar – together with Martha Nussbaum, Elaine Scarry, and others – are helping to accomplish the disconsolation of philosophy. They and the realities to which they point help to convince me that to the extent that Christian theology has embraced "the facility of char-

---

and shelter. For those with such dis-eases, the *Consolation* is a poisonous opiate" (p. 155). Most importantly, he goes on to note that "Boethius argued that the truly wicked cannot harm the truly good person. However, he neglects to mention their bad example and to evaluate the damage they do if they deprive others of the goods (food, etc.) proper to their nature. While they may be in God's providence, the evil they do creates more than misfortune for others . . . A Boethian after Auschwitz and Nagasaki may need to pay more attention to the malignant forces the wicked and thoughtless unloose" (p. 157). I would second this sentiment, emphasizing the vulnerability of virtue itself. In what follows, in any event, I am not so much interested in the quest for the historical Boethius as in what have come to be thought of as "Boethian" themes and theses. False consolation is the primary target, not Boethius *ipse*.

10 Richard Rorty, *Contingency, Irony, and Solidarity*, p. 120; see also his "Method, Social Science, and Social Hope," in *Consequences of Pragmatism* (Minneapolis: University of Minnesota Press, 1982).
11 Rorty borrows the idea that "cruelty is the worst thing we do" from Judith Shklar. See *Contingency, Irony, and Solidarity*, p. xv.   12 Ibid., p. 119.

ity," that theology must also be disconsoled. To preach the self-sufficiency or invulnerability or even certain validity of charity, especially
when that charity is thought to come irresistibly from God and to be
directed more or less exclusively at God, is cruel to both believer and
nonbeliever. I will be arguing, then, that Christian ethics should distance Boethius and go part way down the road with Shklar and Rorty; a
dose of Rortian irony is always salubrious when confronted with one of
"Job's Comforters." I shall also contend, however, that both Rorty and
Shklar misinterpret the nature of Christian charity. More specifically, I
shall address epistemological concerns to Rorty and theological concerns to Shklar. In responding to Rorty, it is paramount to emphasize (1)
the extent to which love admits fallibility and pluralistic visions of the
good, and (2) the extent to which irony fails to support and may actually
undermine the sort of solidarity he cherishes. In reply to Shklar, the key
thesis is that strong *agape* may put charity first among the virtues without
denying the lovability of other human beings for their own sakes or
ignoring the centrality (if not the primacy) of cruelty among the vices.

Christian theology has much to learn from Rortian irony and Shklarian liberalism. These are elegant devices to avoid epistemological and
ethical pretension. Rorty's irony prompts us to see one another as
vulnerable reeds, "fellow sufferers,"[13] rather than to try to annihilate
each other's error or wickedness. Being concerned with "ordinary
vices," Shklar's liberalism helps us to attend realistically to our own
characters without displacing responsibility onto God or cruelly neglecting our neighbors. I shall conclude, nevertheless, that epistemology and
ethics are best served not by a pervasive irony or by putting cruelty first
but by *a chastened view of charity* that appreciates its priority. Charity (like
irony) is, in one sense, beyond both certainty and morality – though in a
way far more powerful than is irony, as I hope to show. And "putting
charity first" emphasizes a positive virtue and the attendant behavior
rather than giving primacy to something negative, even something as
important as the avoidance of cruelty.

To anticipate my conclusions in more detail, I sketch a defense of four
positions: (1) a denial of foundationalism in epistemology that nevertheless embraces moral realism; (2) a denial of the self-sufficiency of virtue
that nevertheless embraces the priority of love; (3) a denial of the
invulnerability of love that nevertheless also doubts the possibility of
moral dilemmas; and (4) a denial of the necessary immortality of love

---

[13] Ibid.

that nevertheless does not plummet into despair. We don't have to endorse a Boethian picture of Reason and Providence to love our neighbors and worship God, but in loving and worshipping rightly we transcend a merely pragmatic fate, a purely bourgeois self-image. This transcendence renders issues of personal immortality largely irrelevant morally.

I. RORTY ON REALISM, CERTAINTY, AND LIBERAL IRONY

In *Contingency, Irony, and Solidarity*, Rorty rejects strong evaluation (and moral realism generally) because its reference to "ethical truth" and "objective value" seems to him to invite oppression and/or various forms of false consolation. Though he nowhere lists them explicitly, it is clear that these unhappy consequences can be sparked in four basic ways – depending on whether we focus on ourselves or others as the objects of evaluation and whether the evaluation is positive or negative.

Consider first *a positive evaluation of ourselves*. If we believe ourselves to possess moral truth and/or to embody objective value, we will tend to a cruel intolerance. The inclination, Rorty suggests, will be to draw invidious contrasts between "Us-in-the-Know" and "Them-Poor-Benighted-Folk" who disagree with us. Inevitably, it is hard for moral realists to resist proto-Manichaean distinctions between Us, the Sons and Daughters of Light, and Them, the Powers of Darkness. Couple realism with claims to know God's will incorrigibly, and pretty soon somebody calls for a *jihad* against the infidels, or, alternatively, we "bash all the genial tolerance out of our own heads," to use Rorty's phrase.[14] Religious certainty in particular makes for cruelty. Even if it were to remain pacific, the conviction that we possess moral truth or realize real value must be offensively smug; even without claiming strict indubitability, it will incline to a crass comfort that is insensitive to the historical relativity of cultures and artifacts.

Consider second *a positive evaluation of others*. If we judge others to possess moral truth and/or to embody objective value, we will tend to a stifling obsequiousness. The Rortian "strong poet" *creates* him- or herself by imaginative redescription, but claims about *discovering* an intrinsic worth in others (or God) retards this process. Strong poetry is incompatible with strong evaluation in the moral sphere. The evaluator's language of "discovery" moves us to think that there are normative ways to

---

[14] Rorty, "Science as Solidarity," in *Objectivity, Relativism, and Truth: Philosophical Papers*, vol. I (Cambridge: Cambridge University Press, 1991), p. 43.

be independent of our private aspirations, natural human kinds that we ought to imitate regardless of our idiosyncratic preferences. And all of this is a threat to our freedom. When couched in terms of their having inherent value, positive judgments of external objects (including God and other people) represent a failure of nerve. We may identify with various human heroes or our larger community, to be sure, but not on the basis of their embodying anything *objectively* good or right. To a certain extent, indeed, "we must, in practice, privilege our own group."[15] But those who long to find meaning in objectivity rather than solidarity would be compelled by a power larger than their social ethos, would find their *raison d'être* outside of their own or any other human wills, would surrender personal liberty and be acted on morally as if by a kind of ray.[16] On Rorty's reading, evidently, the realist's belief in moral truth is akin to, perhaps even a remnant of, the classical theist's belief in irresistible grace – and objectionable for much the same reason. By displacing personal responsibility, truth, like predestination, creates more problems than it solves. It stunts and oppresses us.

Consider third *a negative evaluation of ourselves.* If we deem ourselves to lack objective truth and/or to embody *dis*value, we will surely feel unworthy in one of two ways. Either we will be burdened by guilt, blaming ourselves for not living up to ideals that even we may acknowledge to be humanly impossible, or we will be paralyzed by tragedy, resigning ourselves to an undeserved but perhaps insuperable inferiority relative to other people or impersonal powers. Rorty, in contrast, would deliver us from all such austerities of conscience; he would have us cultivate the kind of "light-mindedness" that glides along the surface of life. Like Sartre's humanist and Kierkegaard's aesthete, Rorty's liberal ironist refuses to take herself and others too seriously. She knows that even her most entrenched vocabulary, even her most cherished self-description, is an ephemeral child of fortune. All are caught in the web of contingency, therefore irony is the great leveller. Though Rorty sometimes sounds a bit flip or even decadent in his comments on ethical matters – e.g., divorce[17] – it is just here that I find him most compassionate. His apparently cavalier attitude is, arguably, the altruism of one who refuses to condemn, the kindliness of a postmodern Sextus Empiricus who declines out of *philanthropia* even to judge in the usual sense. He would not have anyone suffer the painful self-accusations that can

---

[15] Rorty, "Solidarity or Objectivity," in ibid., p. 29.
[16] The analogy is Stanley Cavell's in *The Claim of Reason: Wittgenstein, Skepticism, Morality, and Tragedy* (Oxford: Clarendon Press, 1979).   [17] Rorty, *Contingency, Irony, and Solidarity*, p. 6.

attend an Inquisition, even of one's own mind and heart. Irony is, in this way, also the great liberator; it makes for that kind of gentle self-possession which, paradoxically, can only come by letting go of insistent self-control.

Consider fourth and finally *a negative evaluation of others.* It is enough to characterize this alternative to recall what the Popes used to say about unbelievers: "Error has no rights." If we judge others bereft of the true and the good, then we will likely not bother about them as fellow sufferers. Boethius goes so far, for instance, as to have Lady Philosophy assert that "our main duty is to oppose the wicked."[18] The order of the day is solidarity and imaginative conversation with others, according to Rorty, but these qualities are impeded rather than fostered by moral realism. Such realism generally only makes us petulant and unhappy in the end, both individually and collectively. Better to go thoroughly pragmatic and ironic and cease talking of "the true" and "the good";better to be romantic poets than realist philosophers, much less dogmatic theologians. We don't need theories of the essence of duty or virtue but rather imaginative identification with those, like ourselves, capable of being humiliated.[19]

What can be said by way of critical response to Rorty and liberal irony? I begin with the fact, described by Irving Singer, that love entails both "appraisal" and "bestowal." Appraisal involves judging how well an object, by virtue of its intrinsic properties, meets one's needs or satisfies one's desires or lives up to some more or less objective standard of excellence. To appraise something is to ask: does it measure up to the criteria implicit in my (or my community's) interests, whether aesthetic, moral, or religious? And this is a question to which one might give a wrong answer. Things or people may be deemed desirable or good or holy when in fact they are not. Bestowal, by contrast, is a more subjective affair. "[L]ove [as bestowal] creates a new value, one that is not reducible to the individual or objective value that something may also have . . . Here it makes no sense to speak of verifiability . . . For now [unlike with appraisal] it is the valuing alone that *makes* the value."[20]

In effect, Rorty sees strong moral evaluation (construed as a species of moral realism) as a matter of appraisal only. When taken thus, one must admit that his worries have some justification. Pure appraisal can lead to coercion, the tyrannical effort to change others or oneself into what is

[18] Boethius, *The Consolation of Philosophy*, p. 8.
[19] Rorty, *Contingency, Irony, and Solidarity*, pp. 91–93.
[20] Irving Singer, *The Nature of Love*, vol. I, p. 5.

antecedently judged worthwhile. Aggressive intolerance, insufferable complacency, and a general tendency cruelly to use others may all accompany the coldly critical eye of a pure appraiser. In this case, ethics is reduced to justice and justice to fanaticism. Still, there are two lines of argument open to Rorty's critic at this point. First, one may note that even if moral realism were entirely appraisive, the unwelcome prospects Rorty fears would not be strictly *entailed* by such realism, either logically or psychologically. What Rorty objects to is, in fact, not so much moral realism as epistemic foundationalism, not so much religious faith as headstrong rationalism.

As a correspondence theory of truth and/or an objectivist theory of value, moral realism does not commit one to dogmatic claims to certainty. One can perfectly well be a realist in both alethiology and axiology, yet remain a fallibilist in epistemology. That is, one may affirm (1) that the nature of truth is correspondence between our thoughts and the way the world is and (2) that the world contains, among other things, real values and disvalues (as well as God), yet deny (3) that we have indubitable tests for truth or unmediated access to the real. Realists may mistakenly conflate their position with the foundationalist demand for incorrigible justifications or immediate intuitions, as did Plato and many Enlightenment figures, but they *need* not. Indeed, epistemic humility should prevent this in both philosophical and theological contexts. Self-criticism, not pure irony, is the remedy for epistemic hubris. Unlimited irony makes it impossible to love.

Rather than combining moral realism with epistemological fallibilism and axiological pluralism – what I have elsewhere called "sceptical realism"[21] – Rorty goes to the other extreme and depicts ethical existence as a matter of *bestowal* only. For Rorty, virtue must be totally unmotivated from without; reminiscent of Abelard, he eschews all talk of objective merit (much less external reward) as the ground for right action. Taking various Protestant principles to their limit, Rorty sees affirmation of self and others as entirely gratuitous, a poetic gesture free and unconstrained. He gives us, so to speak, Radical Protestantism without the Deity, *agape* without divine grace. Rorty does fault Nietzsche and Derrida for their views of (moral) truth,[22] but in his more Sartrean moments Rorty himself suggests that instead of recognizing value, we

---

[21] Jackson, "The Theory and Practice of Discomfort: Richard Rorty and Pragmatism," in *The Thomist*, vol. 51, no. 2 (April 1987): 270–298; and "The Possibilities of Scepticisms: Philosophy and Theology Without Apology," *Metaphilosophy*, vol. 21, no. 4 (October 1990): 303–321.

[22] Rorty, *Contingency, Irony, and Solidarity*, p. 8, ftnt. 2.

create it *ex nihilo* – in much the way God was supposed to in better moments. To imagine anything else is bad faith.

The Rortian pragmatist is not novel in attempting to live well without God; this has been the West's central cultural task since the Enlightenment, if not since Constantine. Unlike the various modern attempts to replace God with Reason or Human Nature (and thus theodicy with anthropodicy), however, Rorty spurns all such efforts as false consolations, *merely* metaphysical comforts. This is his distinctive challenge. His vision is the Promethean one of self-creation without *any* objective standards, natural or supernatural. "Do you need objective reasons not to be cruel?" Rorty asks. "Well, if God and Divine Law could not provide such reasons, then, *a fortiori*, neither can Man and Natural Law," he answers in effect. Moral realism is but a last vestige of the theological propensity to project and idealize; reference to "real values" is but Christianity not yet fully disabused of its mythic conception of the world as created by a good God, with humanity made in God's own Image.

Now, part of me admires Rorty's willingness to be so utterly disconsoled: as in Nietzsche, there is a fierce and bracing honesty at work that forces one to introspect. But at the end of the day Rorty urges on us a too extreme form of pragmatism. His "nihilism" is not of the hand-wringing, desperate variety one associates with certain nineteenth-century Russians; it is unmistakably American in its cheerfulness, in what William James would have called its "healthy-mindedness." In Rorty, irony is a form of humility, at times a marvelously self-deprecating brand of humor intended to help us go on living rather than to lead us to despair. Like Nietzsche, Rorty wants us to move from resignation to joy in the face of our contingency – including that of our own consciences – even while playfully appreciating the limits on any "explanation" of such contingency. Nevertheless, Rorty's is an untenable position, I believe: at its worst, a kind of cultural potlatching in which the pragmatist challenges the realist, the theist, *et al.* to see how much they can live without.[23] Rorty's critique of the false consolations of philosophy may suggest that it is better to give up love than to endorse Boethian theodicy or Enlightenment foundationalism, but Christian theologians should know that these do not exhaust the alternatives.

---

[23] Jeffrey Stout has suggested in correspondence that, "despite his typically anti-realist rhetoric . . . Rorty is best read as neither a realist nor an anti-realist." Stout calls this the "pox on both your houses" option, and it is indeed evident in some of Rorty's later work. I do not see how such an a-alethiological stance can be sustained psychologically, however, given that I cannot conceive of how one can live without concern for truth.

This brings me to the second possible line of argument open to Rorty's critic. This line rejects the equation of strong moral evaluation with pure appraisal, even while it deflates the liberal ironist's pretension to pure bestowal. When love is put at the heart of the moral life, that life cannot be seen as exclusively either appraisal or bestowal. If ethics is defined narrowly in terms of accurate appraisal or equal justice alone, putting charity first requires a contradiction or perhaps a "teleological suspension" of the ethical – as when one shows mercy, forgives offense, loves the guilty, gives to strangers, and so on. But it is better to expand our definition of ethics to make love's synthesis of appraisal and bestowal central to morality. Such an expansion is required, at any rate, by putting charity first. As Singer argues, even love of neighbor is both objective and subjective, both appreciative and productive.[24] When evaluating most strongly, we *attend* to the value *in* the loved one, as well as *extend* value *to* him or her. Strong*est* evaluation does not merely discern but also communicates goodness. A Rortian solidarity of pure bestowal, in contrast, is inconceivable – indeed, it is unrecognizable as solidarity since it has no real objects.

Promethean self-creation and utterly gratuitous care for others risk collapsing into their (putative) opposite, a self-destructive and domineering hubris. Romantic self-creation is a very close cousin of wanting to be like God, the original sin. Moreover, it is false to experience: we need each other (not to mention God) more than this, and we know each other (if not God) better than this. Only God can create *ex nihilo*, and with the possible exception of the original act of creation, not even God's *agape* is unalloyed bestowal. God has granted creation a (partially) independent being, called "good" in its own right (Genesis 1); even God is now a strong moral evaluator. The contingency and fallibility of the world do not preclude its having value, any more than the contingency and fallibility of my words preclude, in principle, their being true appraisals of that value. And it is far from loving to be indiscriminate or pervasively ironic toward the world's worth, even if one expresses a care that goes beyond objective merit.

[24] Singer, *The Nature of Love*, vol. III, pp. 391–394. Singer himself contends that "love is not *inherently* moral" and that "ethical attitudes must always be governed by appraisal rather than bestowal" (ibid., vol. I, p. 11). But this is out of step with the spirit of his analysis, especially in subsequent volumes. Some *apparent* bestowals of value may be ill-advised because they move one to fall below justice, but such behavior is not love. If, as I have argued, love's bestowal of goodness (as opposed to mere infatuation or narcissism) never falls below justice, then it is never a moral mistake, however personally costly it may be in other terms.

In seeking to distance a dogmatic foundationalism, then, the Rortian strong poet embraces hyperromanticism; in aiming to rise above a calculating justice, she falls below it; in attempting to acknowledge the contingent possibilities of human selves and their communities, she makes moral selfhood and solidarity impossible. "Respect" motivated by personal convenience or poetic preference alone is not a virtue, for example; if liberal irony does not attend to the worth of others for their own sakes, it is a vice, however otherwise "poetic" or "committed." In short, our reasons for action do matter, at times as much as our overt action itself. Rorty is well aware of the danger that liberal virtues will not be sustainable under an ironist sky – that they may seem to collapse into manipulative self-interest – but his response to this objection turns too much on his evident personal kindliness as opposed to plausible observations on the basis of which one might educate the young. It is not so much that our antecedent "wish to be kind" must be "bolstered by an argument"[25] as that we can't cultivate kindness in the first place, we don't know fully what it means to be kind, without attending to the intrinsic worth (and vulnerability) of others. The highest compliment one can pay Rorty is to note that his minimalist theory cannot account for his charitable practice. Like Hemingway, he seems embarrassed by the finer truths about love.

Rorty grants that "there is no way to bring self-creation together with justice at the level of theory."[26] He allows that irony "seems inherently a private matter" and that it is, "if not intrinsically resentful, at least reactive."[27] But the problem is deeper than the "incommensurability" of private redescriptions and public discourse. Irony is parasitic upon public meaningfulness; it does not itself produce it. More importantly, however, ironism often cuts against meaningfulness, both public and private. Strong poetry can't save us because our self-redescriptions must seem like rather arbitrary fictions if they are not rooted in personal fact and interpersonal community. Rorty believes in group solidarity as a goal, but what he says about contingency and irony tends to undermine such solidarity, in spite of himself. Can one imagine dying for irony's sake? Rorty thinks so,[28] but even Socrates wasn't that "liberal." Even a pragmatic utopia must assert the truth of a shared desire (if not a universal human capacity) for self-creation.

Rorty believes that "if we take care of political freedom, truth and

[25] Rorty, *Contingency, Irony, and Solidarity*, pp. 85 and 91.   [26] Ibid., p. xiv.
[27] Ibid., pp. 87–88.   [28] Ibid., p. 189.

goodness will take care of themselves."[29] But this bourgeois optimism strikes me as itself a false comfort. We can no more reduce social theory to liberal practice than we can segregate private aspirations from public projects or equate love with pure bestowal. Even democracies can be highly self-deluded. A true account of ourselves will not dismiss evil and suffering as illusory or explain away contingency and death as insignificant; it will, instead, allow us to struggle against suffering when we can and to accept it when we must. (We struggle against afflicting contingen*cies* but not contingency as such.) *Pace* Rorty, however, Christianity believes charity rather than irony is the best means of seeing and acting on the truth about our situation, the best means of generating as well as recognizing meaning in the midst of our vulnerabilities. Charity concentrates attention primarily on others rather than self, confident that this will not be futile.

The religious and ethical case against pure ironism was forcefully stated by the young Kierkegaard:

[T]hat for irony nothing is serious . . . may . . . be asserted with reference to the negatively free subject. For he is not at all serious about the virtues he practices, insofar as true seriousness is only possible in a totality, . . . wherein the subject no longer arbitrarily determines himself at each moment to continue his experiment, where he feels the task not as something which he has set himself, but as something which has been set for him.

All things are possible for the ironist . . . For a change he even deems it appropriate to let fate and accident decide for him.[30]

Rorty makes it clear that, for his money, he would prefer "a Kierkegaard without Christianity, one who remained self-consciously 'aesthetic,' in Kierkegaard's sense of that term."[31] Rortian pragmatism, it is evident, is not metaphysically neutral; one can't be an ironist and a theist at the same time.

II. SHKLAR ON PUTTING CRUELTY VS. CHARITY FIRST

Let me turn now to the self-sufficiency of charity and its relation to cruelty as understood by Judith Shklar. In *Ordinary Vices*, Shklar writes:

Putting cruelty *first* is . . . a matter very different from mere humaneness. To hate cruelty more than any other evil involves a radical rejection of both religious and political conventions. It dooms one to a life of skepticism, inde-

---

[29] Ibid., p. 84.
[30] Søren Kierkegaard, *The Concept of Irony*, trans. by Lee M. Capel (Bloomington: University of Indiana Press, 1968), pp. 254 and 299. [31] Rorty, *Contingency, Irony, and Solidarity*, p. 107.

cision, disgust, and often misanthropy . . . To put cruelty first is to disregard the idea of sin as it is understood by revealed religion. Sins are transgressions of a divine rule and offenses against God; pride – the rejection of God – must always be the worst one, which gives rise to all the others. However, cruelty – the willful inflicting of physical pain on a weaker being in order to cause anguish and fear – is a wrong done entirely to *another creature*. When it is marked as the supreme evil it is judged so in and of itself, and not because it signifies a denial of God or any other higher norm . . . To hate cruelty with utmost intensity is perfectly compatible with Biblical religiosity, but to put it first does place one irrevocably outside the sphere of revealed religion. For it is a purely human verdict upon human conduct and so puts religion at a certain distance.[32]

Putting cruelty first among the vices serves the same purpose for Shklar as praising irony does for Rorty. Shklar's emphasis on cruelty-avoidance stems from an insistence that we not denigrate everyday values and disvalues by referring them to something not themselves. Cruelty is evil in itself, not merely instrumentally so. The primacy of cruelty as a vice can act, moreover, as an antidote to the self-sufficiency of charity as a virtue. It points to the goods other than love that we should treasure and may lose.

But must Christian charity inevitably violate Shklarian sensibilities? Is it preferable, or even possible, to promote Christian love as prior to the avoidance of cruelty? Christian orthodoxy holds that selfless love for all human beings is not possible without God, but this does not mean that God is the only object of love. Similarly, the Christian believes that the avoidance of cruelty is not possible without God, but this does not mean that it is exclusively for the sake of God (much less heavenly reward) that we avoid cruelty. If creatures are made in the Image of God, then, we may love "others in God" vs. "God in others." Putting charity first means empathizing with the concrete people before us, with their very real excellences and deficiencies, while also calling them into goods that they may not yet possess. First among these goods is the capacity to love itself: "let us consider how to provoke one another to love and good deeds" (Heb. 10:24). Love creates more love by treating others as lovable, but this is not merely behaving "as if" they were inherently valuable when in fact they are not.

That said, it must be admitted that Shklar has some warrant for her suspicion of Christian theology. As noted in chapter 3, Saint Augustine suggests at times that God is the sole proper object of "enjoyment" (*"frui"*), while Simone Weil holds that we must "decreate" ourselves and

[32] Judith Shklar, *Ordinary Vices* (Cambridge: Harvard University Press, 1984), pp. 8–9.

allow God's love to flow back to God alone. These pious sentiments do indeed risk the cruel worship of a narcissistic Deity. Happily, however, the two Biblical love commandments indicate that God is not so jealous; Matthew 22:37–40 would have us love both God and the neighbor. There is no conflating the two commandments; individuals are to love God with an utterly unqualified obedience, whereas they are to love their neighbors as themselves. Yet, again, we are to love *both* God *and* the neighbor, as well as ourselves.[33]

Charity is neither identical with nor a sufficient replacement for all other goods, but it is important to note how far one may go in putting charity first without cruelly denigrating other values. Thomas Aquinas does say that the neighbor "is loved out of charity for God's sake."[34] But even Thomas, for whom God is always the principal object of charity, does not say that God is the *sole* object.[35] His strong agapism emerges in affirming that "[c]harity is included in the definition of every virtue, not as being essentially every virtue, but because every virtue depends on it . . ."[36] Even when strong *agape* sees charity as a necessary condition for personal fulfillment across the entire range of human capacities (1 Cor. 13:1–3), other goods are acknowledged as such. As important as love is, it is not sufficient for full human flourishing. To have it without health, meaningful work, political enfranchisement, a happy family life, etc. is to suffer genuine loss or deprivation. In short, Shklar accepts too complete a contrast between "a purely human verdict" and one that makes reference to the Deity.

There are two senses, then, in which one must deny that the self-sufficiency of charity follows from putting charity first. First, other human goods (moral and nonmoral) must be deemed genuinely valuable. Second, though loving communion with God and the neighbor is the supreme good, attaining this state is not wholly within human control. The need for divine grace makes it impossible for a Christian to believe that a charitable life is self-sufficient in the way Plato's contemplative life is supposed to be.[37] It is only when we forget these two points that a pragmatic liberalism seems attractive and we are tempted to the overly negative move of putting cruelty first.

[33] In the end, Rorty qualifies his subjectivism by noting that pain and humiliation are nonlinguistic realities, real disvalues to which one ought to attend. One ought to be not ironic but kindly about another's pain, Rorty notes; thus, for him, it seems we can discover disvalues even if we must invent values. See Rorty, *Contingency, Irony, and Solidarity*, pp. 92–94.

[34] Aquinas, *ST*, II–II, Q. 23, art. 5, *ad* 1.

[35] As he puts it, "the aspect under which our neighbor is to be loved, is God, since what we ought to love in our neighbor is that he may be in God" (ibid., II–II, Q. 25, art. 1).

[36] See ibid., II–II, Q. 23, art. 7 and art. 4, *ad* 1.

[37] I owe this point to John Taylor, in conversation.

Shklar emphasized in later work that, for her, "liberalism refers to a political doctrine, not a philosophy of life" and that "[a]part from prohibiting interference with the freedom of others, liberalism does not have any particular positive doctrines about how people are to conduct their lives or what personal choices they are to make."[38] This sounds reminiscent of a Rawlsian procedural account that would be "purely political,"[39] but to the end of her life Shklar made substantive and perceptive claims about what is required for a decent human existence. The "liberalism of fear," as she called her position, was a moral response to such persistent historical realities as torture, war, religious intolerance, and political tyranny. Clearly, Shklar's final version of liberalism was morally basic rather than morally empty.[40] She concentrated on "damage control,"[41] as she did in *Ordinary Vices*, but she acknowledged more overtly the extent to which, in the wake of the religious wars of the sixteenth century, tolerance itself came to be seen by many as an "expression of Christian charity."[42] Even so, her vision remained largely negative and too minimalist to sustain the social practices she treasured, I believe.

Shklar wrote: "[The liberalism of fear] does not, to be sure, offer a *summum bonum* toward which all political agents should strive, but it certainly does begin with a *summum malum*, which all of us know and would avoid if we could. That evil is cruelty and the fear it inspires, and the very fear of fear itself."[43] But can one really say what is *malum in se* without implying a "positive doctrine" about what is *bonum in se*, if not the highest good? For Shklar, the prime object of liberalism was to disperse and restrain governmental power, but what of the need to create and retain civic-minded citizens?[44] One senses cart-before-horse problems here, an overemphasis on the *distribution* of benefits and burdens as opposed to the *production* of persons capable of being benefited or burdened. Shklar counted on "habits of patience, self-restraint, respect for the claims of others, and caution" to be the "indirect" "psychological effect"[45] of the liberal state and its system of education. But when construed negatively such a system is likely to generate "tolerance" by evacuating individuals of conviction rather than by

[38] Shklar, "The Liberalism of Fear," in *Liberalism and the Moral Life*, ed. by Nancy L. Rosenblum (Cambridge: Cambridge University Press, 1989), p. 21.
[39] Compare, for instance, ibid., p. 33.
[40] This point is made emphatically by Shklar in *The Faces of Injustice* (New Haven and London: Yale University Press, 1990), p. 124.   [41] Shklar, "The Liberalism of Fear," p. 27.
[42] Ibid., p. 23.   [43] Ibid., p. 29.
[44] This sort of question is raised by Charles Taylor in "Cross-Purposes: The Liberal-Communitarian Debate," in *Liberalism and the Moral Life*.   [45] Shklar, "The Liberalism of Fear," p. 33.

inculcating real virtue. Some positive conception of political community, coupled with a credible picture of the social self, is required to cultivate the kind of personal autonomy that liberal statecraft is supposed, in turn, to protect. This is why strong agapists speak of "the priority of *agape* to political philosophy,"[46] and why they must ultimately move beyond the liberalism of fear.

Love fears for the defenseless – and most of us are highly vulnerable before the power of modern governments – but even in a limited state, love would cast out fear by offering something more basic: social solidarity based on shared humanity. Shklar's insistence that liberals put cruelty first among the vices will only be an effective deterrent to injustice if we grant moral standing to others as the potential subjects/objects of cruelty. Yet the granting of such status requires empathy with others rather than fear for oneself. Colonial exploiters, racial bigots, and religious zealots are so objectionable not (usually) because they are self-consciously cruel to marginalized and vulnerable people, but because they do not or will not recognize these others *as* people. Putting cruelty first would not have made Christopher Columbus more humane to the Caribs or Andrew Jackson more civil to the Creeks unless each man had antecedently been moved to see the native populations as fellow sufferers.[47] Again, this is accomplished not by self-referential fear – the marginal are seldom a real physical threat – but by other-regarding love.[48]

III. ON INVULNERABILITY

A. Spiritual suffering and harm?

This brings us to the third facet of the facility of goodness, its invulnerability. Is love itself beyond all harm from others? Notoriously, Christ

---

[46] See my "Liberalism and *Agape*: The Priority of Charity to Democracy and Philosophy," in *The Annual of the Society of Christian Ethics* (1993): 47–72.

[47] I offer my thanks to Shelini Harris for helping me to clarify this point.

[48] Shklar's *The Faces of Injustice* goes some way toward remedying the overly negative accent of "The Liberalism of Fear." She claims in the former that "it is evident that when we can alleviate suffering, whatever its cause, it is passively unjust to stand by and do nothing" (p. 81); and she bolsters this view with the political observation that "the democratic sense of injustice cries out ... for a public recognition that it is wrong and unfair to deny to anyone a minimum of human dignity" (p. 86). This is a powerful brief for compassion and social solidarity that, if acted on, would go well beyond strategies of fear-avoidance to a positive program to promote the public good of all. I am a bit mystified, therefore, when Shklar goes on to aver that "[p]assive injustice is a civic failing, not a sin or a crime. It refers to the demands of our political role in a constitutional democracy, not to our duties as men and women in general" (p. 98). Being oblivious to the homeless or the oppressed may not be legally actionable, but it is surely a sin against our common humanity. Avoiding passive injustice is at least a duty of charity.

seems to endorse radical invulnerability for his followers: "See, I have given you authority to tread on snakes and scorpions, and over all the power of the enemy; and nothing will hurt you" (Luke 10:19). Surely this passage is not to be given a literal reading, however. Jesus was well aware of the fragility of the flesh and its subjection to death, often at the hands of unjust others (Luke 21:16). Nevertheless, he appears to subscribe to a kind of *spiritual* invulnerability. He counsels supreme confidence based on trust in and even fear of God: "Do not fear those who kill the body but cannot kill the soul; rather fear him who can destroy both soul and body in hell" (Matt. 10:28). Evidently, God can kill the soul, but other human beings cannot. What are we to make of this?

Spiritual invulnerability has been a very attractive doctrine to many Christians, and it has often gone hand-in-hand with an insistence on radical individual responsibility. In "The Freedom of a Christian," Luther thinks it evident that "no external thing has any influence in producing Christian righteousness or freedom, or in producing unrighteousness or servitude."[49] In *Works of Love*, Kierkegaard writes: "[P]hysically and externally understood I can fall by the hand of another, but spiritually there is only one who can slay me, and that is myself; spiritually a murder is not conceivable – certainly no violent assaulter can murder an immortal spirit; spiritually suicide is the only possible death."[50] In his *Journals*, Kierkegaard puts the point even more strongly: not just spiritual death but "corruption" is exclusively self-wrought.[51] I suspect, however, that our religious and moral lives are more fragile than this, even as accountability is less private. We need each other's help and suffer from each other's harm more than Kierkegaard's comments permit. Some distinctions must be drawn, at any rate, between types of agents and patients and kinds of interpersonal help and harm.

We should distinguish between individuals who have reached a certain threshold of schooling and self-awareness, such that they are fully competent agents, and individuals who are forever stunted or

---

[49] Luther, "The Freedom of a Christian" [1520], in *Martin Luther: Selections from His Writings*, p. 54; see also p. 63, where "nothing can do him [the Christian] any harm."

[50] Kierkegaard, *Works of Love*, p. 308. This quote was called to my attention by Gene Outka. On this and related matters, see Outka, "Equality and Individuality: Thoughts on Two Themes in Kierkegaard," in *Journal of Religious Ethics*, vol. 10, no. 2 (Fall 1982): 171–203; and "Equality and the Fate of Theism in Modern Culture," in *The Journal of Religion*, vol. 67, no. 3 (July 1987): 275–288. See also my "Arminian Edification: Kierkegaard on Grace and Free Will," in *The Cambridge Companion to Kierkegaard* (Cambridge: Cambridge University Press, 1998).

[51] "Physically it is true that a man can fall by the hand of another; spiritually it is true that a man can fall only by his own hand – no one can corrupt him but the man himself." See Kierkegaard, *Journals and Papers*, vol. 1, no. 59, p. 23.

simply still in their spiritual nonage. Undoubtedly, the latter are in many ways more subject to outside help and harm than the former. In the extreme, a child may be so violated by abusive parents, for example, as to be effectively robbed of the prospect of ever trusting (and therefore of ever loving) others. Once the threshold of moral selfhood is achieved, in contrast, a good deal more autonomy and accountability prevails; indeed, a normal adult may always be partly complicitous in any loss of his or her virtue, once acquired. But it is still possible to diminish another by so tormenting her that we are the occasion for her loss of goodness. Shklar writes: "What is moral cruelty? It is not just a matter of hurting someone's feelings. It is deliberate and persistent humiliation, so that the victim can eventually trust neither himself nor anyone else."[52] She spends a lot of time discussing those like Montaigne, Hawthorne, and Nietzsche who see Christianity, "the religion of meekness," as thriving on such cruelty. Christianity, Shklar suggests, plays on our vulnerabilities precisely by pretending that we are invulnerable. Her humane remedy for this is pride in our small competences and even our flaws and needfulness. "Nothing but cruelty comes from those who seek perfection and forget the little good that lies directly within their powers."[53]

Is Christian charity in fact "a vast engine of cultural dishonesty and humiliation," to use Shklar's phrase?[54] It is a troubling prospect indeed that there is an internal relation between Christian love and human misery, but we must distinguish between the ideal of love itself and the various hypocrisies and cruelties that stem from a refusal to acknowledge that we fall short of it. (We ought to note our flaws and vulnerabilities out of charity itself.) The priority of God's love to humanity's is the good news of the gospel, and what makes possible strong *agape*. But it does seem that people can so brutalize others, so "unmake their humanity"[55] – in torture, for example – as to render love humanly impossible for them. An honest examination of the human condition will note the stunning precocity and brutality of evil, as when two Arkansas boys, eleven and thirteen years old, gun down four girls and a teacher out of childish romantic frustration. And it is facile to deny that love suffers physical and emotional harm; real and even irremediable loss are inseparable from many human lives.

There are different sorts of harm, however, and moral vulnerability extends only so far. It seems that happiness can be taken far more easily

[52] Shklar, *Ordinary Vices*, p. 37.   [53] Ibid., p. 39.   [54] Ibid.
[55] Elaine Scarry, *The Body in Pain, passim*.

than ethical innocence, for instance; outrageous fortune, such as the murder of a spouse, can cut us to the spiritual quick without making us blameworthy. The key question is: beyond being contributing factors to spiritual *suffering and harm*, may the world or the people in it actually necessitate an agent's moral *culpability* independently of his or her own actions? May love even suffer *decisive* harm even unto *damnation*, being compelled to sin by another person or unfortunate circumstances involving no fault of one's own? Admitting the vulnerability of charity does not require going that far, I believe, since the idea of necessitated culpability amounts to blaming victims.

B. Genuine dilemmas?

Define a genuine moral dilemma as a situation in which, through no antecedent fault of your own, you cannot but become guilty. Two binding yet mutually exclusive duties/principles/commandments obtain, such that neither one overrides or negates the other. It is not that a *feeling* of guilt is inevitable, but rather that *actual* guilt is unavoidable: you are literally "damned if you do and damned if you don't." For any account of ethics that puts charity first, the existence of such a dilemma would appear to be devastating. If dilemmas were real, there would seem to be times when an innocent moral agent faces only culpable choices, between which he or she is forced to choose and must (in the end) be willing to choose. This would imply, in turn, that it is then immoral to love, if loving would make the agent unwilling to do the "necessary evil." If love never does evil that good might come (cf. Rom. 3:8) – always rejects as hateful the direct killing of an innocent human being, for instance – then the lover would be paralyzed when faced with an exclusive choice between evil (e.g., murderous) options.

Some Christian ethicists endorse moral dilemmas as consistent with, even integral to, religious faith. In a beautifully written piece, Philip Quinn, for instance, holds that "the possibility of a dilemma arising is built into Christian ethics at its foundations . . . it seems clear that it is possible for a situation to arise in which the two parts of the Great Commandment are in conflict."[56] By "the Great Commandment," Quinn refers to Christ's summary of the law and the prophets, quoted

---

[56] See Quinn, "Tragic Dilemmas, Suffering Love, and Christian Life," in *Journal of Religious Ethics*, vol. 17 (1989), p. 171. See also his "Moral Obligation, Religious Demand, and Practical Conflict," in Robert Audi and William Wainwright, eds., *Rationality, Religious Belief, and Moral Commitment* (Ithaca and London: Cornell University Press, 1986).

above (Matt. 22:37–40). Referring to the commands in the singular blurs the fact, however, that they are lexically ordered. There are *two* commandments standing in a priority relation, as Quinn himself apparently grants.[57] This implies that there can be strain between the injunctions, for they are not simply identical, but if they come from the same God, there must be limits to the opposition. If there were a flat contradiction between love of God, love of neighbor, and love of self, the two love commands themselves would be at odds. And if this were the case, God and the Christ would be schizophrenic, demanding actions and dispositions that are mutually exclusive. Yet the thrust of the Gospel witness to the goodness of God seems to rule out the commandments' being contradictory in this way: "the one who loves another has fulfilled the law" (Rom. 13:8).[58]

I discuss moral conflict in much more detail in chapters 6 and 7, but four basic arguments are commonly offered against the possibility of moral dilemmas as technically defined:

(1) *A logical argument*: versions of this argument are as old as Aristotle. If, as realists maintain, moral propositions have truth value, then allowing genuine dilemmas amounts to thinking that a self-contradiction can be true. Granting a dilemma requires asserting, for example: "It is the case that I ought to do action X, and it is not the case that I ought to do action X." But such a self-contradiction is a necessary falsehood, thus exponents of moral realism (e.g., natural law theorists) must reject it as impossible. To introduce a dilemma into practical reasoning would be as devastating as introducing a contradiction into speculative reasoning; even as anything follows logically from a self-contradiction, so anything would follow ethically from a dilemma. There would no longer be a way to speak of moral dispositions or decisions as right or wrong.

(2) *A theological argument*: if, as divine command theorists believe, God's will provides the deontological reasons for human action, then admitting genuine dilemmas amounts to thinking that God is either schizophrenic or cruel. For God to command me to do two incompatible things at one and the same time would be to necessitate my sin, but such

---

[57] Quinn writes in a footnote to "Tragic Dilemmas" that "[t]hough the two commandments are ordered, it does not seem to me that Jesus says or implies that the second is to be subordinated to the first or that the first would override the second in case of conflict" (p. 182). It seems to me that Jesus says or implies exactly this. What else does it mean to call total devotion to God "the greatest and first commandment," with the second being "like" (but not synonymous with) it? If the two commandments are "ordered," moreover, I am not sure why Quinn then continues to refer to them as "*the* Great Commandment."

[58] Even for Quinn, "[i]t is . . . a typically audacious Christian hope that even a tragic ethical dilemma need not spell tragedy for the whole of one's ethical life. Providence may provide a replacement for shattered goodness" (ibid., p. 179).

necessitation would clearly indict the divine wisdom or goodness, or perhaps both. If one holds an Augustinian view of original sin as entailing universal guilt inherited independently of one's own (though not Adam and Eve's) wrongdoing, then *every* human life is now dilemmatic. This may be a pious expression of humanity's need for grace, but it seems irreconcilable with creation of the world by a just and loving God. Bringing into existence a world characterized by undeserved guilt, not to mention biologically transmitted sin, would be morally reprehensible. Sinful structures can be embedded in collective institutions, and sin is certainly tenacious, but to see it as externally necessitated is to explode the concepts of divine and human responsibility.

(3) *A psychological argument*: if sound moral education helps us to lead a life of virtue and to escape a life of vice, then we have pedagogical reasons for denying dilemmas. Talk of dilemmas inevitably accents coping with guilt rather than avoiding it, and this leads in turn to a too ready acquiescence in evil. Hemingway's sentiment that "we are all bitched from the start" can lead us to retreat to the Garden of self-indulgence. And Michael Walzer's contention that in a "supreme emergency" we must be willing to "dirty our hands" can move us sincerely to legitimate mass murder.[59]

(4) *A burden of proof argument*: a central motive for accepting the existence of dilemmas is the desire to do justice to the vicissitudes of the moral life, but we can accomplish this in other ways. Reference to phenomena such as ignorance, ambiguity, weakness of will, and perversity of will – as well as the vulnerability discussed above – accounts for the pathos of the moral life without the problems associated with dilemmas. Sometimes we do not know the good or the right; sometimes we know them but cannot, despite our best efforts, move ourselves to act on them; sometimes we even act for the sake of the bad and the wrong, wanting evil to triumph in the world; but none of these scenarios translates into inescapable guilt imposed from without. Again, we may admit the possibility of unavoidable moral diminishment without associating this with personal guilt or sin.

Even briefly stated, these four arguments suggest that denying the facility of goodness does not dictate an utterly tragic vision of our moral prospects, any more than it requires pragmatic ironism or bourgeois liberalism. It must be admitted, however, that the arguments do not quite constitute a knockdown refutation of the possibility of moral

---

[59] See Michael Walzer, "Political Action: The Problem of Dirty Hands," in *War and Moral Responsibility*, vol. 2, no. 2 of *Philosophy and Public Affairs*, (Winter 1973): 160–180; and *Just and Unjust Wars* (New York: Basic Books, 1977), chap. 16. I discuss Walzer in chapter 7.

dilemmas. As I argue in chapter 7, strong *agape* believes that there is at least one permissible, however painful, alternative in any given situation: to love. But what could count as a proof of this? Love never hates, but this is often in spite of the apparent moral absurdity of the world rather than because of its evident harmony. Conflict and loss can be necessitated by ruthless people or unfortunate circumstances – that much is clear – but the denial of moral dilemmas is ultimately an article of faith. Holding that moral claims have truth value, that God is a loving Parent, that there is always good reason to be ethical, and that human perversity is not the last word are much more *expressions* of a prior commitment to love than *rationales* for being loving to begin with.

To the extent that admitting dilemmas would threaten the propriety of neighbor-love and thus the intelligibility of the moral life as a gift of God, the Biblical Christian will respond by affirming the priority of *agape*, especially its willingness to sacrifice. Sacrifice (in the form of forgiveness, for example) can open individuals to possibilities that add value to an apparently hopeless situation. Even if there is no "happy" outcome to a forced decision, there need not be loss of innocence defined as the necessary betrayal of charity. The example of the cross suggests that it is always possible to love, however taxing or costly this may be; and love's priority renders a despairing vision of our moral prospects implausible, even while it highlights our inescapable dependency on others and our universal tendency to fail others. We are deeply vulnerable but not without resources, predictably sinful but not without redemption.

Allegiance to strong *agape* is not a prescription for moral dandyism, for letting the world go to smash in order to preserve one's priggish sense of self-righteousness. On the contrary, love takes responsibility for the world. This responsibility is critical and creative; it neither despairs over life's trials (including political conflict) nor idealizes ascetic withdrawal. Rather than resignedly accepting the evils of the world, love confronts and seeks to overcome them. Love transforms history not by inattention and disengagement but by willingly accepted suffering. This capacity makes it a "supernatural" virtue. It is experienced as a gift from beyond the self that integrates the personality, and society generally, at a level higher than justice (defined as *suum cuique*) dictates or empowers.

It may well be that we believe so much in dilemmas today because we believe so exclusively in a narrow idea of justice. Justice has been the premier virtue for modernity, and for understandable political reasons, but if justice were in fact the first virtue, moral dilemmas would probably be unavoidable. When interest-based rights are taken to be basic and they conflict, when ethics is pure appraisal but people need more than they have earned, then we are at the limits of justice as giving persons only their due. Indeed, in order to become a person with rational interests, one must first receive a care that outstrips justice based strictly on achieved merit. To dwell on justice alone is to be stymied, for our standing system of moral evaluations (of duty, desert, etc.) moves us to ask questions that cannot be answered within that system. What is required is changing what is due, giving more than is historically earned, or consenting to less in order to redeem. This requires a paradigm shift in which a love open to self-sacrifice (i.e., open to grace) takes priority. Forgiveness is one distinctive fruit of this shift, but I shall delay further discussion of this paschal mystery until subsequent chapters.

IV. THE USES AND ABUSES OF IMMORTALITY

I have argued that charity is neither self-sufficient nor invulnerable, but this still leaves open the senses, if any, in which "[l]ove never ends" (1 Cor. 13:8). In this section, I trace four broad questions through a range of relevant literature: (1) Does love's priority *require* personal immortality? (2) Does love's priority *permit* personal immortality? (3) Is love's priority *required by* personal immortality? And (4) Is love's priority *permitted by* personal immortality? My thesis is that strong *agape* need not win its practitioners immortality (construed as endless life) to be coherent or justified. As an ideal, love perseveres independently of such "external" rewards. As Wendell Berry writes:

> What death means is not this –
> the spirit, triumphant in the body's fall,
> praising its absence, feeding on music.
> If life can't justify and explain itself,
> death can't justify and explain it.

> love is no more than what remains
> of itself.
>   There are no arrivals.[60]

A. Boethius and Feuerbach

Boethian Philosophy insists that the soul is immortal (i.e., endlessly perdurable) and must be so if humanity is to achieve the highest good,

---

[60] Wendell Berry, *Collected Poems: 1957–1982* (San Francisco: North Point Press, 1984), pp. 17 and 10.

happiness. "It is clear . . . that if transitory happiness ends with the death of the body, and if this means an end of all happiness, the whole human race would be plunged into misery by death."[61] But this admits an objectionably external factor into the account of moral goodness. Unless he is arguing that living forever is itself a virtue and being mortal a vice – a dubious proposition – Boethius here departs from a strong view of goodness as its own reward. As a result, Boethian virtue seems after all too easily immiserated, which is as distinct from being disconsoled as despair over human frailty is distinct from compassion.

Boethius may be contending that immortality-as-endless-life is a necessary condition for the realization of virtue, but then this is a point about practicalities, not about the nature of goodness in itself. The practical question is undeniably important. Many sensitive souls have wondered whether, in Henry James's words, "to fructify, to use the material [collected in life], one should have a second age, an extension." But the longing for what James calls "another go, . . . a better chance"[62] – whether this takes the form of reincarnation, resurrection, or resuscitation – construes the relevant "extension" as a means to the end of virtue rather than as part of virtue proper. The point remains that even if goodness is not as invulnerable and self-sufficient as Boethius imagines, death need not diminish or tarnish it as such. Lack of perdurability in the soul might prompt nonmoral regret but not ineluctable guilt, for example. The finality of death would not turn human happiness into baseness or charity into a disvalue; it would merely stop or preclude them as matters of fact.

Some would argue that subjective certitude about an afterlife is indispensable for those who (like the disciples) would endure the suffering attendant upon Christlike love. We just cannot be "patient and kind," "not jealous or boastful," "not arrogant or rude," much less "bear all things" (cf. 1 Cor. 13:4–5, 7) without unshakeable confidence in personal survival of natural death, the argument runs. It is important to note that this is more than the claim that we cannot be good without God, an ontological thesis; it is the psychological speculation that we must unassailably believe a particular proposition about heaven if we are to be able to put charity first. There is considerable force to this conjecture, but I nevertheless doubt any necessary linkage between love's priority and certainty about one's endless longevity. Christ's own example on the cross suggests the possibility of obedience in the midst of

---

[61] Boethius, *The Consolation of Philosophy*, p. 30.
[62] Henry James, "The Middle Years," in *The Figure in the Carpet and Other Stories*, p. 239.

doubt. It does seem possible (perhaps even most admirable) to remain steadfast even in the absence of certainty. At any rate, the indispensability of certitude is again a practical question removed from the nature and proper motivation of love itself.

If life is a pure gift, then its being of limited duration does not impugn the justice of God. If immortality-as-endless-life were a requirement of virtue, essential to a life with meaningful consequences, then the fact that everyone dies a permanent death would mean that all fall short of the good. But God would only be unjust if God (1) promised such immortality to the virtuous and (2) failed subsequently to reward those who are actually good. Whether or not such a divine promise has been given, the fact that, as it happens, no one is good would be a sad commentary on creatures, though not on the Deity. Surely the more plausible thesis, however, is that personal perpetuity is not a necessary condition for all virtue. The doctrine that virtue is its own reward and vice its own punishment flows naturally into the conviction that both virtue and vice are, to some extent, possible for human beings here and now independently of an afterlife, though not independently of other forms of divine grace.

The young Feuerbach went so far as to maintain that virtue is only possible in the *absence* of immortality-as-endless-life. In *Thoughts on Death and Immortality* (1830), he writes:

Love would not be complete if death did not exist. . . . Natural death is . . . the ultimate sacrifice of reconciliation, the ultimate verification of love . . . As you love, you acknowledge and proclaim the nothingness of your mere being-for-self, of your self. You acknowledge as your true I, as your essence and life, not yourself, but the object of your love.[63]

For Feuerbach, the spiritual "surrender of the self" associated with love has a natural counterpart, even a foundation, in physical death. By accepting death one "overcomes" nature and participates in the "universal will" of God. Thus orthodox Christian theology is "most pitiable" and "most immoral" "if it does not recognize in death the action of the most exalted freedom."[64]

Feuerbach defends, then, a very strong thesis indeed about the relation between mortality and love. It would be one thing to say that *im*mortality ought not to be the *motive* for charity, that the desire for eternal life must not be the *reason* one chooses to love others, since this

---

[63] Ludwig Feuerbach, *Thoughts on Death and Immortality*, trans. by James A. Massey (Berkeley: University of California Press, 1980), p. 125; see also pp. 124 and 126. [64] Ibid., p. 126.

would taint the choice with egocentrism. But Feuerbach claims considerably more than this. He contends that the *fact* of immortality, regardless of whether it stands as a motive, would be incompatible with love, that love causally *requires* death. As he puts it in a poetic segment:

> Love has strict properties,
> Has its power in contrasts;
> This, its exacting character,
> Does not tolerate immortality.[65]

What are we to make of this? Does the possibility of charity – not to mention putting charity first – presuppose the permanent reality of death? To the extent that love accepts the world, it will accept the limitations on human nature, including the finality of death (should it be); but this alone does not entail that love requires death for its completeness, that love as a free act would be impossible without the "total surrender of self" Feuerbach equates with natural demise. Perhaps we can be both loving and immortal.

Feuerbach's appreciation of the self-giving quality of love, its extension of the self to others and its liberation of the self from narcissism, is at times astonishingly beautiful. There is clearly an old danger here, however, which we first met in Hemingway (chapter 2) and then saw elements of in Weil (chapter 3) and Foucault (chapter 4). To believe with Feuerbach that the "inner" necessity of death (one's mortality as a member of the species) is the "ground" of love and that the "external" actuality of death (one's concrete demise as an individual) is the "verification" or "manifestation" of love is to come very close to *thanatopsis*, the worshipping of death itself.[66] Feuerbach does more than open love to the possibility of self-sacrifice, he directly corrolates the two, claiming: "[T]he more you sacrifice yourself, the greater and more genuine is your love. For one cannot love without self-sacrifice . . . All love, all modes of love, have in common the fact that they are self-surrender, self-sacrifice."[67] If "self-surrender" referred to letting go a false sense of self-sufficiency and acknowledging (even celebrating) the relational nature of the person, then there would be little to object to in these remarks. If "self-sacrifice" connoted embracing the vulnerability and pain that attends commitment to others, then Feuerbach would be a champion of theological disconsolation in the name of love. But the picture is more troubling than this. The Hegelian insistence on the vacuity of the isolated subject, the emptiness of being-by-and-for-oneself

---

[65] Ibid., pp. 144–145.   [66] Ibid., pp. 125–127.   [67] Ibid., pp. 122–123.

without being-with-and-for-others, gives way in the end to a valorization of nonbeing.

For Feuerbach, a sacrifice of one's individual will before the substantiality of the other is synonymous with love's action, even as recognition of the "destitution" and "nothingness" of one's "mere self" is synonymous with love's knowledge. Thus the fulfillment of love demands – even means – loss of self, the absorption of the personal into something infinite, universal, and impersonal. More to the point, Feuerbach ultimately identifies full self-surrender with death and death with nothingness rather than unegoistical relatedness. He wishes so radically to disconsole us, so thoroughly to distance concern with *im*mortality, that he proposes mortality itself as the lover's proper motive. The desire for (not merely the acceptance of) a permanent death, for self-sacrifice as utter self-destruction, becomes the *basis* of charity as a free act, its source and object. One may not explicitly wish for death on a self-conscious level, but *sub specie aeterni* death is the most meaningful "action" an (erstwhile) agent can perform, since extinction of self is the greatest good. With this, Feuerbach effectively equates liberation with abomination.

Putting charity first does not demand such literal self-denial; indeed, it prohibits it by insisting on the legitimacy of self-love in concert with love of neighbor as *together* reflecting the social character of the person. If the Enlightenment turn to the subject overstates the autonomy of individual agents, denying their historical conditionedness by couching personal identity in Promethean terms, the young Feuerbach goes too far in the other direction.[68] In offering a corrective to the atomism of eighteenth- and early nineteenth-century philosophical anthropology, he risks denying moral selfhood altogether by merging personal identity into a fatalism of impersonal powers. In the name of love, the self must acquiesce in a reality (death) both larger than and finally antithetical to itself. This is a prescription for masochism.

My more modest thesis is that a future heaven and/or hell ought not to play much of a role in ethics, though they may do so in cosmology. Postmortem rewards and punishments may be *consequences* of actions taken in this life, but they ought not to factor much into the *motives* for a moral existence. As a concession to human fear and finitude, one may grant that we sometimes may act with one eye on "treasures in heaven,"

---

[68] I shall not concern myself with the extent to which the mature Feuerbach escaped this excess when he broke free of his youthful idealism. See Van Harvey's *Feuerbach and the Interpretation of Religion* (Cambridge: Cambridge University Press, 1995) for more.

but for the most part one should not be so distracted. Better simply to say that eternal reward is a blessed hope and eternal punishment a prudent fear. As Basil the Great put it: "We can flee evil either out of fear for punishment – like slaves, or out of hope for reward – like hirelings, or out of love of God – like children."[69] Concerning immortality, we may not get "a second chance," a personal extension. Yet this possibility need not daunt us. "The thing is to have made somebody care."[70]

There are resources in Western Christianity to support a courageous acceptance of death without perversity. Even Saint Paul, who usually saw the future resurrection of the dead as an indispensable validation of the sacrificial suffering of Christians in this life, did not emphasize gratitude for deliverance from sin and death as a motive for obedience to God. Paul insisted, rather, that fidelity to God simply expresses the truth of our present situation; to fail to embody faith, hope, and love is to be blind to who God is (gracious Lord) and who one really is oneself (part of the new creation).[71] Indeed, though it may not have actually been written by Paul, the "Pauline" epistle to the Ephesians seems to interpret the resurrection of the dead "as an awakening to moral consciousness (5:14) rather than as a future hope."[72] Such a focus on *aletheia/veritas* as the ground of *agape/caritas* can serve to relativize fear of permanent death, as well as gratitude for eternal life. To be charitable is already to know God, one might hold, regardless of what (if anything) follows this life. Thomas Aquinas, for his part, grants that physical demise is in one sense a natural part of the human life story, that bodily decay and death would have characterized our temporal existence even had moral evil not intruded.[73] Unlike Feuerbach, however, Thomas does not suggest that permanent death is a necessary condition for moral goodness. Clearly, one might contend that love is fully possible *regardless of* mortality, rather than *because of* (much less *only as*) mortality. Burial of the dead may be integral to what makes us human (from "*humare*," to bury), but there is something inescapably sad and troubling about funerals: we hope for life *in spite of* death.

---

[69] Quoted by Kierkegaard in his *Journals and Papers*, vol. I, no. 531, p. 215.
[70] James, *The Figure in the Carpet and Other Stories*, p. 258. In "The Middle Years," Dencombe, James's dying alter-ego, concludes by rejecting the need for more than the creative but flawed life he has had: "A second chance – *that's* the delusion. There never was to be but one. We work in the dark – we do what we can – we give what we have. Our doubt is our passion and our passion is our task" (ibid.). [71] See Richard Hays, *The Moral Vision of the New Testament*, p. 39.
[72] Ibid., p. 64.
[73] Even in the Garden before the Fall, incorruptibility required a supernatural "gift of original justice"; see Aquinas, *ST*, I–II, Q. 85, art. 6. See also *ST*, I, Q. 97, art. 1.

The strong Feuerbachian identification of love and freedom with death and self-denial has a disturbingly gnostic flavor, especially when death is personified and made the source and apparent object of life. Feuerbach writes:

> Death startled matter
> And put nature on its course
> So that it will always run
> From place to place.
> Death alone conducts the dance of the stars
> And the music of the spheres.
> . . .
> Ah, what a miracle, what rich abundance!
> The press of life, the silence of rest,
> The night of pain, the brightness of peace
> Have their source in death.
> I read this in the great book of the world:
> Death is the measure of all things.
> Death is the silent inertia
> In every power and difference.[74]

The New Testament speaks of finding one's life by losing it (Matt. 16:24–25), of serving the neighbor out of a love willing to lay down its life (John 15:13); but the Scriptural emphasis is on annealing, rather than annulling, the self – on purification of the person through the trials associated with compassion rather than extinction through death willed for its own sake. A key New Testament question is whether love is defeated or rendered meaningless by death, and the strong agapist's answer is: "No, we can accept and even profit from the pains of life just so long as we continue to love" (cf. Rom. 8:28). Saint Paul goes farther than this, of course, in holding that love is not only not defeated by temporal death but also wins for believers eternal life. Yet so much certainty is not needed to put charity first. Paul's insistence that love must win immortality strikes me as the complementary error to Feuerbach's insistence that it must not; it borders on a kind of vitalism, however supernaturalized, in which meaning requires permanence.

We need not assert that if personal death is final, then life is wretched; nor need we contend that if we are not risen with Christ, then our faith is "in vain" (cf. 1 Cor. 15:14). Strong *agape* means believing in the value and practicability of love, with God's help, in spite of the exigencies and possible extinction of this life. Putting charity first requires that we

---

[74] Feuerbach, *Thoughts on Death and Immortality*, pp. 147 and 149.

worship neither life nor death. On the one hand, eternal life may be a blessed hope, compatible but not identical with our highest aspirations; on the other hand, temporal suffering and death may occasionally be instrumental goods, vehicles for personal growth (at least among the survivors). The latter is a far cry, however, from willing pain for its own sake or directly equating love with dying. I have emphasized that *agape* is "open to self-sacrifice," but such sacrifice must be voluntary and constructive if it is to be true service of others rather than pandering to evil. Indiscriminate self-effacement too often stems from masochism and too often abets oppression to be the unqualified rule of love. If there is a proper place for self-love, as the second love commandment implies, then utter loss of self cannot be the essence of *agape*.

The question remains, nevertheless, whether agapic love is compatible with *immortality* as its *consequence*, even if distinct from *mortality* as its *motive*. Can we be content with Thomas's acceptance of death as natural and couple this with a "blessed hope" for supernatural resurrection? Many of the early church fathers (e.g., Justin and Irenaeus) denied the natural immortality of the soul as implying the irrelevance of the life, death, and resurrection of Jesus Christ. (If the human soul were intrinsically immortal, there would be no need for a divine Incarnation to win eternal life.) But the fathers did generally believe that Christ had ransomed the elect from the permanent death that is one of the wages of sin. They held, in effect, that inserting the cross of Christ into human immorality guaranteed the immortality of the faithful. Whereas Feuerbach sees a meaningful temporal life and a personal afterlife as mutually exclusive – "if there is life after death, there cannot be life before death; one excludes the other"[75] – many early Christians saw the one as insuring the other. The priority of love allows one to break free of both extremes.

The practical possibility of love, as well as its moral validity, does not turn on the question of immortality either way. I depart from both Saint Paul and Feuerbach in holding that there is no internal relation between charity and an afterlife; they neither require nor exclude one another. To think that the future finality of death would evacuate present love of all meaning is to deny that *agape* is motivated by the well-being of finite others here and now.[76] Strong *agape* affirms, in contrast, that should God

---

[75] Ibid., p. 133.

[76] Glenn Tinder, a wise Pauline Christian, writes: "One cannot live in a truly human way without respect for others and respect for oneself, that is, without love. The comprehensive respect which is love, however, is dependent on faith in the immortality of the individual person. When that

not grant the faithful immortality, this would imply no indictment of God's divinity nor any negation of their humanity. Human beings can and should still, with God's grace, put charity first, and the temporal life of love is anything but wretchedness. Should God grant some or all creatures everlasting life, on the other hand, this would be pure serendipity, unmerited favor rather than deserved reward. As for God's utter condemnation and permanent punishment of some, this too seems neither required nor precluded by divine love. Some divine punishment may be mandated by God's righteousness, but endless torment does not seem necessary for either love or justice. If agapic love is its own reward and if the love of God, freely consented to, is the only necessary condition for the love of neighbors, then neighbor-love need dictate neither perpetual life nor perpetual death.

Putting charity first means that love's willing the good for others insures only the present plenitude of the self. Saint Paul's insistence that "flesh and blood cannot inherit the kingdom of God, nor does the perishable inherit the imperishable" (1 Cor. 15:50) can be read as a reminder of the indispensability of grace: human nature as such and alone is not capable of eternal life, in any sense. Still, God's gift of love guarantees only that the soul exists in its highest relational form, not that it must or must not continue to do so. Love and hope are distinct, then, but not ineluctably at odds. We need not insist on the impermanence of death as a necessary condition for love, since charity is its own reward; but neither should we pine for the finality of death as a consummation of love, since, all things being equal, we would prefer a lasting communion with those we care for.

B. Kaufmann and Lewis

It is possible to indict hope for immortality on grounds other than those elaborated by Feuerbach, even as it is possible to defend insistence on it on bases other than those of Boethius. Walter Kaufmann has suggested, for example, that of the three theological virtues of faith, hope, and love, only the last (at most) is defensible to the truly noble soul. His objection differs from Feuerbach's in being not so much masochistic as Stoic. Kaufmann does not so much long for death as fulfillment as accept it as spur and finally as release:

faith disappears the result is demoralization, a state ensuing upon a twofold loss: of morality and of morale . . . If every reality is at last completely extinguished and forgotten, if every act and event leads finally into oblivion, then it does not matter how one lives." See Tinder, *Against Fate: An Essay on Personal Dignity* (Notre Dame: University of Notre Dame Press, 1981), p. 85.

Our attitude toward death is influenced by hope as much as it is by fear. If fear is the mother of cowardice, hope is the father. Men accept indignities without end, and a life not worth living, in the hope that their miseries will end and that eventually life may be worth living again. They renounce love, courage and honesty, pride and humanity, hoping. Hope is as great an enemy of courage as is fear.

Let people who do not know what to do with themselves in this life, but fritter away their time reading magazines and watching television, hope for eternal life. If one lives intensely, the time comes when death seems bliss . . . The life I want is a life I could not endure in eternity. It is a life of love and intensity, suffering and creation, that makes life worth while and death welcome. There is no other life I should prefer. Neither should I like not to die.[77]

Kaufmann prefers the transitoriness and suffering of human finitude to any conceivable alternative – he even "welcomes" death – but he is resigned rather than perverse. Death is not longed for for its own sake, thus Kaufmann cannot be so easily dismissed on this point as Feuerbach. Does Kaufmann in fact demonstrate that *any* hope for a better life or for a transcendent meaning to this life is contrary to love? No, for the simple reason that he seems to think that eternity must be simply more of the same turmoil that we experience in time. One wants evolution not merely longevity, and the evolution need not be into a godlike self-sufficiency that disdains such "merely human" goods as friendship and love of others.

Pace Kaufmann, it is quite possible to hope for something qualitatively better in a realm beyond everyday life without denying what is good and challenging about this world. Correlatively, only by equating present human existence with perfection, in spite of its trials and tragedies, can one vilify all hope for something better. For my part, I can accept suffering and death as necessities, but I cannot sincerely celebrate them, especially not when they destroy someone else. My description of charity as its own reward, uncoupled from immortality as motive, commits me to neither the uncritical affirmation of nor the cowardly flight from this life. Death may be the end of all personal consciousness – a prospect that we must be willing to face – but we may still *hope* for an afterlife of heightened spiritual stature without categorical *insistence* on it. Again, the crucial move is to place charity ahead of such notions as reward or punishment, personal continuity or impersonal nullity.

No one knows exactly what an afterlife may be like.[78] To hope for

---

[77] Walter Kaufmann, *Existentialism, Religion, and Death: Thirteen Essays* (New York: Meridian, 1976), pp. 212 and 214.

[78] Frank Tipler imagines he has a pretty good idea, though. See his *The Physics of Immortality: Modern*

immortality, however, need not be to despise or be blasé about the finite things that normal human beings now care about. Some temporal activities, such as eating, would no longer make sense in an afterlife set free of bodily need. But one might continue to cherish a range of goods as valuable *up until the time of death*, even if they were to pass away afterward. Theological hope need not undermine all everyday virtues either. Some virtues, such as courage before physical danger, would lose their point if a postmortem invulnerability were achieved. But courage would continue to be a virtue *in this life*, since temporal suffering and loss are real and no one can be certain of her eternal destiny. Steadfast willingness to sacrifice in the midst of ambiguity and pain is often admirable, and ambiguity and pain attend the lives of all existing persons, regardless of their hopes concerning the future. The fact of immortality, which would come to light only eventually, would rule out earthly altruism only if one adopted a dogmatic attitude toward it and disregarded the affliction which even immortal beings undergo at some time in their lives. A person who is evolving into endless life may still be hurt *in this life*, as when his immediate ability to love is thwarted; and sacrifice can be made by "eternal" beings to minimize this injury, as when they freely lay down their lives in defense of the innocent.

Even in an afterlife significantly delivered from earthly limitations, we must be able to recognize ourselves as the persons we are and have been, if immortality is to be meaningful for us. So heavenly creatures must remain finite and caring. Growth in spirituality rules out impersonal merger into the Transcendent. We can in fact imagine, if only to a degree, a durable communion between spiritual individuals without the pretense of their having "overcome" finitude altogether in favor of an abstract impassibility. *Impassibility is not perfection for someone who loves.* The perfection of charity in heaven would be a steadfast concern for all that is, has been, or ever might be true and good and beautiful – especially God and other people – rather than an immutable solipsism.[79] The

Cosmology, God and the Resurrection of the Dead (New York: Doubleday, 1994). If taken as a grand thought experiment, this book is fascinating; if seen as a "proof" of God's existence or of the immortality of the soul, it is (as Kierkegaard said of Hegel) merely comical.

[79] Martha Nussbaum critically discusses these themes in Epicurus and Lucretius. In *The Therapy of Desire*, p. 226, she writes: "Our finitude, and in particular our mortality, which is a particularly central case of our finitude, and which conditions all our awareness of other limits, is a constitutive factor in all valuable things' having for us the value that in fact they have. In these constraints we live, and see whatever we see, cherish whatever we cherish, as beings moving in the way we actually move, from birth through time to a necessary death. The activities we love and cherish would not, as such, be available to a godlike unlimited being." Nussbaum, like Kaufmann, fails to see that a courageous and loving human being might want constancy without

divine love is a model for the human, according to Christianity; but if infinitude were so solipsistic as to love only itself and to absorb everything not itself, then God could not love human beings, much less tenderly incarnate among them.

The challenge is to acknowledge that death may be the end of life (its final termination) without suggesting that death may be the End of life (its purpose or point). I side here, to repeat, with neither Saint Paul nor Feuerbach: I neither assert the necessity of immortality as a consummation of a life of love nor deny the possibility of immortality as a gracious gift of God. Hope is in order, but I would downplay most talk of an afterlife (both positive and negative) as a threat to purity of motive. In this extreme, such talk tempts us to hate life or love death.

Where Walter Kaufmann accents death as needed release, C.S. Lewis emphasizes afterlife as necessary reward. In partial opposition to the middle-of-the-road view I recommend, Lewis writes:

> Those who have attained everlasting life in the vision of God doubtless know very well that it is no mere bribe, but the very consummation of their earthly discipleship; but we who have not yet attained it cannot know this in the same way, and cannot even begin to know it at all except by continuing to obey and finding the first reward of our obedience in our increasing power to desire the ultimate reward [heaven]. Just in proportion as the desire grows, our fear lest it should be a mercenary desire will die away and finally be recognized as an absurdity.[80]

Lewis thinks that a negative attitude toward large desires for our own reward (including personal immortality) "has crept in from Kant and the Stoics and is no part of the Christian faith."[81] Two things may be said in response. First, Lewis himself illustrates the danger of an emphasis on the afterlife. He maintains: "If a transtemporal, transfinite good is our real destiny, then any other good on which our desire fixes must be in some degree fallacious, must bear at best only a symbolical relation to what will truly satisfy."[82] One need not lapse into an idolatrous elevation of created things to find this a troubling denigration of this world. This is especially true if we speak of both good and evil (e.g., others' pain) as

self-sufficiency and that the desire and aptitude for such constancy may be awakened and schooled in time yet come to fruition in eternity. Nussbaum explicitly denies that death is "a good thing" (p. 231), but if it is a permanent and necessary condition for many other values, then it is in fact a good thing. Hope for immortality must be out of place for her. As I interpret them, religious aspirations for a healing of the self beyond the grave may provide an alternative to the celebration of death but need not amount to flight from this life.

[80] C.S. Lewis, "The Weight of Glory," in *The Weight of Glory and Other Essays* (Grand Rapids: Eerdmans Publishing Co., 1979), p. 3.　　[81] Ibid., p. 3.　　[82] Ibid., p. 4.

"fallacious." The more central the moral role played by immortality-as-endless-life, the harder it is to acknowledge human vulnerability; and the less we admit vulnerability, the easier it is to be cruel. Second, it is unclear that endless life is such an inherent "consummation" of Christian discipleship – what I have called "putting charity first" – that its absence would undermine the meaning of that discipleship. Literal deathlessness may be a consummation devoutly to be wished, and nothing I have said rules out a robust desire for this kind of immortality. What I have denied is that immortality-as-endless-life should be a central motive for charity, i.e., that it is an essential part of or otherwise directly entailed by that virtue.

Putting charity first aims at overcoming any sharp dichotomy between a Catholic focus on immortalization and a Protestant focus on justification.[83] Strong *agape identifies* immortalization with justification and both, in turn, with *agape* as participation in the life of God here and now. Considerable (though not total) liberty of heart and tranquility of conscience flow from appreciating the priority of *agape*, and whatever bondage and distress remain would not be alleviated by either an endless lifespan or a complete merger into infinitude anyway. What is wanted in the face of death is a rare combination of acceptance and compassion, *amor fati* purged of Spinozistic fatalism and Nietzschean cruelty.[84]

C. Hebrew and Christian Scriptures

A full survey of Biblical attitudes toward death is far beyond the compass of this chapter, but I want to conclude this section by pointing toward Scriptural resources for the kind of acceptance-cum-compassion just mentioned. The first thing to say is that Hebraic attitudes toward immortality are complex and have changed over time. Simcha Paull Raphael notes:

---

[83] I have in mind Miguel de Unamuno, who expresses sentiments akin to Lewis's: "[W]hat is specific in the Catholic religion is immortalization and not justification, in the Protestant sense . . . It was from Kant, in spite of what orthodox Protestants may think of him, that Protestantism derived its penultimate conclusions – namely, that religion rests upon morality, and not morality upon religion, as in Catholicism. For my part, I cannot conceive the liberty of a heart or the tranquillity of a conscience that are not sure of their perdurability after death." See Unamuno, *Tragic Sense of Life*, trans. by J.E. Crawford Flitch (New York: Dover Publications, 1954), pp. 67 and 70.

[84] Compare the hero of Unamuno's *San Manuel Bueno, Martir*, trans. by M.E. Valdes (Madrid: Editorial Castalia, 1973).

In patriarchal and Mosaic times, even in the days of the Israelite tribal confederacy, the Bible has nothing to say about the fate of the individual after death, and there is certainly no notion of an individual afterlife experience for the soul. There is not even a clear conception of an individual apart from the collective, nor any idea of a soul separate from the body . . . only after the sixth century B.C.E. do any conceptions of an afterlife for the individual begin to appear within Judaism.[85]

Raphael goes on to suggest that the Book of Job may be a turning point: "For the first time in biblical literature, the possibility of an immortal, spiritual existence subsequent to physical death may here [in Job 19:25–26] be glimpsed." But this is a controversial reading, as Raphael grants, and he qualifies his remarks by adding that "the possibility of an individual postmortem immortality is at most glimpsed for a fleeting moment by Job."[86]

A vision of resurrection of the dead appears for the first time in Ezekiel (*c.* 571 B.C.E.) – "Mortal, can these bones live?" (Ezek. 37:3 ff.) – but the only truly positive affirmation of general immortality in the Hebrew Bible comes in the apocalyptic Book of Daniel (167–164 B.C.E.), a late addition to the Old Testament canon:

. . . at that time your people shall be delivered, everyone who is found written in the book. Many of those who sleep in the dust of the earth shall awake, some to everlasting life, and some to shame and everlasting contempt. Those who are wise shall shine like the brightness of the sky, and those who lead many to righteousness, like the stars forever and ever. (Dan. 12:1–3)

Taking some license, it is possible to perceive in the trajectory of Jewish thought between Ezekiel and Daniel two crucial evolutions: (1) from a corporate understanding of identity in which individual agency and responsibility are largely neglected to a more multi-tiered view in which both the Chosen People and specific persons are held accountable before the one true God for their attitudes, actions, and accomplishments; and (2) from a general silence and even avoidance concerning the fate of the dead to more detailed images of Sheol in which it moves from being a dark and amoral realm of shadows to being the positive context of God's justice. Raphael suggests that both of these broad evolutions may be seen as the working out of the foundations of moral monotheism laid on Sinai. He writes, "[a]s the God of Israel eventually became the God of the entire world, the power of YHVH extended throughout the

---

[85] Raphael, *Jewish Views of the Afterlife* (New Jersey: Jason Aronson, 1996), p. 43.
[86] Ibid., p. 64. I would put the point still more strongly and say that Job raises the prospect of personal immortality only to reject it (e.g., Job 7:9). See my "Must Job Live Forever?: A Reply to Aquinas on Providence," in *The Thomist*, vol. 62, no. 1 (January 1998): 1–39.

created universe, including Sheol. This theological shift paved the way for the development of an individual postmortem eschatology and a notion of personal immortality."[87]

The question of immortality probes the extent to which the lives of individuals and communities have meaning before God, as well as the degree to which individuals and communities trust God in the face of their deaths. Strong *agape* maintains, just so, that both the meaning of life and trust in God at death are fostered by shifting the focus away from an afterlife. Really believing that human beings are personally responsible before God does not require the sanction of postmortem reward or punishment, and really trusting that God is righteous in spite of death does not dictate that God guarantee never-ending life.[88] Thus one might extend the trajectory traced between Ezekiel and Daniel to affirm that God's love and power can now be relied upon to redeem our lives here and now with the divine presence. Strong agapists find theophany enough, even without denying the possibility or even desirability of immortality.

A deemphasis on personally surviving physical death is admittedly more Joblike than Pauline. In 1 Corinthians 15:12–19, Saint Paul notoriously contends: "If there is no resurrection of the dead, then Christ has not been raised; and if Christ has not been raised, then our proclamation has been in vain and your faith has been in vain . . . If for this life only we have hoped in Christ, we are of all people most to be pitied." But it is unclear to what extent Christ himself saw eternal life in this way. Although Jesus did speak of the faithful having "treasure(s)" and "reward" in heaven (e.g., Matt. 6:20 and 19:21, and Luke 6:23), he seems not to tie purity of heart so closely to immortality-as-endless-life that the one requires the other. The pure in heart "shall see God" (Matt. 5:8), but it is moot to what degree this need be in an afterlife. Even the "eternal life" promised in John 3:16 – "For God so loved the world that he gave his only Son, so that everyone who believes in him may not perish but have eternal life" – may be seen first of all as present "participation in God's life" (NRSV note) rather than as endless or transtemporal existence.

This is a very old debate, but on the reading I am advocating individuals may have "eternal life" here and now, in love. "Repent, for

---

[87] Raphael, *Jewish Views of the Afterlife*, p. 57.
[88] Miroslav Volf may disagree. He argues that human foregoing of violence is only possible if we assume "divine vengeance" for evildoers "at the end of history." If Volf judges that God's use of violence must extend into an afterlife (hell), immortality is required for some. See Volf, *Exclusion and Embrace: A Theological Exploration of Identity, Otherness, and Reconciliation* (Nashville: Abingdon Press, 1996), pp. 302–304.

the kingdom of heaven has come near," Jesus declares in Matthew 4:17. The repentant may put charity first, and thus know immortality-as-participation-in-the-life-of-God, because Charity (in the form of the Incarnation) has already put them first. "We love, because he first loved us" (1 John 4:19). This does not imply that the eschaton is fully realized or that finite creatures can attain temporal perfection – in the Lord's Prayer, Jesus himself bids "Thy kingdom come" (Matt. 6:10; and see Matt. 24:6, 36) – but it does mean that the injunction to love God and the neighbor is already in force. The past example of Christ and the present reality of the Holy Spirit make it possible, even mandatory, to love come what may. Conversely, "[w]hoever does not love abides in death" (1 John 3:14). Christ is the promise of eternity kept (a question of the quality of one's life, its meaningfulness), so the justice of God cannot be impugned even if there is no future perpetuity for creatures (a question of the quantity of one's life, its perdurability).[89] "And this is eternal life, that they know you, the only true God, and Jesus Christ whom you have sent" (John 17:3).

The genuinely pious will ask at this point: what about the Resurrection? Is this not a promise of a similar perdurance for the faithful; is this not a pledge that eventually death shall have no more dominion, among at least some creatures? In short, is not the empty tomb a central and ineliminable Christian consolation? Two things may be said in response. First, even if the Resurrection is a kind of promise, it is implicit. Even if one takes the reports of the raising of Jesus's body as literal accounts of an historical event rather than as, say, "the welling up of the Easter spirit" among the disciples (Bultmann), the question remains: why should I think the same will happen to me? I may be adopted as a "son," but I am not the Son of God Incarnate. The meaning of sonship, the full redemption of finite life, may be in the grace-filled imitation of Christ's self-sacrificial love on earth. Which brings me to the second response. Any appropriation of the Resurrection as entailing one's own endlessness will be far more akin to hope about divine generosity than to

---

[89] Eternity read as endless temporal duration is what Hegel called the "spurious" or "bad (*schlechtes*) infinite." See Hegel, *Lectures on the Philosophy of Religion*, ed. by Peter C. Hodgson (Berkeley: University of California Press, 1988), p. 170. This is perhaps overly pejorative; we need not despise the desire for some form of perdurability in order to subordinate it to charity. More recently, Eleonore Stump and Norman Kretzmann have drawn an interesting contrast between "sempiternity," defined as "limitless duration in time" or "persistence *through time*," and true eternity, defined as "infinite atemporal duration" or "duration without succession." Only the latter is worthy, in their view, of the title "illimitable life," as this is normally associated with God. See Stump and Kretzmann, "Eternity," in *The Concept of God*, ed. by Thomas V. Morris (Oxford: Oxford University Press, 1987), pp. 220, 238, 233, and 225.

certainty about an owned fact. I would respond to questions about my
own resurrection, then, the way Reinhold Niebuhr once did about
Christ's blood Atonement: I feel "unworthy to enlarge upon the idea."[90]
Dwelling on it or being dogmatic about it seems a temptation to take the
Passion less seriously.

But didn't Jesus himself emphasize the afterlife? Leaving aside his
forlorn appeal to "Eloi/Eli" on the cross, Clifford Herschel Moore
notes that "Jesus apparently took the resurrection of the righteous at
least for granted"[91] (cf. Luke 14:14). Moore goes on to insist, however:
"The significant thing is that Jesus felt the kingdom of God to be a
present reality rather than something to the enjoyment of which man
might attain in the future."[92] With respect to the Johannine writings in
particular, Moore stands in a long tradition when he points out that "the
whole emphasis is on the present experience of eternal life won by faith
in Christ and testified to by love for God and man."[93] He also makes
clear that the Platonic doctrine of the natural immortality of the soul
was rightly seen as a threat by many early church fathers. Such a
doctrine is a denial of the need for God's redemptive sacrifice as a good
gift.[94] The position I want to defend is suggested by a final quote from
Moore: "Before [Plato], . . . confidence in the continued existence of the
soul after death was based on religious hope and intuition: it remained
for the founder of the Academy to give that confidence a rational basis,
or at least a basis that supported human longings with comforting and
assuring arguments."[95] Better to keep immortality-as-personal-endless-
ness a pure hope, a vague intuition/intimation; better to see Christian
ethics as an expression of and reaction to divine compassion, rather than
as an offshoot of Platonic rationality or Pauline retributivism.

Charity wills the good for the neighbor, and for oneself in as much as
one is also a neighbor; but when I will *your* good, it is that willing and that
good themselves that are *my* reward. I may *de facto* bring about my
immortalization by loving you; and I may do some things other than
loving you motivated by the personal quest for a future heaven, even as I
do some things motivated by the desire for descendants. But beyond
this, neither *my* winning heaven nor *my* promoting *my* descendants'
welfare is a proper motive for my loving *you* and *yours*. Any virtue that
could not accept the finality of death would be dubious on the face of it.

---

[90] Niebuhr, *Leaves from the Notebook of a Tamed Cynic*, p. 77.

[91] Clifford Herschel Moore, *Ancient Beliefs in the Immortality of the Soul* (New York: Longmans, Green, and Co., 1931), p. 63.   [92] Ibid., p. 64.   [93] Ibid., p. 69.   [94] Ibid., pp. 71–77.

[95] Ibid., p. 15.

And external personal rewards, post- or premortem, just should not occupy us. What we ought to fear is not so much death as meaninglessness. Creatively to echo Matthew 6:34: "Sufficient unto the day is the *good* thereof."

In 1 Corinthians 15, Paul insists on personal resurrection in an age to come, and he understandably criticizes the view apparently held by some Christians at Corinth that they had already ascended to heaven. But death and how bodily to overcome it – in the past, present, or future – is not the most decisive question raised by Christ's good news. Hatred and despair over sin are the foremost enemies, as I read the Bible. Paul's authority to interpret Scripture, including his own epistles, is uniquely weighty, yet it is not unquestionable – even as authorial intent is not always the last word in contemporary debates over the meaning of literature. Moreover, willingness to let go of insistence on immortality can be seen as an implication of *Paul's own* claim that, of faith, hope, and love, "the greatest" is love (1 Cor. 13:13). For the strong agapist, love can endure even without faith in one's own resurrection and even when hope for same is muted.[96]

If the human species is not perpetual, then the human experience of love will be no more permanent than that of faith and hope. Still, love connotes a wholeness and inspiration not evident in faith and hope, both of which suggest insufficiency. Complete knowledge and realized desire would make faith and hope obsolete, as Paul saw, but perfect communion would be the fulfillment rather than the negation of agapic love. (It makes sense to speak of the Persons of the Trinity "loving" one another "eternally," for instance, but not of their "believing" forever in things unseen or "hoping" forever for things to come.) *Agape* persists in spite of alienation, in short, but its ideal is unity within diversity. Imitation of God's love has primacy for creatures here and now, because it is an inkling of divine fullness and a partial remedy for human neediness. The inkling need not be a literal fore-taste of heaven, however, any more than the eventual passing away of the earth need make love pointless or obsolete.[97] The avoidance of obsolescence does not

---

[96] In *The Resurrection of the Dead* (New York: Fleming H. Revell Co., 1933), Karl Barth objects to the kind of reading I offer. He writes: "It will not do to reject Paul here [1 Cor. xv. on the bodily resurrection of the dead], whilst finding his words in Rom. viii. 28 or 1 Cor. xiii. marvelously true and edifying; for if we reject him here we prove that we have understood even Rom. viii. 28 and 1 Cor. xiii. quite differently from him . . ." (p. 123). Paul did see scepticism about bodily resurrection as threatening "in the most vital point, not only himself, but the gospel, the work of the Lord," as Barth puts it (p. 122). On rare occasions, however, the gospel may be one thing and Paul's interpretation of it another (cf. Barth, p. 116).

[97] Cf. Richard Hays, *First Corinthians*, pp. 230–231 and 233.

require that something go on without ceasing forever, only that it never be surpassed in time. If human life and chronological time themselves ended, this would not render everything mortal obsolete but rather put an end to obsolescence itself.

I do not deny the possibility of immortality-as-endless-life, to reiterate. I merely suggest that to the extent that Christian theology indulges in comforting arguments here, we should assert the priority of love to that theology. The risk of false comfort, as Rorty and Shklar point out, is a tendency to cruelty. The temptation to "fend off thoughts of mortality" with ideas that blunt the present urgency of love for God and our fellows is very great indeed. So, in quasi-Rortian fashion, charity tends to change the subject when the topic of heaven arises, without thereby doubting the validity of Christ's "new commandment" to "love one another, even as I have loved you" (John 13:34). If I am right, the deliverance from fear Rorty so admirably longs for cannot be achieved via irony, even liberal applications thereof; the road on which he and Shklar travel in order to avoid vice leads only part way to virtue. The requisite virtue – that which convinces us we have lived (however fallibly) and thus that we need not fear dying (however permanently) – is love.

VI. THE LOVE OF GOD AND THEODICY/ANTHROPODICY

One crucial issue remains to be considered. If *agape* is primordial, must it not also be eschatological? Even if God cannot be indicted as *unjust* for not promising (and consequently not granting) an endless afterlife to the righteous, would God not be *unloving* if God didn't promise (and consequently didn't grant) such an afterlife? If *agape* outstrips the demands of contractual justice in favor of a self-giving benevolence, as I have claimed, wouldn't a supremely excellent Creator (who is simultaneously omnipotent and omniscient) extend all genuine benefits to creatures whether or not this is a matter of strict obligation, so long as no other moral requirements were violated? If, as some have maintained, moral praise is due only to acts of supererogation, must not a praiseworthy God show mercy and preserve at least some human beings forever?[98] The answer to all of these questions clearly turns on whether immortality-as-endless-life is in fact a genuine human good and, if so, how it relates to immortality-as-participation-in-the-life-of-God, which is the

[98] The urgency of these sorts of questions was pressed on me by members of the Society of Christian Philosophers, especially Larry Lacy, when I read a version of this chapter at a regional meeting at Rhodes College in Memphis.

greatest good. The answer turns, that is, on how perdurability relates to strong *agape*.

Though it is hard to know to what criteria to appeal, I am inclined to think that perdurability would, *ceteris paribus*, be a real benefit and thus that it is properly a blessed hope – what used to be called an "utinam." Self-love permits us to wish for survival of death as a happy upshot of faith, though not as its primary motive. But, again, putting charity first implies that this kind of immortality is not the greatest good nor probably a necessary means to the greatest good. To have love is not to have all good things, but it is to have the *best* thing. An omnibenevolent Creator would no doubt help creatures realize the best, but not all good things (including perdurability) may be compossible with that best (*agape*). More importantly, whether we in fact get maximal compossible goods may depend on our not self-consciously grabbing for them as such. Putting charity first, in any case, means that we can be supremely confident that an agapic God grants perdurability to the righteous *if* their ever being loving itself requires this, and we can be equally confident that God withholds perdurability *if* their ever being loving requires this. (Above all else, love would see others become loving.) Beyond that, making love your aim suggests leaving the matter of an afterlife largely to the womb of time. There is no certainty about which alternative God has promised (and thus realized), nor need there be.

If human love *for God* must be endless to be ever efficacious, then of course there must be an afterlife. But I don't see that endlessness is in fact a necessary condition in this way. Similarly, if divine love *for humanity* itself requires our endlessness for its efficacy, then we must live forever. But there seems to be no *necessary* connection between God's being and any of us continuing. Just as God might not have created the world and with it the beginning of time, so God might not bestow endless life on any creatures at the end of time. Even if friendship with God is seen as the key virtue, it need not be permanent to be real. We tend to insist on such permanence, I suspect, because we are engaged in theodicies or anthropodicies that have more to do with human justice than with divine love.

Whether justifying God or justifying humanity is the goal, insistence on immortality-as-endless-life has three general inspirations: (1) a *distributive justice* in which human virtue is permanently rewarded, (2) a *retributive justice* in which human vice is permanently punished, and (3) a *compensatory justice* in which human suffering is permanently made up for. It is right to insist on the divine promises, as I have emphasized, but short of a direct promise of perdurability, I do not see that any combination of (1) – (3) is required of God. Anthropodicy would make sure that human beings get their due, even as theodicy would make sure that God gives it, but these concerns are secondary to the question: how do we become the kind of people who love as God loves?[99]

When God touched Martin Luther King, Jr., in what came to be known as "the kitchen table epiphany," the frightened young preacher facing death threats in Montgomery reported the 1956 event this way:

> And it seemed to me at that moment that I could hear an inner voice saying to me, "Martin Luther, stand up for righteousness. Stand up for justice. Stand up for truth. And lo I will be with you, even unto the end of the world." . . . I heard the voice of Jesus saying still to fight on. He promised never to leave me, never to leave me alone. No never alone. No never alone. He promised never to leave me, never to leave me alone.[100]

Note that the promise was not of physical safety, nor of endless communion with God, but of never being abandoned. Jesus assures King of his steadfast presence with him, and King recalled this assurance in times of trouble for the rest of his life. But one has to exist in order to be abandoned, so King's assassination in 1968 does not mean a failure of the divine promise; we presume that God was with him even on the balcony of the Loraine Motel. (We are left, of course, to wonder how to interpret the phrase "even unto the end of the world.") Even if we go so far as to say that there is a "call of love" from God to God for a granting of never-ending life to faithful servants, like King, this is not a divine duty of justice. An answered "*Nunc dimittis*" does not *require* that one be departing for immortality, only that one be given the peace of God.

Both theodicy and anthropodicy seem doubtful, then, despite the powerful cases recently made by John Hick and Robert Adams. Hick has argued that an afterlife is "crucial for theodicy," asking: "Would it not contradict God's love for the creatures made in His image if He caused them to pass out of existence whilst His purpose for them was still so largely unfulfilled [due to sin, suffering, premature death, etc.]?"[101] But God's necessary goodness and supreme praiseworthiness are compatible, for example, with a possible world in which all creatures freely and perpetually sin and/or ineluctably and permanently die. Both love

---

[99] See Stanley Hauerwas, *God, Medicine, and Suffering* (Grand Rapids: Eerdmans, 1990) for a powerful critique along these lines of theodicy in medical ethics.

[100] Quoted by David J. Garrow in *Bearing the Cross: Martin Luther King, Jr., and the Southern Christian Leadership Conference* (New York: Vintage Books, 1988), p. 58.

[101] John Hick, *Evil and the God of Love*, revised edition (New York: Harper and Row, 1978), p. 338. A similar point is made in Hick's *Death and Eternal Life* (San Francisco: Harper and Row, 1976).

of neighbor and trust in God may be *possible* in such a world – i.e., neither the reality of nor certitude about an afterlife seems practically necessary for an agapic existence – whether or not these virtues are caused or permitted by creatures to become *actual*. And if, as Hick believes, freedom is required for the development and proper employment of moral qualities, then all one can assert as entailed by the love of God is that all creatures have a *chance* at the highest virtue, not that they will *de facto* achieve it, either in this life or a next.

Again, with freedom comes vulnerability: we can so wound ourselves and others as to preclude us/them from ever realizing the human capacity for love. In this sense, the final goodness of the world, i.e., whether God's gift of finite freedom is worth it to all God's creatures, depends in part on us. Hick writes that "Christian theodicy must point forward to . . . final blessedness [beyond death], and claim that this infinite future good will render worth while all the pain and travail and wickedness that has occurred on the way to it."[102] But if love is the great good for the sake of which God permits evil, and if love itself can only be cultivated in and exercised by free beings, then there is no guarantee that evil will ever be overcome or compensated for. That God loves creation and has extended to creatures the wherewithal to love God in return (even in and through their affliction), is forever established by the Incarnation; but that we accept this love is not fixed, unless we endorse some version of divine fatalism.

All creatures need do for salvation is consent to the grace that would make them loving, and we may suspect that eventually God's wisdom and steadfastness will win over even the hardest of hearts. But it is nevertheless possible that a universal (or even majority) "Yes" to blessedness may never come, even if human beings live forever and suffer greatly. Indeed, our continued free "No" is what makes for the pathos of history and the enduring sorrow of God. Hick himself acknowledges that it is "not logically impossible" that God's purposes should be "eternally frustrated," but he still considers it "morally" impossible; universal salvation in an endless afterlife is, for him, "a practical certainty," something that "the needs of theodicy compel us" to affirm.[103] This significantly overstates matters, I believe, given that freedom is an *internal* component of the *agape* that God would elicit in creatures. If infinite love does not override finite liberty, as Hick elsewhere grants,[104] then must we not admit that infinite love does not

---

[102] Hick, *Evil and the God of Love*, p. 340.   [103] Ibid., p. 344.
[104] Hick, *Death and Eternal Life*, pp. 254–258.

override its own liberty either? Nothing forces God's hand here. God's experiment may yet turn out badly, though if it does we have no one to blame but ourselves. God remains omnibenevolent, but God's creation of a world inhabited by free beings implies that ascriptions to God of "absolute sovereignty" or "ultimate omni-responsibility"[105] can only be misleading.

Like Hick, Robert M. Adams has maintained that a successful theodicy must assume "that every created person will have, in the end and on the whole, a life history that is good for him, or at least worth living (unless perhaps he has brought something worse on himself through some free and commensurate fault of his own)."[106] The apparent unhappiness of some people's earthly lives suggests to Adams, in turn, that this assumption "seems unlikely to be true unless there is life after death, at least for some of us."[107] The picture of immortality-as-compensation-for-ills-suffered-or-opportunities-missed seems considerably more plausible than that of immortality-as-reward-for-merits-accrued-or-punishment-for-faults-displayed; but it also seems, ironically, at most a case for life after death for pure victims and unrepentant sinners, rather than for the righteous. Even the radically harmed and harmful, however, may be loved by God in ways that do not entail an afterlife. (God may simply grant them release, for example.) The *possibility* of love is all that even an infinite Charity can offer a finite creature. And presumably it was *once* possible (however early in their careers) for all human beings to be or become agapic lovers, even if subsequently some were stripped or stripped themselves of this potential. In short, I do not find what might be called the Argument from Chaos or Unhappiness a *proof* of personal durability, even as I do not find the traditional Argument from Design a proof of a personal Deity.

We cannot argue cogently from the apparent orderliness or partial goodness of the present world to the existence of an omnipotent and omnibenevolent Designer; we can, however, reverse the direction of our "argument" and move from a faith in the trustworthiness of God to an understanding and acceptance of God's creation.[108] Similarly, we cannot argue from the apparent need of or undeniable longing for perdura-

---

[105] Hick, *Evil and the God of Love*, pp. 352–353.
[106] Adams, *The Virtue of Faith*, p. 68.   [107] Ibid.
[108] This is what Jonathan Wells, *Charles Hodge's Critique of Darwinism* (Lewiston, NY: Edwin Mellen Press, 1988), pp. 9, 93–101, and 215–223, calls the distinction between "the Argument *from* Design" and "the Argument *to* Design." Louis Dupré makes a related point in "Evil – A Religious Mystery: A Plea for a More Inclusive Model of Theodicy," in *Faith and Philosophy*, vol. 7, no. 3 (July 1990), pp. 267–268.

bility to the existence of an afterlife spent with God; we can, however, reverse the direction and move from a faith in the benevolence of God to a hope for personal continuity if this be for our good. In the absence of an antecedent divine promise, the granting of eternity-as-perdurability (as opposed to eternity-as-charity) is not required by God's justice; and in the absence of an internal connection between endless duration and our own ability to love, it is not required by God's charity. God may bestow endless life upon us, but it would be utter serendipity. (Furthermore, neither love nor trust is likely to be induced by attempts to demonstrate rationally the reality of life after death.) This accent on the pure graciousness and unpredictability of an afterlife is the difference between the best of Biblical piety – for example, Abraham and Job, neither of whom evidently believed in immortality – and much of modern theodicy (though not, in the end, Hick's or Adams's[109]). And any tale of "necessary evolution" between this life and a next will tend to do violence to that piety.

CONCLUSION

Letting go of traditional immortality as an element in theodicy is part of what I mean by "the disconsolation of theology." Similarly, part of what I mean by "putting charity first" is disconnecting that virtue from "eternal rewards" and "external triumphs." I am Gustafsonian enough to suspect a too easy anthropocentrism in such language.[110] The virtues are their own rewards, as Boethius believed, but Boethius went wrong in thinking that they are the *only* goods. Love is for the strong agapist the greatest good; it does trump in cases of conflicting values. (To love is to know God, the Highest, even as to know God is to love.) But charity, however necessary, is not a sufficient condition for full human flourishing. Love is the *summum bonum* but not the *solum bonum*; nor is it a guarantee of an afterlife. What charity is sufficient for is the acceptance (even the promotion) of disconsolation, when this makes us more attentive to each other's joys and afflictions. The greater the love, in fact, the more it will be disconsoled and disconsoling, yet without despairing of the works of love in caring for others.

Another aspect of "theological disconsolation" is abandonment of

---

[109] Hick's references to "mystery" and the world as "ambiguous" and Adams's to "ambivalence" and what is "probably" the case save them from the worst of modern theodicy's tendency to rationalize away human suffering or to take for granted an afterlife. See Hick, *Evil and the God of Love*, pp. 333–335, 373, and 386; and Adams, *The Virtue of Faith*, p. 76.

[110] Cf. James Gustafson, *Ethics from a Theocentric Perspective*, vol. I (Chicago: University of Chicago Press, 1981).

such notions as the irresistibility of grace and the unlovability of men and women for their own sakes. I argued in previous chapters that a tradition of Christian consolers goes wrong in deeming charity to be aimed primarily (if not exclusively) at God,[111] fully guaranteed (if not necessitated) for some people by God, and/or exquisitely invulnerable (if not solitarily self-sufficient) in relation to other creatures. Divine grace is a necessary condition for charity, even as charity is a necessary condition for a well-lived life. Grace is not a necessita*ting* condition, however. Boethius, like others after him, wanted to demonstrate the *compatibility* of the divine attributes (including omniscience and omnipotence) with human freedom. But his rendition of Providence ends up rather fatalistic: God sees and controls all from an eternal present, such that being graced is a sufficient condition for being good, regardless of what we or others might do on our own.

I hold with Arminius and Kierkegaard that human beings are free either to accept or reject God's assistance in loving. Irresistible grace is just as problematic in theology as indubitable value is in ethics. We do not need and cannot have *a foundationalism of the intellect*, in which our knowledge of the good is necessitated by something outside ourselves; correlatively, we do not need and cannot have *a foundationalism of the will*, in which our performance of the good is necessitated by something outside us. Both of these represent false facility. I go farther than Kierkegaard in maintaining that even other creatures can substantively help and harm us in loving; but nobody can necessitate the process. The intellect remains free (we must believe in order to understand), even as the will remains free (we must love in order to act).

What sense, then, is left to the idea of "grace"? Love is, in the scholastic phrase, a "passive potential" which must be triggered by the gratuitous care of others, including preeminently God. We are able to love love, so to speak, because God loves us first. There may be no future reward for our being loving – no perdurability of the soul after death (a disconsoling thought) – but we may know the eternal God in time by Her steadfast love for us in Christ and suffering presence with us in the person of the Holy Spirit. And this is enough to empower our own love both of Her and of one another; this is the sense in which the Word is a performative utterance. The love of God (subjective genitive) makes possible the love of God (objective genitive), but it also makes possible love of neighbors for their own sakes. This is not to say, need I repeat,

---

[111] This general tendency is not unique to Roman Catholic moral theologians, for Martin Luther is capable of writing that the sinner "is loved of the Father, not for his own sake, but for Christ's sake, whom the Father loveth." See Luther, "A Commentary on Galatians," p. 133.

that charity's synthesis of appraisal and bestowal is necessitated by God. A Christian believes that she has a model of love in the Incarnate Christ and that the beauty and strength of this example is enough for her to put charity first. But the human will remains free as well as vulnerable to outside influences. Both the Hebrew prophets and Saint Paul most of the time knew that we are more needful of, and dependent on, one another than Greek and Roman philosophy usually cares to admit.

I suggested above that, in a sense, charity is beyond both certainty and morality. I am now in a position to conclude by summarizing, briefly, what this means. Charity is like irony in being beyond foundationalist claims to certitude, but in charity's case this is not because there is no truth or falsity to love's beliefs about God and the created order. Love is beyond certainty in that its knowledge of others is premised on its free commitment to them rather than on incorrigible apprehensions or logically necessary deductions. Posterior to commitment, however, love appreciates others for who they are and responds to them on the basis of what they need. Charity is beyond morality (narrowly construed) in that mercy is prior to, the source and object of, a calculating justice. Again, love bestows value as well as appraising it; or, better, love outstrips valuation and respects the sanctity of other persons rather than merely computing their utility. Given these facts, putting charity first is actually the surest means to the *avoidance* of cruelty. It is, furthermore, a limiting factor on the sort of ubiquitous irony that must eventually be self-defeating because it is insufficiently other-affirming.

Even as Kant sought to deny dogmatic knowledge "in order to make room for faith,"[112] so strong *agape* would deny both dogmatism and ironism to make room for love. (Hope then takes care of itself.) This is neither Stoicism, nor the Enlightenment, nor even postmodernism diluting Christian charity, but rather charity itself reining in (more or less) constant human pretensions and drawing out (more or less) common human potentials.[113] When the priority of charity is coupled with the kind of epistemic humility I described earlier, we may yet evade those temptations to pride and cruelty that so concern Richard Rorty and Judith Shklar. We may yet, with Love's help, take joy in our imperfect lives without lapsing into Boethian false consolation.

[112] Immanuel Kant, *Critique of Pure Reason*, trans. by Norman Kemp Smith (New York: Saint Martin's Press, 1965), p. 29.

[113] For a discussion of Christian virtues, including charity, in relation to Stoic and Enlightenment alternatives, see Stanley Hauerwas and Charles Pinches, *Christians Among the Virtues*. I suspect that Hauerwas and Pinches would find my remarks on disconsolation, especially on immortality, rather more Stoic than Christian.

CHAPTER 6

Is Isaac our neighbor?

After these things God tested Abraham. He said to him, "Abraham!" And he said, "Here I am." He said, "Take your son, your only son Isaac, whom you love, and go to the land of Moriah, and offer him there as a burnt offering on one of the mountains that I shall show you." So Abraham rose early in the morning . . .

Genesis 22:1–3

. . . those who believe are the descendants of Abraham.

Galatians 3:7

The sacrificial system is virtually worn out, and
that is why its inner workings are now exposed to view.

René Girard[1]

INTRODUCTION

"Is Isaac our neighbor?" This question captures the tension between two Christian commandments, to love God unreservedly and to love the neighbor as oneself (Matt. 22:37–40). It also captures the tension between two books by Søren Kierkegaard, *Fear and Trembling* and *Works of Love*. In *Fear and Trembling*, Kierkegaard's pseudonym Johannes de Silentio characterizes Abraham as willing to act on an absolute duty to God and thereby to suspend ethical obligations to other human beings. The "dutiful" action is the sacrifice of his beloved son Isaac following God's direct order. In *Works of Love*, Kierkegaard enjoins us to will the good for others by making "the eternal" (duty to God) the middle term in human relations. This "dutiful" willing embodies an agapic love that relativizes all erotic and philial preferences and "builds up" the neighbor for her own sake. Such upbuilding, when truly Christlike, accepts suffering and death for the other's good.[2]

---

[1] Girard, *Violence and the Sacred*, p. 295.   [2] Kierkegaard, *Works of Love*, esp. pp. 58–72 and 199–212.

Does de Silentio's Abraham love Isaac in a way that the author of *Works of Love* (and we) could or should endorse? My answer in this chapter is: no. De Silentio's reading of Abraham only makes sense if the first love commandment can conflict with the second such that obedience to God can require murder of the neighbor. The unity of the love commands is a central message of *Works of Love*, however, and indeed of the Gospels themselves. (Matthew uses one and the same word, "*agape*," for both love for God and love for the neighbor.) The adoration owed God is distinguishable from the charity owed any creature, and the two love commandments of Matthew 22 are clearly lexically ordered. But Kierkegaard's own account of eternal love would seem to preclude directly killing an innocent like Isaac. The faithful are called to imitate Christ, but Christlike love typically embraces a *self*-sacrifice that eschews violence against the innocent: "This is my commandment, that you love one another as I have loved you. No one has greater love than this, to lay down one's life for one's friends" (John 15:12). So how can the God who is Love command a "teleological suspension" like that attributed to Abraham in *Fear and Trembling*? How, more generally, can we square Genesis 22, Matthew 22, and John 15?

One conceivable way is radically to reinterpret the literal meaning of Scripture. One might argue that the divine "command" of Genesis 22 comes not from the Deity but from the cultic religion of early Israel. God is not the middle term between the be(k)nighted Abraham and Isaac; primitive patriarchy is. As William Blake maintains, anachronistically: Abraham is the last of the "Druids," the end of the Hebrew line of child-sacrificers who would uphold a hierarchical social order by slaying the beloved son. *Pace* de Silentio, Abraham is to be admired not because he is willing to burn his son but because he is willing to substitute the ram. On a Blakean reading, it is obedience to a revelation of *self*-sacrificial love that moves Abraham to surrender paternal hegemony and refuse to murder. That revelation comes from his own poetic imagination.

The problem with the Blakean move, of course, is that it obliges us to do real violence to the Biblical text. The passage in Genesis does in fact say, "God tested Abraham . . ." For this reason, a third alternative to both the de Silentian and the Blakean views seems called for. Fully articulating such an alternative is beyond the scope of this chapter, but I can gesture toward it by noting the shortcomings of its competitors. As cogent as a Blakean analysis is, for instance, it fails to uncover the *eternal means* whereby violent other-sacrifice is transmuted into compassionate self-sacrifice. The emphasis is on Abraham's own emergent sensibilities with little or no place for revelation and grace as superhuman categories. More specifically, a Blakean analysis is insufficiently attentive to the possibility that God's "command" is real but nonliteral, redemptive but rhetorical. I find this possibility particularly compelling, since it takes up Kierkegaard's suggestions (pseudonymous and nonpseudonymous) that indirect communication is employed by God. As Johannes Climacus observes: ". . . no practitioner of the maieutic art can more carefully withdraw himself from the direct relationship, than God . . . And why is God elusive? Precisely because He is the truth, and by being elusive desires to keep men from error."[3]

My central thesis, then, is that God's "command" in Genesis 22 that Abraham sacrifice Isaac is disconsoling irony, not abusive tyranny. The "command" actually empowers Abraham to abstain from bloodletting by bringing his conscience to a crisis, a crisis that requires a new understanding of divine love. In the new dispensation, Abraham learns that God "desire[s] mercy, not sacrifice" (Matt. 9:13; see Hosea 6:6). I defend this thesis as the best way to square two basic normative commitments: (1) that the Genesis narrative of Abraham and Isaac, like the Bible generally, is regulative for Christian theology and ethics, and (2) that religious and moral duty, like the two love commandments, do not finally contradict one another. By showing that both Johannes de Silentio's and William Blake's exegeses of Genesis 22 are, by themselves, inadequate, I hope to build the case for my "ironic" alternative in which God's "command" schools Abraham *away* from infanticide. (God would not have Abraham be a slave but rather a son; the question is in what sonship consists.) Blakeans lose sight of (1), thus neglecting the role of divine imperatives in transforming human life; while Kierkegaard's pseudonym de Silentio loses sight of (2), thus inviting us to think of human life as dilemmatic or genuinely absurd. My alternative reading is inspired most directly by a third normative commitment: (3) that the kenotic love manifest in the cross of Jesus Christ is the key to resolving moral and religious conundrums, the fulfillment of Abraham's legacy.

This chapter focuses on a painting as well as texts, but all tell the story of the *font et origio* of the Western religious self. In Abraham, we see the

---

[3] See *Concluding Unscientific Postscript*, trans. by David F. Swenson and Walter Lowrie (Princeton: Princeton University Press, 1968), p. 218. Kierkegaard echoes Climacus's comments, under his own name: ". . . the grace of God does not express itself in the way a person would like to understand it but speaks in a way that is more difficult to understand." See "To Need God Is a Human Being's Highest Perfection," in *Eighteen Upbuilding Discourses*, ed. and trans. by Howard and Edna Hong (Princeton: Princeton University Press, 1990), pp. 301–302.

impulse to sacrifice another for God's sake transformed into the willingness to sacrifice oneself for another's sake. This evolution I take to be
one of the underlying dramas common to Hebrew and Christian Scripture. Abraham's willingness to surrender absolute authority over Isaac,
to deny himself the ancient paternal identity, marks him as the captain
of charity and the embodiment of a new brand (a distinctively Biblical
brand) of righteousness, where the strong attend to the weak on equal
terms. This attention is at once free and abetted by grace, at once a
disconsolation and a perfection of power.

I. GENESIS 22: THE TRADITIONAL VIEW AND ITS PROBLEMS

Genesis 22 begins with the naming of the father of the faith, a naming
closely tied to a command to sacrifice his beloved son. The self-conscious presence of Abraham ("Here I am") is linked with the compul-
sory absenting of Isaac ("Take . . . go . . . offer . . . "). How are we to
understand this connection between the identity of the father and the
offering of the son? Kierkegaard is notorious for emphasizing, in his own
voice, the categorical character of fidelity to the Heavenly Father. Other
creatures are to be loved as oneself, but they are not due worship. In
relation to God, in contrast, one is to hold nothing back: "A man should
love God in unconditional *obedience* and love him in *adoration*."[4] Some
read Genesis 22 as teaching this same lesson, that one must be willing to
surrender anything, including persons dear to you, before God. Father
Abraham must not prize even the promised Isaac above obedience to
Yahweh. The God-relation trumps moral relations between human
beings, even the special bonds between parent and child; and nothing
God requires of a creature can be called unjust or unkind, for God is the
utterly sovereign Creator to whom everything is owed.[5] Thomas
Aquinas states the position with admirable clarity: "God is Lord of
death and life, for by His decree both the sinful and the righteous die.
Hence he [like Abraham] who at God's command kills an innocent man
does not sin, as neither does God Whose behest he executes: indeed his
obedience to God's commands is a proof that he fears Him."[6] The place
of the creature is simply to obey, not to question why.

There is undeniable piety in this view. De Silentio's *Fear and Trembling*
is an effort to appreciate the sizeable depths of such a perspective in

---

[4] Kierkegaard, *Works of Love*, p. 36.
[5] For a discussion of this general point, see my "Is God Just?," in *Faith and Philosophy*, vol. 12, no. 3
(July 1995): 393–408.   [6] Aquinas, *ST*, II–II, Q. 64, art. 6, *ad* 1.

which the supreme power and majesty of God radically subordinate creatures and creaturely relations, however beloved. Christ himself says, "Whoever comes to me and does not hate father and mother, wife and children, brothers and sisters, yes, and even life itself, cannot be my disciple" (Luke 14:26). And this may seem consistent with the suggestion that any consideration that God extends to human beings, including not requiring burnt offerings of their children, is pure grace. This may appear to be the case, at any rate, after the Fall of the original parents into sin. Faithful Abrahams must always be willing to kill Isaacs; indeed, we all now *deserve* to be burned alive on the altar of the righteous Yahweh.

For all its supposed theocentricity, there are at least three related problems with this position. First, the traditional "pious" reading would seem to rob creation (including human beings) of any intrinsic worth or sanctity. There are no finite needs or interests or rights or values that the Deity is inclined, much less bound, to respect for their own sakes. It is no longer intelligible, therefore, why the God of Genesis should have called creation "good." Second, the position would seem to corrupt individual consciences. God's authority seems to flow from a cavalier and inscrutable power rather than from an essential benevolence. Thus the veneration of a homicidal Abraham leaves persons worshipping might rather than goodness. Third, and most important, the "pious" view would seem to evacuate God's own *agape* of any meaningful content. God seems capable of commanding anything at all with sublime indifference, hence He becomes the perfect martinet, entirely unprincipled. We are back with Plato's Euthyphro and a potentially perverse Deity.

So how may we understand the legacy of Abraham's sacrifice without valorizing sheer force or placing obedience to God at odds with merciful service to the neighbor?

II. POETICIZING MERCY: BLAKE ON THE COMMAND AS PRIMORDIAL RELIGION

William Blake's tempera work, *Abraham and Isaac* (1799–1800; figure 3), is a powerful reversal of the way we usually think of Genesis 22. We tend to picture Abraham as being willing to sacrifice his son at God's direct command, but only regretfully. We imagine Abraham, the loving patriarch, all the while hoping that God will provide a way out, and we share in his joy when God in fact supplies the ram. Even a "de Silentian" reading of Abraham's faith as absurd rather than merely resigned – as

Figure 3. *Abraham and Isaac, c.* 1799–1800, by William Blake (Yale Center for British Art, Paul Mellon Collection).

paradoxically believing both that Isaac is the child of promise through whom God will bless the nations and that Isaac must be killed for God's sake – leaves us with a tender old man obedient to God but happy to spare his son once the wherewithal for doing so has been discerned. This conception of the father of the faith is not Blake's, however.

Blake gives us an Abraham who is yet to resolve his ethico-religious quandary, who still straddles (both physically and morally) the two alternatives of animal and human sacrifice, *even after he is aware of the presence of the ram.* In his description of the painting, Raymond Lister contends that "[t]he bearded Abraham looks upwards with an expression of thankfulness, one outstretched hand on the ram, the other poised on the altar and holding a sacrificial knife."[7] But this is not how Abraham actually appears. Blake's Abraham does have one hand on the ram while the other (holding a knife) rests on the pyre, but his face is somber, even anguished. There is no sign of thankfulness. With his head upturned to his father, the nude and diminutive Isaac gestures excitedly toward the ram, seeming to entreat the clothed and massive Abraham to

[7] Lister, *The Paintings of William Blake* (Cambridge: Cambridge University Press, 1986), no page number.

take this nonhomicidal option. Yet Abraham himself is ambivalent, still standing immobile as if crucified on the horns of a dilemma. He does not look down at Isaac but up to heaven, disconsolate.

Whereas the sin of Ham was to look unabashedly on his father's nakedness (Noah's guilt and shame), the potential sin of Blake's Abraham is to *refuse* callously to see his son's nakedness (Isaac's innocence and vulnerability). Abraham is said to love his son (v. 2), yet he is still inclined to take Isaac's life. This is the vexing core of this rich text: a genuine love that is nonetheless directly homicidal. Blake captures this tension by depicting Abraham as momentarily self-absorbed. Such self-preoccupation is a failure of care, if "caring is always characterized by a move away from self."[8] But why such conflict in the paradigm of Hebrew love?

Again, Blake's Abraham hesitates even after he is aware of the ram. The red cloud in the upper right of the painting is sometimes interpreted as the angelic presence, informing Abraham of the animal given by God and telling him not to kill his son. Yet Abraham is still tempted to engage in human sacrifice. The difficulty is *not epistemic*; it is not mere knowledge of the availability of an alternative sacrifice that settles the deep issue here. For Abraham literally feels the ram beside him but continues to struggle with two minds (and hearts) about what to do. The problem is *not intellectual but volitional*; a creative act of will is required, a decisive turning away from the letting of human blood, but the father pauses. Blake's picture moves one to conclude that, on some level, Abraham *wants* to take Isaac's life. Abraham is drawn to infanticide, however equivocally, not out of hatred or simple bloodlust but precisely because he loves Isaac and deems him to be the most precious sacrifice he can offer to a sovereign God.[9] (Abraham "loves" Isaac – the Hebrew root is *"aheb"* – but he would worship God.) This sympathy for the abominable is the troubling implication of Blake's thesis that Abraham was among those who wielded "the Druids['] golden Knife."[10]

It is not the Heavenly Father's lethal command that is the source of pathos but rather the ambivalence of the father in the flesh, Blake

---

[8] Nel Noddings, *Caring*, p. 16. Noddings's discussion of care is very helpful, though I would take exception with her analysis of *Fear and Trembling* (pp. 43–44, 98) for too readily identifying de Silentio with Kierkegaard.

[9] See Jon D. Levenson, *The Death and Resurrection of the Beloved Son: The Transformation of Child Sacrifice in Judaism and Christianity* (New Haven and London: Yale University Press, 1993), p. 21.

[10] Blake, *Jerusalem*, plate 27, in *The Complete Poetry and Prose of William Blake*, ed. by David V. Erdman (New York: Anchor Books, 1988), p. 172; see also p. 171. Harold Bloom avers that "Blake's 'Druidism' is the primordial religion of human sacrifice, and therefore equivalent to all natural religion whatsoever . . ." See his "Commentary" in *The Complete Poetry and Prose*, p. 952.

suggests. To embrace this thesis is to revive an ancient understanding of Genesis 22 and to begin to read much of Scripture in a distinctive (though not a new) way.[11] It is to identify the central drama of the text as *temptation*[12] instead of trial, to construe Abraham's "faith" as at least as much a matter of *self-overcoming* as of piety. This is not to say that Blake was a naturalist. He did identify God with creatures, as well as equate the gospel with liberation of humanity's poetic imagination;[13] but he did not endorse materialism, much less legitimize all *de facto* human practices. It is doubtful that Blake has room for truly transcendent divine commands, but his depiction of Abraham implies that an immanent *moral* power would draw him into a deeper love of human life rather than test him with an arbitrary order.

One rather distasteful Blakean possibility is to imagine that Abraham is drawn to a scapegoating of Isaac. Jon Levenson has argued that, in spite of the prophetic attack on child sacrifice by Jeremiah and Ezekiel and the eventual cessation of the *practice*, the roots of infanticide as a theological *ideal* continued to run deep in Hebrew (and later Christian) culture. The literal sacrifice of the first-born son was once considered a pious means of honoring God and/or expiating the sin of the father – cf. Micah's "Shall I give my firstborn for my transgression, the fruit of my body for the sin of my soul?" (6:7) – and the symbolic reenactment lives on.[14] Though Isaac is not Abraham's first-born, he is the first fruit of Sarah's womb and the preferred son of his father. Abraham may be thought to benefit personally from the binding of Isaac, therefore, in

---

[11] The construal of the Biblical story such that the original idea of sacrificing Isaac is Abraham's rather than God's has several precedents. Some rabbinical commentaries offer the same basic hypothesis. See David Pailin's "Abraham and Isaac: A Hermeneutical Problem Before Kierkegaard," in *Kierkegaard's Fear and Trembling: Critical Appraisals*, ed. by Robert L. Perkins (University, AL: The University of Alabama Press, 1981), esp. the discussion on page 17 of Bayle's *General Dictionary, Historical and Critical* (1734).

[12] Gerhard von Rad calls Genesis 22:1–19, "The Great Temptation" (*Anfechtung*), even as John Calvin refers to it as "the patriarchal temptation." But von Rad defines "temptation" as "a pedagogical test which God permits men to endure in order to probe their faith and faithfulness." See von Rad, *Genesis: A Commentary* (Philadelphia: The Westminster Press, 1972), pp. 237–239. I use the word "temptation" in its more everyday sense to describe a situation in which one sees (or begins to see) the wrongness of an action but inclines to do it anyway out of weakness or perversity.

[13] Blake writes in *The Marriage of Heaven and Hell*, plate 16: "God only Acts & Is, in existing beings or Men"; similarly, he says in *Jerusalem*, plate 77: "I know of no other Christianity and no other Gospel than the liberty both of body and mind to exercise the Divine Arts of Imagination." See *The Complete Poetry and Prose*, pp. 40 and 231.

[14] Levenson, *Death and Resurrection*, p. 55, writes: "That the impulse to sacrifice the first-born son never died in ancient Israel but was only transformed is hardly surprising. For the special status of the oldest boy continued to be a point of great significance in the society and of noteworthy resonance in its law."

finding relief from guilt (e.g., over having pushed Sarah into near adultery). This reading is highly speculative, however.

It may be that it is not so much personal gain that tempts Abraham to be willing to slay his son Isaac as, paradoxically, the stability of the nation of Israel which the son will help sire. But the key issue I want to raise in the shadow of Blake's painting is: how may *God* be thought to benefit from the *Akedah*? What could an omniscient God learn from testing Abraham? How could an omnibenevolent God be so unjust as to order the sacrifice of an innocent child? These familiar questions must occur to us, even if they seem not explicitly to occur to the narrator of Genesis 22. It is often averred and just as often denied that in the story of Isaac we see, not God's command of child sacrifice, but His rejection of it: God supersedes human sacrifice by supplying a ram as substitute offering. Yet Blake's work suggests a more interior reading of the story in which conscience overcomes the human impulse to sacrifice another person not simply by displacing it onto an animal but by transmuting it into the willingness to sacrifice oneself.

The eloquent sequel to the passage quoted from Micah is:

> He has told you, O mortal, what is good;
> and what does the Lord require of you
> but to do justice, and to love kindness,
> and to walk humbly with your God? (6:8)

This question may also be addressed to Abraham: what does the Lord require of you? The breakthrough awaiting Abraham's decision is a deeper understanding both of fearfulness and its proclivity to violence and of charity and its remedy for that violence. The moment depicted by Blake involves the painful reform of Abraham's character, not just the abandonment of external acts of homicide. There is, in fact, no clear distinction here between Abraham's enduring identity and his contingent aims and actions; his very soul, as well as that of his son, is at stake on Mount Moriah. A sacrifice is called for in the name of a finer love, but it is a *self*-sacrifice: Abraham must die to his own ancient cultic instincts rather than kill Isaac. Abraham must sacrifice sacrifice in order fully to realize himself as a creature of conscience. To become the "father of the faith," he must not only forego bloodletting but accept a crucifixion of his identity as (1) *paterfamilias* with unlimited power over his son and as (2) founder of a great nation with unlimited power over his subjects. The first feature may tempt him to sacrifice Isaac to expiate his sins, but, more importantly and plausibly, the second feature may tempt him to sacrifice any innocent party in the name of the chosen people, the state of Israel that is to spring from his loins. The first temptation is the voice of Molech, the second the voice of Caiaphas (cf. John 11:49–50).

Abraham must ask himself: in what does sovereign power consist? Michel Foucault has written that

[f]or a long time, one of the characteristic privileges of sovereign power was the right to decide life and death. In a formal sense, it derived no doubt from the ancient *patria potestas* that granted the father of the Roman family the right to "dispose" of the life of his children and his slaves; just as he had given them life, so he could take it away.[15]

If tyranny is the state of absolute injustice, the refusal by the powerful to be bound by any norms or rules in dealing with the relatively power-less,[16] then the "Druidian" Abraham is a familial tyrant. In Blake's painting, however, we see the moment of auto-tyrannicide in which Abraham surrenders the *patria potestas* and binds himself to respect his child's life. This binding is not itself the work of justice, as then under-stood, but of love; charity is the goad that revolutionizes Abraham's self-understanding, and Blake lets us see Abraham directly, pining for the afflatus that will transform his heart and stay his hand. His willing-ness to sacrifice his son must become a willingness to surrender his absolute sovereignty as father, even though that sovereignty has been the erstwhile bulwark of archaic social order.

Blake would also revolutionize our conception of Isaac, for the latter is no longer the bound and passive accepter of his father's designs but rather an agent of moral advance.[17] "The binding" in the story is now centrally that of Abraham rather than of Isaac; the son challenges the father *for the father's sake*. The standard exegetical line on Abraham (partially echoed by Lister) has a seemingly cavalier Yahweh demand of a righteous man that he kill his pliant son, only to rescind the "unjust" demand in the nick of time thereby eliciting the man's gratitude and the son's relief. But Blake's vision of grace as channelled through Isaac (unclothed but unashamed) is arguably much closer to the essence of true charity. It is also a subtler view of the constructive purposes to which youthful rebellion may be put than one that would praise Isaac for sheer quietism.[18] Blake's Isaac respects parental authority but does not simply

---

[15] Foucault, *The History of Sexuality*, vol. I, p. 135.

[16] See Agnes Heller, *Beyond Justice* (Oxford: Basil Blackwell, 1987), p. 15. [17] As Lister notes.

[18] As R.D. Laing observes, "When family relations are no longer harmonious, we have filial children and devoted parents." See his "Violence and Love," in *Counter-tradition: The Literature of Dissent and Alternatives*, ed. by Sheila Delany (New York: Basic Books, 1971), p. 358.

acquiesce to the potential abuse of it; his love and active defense of his own life highlight the *limits* on self-sacrifice. It would be abominable for Isaac to despise himself and so indulge his father's assault, however much he is rightly in awe of his parent. But if there is any abomination about, it is Abraham's, not God's or Isaac's, in Blake's view.

Isaac is often described as "the type of Christ," but though there are profound similarities, there are also palpable differences. Both "sons" are candidates for sacrifice, most obviously, and the image of Isaac's carrying the wood for his own pyre atop Moriah (v. 6) directly anticipates Christ's bearing his cross to Golgotha. In addition, Isaac's asking his father "[W]here is the lamb for a burnt offering?" (Gen. 22:7) distantly intimates Jesus's asking his Father if He might not "let this cup pass from me" (Matt. 26:39). But the salient distinction is that Christ knows in advance that he is the lamb to be slaughtered and still acquiesces: "yet not what I want but what you want" (Matt. 26:39). Christ freely accepts his suffering and death while Isaac is kept in the dark; in Blake's painting, in fact, Isaac actively seeks to avoid his immolation. Unlike Isaac, Christ is not an initially unwary victim but a willing self-sacrifice, and his demise is intended not to placate divine wrath but rather to quiet the human violence that flows out of fear or a murderous sense of one's own righteousness. Correlatively, while Abraham ambivalently wills to sacrifice his son for "the Father's" sake, the New Testament God kenotically sacrifices His son (His very self) for humanity's sake.

I must be careful not to overstate the Blakean case against Abraham. A father who is willing to kill his son, either as a testimony to the father's power or as a scapegoat for his own sins, seems horrific. Why not *condemn* Abraham, then, at least prior to his conversion? Our sympathy is much more fully engaged than this because Abraham is required to make a truly taxing leap of faith. What he must surrender – the awesome mortal authority of the father over the son – is *perceived* by him to be of profound value, and not only to himself. In reforming himself, he is revising the received paradigm of fatherhood and thus performing a valuable service for future generations ("the nations"). The reformation does not come easily, however, and it is not at the time morally unambiguous. There would be little pathos if what had to be overcome were antecedently regarded by Abraham, as well as by us, as a personal vice or a social injustice. But this is not how things stand; Abraham does not (yet) understand himself as a sinner. The problem for Blake's Abraham, to repeat, is not the epistemic one of determining whether there is an alternative to sacrificing Isaac – he knows that the ram is available – but the moral one of establishing which choice is better and then actually acting on it.

We perceive Blake's Abraham as tempted by blood, and so he is; but from his own vantagepoint, he wrestles with the implications of freely undermining what has heretofore sustained order and integrity in his household and in society at large. Others have depended on him as their head, as the one who defines them as subordinate but who is also responsible for their welfare. And this is what makes Blake's patriarch a powerful moral figure: he is sincerely ambivalent about the good of ceasing to be the familial equivalent of Leviathan.[19] We can identify with his inward struggle, moreover, even though we imagine ourselves to be largely on the other side of it. We are supposedly "liberated" from such family hierarchies, but the allure of the absolute sovereign with unqualified power lives on. It promises a stable peace, internal to the home and to the self, though at a terrible cost to respect for individuals. To see the sparing of Isaac as a decisive moral advance is not to deny the courage and simple will-power involved in Abraham's self-sacrifice.

Still more general lessons can be drawn from the story of Abraham and Isaac when interpreted along the lines suggested by Blake's picture. I read the story as, most fundamentally, a parable about love and justice, about how love may transform a limited or nonexistent conception of justice into something higher. I begin with the assumption that human sacrifice was once acceptable among the ancient Israelites. The unabashed directness with which God is said to command Abraham to make a burnt offering of Isaac suggests a standing homicidal ritual. And David P. Wright straightforwardly asserts that "[t]he Israelites practiced this type of worship [child sacrifice] from about 735 B.C. until about 575 B.C."[20] The practice seems based on the profound authority accorded to paternal power – God's and, by analogy, Abraham's. There was a time, apparently, when a Hebrew father held the power of life and death over his children, even as God the Father had absolute provenance over the created order. What God had made He could properly destroy, and so too with the patriarch in so far as he was an agent of and symbol for the Almighty. ("Abraham" literally means "the [divine] Father is exal-

---

19 Blake's patriarch actually has more power over life and death than Hobbes's sovereign, in as much as the latter is bound by the law of nature that makes self-preservation the highest principle, one that no one can be forced to abdicate in their own case.

20 David P. Wright, "Molech," *Harper's Bible Dictionary*, ed. by Paul J. Achtemeier (San Francisco: Harper and Row, 1985), p. 646. This claim is supported by *The New Standard Jewish Encyclopedia*, ed. by Geoffrey Wigoda (New York: Facts on File, 1992), p. 668.

ted."[21]) So Israelite justice was partially defined by an unquestioning deference to the magisterial, ordering power of the F/father. Only a revolutionary conception of divine mercy could trump such traditional justice.[22]

If Kierkegaard's pseudonym Vigilius Haufniensis takes the prohibition in the Garden of Eden to be Adam *himself speaking*,[23] Blakeans take the "command" in Genesis 22 to be Abraham speaking *to himself*. In denying that the command to sacrifice Isaac could come from a loving God, however, is not a Blakean overly poeticizing the text? Is Blake not limiting God's authority and refusing to take Genesis 22 on its own terms? Aharon Agus has lately claimed:

> It would be trivial to suppose that we are being told [in Genesis 22] how Israel, in its "spiritual infancy," came to the realization that human sacrifice is abhorrent . . . The frightening demand made of Abraham is the demand to give up everything. It has nothing to do with the pagan custom of child-sacrifice . . . and it is the deaf listener to biblical tradition who hears that dissonant chord in the straightforward story.[24]

Blakeans can only read these words as reactionary backlash. It is worth remembering that the original covenant with Abraham was, by definition, a promise extended by a superior, paternal power to an inferior, filial one. Hereby a deep ambivalence entered into the Hebraic self-image. Although the covenant was a gracious guarantee of material prosperity and divine concern to Abraham and his descendants, it also served to highlight their vulnerability and dependency. The steadfastness of God's love, but also the irresistibility of God's power, are symbolized, most graphically, by God's instruction that every male be circumcised. The sign of God's "everlasting covenant" (Gen. 17:7) was to be marked in "the flesh" (17:11) and to involve the letting of blood. (Abraham himself was circumcised to illustrate his relation of sonship to

---

[21] This is the RSV's translation; the NRSV interprets "Abraham" to mean "the [divine] ancestor is exalted." See *The New Oxford Annotated Bible*, ftnt. p. 20.

[22] An anonymous reader has objected that Abraham was allegedly raised in Ur of Chaldea, where child-sacrifice apparently was not part of ritual practice, thus he was not breaking on Moriah with traditions that formed his own religious/moral sensibilities. But even if Abraham was not brought up in the ways of infanticide from his youth, he still had to struggle to depart from them as part of his later identity. Perhaps it took an erstwhile outsider, someone already called by God into a new land, to make the prophetic "migration" from organized violence. One recalls, in a similar vein, Freud's provocative claim that Moses was an Egyptian; see *Moses and Monotheism*, p. 16 and *passim*.

[23] See *The Concept of Anxiety*, ed. and trans. by Reidar Thomte in collaboration with Albert B. Anderson (Princeton: Princeton University Press, 1980), p. 47.

[24] Agus, *The Binding of Isaac and Messiah: Law, Martyrdom, and Deliverance in Early Rabbinic Religiosity* (Albany: State University of New York Press, 1988), pp. 2–3.

the Father.) Circumcision is a rather mixed blessing, a painful mini-sacrifice of the newborn son by the father or by a rabbi as agent of both God and the father. The call to Abraham to sacrifice Isaac may be seen as the law of circumcision writ large or taken to extremes. Blake asks if the call is symptomatic of our desperate desire to sacrifice the flesh for something larger than ourselves: God, country, family.

Abraham's obedience to God's putative call by no means indicates a lack of affection for his son. We are told explicitly that Abraham loves Isaac (22:2), as de Silentio emphasizes, and for Abraham to be ordered to kill his child of promise is to have undeniable violence done to his parental instincts – to "test" him (22:1). But the action is nevertheless tempting in being an affirmation of the hierarchical order of things. Especially if seen as an expiation for his own transgressions against the Heavenly Father, Abraham's scapegoating of Isaac reaffirms and there-by sets right the relative power relations governing the universe: God over fathers in the flesh, fathers in the flesh over their sons (not to mention wives and daughters). Abraham's sacrifice would both partici-pate in and perpetuate this inegalitarian scheme, from which he both suffers and profits. (It is significant that, in the NRSV, Isaac's dear but subordinate status as "son" is referred to no less than thirteen times in nineteen verses.) The sacrifice of Isaac would, in short, do justice as the Hebrews at that time understood it; it would give God His due, His pound of filial flesh, in return for withholding hearth and nation from chaos.

The point for a Blakean of the Genesis story, however, is that Abraham's initial conception of God's way with the world (and hence of an earthly father's proper way with his children) is badly flawed. Ab-raham is not to be admired because he is willing to kill Isaac but because he eventually turns away from the traditionally "just" practice of infan-ticide as incompatible with love for the defenseless. It is indeed difficult to imagine that God wants him to slay his son, but it is harder still for Abraham to accept that God's love is unconditional and unmerited, and thus that the covenant requires no paternal bloodletting. In order to know God's *'hesed*, Abraham must forego the false consolation of vio-lence and punitive "justice" generally. It is not the "obedient" harshness toward his son, nor even the free acceptance of the ram, that is the decisive "leap" for which Abraham is to be remembered and venerated. It is Abraham's sacrifice of himself, of his identity as omnipotent father, that is the decisive manifestation of the kenotic dimension of agapic love. It is not the binding of Isaac but the unbinding of his own ritual conscience that delivers Abraham from a *thanatos* masquerading as righteousness.[25]

Of course, interpreting love of neighbor to preclude a divine mandate to murder is not uncontroversial. The sentiment from Agus, quoted above, is not idiosyncratic. Both Gerhard von Rad and E.A. Speiser would also object to a Blakean reading. Speiser writes:

Certainly, the object of the story had to be something other than a protest against human sacrifice in general, or child sacrifice in particular – an explanation that is often advanced. To be sure, the practice is traced to Israel's neighbors . . . Yet here the subject comes up indirectly, as something not normally expected, and all the more terrifying because demanded by God himself. More important, the sacrifice is characterized at the outset as unreal, a gruesome mandate to be canceled at the proper time.[26]

But, once more, one must ask: can God really issue an "unreal" and "gruesome" call for the direct killing of an innocent? Is not such a pandering Jehovah a contradiction, a hard paradox? Divine love is often iconoclastic, and we cannot anticipate in detail all that God may ask of us; but unswerving faith is given to a *righteous* Lord, after all, not to brute force or saturnine will. Augustine held that, given general facts of human psychology, the direct killing of a human being even in self-defense carries with it a morally brutalizing motive, a "lust" for created things.[27] The same may be said, with even more plausibility, for the sincere *intention* directly to kill the *innocent*; however supposedly good its consequences, such an intention is always tainted by hatred. So how could a God who is Love and who would conform creatures to His own Image mandate this killing, or even knowingly elicit the intention?

A central Blakean contention is that there can be no good purpose

---

[25] Fate moving a son ineluctably to kill his father is the pinnacle of Greek tragedy (Oedipus), while faith moving a father freely to spare his son is the paragon of Jewish religion (Abraham). In sparing Isaac, rather than himself, Abraham foreshadows the triumph of Gospel over Law. The law of sacrifice of the first-born son is supplanted by the gospel of parental suffering, which, in turn, makes a new law possible. With respect to American civil law, Ronald Dworkin notes that "the law does not generally require people to make a sacrifice in order to save the life of another person" but that "parents are invariably made an exception to the general doctrine because they have a legal duty to care for their children." See Dworkin, *Life's Dominion* (New York: Alfred A. Knopf, 1993), pp. 109–110. Is it far-fetched to thank father Abraham for helping to establish as a matter of "jural love" (Greenlee), the convergence of love and justice, what once required an extraordinary suffering and self-sacrifice?

[26] Speiser, trans. and commentator, *The Anchor Bible: Genesis* (Garden City, New York: Doubleday 1964), p. 165.

[27] Augustine, *On Free Choice of the Will* [395], trans. by Anna S. Benjamin and L.H. Hackstaff (Indianapolis: Bobbs-Merrill, 1979), bk. 1, chap. V, pp. 10–13.

behind the putative divine command to sacrifice Isaac. The "suspension of the ethical" called for fails the normative teleology test. The command to burn Isaac is transgressive, but it is not goodness-generating. For Blakeans, to repeat, Abraham's supposed trial is in fact a temptation; the command comes not from a transcendent God but from Abraham and his primordial context. The "miracle" described in Genesis 22 is not the instruction to bind Isaac but the sensitizing of Abraham's own conscience: "In families we see our shadows born. & thence we know / That Man subsists by Brotherhood & Universal Love."[28] We are not dealing in the Biblical text with a "utility monster" that maximizes results though it threatens to take innocent life, for no merciful Power would employ hateful means to a benevolent end. "Can that be Love, that drinks another as a sponge drinks water?"[29]

III. ABSOLUTIZING OBEDIENCE: DE SILENTIO ON THE COMMAND AS PARADOXICAL RELIGION

Any Blakean reading of the *Akedah* must come to grips with Johannes de Silentio's brilliant commentary in *Fear and Trembling*. There are three important convergences between a Blakean account and that of Kierkegaard's pseudonym, de Silentio. First, both accounts accent the fact that Abraham must resolutely choose rather than reason or gather empirical data:[30] he faces a situation rendered problematic not by lack of objective information but by the need to redefine himself subjectively. He has previously understood himself as the upright servant of God yet also as the privileged father of Isaac, through whom the nations are to be blessed; and this identity is now disturbed by new and unexpected circumstances, ambiguously engineered by a Higher Power. Second, both accounts see Abraham as essentially isolated. His choice must be made alone, divorced from social institutions and fixed standards shared with others, since these institutions and standards are exactly what are at issue. There is no partnership here. Third, both accounts highlight the limits of ethics, defined in terms of universal rules and extant institutions. Abraham must decide both his and Isaac's fates, and this decision requires a daunting self-renunciation. The fate of traditional ethics

---

[28] Blake, *The Four Zoas*, "Night the Ninth," in *The Complete Poetry and Prose*, p. 402.

[29] Blake, *Visions of the Daughters of Albion*, plate 7, in *The Complete Poetry and Prose*, p. 50.

[30] Cf. de Silentio on faith with Blake on "perswasion": "Then I asked: does a firm perswasion that a thing is so, make it so? He replied. All poets believe that it does, & in ages of imagination this firm perswasion removed mountains; but many are not capable of a firm perswasion of any thing." See *The Marriage of Heaven and Hell*, plate 12, pp. 38–39.

rides, in turn, on just how this self-overcoming is understood. On these three points Blake and de Silentio agree.

For Blakeans, however, the chief problem with de Silentio's analysis is its assumption that Abraham's contemplated sacrifice is morally forbidden yet religiously required. If the Highest Power is love, Blakeans reason, then murderous sacrifice must also be ruled out by true religion. For Kierkegaard's pseudonym, "the ethical" forbids directly killing the innocent, while God may command it as an "absolute duty."[31] Blakeans contend, in contrast, that the killing of Isaac is much more likely to be licensed by "ethics" (construed as ossified social consensus) but prohibited by faith (construed as individual self-revelation). De Silentio insists the paradox of faith is that the singular is higher than the universal, that the individual's duty to God trumps any and all social mores. But one can accept this without agreeing that "[t]he ethical expression for what Abraham did is that he meant to murder Isaac; the religious expression is that he meant to sacrifice Isaac."[32] When de Silentio writes that Abraham's faith "makes a murder into a holy and God-pleasing act,"[33] this is a nonChristian author setting ethics and religion needlessly at odds. It is a radicalization of the vertical dimension of love, such that love of God virtually negates horizontal love of neighbor. Not only can God take innocent life, but individuals can be chosen as God's agents and obliged to do the same, however horribly. Thus does *agape* lose all content.

De Silentio is unable to imagine an alternative grounded in faith to this dilemmatic view of Abraham; as he frequently notes, he cannot make the leap. Yet a teleological suspension of the ethical that requires direct killing of the innocent is indistinguishable from a destruction of the truly ethical, for again a higher end is lacking. Or, conversely, if the higher end were present, then the ethical would not need to be suspended. Writing from a religious point of view, Kierkegaard (but not de Silentio) can hold that what is forbidden by Christian ethics must also be forbidden by Christian faith, because God is the author of both. When de Silentio writes, "The absolute duty [to God] can lead one to do what ethics would forbid, but it can never lead the knight of faith to stop loving,"[34] he sets ethics and faith too completely in opposition. De Silentio cannot make the leap out of a regnant moral paradigm and seems not a little fascinated by a raw power that must be obeyed. The

---

[31] Kierkegaard (Johannes de Silentio), *Fear and Trembling*, ed. and trans. by Howard and Edna Hong (Princeton: Princeton University Press, 1983), p. 70.
[32] Ibid., p. 30. [33] Ibid., p. 53. [34] Ibid., p. 74.

power is sacred rather than profane, Jehovah rather than the Hegelian state, but the pseudonym still seems latently authoritarian.[35]

For Christians, the two great love commandments ground all morality and piety: "'You shall love the Lord your God with all your heart, and with all your soul, and with all your mind.' This is the greatest and first commandment. And a second is like it: 'You shall love your neighbor as yourself.' On these two commandments hang all the law and the prophets" (Matt. 22:37–39). God, unlike creatures, is to be worshipped; to think that the two commands can be fully at loggerheads, however, is to make God schizophrenic. The likeness of the two dimensions of love rules out radicalizing one at the expense of the other, even as their lexical ordering rules out poeticizing one into the other.

A chief source of distress for Abraham is that the divine promise (that, through Isaac, Abraham will be the father of many nations) seems incompatible with the divine command (to make of the adolescent Isaac a burnt offering). One way to arbitrate the dispute between Blake and de Silentio on how to alleviate this distress is to examine at more length the differences between de Silentio and Kierkegaard himself. Why isn't the "knight of faith" described in *Fear and Trembling* a deluded and potentially murderous monster? I do not think that de Silentio can adequately answer this question, but this is not to say that Søren Kierkegaard cannot.[36]

IV. KIERKEGAARD ON FAITH AS ABOVE REASON AND ETHICS, NOT AGAINST THEM

It is common to think of Kierkegaard and his pseudonyms as either irrationalists or immoralists or both,[37] but above all it would be *impious* to think that God actually commands murder or that religion contradicts ethics. The alternative is a faith that begins with an *apparent* contradic-

[35] In *Existentialism, Religion, and Death*, p. 13, Walter Kaufmann declares: "Kierkegaard revered Abraham for the unflinching authoritarianism and the ethic of utterly blind obedience that he attributed to him, however mistakenly. He admired Abraham for not looking at the content of the commandment to sacrifice his son, and for not concluding that it was not divine and could not come from God." As I argue below, these remarks are a cogent critique of Johannes de Silentio but not of Kierkegaard.

[36] Walter Lowrie reminds readers of this point in his "Translator's Notes" to *Fear and Trembling* (Princeton: Princeton University Press, 1970), ftnt. 27, p. 265.

[37] See, for instance, Alasdair MacIntyre, "Søren Aabye Kierkegaard," in *The Encyclopedia of Philosophy*, vol. IV (New York: Macmillan and the Free Press, 1972); Roger Poole, *Kierkegaard: The Indirect Communication* (Charlottesville and London: University Press of Virginia, 1993); and Stanley Rosen, *Nihilism: A Philosophical Essay* (New Haven and London: Yale University Press, 1969).

tion – one that reason alone cannot decipher – and then by virtue of a *veridical* paradox achieves a higher understanding. De Silentio appreciates the seeming absurdity facing Abraham but is unable to move beyond resignation to faith's higher understanding. He fails to see how Abraham's teleological "suspension" of the ethical can be a matter of love *transforming* justice, not merely a trumping or justified infringement of an otherwise cogent concept of justice that remains nominally intact but a paradigm shift in which the definition of justice itself changes in the light of a better appreciation of God's love. A false or limited conception of ethics and human nature is overcome, not by deontic logic but by an act of will and a purging of emotion. An act of will is called for since there are no "neutral reasons" to appeal to in "leaping" from one conception of ethics to another. Such a paradigm shift looks "absurd," in the sense of antinomical, to someone (like de Silentio) still on this side of it. But Kierkegaard himself has made the leap, as *Works of Love* and other books attest.

Kierkegaard tends to see the higher forms of religion (Judaism and Christianity) in terms of truths that outstrip reason but not passion (e.g., the Incarnation). Unlike de Silentio, therefore, he can construe Abraham as also facing a veridical paradox. The veridicality can only be seen with the eyes of faith, however. To anyone who has not made the leap of faith, there is no way to explain how Genesis 22 does not amount to a hard antinomy. But for Kierkegaard, the mature believer, Abraham's paradox is above reason rather than against it, even as Abraham's action is an elaboration of ethics rather than a violation. As Kierkegaard says in his *Journals*,

What I usually express by saying that Christianity consists of paradox, philosophy in mediation, Leibniz expresses by distinguishing between what is above reason and what is against reason. Faith is above reason. By reason he understands, as he says many places, a linking together of truths (*enchainement*), a conclusion from causes. Faith therefore cannot be *proved*, *demonstrated*, *comprehended*, for the link which makes a linking together possible is missing, and what else does this say than that it is a paradox. This, precisely, is the irregularity in the paradox, continuity is lacking, or at any rate it has continuity only in reverse, that is, at the beginning it does not manifest itself as continuity.[38]

Kierkegaard goes on in the sequel to this passage to declare that faith is able to "solve" the "divine paradox" of Christ,[39] and it is but a small step to imagine an analogy to the Hebrew Abraham's "solving" the paradox of Isaac. As Anti-Climacus, the superlative Christian and the pseudonym

---

[38] Kierkegaard, *Journals and Papers*, vol. III, no. 3073, pp. 399–400.   [39] Ibid., p. 401.

closest to Kierkegaard own personality, writes in *The Sickness Unto Death*: ". . . salvation is, humanly speaking, utterly impossible; but for God everything is possible . . . The believer has the ever infallible antidote for despair – possibility – because for God everything is possible at every moment. This is the good health of faith that resolves contradictions."[40]

Faith (re)solves paradoxes, but, again, de Silentio is without this key that Abraham and Kierkegaard possess. Having not made the leap of faith, de Silentio is like someone who is unaware of leap-year day coming every four years and thus cannot understand how someone can be twenty-one having had but five birthdays.[41] He lacks the crucial principle that would clarify how Abraham's paradox is truth-telling, how Abraham can be true to both God/religion and Isaac/ethics. And what is that principle? Some commentators have held that the (re-pressed) premise in Genesis 22 is resurrection. For his part, Kierkegaard clearly believed in some form of immortality as the destiny of the faithful. He might argue, then, in his own voice, that what makes it possible for Abraham to hold the divine promise and the divine command in a passionate unity is faith in the post-sacrifice resurrection of his son. Even if God requires Isaac's life, Kierkegaard might allow, it will be restored in a way consistent with Abraham's fathering many nations; Abraham need only trust in the Lord's veracity and power to perform a miracle.

Whether or not Kierkegaard was attracted to it,[42] there are two problems with this reading. First, resurrection is nowhere explicitly mentioned in Genesis 22. Some think it is implied in verse 5 – when Abraham says to his "young men," ". . . the boy and I will go over there; we will worship, and then we will come back to you" – but in fact we do not see Isaac return with his father from Moriah. Isaac seems to disappear, only to reappear in chapter 24. Second, even if Isaac had been sacrificed then reanimated, this would not change the fact that Abraham had to be willing directly to kill the innocent. The issue remains whether divine love can be the source of a command directly to

---

[40] Kierkegaard (Anti-Climacus), *The Sickness Unto Death*, ed. and trans. by Howard and Edna Hong (Princeton: Princeton University Press, 1983), pp. 38 and 39–40.

[41] I take the example from Willard Van Orman Quine, "The Ways of Paradox," in his *The Ways of Paradox and Other Essays* (Cambridge: Harvard University Press, 1977), p. 1.

[42] In his *Journals*, Kierkegaard connects immortality with sacrifice, but not with Abraham: "On the whole, immortality first appeared with Christianity, and why? Because it requires that a person shall die to the world. In order to be able and willing to die to the world – the eternal and immortality must remain fixed. Immortality and dying away correspond to each other." See *Journals and Papers*, vol. II, ed. and trans. by Howard V. and Edna H. Hong, assisted by Gregor Malantschuk (Bloomington: Indiana University Press, 1970), no. 1952, p. 381.

take an innocent human life, whether one calls this "murder" or "sacrifice." For, again, what could be the point of an omniscient God's ordering Abraham to burn Isaac?[43] Let me, at last, answer that question.

A KIERKEGAARDIAN CONCLUSION: THE CROSS AS KEY

"One can deceive a person for the truth's sake, and (to recall old Socrates) one can deceive a person into the truth."[44] Blake is a lover of Christ and the Hebrew prophets, as well as a master of irony, yet Kierkegaard adds to the Blakean reading of Genesis 22 a sensitivity to how God might "deceive" creatures into virtue by means of "dreadful" prohibitions (to Adam and Eve) or "homicidal" commands (to Abraham about Isaac). Kierkegaard is too Kantian to extol the heteronomy of brute force blindly obeyed, but he is too orthodoxly Christian to extol abstract autonomy or artistic self-creation.[45] His *via media* is to describe how divine love engineers individuals' inwardness nonrationally and theonomously. Vigilius Haufniensis points out how God's command not to eat of the tree of knowledge (Genesis 2) helps precipitate what it forbids: the prohibition awakens self-knowledge (dread) in Adam and Eve, though it does not necessitate sin (despair). Johannes de Silentio is rather quiet about how God's command to sacrifice Isaac (Genesis 22) might forbid what it requires, for how can a loving Deity demand the holocaust of the innocent? But Kierkegaard himself opens us to the prospect that God does not intend Abraham literally to carry out the "command."

---

[43] My argument in chapter 5 that any correspondence between *agape* and immortality is, at most, very loose, is largely inspired by the examples of Abraham and Job. Abraham's decision to spare Isaac has little or nothing to do with whether Isaac is immortal, even as Job's reconciliation with God has little or nothing to do with his receiving new children in the end to replace those previously lost. See my "Must Job Live Forever?," p. 30.

[44] Kierkegaard, *The Point of View for My Work as an Author*, trans. by Walter Lowrie (New York: Harper and Row, 1962), p. 39.

[45] See Ron Green, *Kierkegaard and Kant: The Hidden Debt* (Albany: State University of New York Press, 1992), esp. chap. 3. See also Green, "Enough Is Enough!: *Fear and Trembling* Is Not About Ethics," in *Journal of Religious Ethics*, vol. 21, no. 2 (Fall 1993): 191–209. Green argues in the latter piece that, although Abraham is not a sinner, his "teleological suspension of the ethical" is symbolic of the problem of human sin and points the way to divine grace, a grace that forgives sin by suspending justice and transcending ethics generally. *Pace* Green (p. 203), I would contend that God's graciousness toward Abraham is not first of all a suspension of God's justice, but rather a leavening transformation of Abraham's own. For an excellent review of the rabbinical commentaries on the *Akedah* and its vindication of God's righteousness, see Green, *Religion and Moral Reason: A New Method for Comparative Study* (Oxford: Oxford University Press, 1988), chap. 4. Green's discussion (pp. 100–101) of divine mercy prevailing over divine justice is edifying, but it needs to be brought more directly to bear on *human* mercy and justice.

De Silentio writes: ". . . it is a duty to love one's neighbor. It is a duty by its being traced back to God, but in the duty I enter into relation not to God but to the neighbor I love"; Kierkegaard, in contrast, ties neighbor-love inextricably to a relation to God: ". . . in love to find one's neighbor a person must start with God and in loving his neighbor he must find God."[46] God's tactic in Genesis 22 may seem brutal, but it becomes intelligible if seen as an ironic way of moving Abraham to leap out of an abominable ritual. Sounding rather de Silentian, Kierkegaard writes in *Works of Love*:

. . . God you are to love in unconditional obedience, even if what he demands of you may seem to you to be to your own harm – yes, harmful to his cause. For the wisdom of God is not to be compared with yours, and God's governance is not, in duty bound, answerable to your prudence.[47]

Note, however, that Kierkegaard preserves the distinction between an apparently harmful command and a really harmful one. God's commands may "seem" harmful, and God's governance outstrips rational human categories, but none of this settles whether a divine command is literal or ironic. This is the determination of faith, but Biblical faith worships a God who is both good and powerful. Faith is schooled by love, moreover, and "a man's love mysteriously begins in God's love."[48]

"God tested Abraham" for God's sake, to see whether Abraham would be obedient to a withering command? No, for this makes God an ignorant schemer. (God did not test Abraham the way the Pharisees tested Jesus.) But if "God *tempted* Abraham" for *Abraham's* sake, hoping that he would feel pity and be *un*willing to kill, this upbuilding is compatible with Kierkegaard's definition of neighbor in *Works of Love*: "*Neighbor* is what philosophers would call the *other*, that by which the selfishness in self-love is to be tested."[49]

An angel of the Lord says, in Genesis 22:12, "Do not lay your hand on

[46] *Fear and Trembling*, p. 68; *Works of Love*, p. 141. See also *Works of Love*, p. 94: "Truly, only by loving one's neighbor can a man achieve the highest, for the highest is the capability of being an instrument in the hand of Governance."

[47] Kierkegaard, *Works of Love*, p. 36.   [48] Ibid., p. 27.

[49] Ibid., p. 37. Compare Kierkegaard's comments on God's demand that Abraham "wound selfishness at the root," in *For Self-Examination*, ed. and trans. by Howard and Edna Hong (Princeton: Princeton University Press, 1990), p. 79. This brief discourse, written under Kierkegaard's own name, does not say that the divine demand is ironic, but it makes clear that God is engineering Abraham's self-overcoming rather than showing off God's own hegemony. Even the thought "that before God a man is always accounted guilty" throws a person back on the conviction that God is love rather than on a despair in which God is an incomprehensible cunning. I take the comment on guilt, that is, to be a provocative formula for the primacy of divine love over human justice. See Kierkegaard, *Gospel of Sufferings*, trans. by A.S. Aldworth and W.S. Ferrie (London: James Clarke & Co., 1955), esp. pp. 69–71.

the boy or do anything to harm him; for now I know that you fear God, since you have not withheld your son, your only son, from me." This does indeed seem to praise Abraham for being willing to sacrifice Isaac, but it is crucial to note that it is not the Lord Himself speaking here. God provides the ram, it appears, but the angel is a genuinely intermediary figure who is not simply to be identified with either God or Abraham. (That said, it is tempting even for nonBlakeans to associate the angel with Abraham's conflicted conscience.) Most importantly, the angel calls to Abraham a second time, after Abraham has *spared* Isaac, and this time the angel quotes the Lord directly with: "Because you have done this, and not withheld your son, your only son, I will indeed bless you . . ." (22:16–17). How are we to understand the "this?" My thesis is that Abraham's not withholding Isaac from God is a different act from his not withholding him from the angel, from the surrounding Israelite community, or from Abraham himself. The angel notwithstanding, I interpret God's blessing to be motivated by Abraham's showing mercy to his son. From God's own point of view, that is, Abraham's not withholding his son is a matter of his being willing to see Isaac as a vulnerable child of God, worthy of respect and protection, rather than his being willing to slaughter him as the (earthly or heavenly) father's personal property.

De Silentio goes wrong in taking the "command" of Genesis 22 to be a *direct* communication from God, something God wants Abraham to act on. Blake, in turn, fails to see how the "command" to sacrifice Isaac might actually come from God but be an exercise in *indirect* communication. Failing to consider a real but ironic Deity, both fail to see that the divine "command" is an indirect indictment aimed at "a prior irruption of inwardness"[50] that schools Abraham in a more egalitarian, even a selfless, love. Without an appreciation of how human love of God and neighbor are both to be based on God's kenotic love of humanity, we are in danger of seeing the two love commands of Matthew 22 as unrelated or actually opposed.[51] We then risk, like de Silentio, construing religion (whole-hearted fidelity to God) as the enemy of ethics (rational justice to human beings). Or we risk, like Blake, constructing religion out of our own good will for our fellows, with "God" as a

---

[50] This phrase is from *Concluding Unscientific Postscript*, p. 219.

[51] Philip Quinn has recently argued for such a potential dilemma at the very root of Christian ethics. See Quinn, "Tragic Dilemmas, Suffering Love, and Christian Life," pp. 171, 179, and 181. See also his "Moral Obligation, Religious Demand, and Practical Conflict," and his "Agamemnon and Abraham: The Tragic Dilemma of Kierkegaard's Knight of Faith," in *The Journal of Literature and Theology*, vol. 4, no. 2 (July 1990): 181–192.

metaphor for poetic genius. Both of these options forget, to put it anachronistically, that Isaac is a neighbor for whom an Incarnate Redeemer died.

When Christ freely sacrificed his life for others, at the behest of his Father, Abraham's legacy came to full fruition. The cross, intersection of the vertical and horizontal axes of love, is the key to solving Abraham's paradox: *to show mercy to the vulnerable creature is to obey the righteous Creator.* If the strong would be children of God, they must spend themselves for the weak, even as God empties Herself for all. At the core of Biblical love is a refusal to turn directly against the life of an innocent, indeed "the willingness to stick it out agapically even to the edge of doom."[52] This is the lesson ironically intimated in Genesis 22, made explicit in John 15, and reiterated by Kierkegaard in *Works of Love*. With some form of child-sacrifice seemingly a perennial temptation, we would do well to learn the lesson anew – with God's help.

[52] The phrase is Jeffrey Stout's, in correspondence of August 17, 1998.

CHAPTER 7

Love on the cross

"Eloi, Eloi, lema sabachthani?"   Mark 15:34

Do nothing from selfish ambition or conceit, but in humility regard
others as better than yourselves. Let each of you look not to your
own interests, but to the interests of others. Let the same mind be in
you that was in Christ Jesus, who, though he was in the form of
God, did not regard equality with God as something to be ex-
ploited, but emptied himself, taking the form of a slave, being born
in human likeness. And being found in human form, he humbled
himself and became obedient to the point of death – even death on
a cross.   Philippians 2:3–8

INTRODUCTION: OPTIMISM AND PESSIMISM

I begin the body of this final chapter with a quote from George Orwell,
seemingly as kenotic and disconsoling as Saint Paul's epistle to the
Philippians:

The essence of being human is that one does not seek perfection, that one *is*
sometimes willing to commit sins for the sake of loyalty, that one does not push
asceticism to the point where it makes friendly intercourse impossible, and that
one is prepared in the end to be defeated and broken up by life, which is the
inevitable price of fastening one's love upon other human individuals.[1]

Orwell's lines raise two related but distinct questions: (1) Is the world
known to be structured in such a way that unfortunate circumstances or
malevolent agents can compel one to sin, and (2) What should we do in
the face of doubts about the goodness or harmony of the world and

---

[1] Orwell, quoted by Samuel Haynes in "Not Just Another Apocalyptician," a review of *Orwell: The
Authorized Biography* by Michael Sheldon, in *The New York Times Book Review* (November 3, 1991), p.
30.

about the avoidability of personal guilt?[2] Question (1) asks how fragmented our moral existence can be determined to be, while (2) asks how disconsolate, not to say despairing, we should be in reaction to any actual or apparent fragmentation. The former is a matter of metaphysics and epistemology, the latter of moral psychology and faith.

With respect to question (1), there are two general schools of thought. The first may be called "Axiological Optimism." It holds that certain values or principles can always be shown to outweigh others, so one can have a rational certitude about the moral coherence of the universe. Reality is structured such that we have at least one blameless course of action in any circumstance, and this can in principle be demonstrated. Any confusion or hesitation we may experience here is due to ignorance, weakness of will, or perhaps perversity of will. Either we don't know what to do, or we know and want to do the right but still can't move ourselves to act accordingly, or we are so warped as knowingly to reject goodness as such. In all three cases, however, the limitation is within us, not in the external situation; all moral difficulties are traceable to ambiguity, lack of fortitude, or abomination, none of which is the same as a genuine moral dilemma.

A moral dilemma, as defined in chapter 5, is a situation in which, through no antecedent fault of your own, you can't avoid real guilt. Real guilt is, by definition, blameworthy; and being blameworthy ought to elicit remorse. In a dilemma, then, no possible knowledge or will-power or liberation would deliver you from appropriately feeling remorse. You would suffer significant moral loss, become vicious and blameworthy, no matter who you are, how you behave, or what you achieve. You would be faced with extreme moral tragedy, not just moral perplexity or frustration; at the limit, you would have to betray charity itself. To repeat, however, an axiological optimist claims to know that matters never come to this.

Two further contrasts are in order, by the optimist's lights. First, (a) remorse should be distinguished from nonmoral regret. To feel nonmoral regret over an action is to judge it, all things considered, an unhappy necessity. A doctor may feel such regret over the decision to amputate a patient's gangrenous leg, for instance, even after full consultation and with informed consent. There is no guilt in this case, though there is genuine loss; one would not, under the circumstances, have

---

[2] I thank Jeffrey Stout, in correspondence of August 17, 1998, for helping me to see the importance of this distinction, as well as for suggesting some of the implications of strong *agape* with respect to it.

acted differently. Remorse, in contrast, implies self-reproach; one wishes one had not done what one did, not just because it was costly but because it was morally wrong. Second, (b) real guilt should be distinguished from a subjective *feeling* of guilt. Feeling guilty may often be inescapable, given our psychological makeup, but "real guilt" refers to the objective culpability that a wise third party would ascribe to another agent under conditions of knowledge. If I blame myself morally in ways that are unjustified, a wise judge will encourage me to seek therapy for the irrational feeling rather than to reproach myself and repent an immoral deed. This encouragement recognizes that even sincere and highly tenacious feelings of guilt can be mistaken.[3]

In light of (a) and (b), Axiological Optimism can be defined as the view that, however empirically universal they may be, moral remorse and objective guilt can be shown to be not practically necessary. Moral rigor is a real and demonstrable possibility, and this reassures the optimist of the rational intelligibility (if not the ultimate profitability) of virtue.

The second school of thought on the metaphysical and epistemological issue, which I will call "Axiological Pessimism," argues that true dilemmas can be shown to arise. The ethical pessimist does not simply worry over or wonder about moral disorder; he or she asserts it as provable. The sources of human meaning and obligation can be known to be multiple, conflicting, and finally incommensurable.[4] In the extreme, the gallimaufry of hopelessly competing goods leaves us with dilemmas in which we cannot but sin against some dear person or binding principle; obligations to promote mutually exclusive ends sometimes entail culpability no matter what one intends, does, or accomplishes. Indeed, incompatible loyalties are sometimes *equally* weighty; thus we are left with no way to avoid dereliction of some duty of justice or some call of love. Because we cannot avoid real personal guilt, it is as though interpretation of our character, action, and effects oscillates

---

[3] Cf. Herbert Morris, "Nonmoral Guilt," in *Responsibility, Character, and the Emotions*, ed. by Ferdinand Schoeman (Cambridge: Cambridge University Press, 1987). Morris argues against "the hegemony of moral guilt" (p. 222) and in favor of a form of guilt that is real and reasonable but morally blameless. Morris's interesting analysis of "unjust enrichment" and "vicarious guilt" notwithstanding, I prefer to speak of "nonmoral regret" or "subjective shame," finding the idea of morally blameless guilt to be unintelligible. It is important to note, however, that even if one allows as inevitable some form of nonmoral guilt (e.g., for base thoughts not acted upon), this would still not amount to a *moral* dilemma – since such a dilemma requires unavoidable *moral* guilt.

[4] Cf. Thomas Nagel, "The Fragmentation of Value," in *Moral Dilemmas*, ed. by Christopher W. Gowans (Oxford: Oxford University Press, 1987).

between moral justification and causal explanation, between reference to freedom and to necessity. We are trapped by fate but nevertheless morally blameworthy, Agamemnons all.

Consider a woman whose alcoholic husband abuses their young children. She feels bound by the marriage vow to remain with her husband through hard times, but she also feels she must attend to the safety and well-being of her offspring. She may well judge herself guilty if she leaves home or if she stays. Consider a lawyer whose professional obligation zealously to defend her client (whom she believes to be guilty) comes into conflict with the normal obligation to promote justice. She is sworn to uphold due process but worries that she is being complicitous in a crime. Consider a young Christian male wrestling with whether to register for the draft or to listen to his pastor who claims that Christians ought to be nonviolent. He may feel a patriotic urgency to defend the common good from which he daily benefits, but he may also be haunted by Jesus's injunction to turn the other cheek. The pessimist maintains that we should see these and similar cases as involving inevitably dirty hands.

With respect to question (2), concerning moral psychology and faith, there are again two general schools. Axiological optimists tend to endorse "Natural Facility." They reason that because reality is determinably user-friendly, so to speak, we may set our ethical aim quite high and hold individuals to categorical standards of action and intention. Doubts about the goodness of the world and the perfectability of humanity are misplaced; "ought" implies "can," so there is no excuse for not treating everyone as fully accountable for virtue. Axiological pessimists, in turn, tend to underwrite "Social Minimalism." They conclude that because reality is determinably hostile or absurd, we should surrender traditional ideals of purity and resign ourselves to the inevitability of dirty hands. Classical aspirations to moral wholeness are cruel and should be replaced by ironic attitudes toward our multiple roles and humorous attitudes toward any power that promises to unify those roles. Pessimism does not directly entail Minimalism, even as Optimism does not immediately translate into Facility, but they are easy allies.

Throughout this book, I have advocated a single virtue, charity, as having moral primacy. Yet I have also argued that this virtue must be weaned away from traditional claims to certainty, invulnerability, immortality, and irresistible grace. Should the priority of agapic love move one to reject the metaphysical possibility of dilemmas, or should the disconsolation of that same love lead one to accept this possibility?

Obviously, if putting charity first is to be adequate, it must be able to respond to Axiological Pessimism in *some* fashion. If the moral life is demonstrably futile or contradictory, no good or goal can serve as a metavalue. In addition, if *agape* is to be strong, it must be able to fend off Social Minimalism. If irony and irreverence are at the heart of our moral psychology, religious piety is impractical. These hypothetical observations do not settle anything, of course; they merely ask anew our two basic questions about metaphysical structures and psychological reactions.

In part I of this chapter, I look at the relevant work of two contemporary philosophers. The first, Michael Walzer, denies the *possibility* of moral rigor by affirming the real existence of moral dilemmas. He contends that on occasion we cannot avoid dirtying our hands, in an ethical sense. The second, Susan Wolf, questions the *desirability* of a rigorously moral life. She focuses her discussion on the psychology of moral saints, asking: should we *want* to lead a saintly existence even if we could? Her answer is "No," it would be too one-dimensional and dispiriting. In part II, I consider in detail how a strong agapist would respond to Walzer and Wolf. In part III, I examine two contemporary theologians, Helmut Thielicke and Gilbert Meilaender, who defend the impossibility and perhaps (also) the undesirability of moral rigor. The most vexing prospect suggested by the theologians is the Orwellian idea that love itself sacrifices moral innocence in order to serve others.

My conclusion is that the strong agapist should affirm *neither Axiological Optimism nor Axiological Pessimism, neither Natural Facility nor Social Minimalism*. If the putative fragmentation of value cuts against any virtue's having practical priority, then strong *agape* will consider it unproven. For all its veneration of the power of love, however, strong *agape* is not what Isaiah Berlin rightly rejects as "a final solution" to all conflicts of value. Berlin is surely right in saying that "not all good things are compatible, still less all the ideals of mankind."[5] So the strong agapist resists a monism that reduces every good thing to one end or precept, even as she dismisses a foundationalism that claims perspicuous knowledge of the ways of the world. What she stumps for, in contrast, is the priority of love among genuine values and the steadfastness of love amid real doubts. The priority presumes metaphysical unity behind diversity, and the steadfastness provides psychological coherence in spite of ambiguity and conflict.

---

[5] Berlin, *Four Essays on Liberty*, p. 167.

Love does not console itself by beginning with observations of the
world, then deducing that it cannot possibly be dilemmatic even after
the Fall of humanity into sin. (This would be another dogmatic version
of the Argument from Design.) But neither does love conclude that
human lives are "bitched from the start," in Hemingway's words, and
thus that insouciance must replace charity. Rather, love starts with a
supreme confidence in the grace of God that sustains human beings in
crisis, then perseveres in willing the good for itself and others even to the
brink of hell. Nothing is permitted to override the will-to-love, nor to
move one to turn directly against the innocent, even when things look
darkest. (This is the psychological commitment behind "the Argument
to Design."[6])

To the extent that Social Minimalism prompts one to abandon the
quest for an exacting moral ideal, strong *agape* will find it falsely consoling (a too easy despair) rather than disconsoling. By the same token,
however, a Natural Facility that sees individuals as sublimely autonomous and self-sufficient is not true to experience. What is wanted is an
appreciation of human finitude wedded to a faith in something higher.
Orwell gestures towards this in the lines quoted above, but in recommending sin he contradicts his own aspiration to love. The Christian
finds a fully reliable example in Jesus at the height of his Passion – the
Jesus, who, though still perfectly loving, asked God why He had forsaken him.

I. THE PHILOSOPHICAL ANATOMY OF DILEMMAS: WALZER AND WOLF

It is a commonplace among modern moral philosophers that there is
friction between deontology and consequentialism. Deontologists
maintain that certain moral duties are absolutely binding regardless
of circumstances, while consequentialists look to maximize future welfare (defined in terms of pleasure, happiness, or some other criterion
of satisfaction) and thus their judgments are more open-ended. Practices such as torture and murder are usually thought by deontologists
to be intrinsically unjust and thus things we must never do. But under
rare conditions these practices may satisfy the criterion of bringing
about the greatest happiness for the greatest number or of avoiding a
comparable harm and thus, by the consequentialist's lights, be re-

---

[6] See Jonathan Wells, *Charles Hodge's Critique of Darwinism*, pp. 9, 93–101, and 215–223.

quired. Is it always possible to order these two basic intuitions? Can we always give priority to one over the other, or may they sometimes demand two contradictory actions with equal cogency? May the unavoidable guilt associated with moral dilemmas be the result of the right action irremediably conflicting with the best consequences? Opinions vary.

In a 1973 edition of *Philosophy and Public Affairs* dedicated to the topic "War and Moral Responsibility," Michael Walzer defends the thesis that genuine moral dilemmas may sometimes arise, while R.B. Brandt and R.M. Hare deny this possibility.[7] Walzer's account is especially interesting because of its frank thesis that political utility must sometimes "override" justice. Such cases do not merely represent unhappy duties, because cogent moral principles are not merely suspended but *violated*. Yet neither are they simple mistakes, for the violations involved are deemed proper under the circumstances. As Walzer puts it, "a particular act of government (in a political party or in the state) may be exactly the right thing to do in utilitarian terms and yet leave the man who does it guilty of a moral wrong."[8] Walzer contends that torturing a prisoner to save lives, although always a "moral crime," may at times be the thing to do. Hence the paradoxical notion of unavoidably "dirty hands."

In his 1977 book *Just and Unjust Wars*, Walzer goes even further. He contends that when a nation is confronted by a "supreme emergency" and its very survival is threatened by unjust attack (e.g., Britain at the start of World War II), the normal moral rules self-destruct. So great is the value of preserving the nation from catastrophe that the usual moral restriction against directly attacking noncombatants may have to be violated. Walzer emphasizes that the threat to one's own country must be both close and serious, and that in terror bombing the civilians of the enemy country one is guilty of "a kind of blasphemy against our deepest moral commitments."[9] There is no escaping the fact, however, that here mass murder is defended as an occasional political makeshift. Dirtier hands one could hardly imagine.

Gilbert Meilaender has suggested that, rather than morally *justifying* murder in the name of social utility, Walzer is concerned chiefly with the unhappy *necessities* faced by politicians, necessities that bear down on

---

[7] *War and Moral Responsibility*, ed. by M. Cohen, T. Nagel, and T. Scanlon (Princeton: Princeton University Press, 1974), pp. 3–82.
[8] Walzer, "Political Action: The Problem of Dirty Hands," in ibid., p. 63.
[9] Walzer, *Just and Unjust Wars*, p. 262.

them with brute force.[10] The prominence of necessity in *Just and Unjust Wars* is undeniable; the book is often a profound reflection on what it means to be coerced by circumstances. Nonetheless, Walzer's basic claim is moral rather than merely political. His thesis is that ethics is sometimes divided against itself, not just that ethics is occasionally trumped by an alien, communal fate. When faced with a supreme emergency, utility "overrides" deontology such that we *ought* to suspend the principle of discrimination and target civilians, even though this is a "kind of blasphemy." We are faced in this case not with pure fatalism, à la Oedipus, but rather with moral fragmentation in which we can pick, in some sense, our poison. Ethics, that is, is *internally* inconsistent; there can be a hopeless "tension between *jus ad bellum* and *jus in bello*," or between what Walzer has called "a rights normality" and "the utilitarianism of extremity."[11]

At the very least, one must say that, according to Walzer, we may be *both* compelled *and* obligated to violate justice in the name of the general welfare.[12] Paradoxically, it is meet and right to accept "the burdens of criminality"[13] when there is no other way to save one's people and their political traditions. As Walzer puts it:

> . . . it is not usually said of individuals in domestic society that they necessarily will or that they *morally can* strike out at innocent people, even in the supreme emergency of self-defense. They can only attack their attackers. But communities, in emergencies, seem to have different and *larger prerogatives*.
>
> . . . it does seem to me that the more certain a German victory appeared to be in the absence of a bomber offensive, the more *justifiable* was the decision to launch the offensive . . . Here was a supreme emergency where one might well be *required* to override the rights of innocent people and shatter the war convention.
>
> *Utilitarian calculation* can force us to violate the rules of war only when we are face-to-face not merely with defeat but with a defeat likely to bring disaster to a political community.[14]

Note the use of the words "morally can" and "justifiable." Meilaender takes the term "required" in the second quote "to point to the realm of

---

[10] Meilaender, in correspondence of March 4, 1993.

[11] Walzer, *Just and Unjust Wars*, p. 265; and Walzer, "Emergency Ethics," The Joseph A. Reich, Sr., Distinguished Lecture, no. 1 (Colorado: United States Air Force Academy, November 21, 1988), p. 11.

[12] Meilaender himself writes in "*Eritis Sicut Deus*: Moral Theory and the Sin of Pride," *Faith and Philosophy*, vol. 3, no. 4 (October 1986), p. 409: "An emergency is 'supreme' when it is both *morally* and *strategically* necessary to break the moral rule for the sake of the desired outcome."

[13] Walzer, *Just and Unjust Wars*, p. 260.   [14] Ibid., pp. 254, 259, and 268, emphases added.

necessity into which one has fallen when one must override the rights of the innocent."[15] But this fall is a *felix culpa*, for Walzer; he is recommending a particular action, however ambivalently and mournfully. As Walzer puts it, "men and women with dirty hands, though it may be the case that they had acted well and done what their office required, must nonetheless bear a burden of responsibility and guilt."[16]

When Winston Churchill targeted German civilians in 1939–1940, he did not remain morally innocent, according to Walzer; nevertheless, one is given the impression that Walzer would *fault* any leader who *refused* to kill noncombatants if this were the only way to defend his country against imminent, utter defeat at the hands of a barbaric aggressor. What else does it mean to call the defensive murder "indispensable," normally a probitive term? Admittedly, it is difficult to state Walzer's position exactly, but this is a function of his own ambivalence about which trumps: freedom or necessity, deontology or utility? He is a just war theorist, but only so far, when he writes: "The effect of the supreme emergency argument should be to reinforce professional [military] ethics and to provide an account of when it is permissible (or necessary) to get our hands dirty."[17]

A second challenge to Axiological Optimism, distinct from the foregoing, may be formulated. Whereas Walzer concentrates on the incompatibility of recognizably moral values, others perceive an antagonism between such values and *non*moral goods. It may be feasible, they reason, to live a consistently ethical (even a saintly) existence, but this requires a sacrifice of certain character traits and aesthetic enjoyments which makes it undesirable (even irrational). There are a number of positive ways to be which depart from, even preclude, an overriding desire always to be moral, whether this is defined in terms of virtuous character, just action, or best consequences. The cultivation of strong personal interests, talents, and relationships – from expertise at chess to depth of friendship – cuts against the selflessness required by constant attention to virtue, duty, and/or the common good. But such cultivation is part of a well-lived life; it represents an extra-moral dimension to existence (self-interest, broadly construed) that is irreducibly valuable for its own sake.

As Susan Wolf puts it, "a person may be *perfectly wonderful* without being *perfectly moral*."[18] Rather than being an impossible ideal, saintliness

---

[15] Meilaender, in correspondence of March 8, 1993.   [16] Walzer, *Just and Unjust Wars*, p. 323.
[17] Walzer, "Emergency Ethics," p. 16; the phrase "permissible (or necessary)" is used by Walzer more than once in this essay and sums up the admitted paradoxicality of his stance.
[18] Wolf, "Moral Saints," in *The Journal of Philosophy*, vol. 79, no. 8 (August 1982), p. 436.

is no ideal at all for Wolf; human life would be the lesser for it, less rich
and spontaneous, if we all sought moral perfection. She writes, "[M]oral
perfection, in the sense of moral saintliness, does not constitute a model
of personal well-being toward which it would be particularly rational or
good or desirable for a human being to strive."[19] On this view, moral
rigor is itself a kind of temptation. Wolf's point, again, is not that
dilemmas sometimes render the pursuit of virtue impractical, but rather
that the single-minded pursuit of virtue is unpalatable.

What might the strong agapist say in response to Walzer and Wolf
and the challenges they represent to rigorous moral aspirtion?

II. THE PRIORITY OF *AGAPE* TO MORAL PHILOSOPHY

For Christians, faith in God orders those ends (moral and nonmoral) in
whose service one acts or refrains from acting – including justice, utility,
and future human interests. Because of the Atonement accomplished by
Christ, Christians need not embrace works righteousness; in order to be
justified before God, believers need not "accomplish" anything temporal as an external product of action. Sanctification as growth in
holiness involves freely responding to God and both furthering God's
will and meeting humanity's needs, but no human achievement has
salvific significance. Thus Christian ethics tends to be suspicious of
strongly consequentialist claims.

Christian liberty does have content, however. If the life, death, and
resurrection of Jesus Christ set the pattern for human self-realization,
then self-preservation is not the supreme good (nor is self-denial) but
rather obedience to God and love of neighbor. To love God and
neighbor is, in fact, to promote self-perfection; such perfection does not
prevent suffering and loss – just the opposite – but it averts despair.
Trust in Christ implies confidence in God's sovereignty over history,
which in turn implies that Christians must not (and need not) do evil that
good might come. They need not fear the stranger and must not be
moved directly to harm the innocent, for example. Specifically, the
redemption and forgiveness made real by the cross of Christ precludes
affirming the Walzerian scenario of "supreme emergency" or "dirty
hands." Such an affirmation would be faithless.

Walzer lacks the ordering principle, the fourth dimension, that would
allow him to regulate character, action, and consequences so as to avoid

---

[19] Ibid., p. 419.

paradox and self-contradiction. The strong agapist, in contrast, finds this principle in agapic love empowered by the grace of God. Strong *agape* is not blind to the heterogeneity of moral and nonmoral goods, but heterogeneity is not the same as utter incomparability. There can be comparability of goods without literal commensurability, in part because of the priority of love. As a metavalue and thus a necessity for the substantive enjoyment of other goods, *agape* provides a unifying perspective that permits an intelligible balance of, and/or choice between, values. This perspective falls short of full commensurability, a single yardstick on the basis of which direct ranking is possible. Such ranking would only be feasible if all goods were reducible to or deducible from *agape*, but strong *agape* does not claim so much. It sees love as foundational to, but neither strictly identical with nor incorrigibly revelatory of, all other human desiderata.[20] There is, to repeat, a plethora of goods.

When understood in conjunction with the other theological virtues, especially hope, strong *agape* rules out asserting genuine moral dilemmas. An agapic theology of the cross is not a knockdown argument, however, based on logic or empirical evidence; it is, instead, an expression of the commitment to serve that grows out of encounter with a suffering God and empathy with vulnerable creatures. Metaphysical data paint a mixed picture of human problems and prospects, and no Christian ethic can fail to take with utmost seriousness the breadth and depth of human depravity. But love waits for neither external evidences of the harmony of the moral life nor internal evidences of its own innocence. Strong agapists accept that they cannot prove that the world is a moral cosmos rather than an amoral chaos, even as they acknowledge that they cannot be moral on their own steam. Since before Job's torments, human minds have wondered about the goodness of God and the point of finite existence, even as human hearts have not been up to the task of charity. The strong agapist simply assumes (or perhaps prays) that, in Shakespeare's famous words,

> Men at some time are masters of their fates:
> The fault, dear Brutus, is not in our stars,
> But in ourselves, that we are underlings.[21]

Neither social utility, personal interest, nor plain bad luck may ever override the obligation to love, for such an obligation is the highest

---

[20] The discussion of comparability vs. commensurability in this paragraph relies on Charles Larmore, "Pluralism and Reasonable Disagreement," a paper delivered at Yale University, April 8, 1993. Larmore does not relate the distinction to charity, however.

[21] Shakespeare, *Julius Caesar*, spoken by Cassius, act I, scene ii, lines 139–141.

expression of God's own holiness. And love never visits injustice upon the neighbor, even if the heavens (or the nation) tumble, since this would be to despise a fellow creature's life. To think that sin can compel us to hateful motive or murderous action is to think that the fall of humanity has completely thwarted God's desires for creation, the very definition of faithlessness. For a moral vision in which justice (defined as *suum cuique*) is the preeminent virtue, dilemmas may well appear unavoidable. Strong *agape* is convinced, however, that a calculating justice is neither the first word nor the last in our lives.[22] Something more must be called on to assure us that giving people (and nations) their due is not self-frustrating, that respecting both guilty and innocent life is not profligate. This something more is faith that in caring for the needy, forgiving the guilty,[23] refusing to murder enemy civilians, etc., agapic love embodies the highest virtue, one that undergirds and transcends but does not violate reciprocal justice.[24]

This is not a "proof" of Axiological Optimism, any more than it is a "disproof" of Axiological Pessimism. The very ideas of rational proof and disproof are internal to systems of appraisive axiology that strong *agape* would rise above. The strong agapist's insight is that even as an individual who always counts costs and puts self-preservation first will subvert his moral character, so a nation or people that claims supreme emergency and commits murder in its own defense will subvert international peace. Personal virtue and international society both require that

---

[22] The system of appraisive justice is incomplete, one might say, in ways roughly analogous to the incompleteness of mathematics, formal number theory. In 1931, Kurt Gödel demonstrated that in any formal system adequate for mathematics it is possible to construct an axiom that is neither provable nor disprovable within that system. This entails that the consistency of the system cannot be proved from within either; methods of proof, imported from outside the system, are required to show whether it is contradictory. (See J. van Heijenoort, "Gödel's Theorem," *Encyclopedia of Philosophy*, vol. 3, Paul Edwards, ed. (New York: Macmillan, 1967), pp. 348–349.) The thesis of strong *agape* is that one cannot prove the self-consistency of modern theories of justice, e.g., one cannot rationally demonstrate the impossibility of dilemmas like Walzer's supreme emergency, but one can appeal to a more ancient and "meta-" charity for the strength to carry on even so.

[23] "Forgiving the guilty" does not mean that one stands by and allows the wicked to have their way in the world; it implies, rather, that one never despises or hates them. Some wars are just, I believe, and even the plot to kill Hitler was compatible with agapic love for Hitler himself: it would have been better, for his sake and others', had he been prevented from becoming such a "successful" mass murderer. I discuss these matters in more detail in *The Priority of Love: Christian Charity and Social Justice* (forthcoming from Princeton University Press).

[24] As Miroslav Volf notes, "the will to embrace the unjust precedes agreement on justice." "If you want justice and nothing but justice, you will inevitably get injustice. If you want justice without injustice, you must want love." See Volf, *Exclusion and Embrace*, pp. 215 and 223. Volf speaks of the "'injustice' of God's grace" (p. 221), but this is meant to prompt us to "rethink the concept of justice" (p. 221) rather than literally to indict God for wrongdoing.

persons be nurtured and respected in ways not specifiable in terms of adjudicated interests, historical claims and counter-claims, alone. Reciprocity is not enough, and W.H. Auden speaks of both the English and the Germans (and later the Americans) when he writes in "September 1, 1939":

> I and the public know
> What all schoolchildren learn,
> Those to whom evil is done
> Do evil in return.[25]

Even in history's darkest moments, in contrast, the strong agapist refuses to return evil for evil, declines to murder in London or Dresden or Hiroshima or Belgrade – even to prevent other murders.

The inability of Walzer's account of political justice to put limits on what might be done to preserve justice itself suggests why terrorism, for instance, is such an intractable problem today. Without empathy for others and a basic honoring of the sanctity of all human lives, even unjust or burdensome or strategically "useful" lives, justice will license endless retaliation. Indeed, without love, there is no escape from "competing justices"[26] – Israeli vs. Palestinian, American vs. Russian, Serb vs. Croat. "Justice" may finally enjoin mass murder. Socrates considered it always better to suffer an injustice than to commit one, and harming another was always for him an injustice;[27] Christianity claims, more positively, that it is always mandatory to love, and that failing actively to support the neighbor is ultimately a betrayal of the God who created the neighbor in God's own Image. Some actions (e.g., terror bombing) and some states of character (e.g., hatred) are forever incompatible with the love of God that individuals are called to reflect in their lives. To embrace them would inevitably be to succumb to the sin of pride, the desire to transcend all personal limitations.[28]

In short, Christianity believes that, though human nature is fallen, a redemptive act (Christ) has made and continues to make love possible, even in the worst cases. This means, in turn, that we may never imagine ourselves compelled/required/forced/obliged/necessitated/or even permitted to hate. This is not to say, to reiterate, that we will always succeed in not hating or that Axiological Pessimism can be decisively

---

[25] Auden, *Selected Poems*, ed. by Edward Mendelson (New York: Vintage Books, 1979), p. 86.

[26] Volf, *Exclusion and Embrace*, p. 196.

[27] See Plato's *Crito*, in *The Last Days of Socrates*, trans. by H. Tredennick (Harmondsworth: Penguin Books, 1969), 49b8–d5.

[28] This point is made repeatedly by Meilaender in "*Eritis Sicut Deus.*"

refuted; it is only to say that, with grace, we can be confident in the capacity to put charity first. Christian confidence does not stem from faith in Natural Facility, but from the conviction that "God first loved us." "In the world you face persecution [RSV: have tribulation]. But take courage; I have conquered the world!" (John 16:33) "I am giving you these commands," says Christ, "so that you may love one another" (John 15:17). God never commands what God does not also first empower, even while leaving creatures meaningfully free.

May the strong agapist say, then, that human beings can never lose something of decisive moral import through no fault of their own? We are vulnerable to physical harm, to be sure, but can we be morally undone from without? The strong agapist holds that we may be spiritually *devastated* by another's cruelty or neglect, even to the point of being stripped of our capacity to love, but she has faith that we cannot be made *guilty* or *hateful* without our own voluntary (and culpable) cooperation. A child's moral agency may be deeply thwarted, as in sexual abuse; an adult's very sanity may be unravelled, as in torture. Thus strong *agape* says farewell to all spiritual invulnerability doctrines as unrealistic (chapter 5). But once we have reached our moral majority, responsibility is presumed to be radically individual and so "necessity" ceases to be an explanation or justification for vice.

The theological ethic I have outlined is not merely another form of pure deontology. Strong *agape* insists that we are always called to do the loving thing, but it does not deny the relevance of agent-character or action-consequence. Rather, it takes up aretology, deontology, and consequentialism into a higher unity. Doing what is right always supersedes achieving any *finite* good; but when the *ultimate telos* of human nature is understood to be communion with God, the question of ordering rightness and goodness becomes moot. The premise of faith is that the right and the good, moral duties and personal values, have been reconciled in Christlike love. There can be tradeoffs but no final contradiction between doing what is right and gaining or preserving what is truly good – including a virtuous personality – because salvation has been secured by the cross. To love in the midst of suffering is to know God, others, and oneself as they really are.

The cross secures salvation in part by revealing how love may accept self-sacrifice. The Passion of Christ has a performative as well as an epistemological dimension, however; it does not merely disclose a gracious pattern to be emulated but also makes possible that very spirit of God without which *agape* is humanly impossible. Two features of the

Passion are especially significant. First, it suggests that unearned suffering does not necessitate guilt, however harmful it may otherwise be: Christ experiences the dreadful absence of God ("*Eloi, Eloi, lema sabachthani?*," Mark 15:34), but he does not sin. Second, the Passion symbolizes the fact that unearned suffering freely accepted is redemptive rather than dilemmatic: Christ is afflicted but not damned, dies but is resurrected thereby reconciling the world with God and itself.

Accent on the redemptive power of suffering in no way minimizes the real pain and loss to which human flesh is heir. There will be tensions and tradeoffs between genuine human goods in this life, and some temporal losses may never be restored. (There may be no personal immortality.) But for Christian love, unlike Social Minimalism, this is not the end of the story. The consummation represented by the cross and Resurrection of Christ obviates, for strong agapists, any pure and permanent moral tragedy. This consummation is not a matter of heavenly reward or compensation; any morally acceptable account of a possible afterlife must be compatible with the highest virtue being its own reward, or else the motive for charity is tainted by self-seeking. Still, the life and death of Jesus vindicates the trust placed in *agape*, not by adding something extraneous to the life of love but by giving individuals more power to realize love itself.

In Mark 10:29–30, Jesus says:

"Truly I tell you, there is no one who has left house or brothers or sisters or mother or father or children or fields, for my sake and for the sake of the good news, who will not receive a hundredfold now in this age – houses, brothers and sisters, mothers and children, and fields with persecutions – and in the age to come eternal life."

If this implies the interchangeability or replaceability, in time, of dear persons who have been lost, then the sanctity of individual lives is denied. It is unkind, a false consolation, to see people as substitutable. If, in contrast, Jesus's words are meant to indicate the incalculable value of relation to God and the acceptability of any earthly sacrifice for the sake of that relation, then it is symbolically cogent. To say that those who suffer for the gospel will "receive a hundredfold now in this age" is a hyperbolic way of saying that with the good news of God's love, everything in this world is more than bearable, and that without the good news, nothing in this world is existentially good. As for "eternal life" in "the age to come," it is a blessed hope for those with faith, but neither a dogmatic certainty nor a fated destiny.

In affirming genuine but limited human freedom, strong *agape* rejects a fatalism of both evil and good. Losses in time are genuine, but any "unredeemable" losses will not be judged ineluctably to alienate their bearers from God. The victims of the Holocaust, for example, were afflicted but not necessarily corrupted. Though we know of no present person who is not guilty, strong agapists presume that ineluctable guilt is unproven (if not unprovable); similarly, though Christians trust that one past person did not sin, strong agapists presume that even Jesus's virtue was not necessitated (or necessitatable). Jesus's freedom before God is illustrated by his requesting in Gethsemane that the cup of self-immolation pass from him, as well as by his experience of abandonment anxiety atop Calvary. The request and the anxiety point to the *need* for responsible agency, even when liberty seems to have evaporated and God seems to have flown. When Jesus says ". . . not my will but yours be done" (Luke 22:42) and then goes on to accept sacrifice on the cross, he embodies the *reality* of loving agency.

What of the conflict of *nonmoral* ends with *agape?* Is it conceivable that a life of love is possible but undesirable, because various other worthy purposes are ill-served by it? Must I truncate my personality by sacrificing ego to conscience, temporal goods to eternal verities? If Christian love and self-interest were forever incompatible, this would entail a Wolfian rift between *agape* and a range of values dependent upon self-interest. Rejecting out of love the means necessary to secure an end requires, in effect, rejecting that end itself. But here too, theological premises make a critical difference.

If many theologians see Christianity as ruling out morality's demonstrably contradicting itself, still more see it also as ruling out morality's being palpably contradicted by self-interest. This compatibility thesis may take one of two forms. Either self-interest is itself counted a moral virtue, and one then falls back on the notion that morality is consistent; or self-interest is reckoned subservient to genuinely moral considerations, and one then looks up to the cross of Christ. On the latter view, the example and teaching of Jesus make love an absolute: an expression of God's holy will and a mandate for human imitation that trumps everything, including (apparent) self-interest, without however rendering other goods nugatory. Jesus appreciated the full range of human wants and needs – from food and shelter to compassion and friendship – yet he gave up his very life rather than stop loving.

It is one thing to give priority to virtue, quite another to belittle or to deny altogether nonmoral goods. Socrates repeatedly describes the virtues (justice, temperance, courage, piety, and wisdom) as the only things good in themselves. They cannot be misused and take radical precedence over the other classes of goods, which we may loosely identify as "nonmoral" (material, social, and intellectual goods).[29] For its part, Christian ethics is more incarnational. Strong *agape* may be non- or even anti-prudential when prudence is narrowly defined as pursuing temporal goals; but this is not the case when prudence encompasses ultimate felicity, i.e., *genuine* self-interest. In addition, a Christian conception of ultimate felicity (one based on the social activism of the Gospel of Luke and Acts, for example) will encompass both moral and nonmoral goods as genuinely valuable for their own sakes, even while subordinating the latter. Anything else would be to despise the wants and needs of incarnate human existence and, therefore, to hate the God who created that existence.

Strong *agape* does not translate into a Socratic self-sufficiency in which no externals are necessary for the acquisition or exercise of virtue. We require care from and for others to realize charity, and we may be thwarted in our development by other people and contingent circumstances (cf. chapter 4). Nevertheless, being contingently thwarted does not imply being made ineluctably guilty; only free agents can become guilty, and that must be by their own hand. For the strong agapist, a hard moral dilemma, in which one obligation must be culpably violated in order to meet another, is inconsistent with ethical monotheism and not a part of the disconsolation that Christian theology rightly accepts. We should always try to love; once personhood is achieved, any failure to love is our own fault, a lack of openness to grace; and to love is to fulfill the law, i.e., to meet all obligations. Because *agape* also supersedes all nonmoral goods, furthermore, there can be no utterly tragic choice between aesthetic fulfillment and ethical uprightness. Cultivation of artistic talent, nurturance of a romantic relation, and the like, are goods in themselves and may even contribute to the exercise of moral virtue; but it is never worth it to forsake *agape* in favor of such goods, for they will not in fact be appreciable in the absence of charity. To love God, oneself, and others is to be deeply realized as a human being, regardless of what one must sacrifice to do so.

Again, there can be conflicts between aesthetic and ethical goods, such that tradeoffs are unavoidable. One thinks of Paul Gauguin's decision to leave his wife and family and sail to Tahiti to find fulfillment

---

[29] See Plato's *Euthydemus*, trans. by W.R.M. Lamb (Cambridge: Harvard University Press, 1977), 281d2–e1; and *Crito*, 48c6–d5.

as an artist. (Gauguin's efforts to find peace in "unspoiled nature" – from taking youthful mistresses to departing for "primitive" islands – remind one of Hemingway.[30]) But this is not to say that *real guilt* is inevitable. To assert the priority of love is not simply to allow ethics to abrogate aesthetics, moreover, since love is essential to the balance of moral and nonmoral goods that makes for human flourishing. Love is concerned with preserving and enhancing *all* good things, to the greatest extent possible: with producing beauty, cultivating talent, keeping promises, etc. This means that reconciling self- and other-regard – more generally, aesthetics and ethics – is at the heart of love's project. One feels that Gauguin failed in this project – we all do, to one degree or another – but not that he *had* to fail.

Neither aesthetic geniuses nor moral saints require dirty hands. A saint is someone who enjoys being altruistic, who loves loving others, even given the hazards. His charity is not spotty or grudging. Put abstractly, the saint's self-regarding and other-regarding ends substantially overlap. There are authentic and inauthentic ways to try to bring about such "charitableness," however. One might repress or even seek to extinguish the self, thus making other-regard hegemonic. In this case, individuality becomes a sin and escape from personality the means and end of virtue. No self means no self-regarding concerns to conflict with attention to others. Yet this generates the kind of vapid and slavish "martyrs" to which feminists and Nietzscheans rightly object. It is a form of masochism, a perversion of *agape*. Alternatively, one might try to eliminate the other pole of the self/other contrast and go idealistic, seeing all of humanity as but a projection of oneself. Here individual identity is expanded to engulf the world and bring it under a single, self-referential project – such as will-to-power. The upshot of this, however, is a paternalism or megalomania in which other-regard is literally impossible. The "other" is then my invention and thus either unreal or, at best, my possession. Such solipsism must, in the end, be sadistic, a perversion of *eros* as well as *agape*.

A third possibility is to cultivate a lively sense of self, one with a rich history and set of commitments (aesthetic, ethical, and religious), and to seek to integrate this identity into concern for neighbors as equals. Mutual relation is the straightforward aim, and self-respect now becomes foundational for authentic respect for others. Sympathy is

---

[30] See Françoise Cachin, *Gauguin: The Quest for Paradise*, trans. by I. Mark Paris (New York: Harry N. Abrams, Inc., 1992), p. 67. Bernard Williams discusses Gauguin's case, somewhat fictionalized, in *Moral Luck* (Cambridge: Cambridge University Press, 1981), chap. 2; Williams is an ethical pessimist (p. 37).

thought to create a bond between two or more persons, even relative strangers; empathy may sustain remarkably intimate communions, as between spouses; but in all these cases there is unity within diversity, a "We" rather than a valorization of the "Thou" or the "I" alone. This is an approximation of charity, but it is still not quite the Christian form of the virtue. As I have emphasized in chapter 1, strong *agape* looks first to obedience to God and passionate service to the neighbor, rather than to self-cultivation, for its impetus.

It is this fourth option that invites elaboration and defense in the light of apparent moral dilemmas. Saintliness is self-perfection, not self-destruction or self-aggrandizement, but self-perfection is not the saint's chief motive. Identification with others must go hand-in-hand with individuation of self, but God's holiness and the neighbor's good take priority. True saintliness is a broad intersection between two recognizable sets of goods (self-realization and other-regard), rather than a single universal set of goods (general utility) that destroys the I/Thou distinction. Even in authentic altruism, self and other can never be simply equated, without remainder. As finite persons, we remain ourselves with interests and needs not fully continuous with those of others. Even saints, therefore, can suffer real loss in serving others; indeed, they normally do sacrifice something of true value.[31] But, again, willingly losing a human good is different from ineluctably losing moral innocence. Calloused or pierced hands need not be dirty.

Too many good people have suffered unjustly and died miserably to think that moral excellence guarantees happiness or prosperity in this life – it will likely do just the opposite. Similarly, some temporal losses even God cannot redeem; that's what it means for creatures to have

---

[31] This simple point is worth emphasizing because it is tempting to some to think of saints as happy self-actualizers who don't really suffer, even in laying down their lives for strangers. Jean Hampton, "Selflessness and the Loss of Self," in *Altruism*, Ellen Frankel Paul, Fred D. Miller, Jr., and Jeffrey Paul, eds. (Cambridge: Cambridge University Press, 1993), p. 159, for example, writes: "On my view, when we commend real altruists, we celebrate not only the authenticity of their choices, but also the point of view they have (authentically) adopted that has resulted in them wanting to make such choices. We commend their deeds not because these deeds are extraordinary acts of self-sacrifice; they *aren't* – real altruists do not understand their actions in this way." For Hampton, despite her emphasis on self-development and duties to oneself, the height of altruism is so freely and intelligently to identify with others as to make self-sacrifice impossible. Others' interests fully become my interests. But this account blurs the first-person and third-person perspectives on charity, and it privileges what is arguably a common self-misunderstanding of the saint. Saints may not feel or dwell on their losses, but they typically *are* sacrificial. Love *accepts* the loss as such, perhaps without thinking but freely and in fact. What saints have given up (e.g., life, limb, freedom, security) is evident to us observers, and we should not deny the goodness of these things even if the saint does so him- or herself. Acting charitably does purify the self, but even the finest altruism is not invulnerable.

some measure of real autonomy and the world to be subject to genuine contingency and malevolence. But the "eternity" that is the experience of love is still of surpassing value, whether or not this entails temporal happiness or a sublime afterlife (chapter 5). This means that, for Christians, life is still worth living in spite of any gap between being good and living well.[32] However taxing or "costly," the potential for charity may justify God's creation. Again, this is not an Axiological Optimism deduced from observations of the world; it is a faith generated by encounter with the Spirit that created the world. Communion with God is the highly desirable upshot of a well-lived life, not an external consequence added after the fact but an internal concommitant always present if not apparent.

Putting charity first means never foregoing love for the sake of nonmoral values, even though this may mean accepting crucifixion. *Pace* Susan Wolf, this does not necessitate melodrama or dullness, however. Saint Paul has the last word on any competition here:

If I speak in the tongues of mortals and of angels, but do not have love, I am a noisy gong or a clanging cymbal. And if I have prophetic powers, and understand all mysteries and all knowledge, and if I have all faith, so as to remove mountains, but do not have love, I am nothing. If I give away all my possessions, and if I hand over my body so that I may boast [other sources: my body to be burned], but do not have love, I gain nothing. (1 Cor. 13:1–3)

III. TWO THEOLOGICAL OBJECTIONS AND A REPLY

How well does the religiously based agapism I have outlined stand up to *theological* criticism? I will let Helmut Thielicke and Gilbert Meilaender, two astute Christian pessimists, mount the attack. Thielicke offers a subtle positive argument for the reality of moral dilemmas, what he calls (following Karl Jaspers) "borderline situations"; Meilaender's "argument for limited responsibility" is a powerful critique of the attempt to lead a rigorously *consequentialist* life, but it also threatens the more general case for the possibility of moral rigorism. Both men appeal to distinctively moral reasons, but both either misstate or fail adequately to spell out the place of strong *agape* in Christian ethics, I believe.

Thielicke holds that when sin has been institutionalized and injustice reigns supreme, there can be "an inescapable conflict of values . . . so that whichever way I go I am guilty."[33] He explains:

---

[32] Cf. Martha Nussbaum on Aristotle's account of *eudaimonia*, in *The Fragility of Goodness*, p. 380.
[33] Thielicke, *Theological Ethics*, vol. I (Grand Rapids: Eerdmans, 1979), p. 583.

The borderline situation is characterized above all by the fact that in it one is confronted by an opponent who is known to be bent wholly on the exercise of power, and who is obviously on the side of evil . . . To fight such an opponent is an obvious duty. But if this is so, the duty is one which can be fulfilled only as we adopt the methods of the opponent. One must necessarily – and this means willingly going against one's own will – share in the depravity of these methods, i.e., get one's hands dirty.[34]

The language here is quite similar to Michael Walzer's, as is the message: in certain extreme circumstances, we must be ready to do wrong in order to prevent something worse. Unlike Walzer's secular account, however, Thielicke's rests on a Lutheran view of our postlapsarian lot. After the Fall, we may not appeal to anything like practical reason or the goodness of creation to explain away dilemmas. Thomas Aquinas claimed that "no man can of himself be the sufficient cause of another's spiritual death, because no man dies spiritually except by sinning of his own will,"[35] but Thielicke contends (citing Jaspers) that borderline situations occur "in which I cannot live without conflict and suffering, in which I take upon myself unavoidable guilt, in which I *must* die."[36] An example of this might be an inmate in a Nazi concentration camp having to choose who will work and who will be gassed on a given day, or another variation on "Sophie's choice" in which a mother must decide which of her two children will be killed by a tyrannical power in order to spare the other.

Thielicke's defense of moral dilemmas is a pious attempt to acknowledge the extent of human rebellion against God; it can even be seen as the flip side of a doctrine of irresistible grace. Just as some theologians (e.g., Augustine and Luther) would accent the majesty of God by insisting on God's sovereign causation of all actions and events, so Thielicke would accent the depravity of humanity by insisting on God's

---

[34] Ibid., p. 585.   [35] Aquinas, *ST*, I–II, Q. 73, art. 8, ad 3.

[36] Thielicke, *Theological Ethics*, vol. I, p. 580; emphasis added. Thielicke cautions us that the conflict he describes is not finally to be attributed to some tragic flaw in the structure of the world but to original sin. The guilt in which we are now implicated flows out of a complex of wrong decisions traceable all the way back to the Fall. Because of this it may seem that, for Thielicke as for Thomas, all dilemmas are *secundum quid* after all: they stem from antecedent wrongdoing for which we are ourselves culpable. This move depends, however, on the plausibility of inherited guilt and corporate sin. It depends upon the traditional but problematic idea that I stand in need of forgiveness not only for my personal sins but also for the sins of the race. As Thielicke puts it, "I bring to the reconciling sign of the cross not merely my own 'individual sins' – indeed such an abstraction is impossible – but 'the guilt of the world.' For I am a participant in the guilt of the 'one man' Adam (Rom. 5:12)" [ibid., p. 597]. These notions complicate the picture, but for my purposes it is enough that Thielicke wants to defend the reality of moral dilemmas that do not stem from "actual sins" committed by an individual. This satisfies my technical definition.

systematic alienation from some actions and events. Whether the emphasis falls on divine control or human sin, meaningful creaturely freedom is denied in both cases. When this happens, we move beyond frank disconsolation to assert the amorality of the world.

For all its piety, Thielicke's position can be criticized on at least three specific grounds. First, Edmund Santurri has pointed out, as did Aristotle, that moral realists have *logical* reasons to deny dilemmas. If moral propositions have truth value, as realists assert, then admitting that "I ought to do X" and "I ought not to do X" entails accepting a self-contradiction as true. Logical consistency precludes this possibility, however, since a self-contradiction is a necessary falsehood.[37] These observations do not count as a refutation of Axiological Pessimism, since, as Santurri also notes, the argument from consistency will have no force for someone who denies moral realism's thesis that ethical claims have truth value.[38] (Realism is itself an article of faith that presumes we can touch and be touched by realities other than ourselves.) But Thielicke does seem to be a moral realist of sorts; he denies that a stable "natural theology" can provide guidance in borderline situations, but his analysis seems intended to capture the truth of our "total corruption."[39]

Second, a *theological* point can be made about the goodness and consistency of the created order and of its Creator. Particularly if one takes ethical duties to be a function of divine commands, to admit moral dilemmas would be to charge God with sadism, or at least with schizophrenia. God would command mutually incompatible things. Though this picture at times prevailed in Greek tragedy (though not in Plato), it is inconsistent with the traditional Judeo-Christian understanding of God as omnibenevolent. I discussed in chapter 6 the problems associated with driving a wedge between the two love commands of obedience to God and service to the neighbor, so I will only observe that, were dilemmas admitted, we would be back with Abraham before his conversion on Moriah. In the *Akedah*, Abraham recognized that sparing the innocent neighbor (whether one's own son or the children of the enemy) is itself an upshot of fidelity to God. Abraham's post-Moriah vision of love as kenotic requires faith, but it anticipates as such the cross of Christ as God's characteristic way of overcoming sin. Rather than either

[37] Santurri, *Perplexity in the Moral Life* (Charlottesville: University of Virginia Press, 1987), pp. 19–35.
[38] Ibid., pp. 31–32. For a defense of the dilemmatic, see Walter Sinott-Armstrong, *Moral Dilemmas* (Oxford: Oxford University Press, 1987); and Martha C. Nussbaum, *The Fragility of Goodness* and *Love's Knowledge*.   [39] Thielicke, *Theological Ethics*, vol. I, p. 579.

directly doing evil that good might come or merely abdicating all responsibility, Christ in his Passion embodies the power of sacrifice and forgiveness to heal the most tragic circumstance.

Third and finally, I would make the *practical* point that, in spite of his best intentions, Thielicke's views risk replacing trust in providence and obedience to God with what Dietrich Bonhoeffer called "cheap grace without discipleship."[40] Thielicke himself notes that "readiness to do wrong" is "a very dubious principle," yet he maintains that on occasion it has "ethical justification."[41] Having admitted so much, we will almost surely worry more about coping with guilt and assuming forgiveness for ourselves than about avoiding guilt and extending forgiveness to others. In this way, Bonhoeffer warns us, "the justification of the sinner in the world" degenerates into "the justification of sin and the world."[42] Such a slippery slope provides no way to guarantee Thielicke's "casuistical minimum" of standards below which we may never fall even in relying on divine grace.[43] If I manifestly *have* to become guilty at times, through no antecedent fault of my own, how can I draw the line against any particular crime when "necessity" becomes pressing?

Indeed, hand-in-hand with the problem of cheap grace comes that of *cheap sin*, in which transgressions large and small bleed together because the fringes of our lives are thought marked by utter tragedy. The prostitute Sonia in Dostoevski's *Crime and Punishment*, in contrast, is a saint precisely because she refuses the Hemingwayesque logic of: "We're all bitched from the start, so it makes little or no difference what we do." As Thielicke observes, Sonia takes moral responsibility for her actions and lives by the miracle of forgiveness from God. *Pace* Thielicke's eloquent yet ultimately curious discussion, however, she does so by *refusing* to plead external "necessity."

Thielicke is not alone in associating admission of moral dilemmas with candor about the tenacity of institutional evil, the ubiquity of original sin. We are all enmeshed in systems of corporate prejudice and injustice, a common argument runs, and these systems outstrip the capacity of any individual to escape or even perhaps to understand. Thus one can only "sin boldly," in Luther's oft-repeated phrase, and admit the depth of human depravity. After the bloody twentieth century, however, when institutional evil became unimaginably "efficient," such an analysis tempts us to cheap sin. With Eichmann's

---

[40] See Bonhoeffer, *The Cost of Discipleship* (New York: Simon and Schuster, 1995), p. 50.
[41] Thielicke, *Theological Ethics*, vol. I, pp. 590–591.
[42] Bonhoeffer, *The Cost of Discipleship*, p. 50. [43] Thielicke, *Theological Ethics*, vol. I, p. 643.

claims to be but a minor and uninformed functionary in the Nazi state still ringing in our ears, we cannot find such avoidance of responsibility plausible. Albert Speer himself noted that the Third Reich bureaucracy was designed so that questions of conscience would not arise, so that one would not think of oneself as personally accountable to living human beings but rather as caught up in a collective necessity larger than oneself.[44] To the extent that admitting moral dilemmas contributes to this distressing chorus of "I had no choice," it is practically objectionable. The fault for "having" to murder, say, to avoid loss of what we hold dear lies "not in our stars [or in our nation state], but in ourselves."

As I have indicated, Gilbert Meilaender offers a shrewd defense of Walzer's doctrine of supreme emergency – more generally, of the occasional unavoidability of doing what is morally wrong. Meilaender rejects pure consequentialism, arguing eloquently that the requirement to do evil that good (i.e., the best) might come is a species of pride and a mistrust of God's providence. But he nonetheless grants that a moment may arise in which we confront the catastrophic necessity of doing evil. This is a time "in which necessity truly has us in its grip – the moment when either we accept the rule of evil or, refusing to do that, invest evil with the involvement of our own purpose."[45] Once that much is granted, however, I find it unintelligible to assert that "if a moment of supreme emergency should arise, the Christian can and will offer no justification for overriding the moral rules which bind us to our neighbors and thereby limit us."[46] For that makes it impossible to comprehend why one is "refusing" to "accept the rule of evil."

Meilaender has faulted consequentialists like Sidgwick for teaching one thing in theory (the universal obligation to maximize the good) while conceding another thing in practice (that it would be better if everyone did not try to be consequentialist all the time). But I don't see how Meilaender himself escapes a measure of inconsistency. It turns out on his view that trust in God and love of neighbor – confidence in and imitation of God's *agape* – cannot integrate the moral life sufficiently to obviate palpable moral dilemmas. Christian charity degenerates into practical fatalism on occasion. But then why not just grant that Christi-

[44] Speer, *Inside the Third Reich*, pp. 10–11.
[45] Meilaender, "*Eritis Sicut Deus*," p. 409. For Meilaender's discussion of Thielicke on "conflict cases," see *The Limits of Love: Some Theological Explorations* (University Park and London: The Pennsylvania State University State Press, 1987), pp. 71–72.
[46] Meilaender, "*Eritis Sicut Deus*," p. 410.

anity is false, that God's commands themselves cannot be trusted and that the created world is itself evil?

Despite the many insights of Meilaender's critique of consequentialism and of the thesis that every "ought to be" implies an "ought to do," he leaves primarily a negative impression about Christianity as an alternative. His rejection of all forms of teleological rigorism seems more a negative concession to human finitude than a positive exploration of the inner logic of faith, hope, and love; it is more an acknowledgment of natural limitations *on* love, in particular, than a celebration of the supernatural expansiveness *of* love. Meilaender points out that he is not simply extolling an ethic of "my station and its duties" and notes that God has made us finite but also free, conditioned by a particular time and place but also capable of transcending our limited interests and perspectives.[47] Yet he does not explain why this "incarnational" mode of creation should be more loving than possible alternatives. In accepting moral dilemmas, he seems to reject the priority of *agape* itself: Christians may be overwhelmed by necessity to the point of moral breakdown and inescapable guilt. If such breakdown translates into being forced sinfully to renounce God, outwardly or inwardly, this sounds indeed like the voice of the serpent.

To the question whether the prospective "triumph of evil" might require the repudiation of *agape* and the actual embracing of its opposite, a Christian must answer "No." If faith, hope, and love abide, with the greatest of these being love, then we can trust in *agape*'s capacity to integrate all three temporal dimensions of the moral life. Some actions are forever proscribed, in spite of their producing the best overall consequences, not because they are too taxing or would make us like God but rather because they are incompatible with the virtue of benevolence which is the true essence of God. The sin of pride is in thinking that we are capable of performing an act lovingly when in fact we are not – when our supposed altruistic motives are tainted by fear, resentment, or self-deception – not in thinking that we are called to lead a rigorously agapic existence. We must not confuse the false indicative of the serpent ("*Eritis sicut Deus*") with the primary imperatives of the Son. "Be perfect, therefore, as your heavenly Father is perfect," Jesus says in Matthew 5:48, and he himself provides the practical example: "This is my commandment, that you love one another as I have loved you" (John 15:12).

---

[47] Ibid., p. 407.

Though partially corrupted after the Fall, creation still bears the stamp of the Creator; if it didn't, if it were utterly debased, it would cease to exist, as Roman Catholic theologians often remind us.[48] Moreover, if God is to be just in holding creatures accountable, as Scripture suggests, then our faculties must be a potentially reliable guide to moral uprightness, however also limited and in need of revelation. Descartes's epistemological axiom that "God is no deceiver" has the ethical analogue that "God is no seducer." Our conscience may fail to apply the principles of practical reason to specific cases or to enact obedience to God's commands in specific contexts. But to believe in God is to trust this failure, however obtuse or sinful, is not dilemmatic; it does not imply unavoidable guilt flowing from no fault of our own.

If Christianity is true, the world's supremest emergency was overcome on the cross by a love whose hands were physically pierced but not morally sullied. The incarnate Christ did not deny the terrible reality of death, but neither did he sin in the face of it. As Peter van Inwagen observes,

in the death of Jesus . . . we see an absolutely perfect man facing death *on his own*, without the illusions about death that comforted Socrates and without the presence of the Holy Spirit, who comforts Christian martyrs. . . Socrates' illusion was this: that it was not *he* who would die but simply an adjunct, his body – a thing that was not only not himself but a prison, a coil to be shuffled off with relief. Jesus, however, knew that it was he himself, and not another thing, who would die, who would become a corpse, who would be composed of nonliving matter. Therein lies the suffocating horror of death.[49]

A love that neither claims ghostlike invulnerability, nor lashes out at the innocent, nor curses God in utter dejection is nothing short of miraculous. Yet Christians are called to imitate that love, not legalistically but joyfully, not "on their own" but with the ineffable "comfort" of the Holy Spirit that dispels false comforts.

---

[48] On a common reading of Thomas Aquinas, he admits dilemmas "*secundum quid*" but not moral dilemmas *simpliciter*. *Secundum quid* cases involve some antecedent wrongdoing on the agent's part (such as promising to lie), thus the inability to avoid guilt is itself due to culpable action or intention (one should not promise to do something immoral). To think otherwise would be to indict the goodness of God. Whether or not we act on it, it will always be a duty to keep God's ordinances and a virtue to imitate God's holiness, and God is not self-contradictory. Neither is creation as such evil, however filled at times with pathos and depravity. (See Aquinas, *Truth* [1256–1259], vol. II, trans. by James V. McGlynn, S.J., (Chicago: Regnery, 1953), Q. 17, art. 4.) Edmund Santurri probes this "standard interpretation" in *Perplexity in the Moral Life*, chap. 3, esp. pp. 91–98, concluding that there is reason to doubt that Thomas allowed genuine dilemmas of *any* kind, even *secundum quid*. If Santurri is right, then Aquinas's ethics is even more antidilemmatic than I suggest.

[49] See van Inwagen, *The Possibility of Resurrection and Other Essays in Christian Apologetics* (Boulder, Colorado: Westview Press, 1998), p. 63.

Strong agapists do not claim that all (or even some) Christians actually have achieved or will achieve moral perfection. Their thesis is the much more modest one that considering such achievement both practically desirable and theoretically possible, with the help of grace, is an upshot of faith in a loving Deity who has made human beings in the divine Image and who died on the cross for their sakes. Though no human being in this life is without sin, human finitude is not as such sinful. If it were, the desire to be holy would be a denial of who we are. As it is, the aspiration to be steadfastly loving (to oneself and to others), even as is God, is not a prideful attempt to escape finitude but a commanded project to realize finitude's full potential before the cross of Christ. To believe that finitude is realized, not denied or destroyed, by the *Imitatio Christi* is to believe in the power of God "unto resurrection," whatever that might mean for one postmortem.

One cannot write off dilemmas as simple fallacies, even as it would be Pollyannaish to defend Axiological Optimism as provable. (Faith, hope, and love are inspired theological virtues, not demonstrable philosophical conclusions.) Some of our best minds and most sensitive souls (including Thielicke and Meilaender) have accepted dilemmas as part of the pathos and complexity of the moral life. My contention, nonetheless, is that in light of Jesus's Passion (a) it is plausible to account for this pathos and complexity with reference to accident, ignorance, weakness of will, and perversity, and (b) it is all but mandatory, given a strong conception of *agape*, to embrace such an account rather than admit genuine dilemmas. Anything less is not disconsolation but despair.

IV. THE MOST DIFFICULT QUESTION OF ALL

Even if one grants, on faith, that no *extrinsic* ground – neither unscrupulous people nor unfortunate circumstances – can compel one to forsake charity, one question remains. *Does charity ever dirty its own hands out of love itself?* This is the most difficult question of all for a defense of the priority of agapic love that would avoid pure pessimism. An affirmative answer is evident in George Orwell's claim, quoted at the start of this chapter, that "one *is* sometimes willing to commit sins for the sake of loyalty." A similar answer is also more or less explicit in the work of Thielicke and Meilaender, as well as that of philosophers as different as Philip Quinn and Jacques Derrida.[50] If *agape* ever willingly violates itself, however, we are faced with more than conflicts across the three dimensions of ethics,

---

[50] See Derrida, *The Gift of Death*, trans. by David Wills (Chicago and London: University of Chicago Press, 1995), esp. pp. 64–68. For references to Quinn's work, see my chapter 6.

we have a contradiction at the very heart of Christian monotheism. What if God Himself were to ask me to sin?, the pessimistic theologian asks. Might I not be moved to do so, "to descend into hell," out of love for the Almighty (cf. Abraham)?

Much that I have already defended cuts against such a prospect. To summarize: (1) love for God and love for the neighbor are not antithetical but complementary, (2) love for the neighbor and self-love are similarly symbiotic, and (3) the Imitation of Christ holds the key for all three love commandments (Matt. 22:37–40 and John 13:34). I have maintained that one never redeems others by becoming genuinely guilty with or for them, only by innocently suffering with or for them. Hemingway's David Bourne never learns this lesson, and when Fitzgerald's Dick Diver forgets it, he ceases to be virtuous and to be of help to Nicole Warren (chapter 2). I have also contended that what may look like the incurring of genuine guilt may actually be liberation's rising above a limited conception of justice to embrace a truer love. When Genesis's Abraham sees and acts on this with reference to child-sacrifice, he becomes the father of the faith (chapter 6).

In the end, however, one must turn to the meaning of the cross of Christ. Christ continued to believe in God and to uphold the world even when the cup of sacrificial death could not be avoided. It would be uncharitable to call perfect Love "guilty," even as it hangs on the cross, and nothing in the Gospel narratives requires us to do so.[51] Jesus remains the Christ even in dying; love disconsoled remains charitable. In fact, nowhere is Jesus so palpably divine as when he forgives his tormentors from the cross (Luke 23:34) and instructs his disciples to love beyond conventional boundaries: saying to his mother, "Woman, here is your son" and, to John, "Here is your mother" (John 19:26–27). The message of Golgotha is not that one ought to surrender love for another's sake, and thereby destroy one's very soul, but that so long as the soul exists one may always take love up for another's sake, and thereby rely on God to save one from sin.

CONCLUSION

Strong agapists take the deep structure of the world to be too ambiguous either to prove or to disprove a pessimistic axiology. They grant that at times our moral options seem profoundly conflicted, even chaotic, but they note that at other times we sense and act on an underlying beauty

---

[51] I owe the phrasing in this sentence to Jeffrey Stout; see also my discussion, in chapter 2, of Christ's "becoming sin for our sakes."

and harmony in life. There are counter-arguments to Pessimism, such as those alluded to in chapter 5, but their inconclusiveness means that ultimately our emphasis must shift to practical questions of commitment and perseverance. The strong agapist's actions will be based on fallible judgments about God, humanity, and the universe – here is no mere emotivism or fideism – but these actions will express a will-to-love that is psychologically durable in spite of metaphysical uncertainty. Even though agapic love is directed to the world for its own sake, the will-to-love stems first from epiphanies of God rather than analyses of nature or culture.[52]

A charity without consolation must react with mixed feelings, then, to my opening quote from Orwell. On the one hand, strong *agape* accepts the vulnerability that accompanies any effort to identify with and serve other people. Compassion, by definition, means feeling another's pain; beyond this, the active promotion of another's good entails running risks and making sacrifices precisely so that the other may be safe and well. The giving does not run in only one direction, of course. We are all needy, and, if we are lucky and virtuous, we grow old both relying on others and getting used up. In the process, tears fall in our lives like leaves from a tree. Our finitude is not to be regretted or despised, however; it is what makes giving and receiving possible. So while the strong agapist is, in Orwell's words, "prepared in the end to be defeated and broken up by life," he must also be counted happy – not like the absurd Sisyphus but like the Suffering Servant.[53]

On the other hand, strong *agape* does seek a kind of perfection; it strives to uphold an unconditional standard, the holiness of God, in a conditioned and flawed world. This is not done to exploit "equality with God," but to obey God and to serve others. Given human nature and the mystery of why meaningfully free creatures seem uniformly to sin, no one may plausibly claim to have *achieved* perfection in this life. But the ideal of steadfastly willing the good, in imitation of God's Son, remains

---

[52] The witness of Martin Luther King, Jr., is a case in point. King's firsthand experiences of racial prejudice and political violence left him with few illusions about human innocence and guilt, but for all his hardwon realism he could still say: "I believe that unarmed truth and unconditional love will have the final word in reality." Though he could give reasons for his nonviolence – e.g., that violence "thrives on hatred rather than love" and that it "ends by defeating itself" – his position did not flow out of an Axiological Optimism thought to be rationally demonstrable or indubitable. King's conviction that "the universe is on the side of justice" was, most fundamentally, an expression of his faith in God's ability "to make a way out of no way" and of his "hope for becoming better men." See King, *The Words of Martin Luther King, Jr*, ed. by Coretta Scott King (New York: Newmarket Press, 1987), pp. 91 and 73; *Stride Toward Freedom* (San Francisco: Harper and Row, 1958), p. 106; and *Strength to Love* (Philadelphia: Fortress Press, 1981), p. 114.

[53] See my review of Shel Silverstein's *The Giving Tree* in *First Things*, no. 49 (January 1995): 43–44.

intelligible. This means that the strong agapist is not willing to elevate any material value or temporal relationship to the status of *Summum Bonum*. She is *not* prepared "to commit sins for the sake of loyalty" to other human beings, for instance, and she is confident that loyalty to God cannot mandate murder, cruelty, or any other form of injustice.

Looking to eternity's entrance into time for a model of virtue, Christians see in the cross the limit of love's disconsolation – both its extreme form (Jesus's suffering death) and its outer bound (Christ's sinless obedience). The Passion is the indispensable model of how one is to hold together both *askesis* and *agape*, both Orwellian realism and Abrahamic idealism, without lapsing into either despair or delusion.

Bibliography

Abbott, E.A., *Flatland: A Romance of Many Dimensions* [1882], New York, Dover, 1952.

Adams, R.M., *The Virtue of Faith*, Oxford, Oxford University Press, 1987.

Agus, A., *The Binding of Isaac and Messiah: Law, Martyrdom, and Deliverance in Early Rabbinic Religiosity*, Albany, State University of New York Press, 1988.

Aiken, C., *Preludes for Memnon*, New York, Charles Scribner's Sons, 1931.

Alain, *The Gods*, tr. R. Pevear, New York, New Directions, 1974.

Andolsen, B.H., "Agape in Feminist Ethics," *Feminist Theological Ethics*, ed. L.K. Daly, Louisville, Westminster John Knox Press, 1994.

Aquinas, T., *Summa Theologiae* [1256–1272], tr. Fathers of the English Dominican Province, New York, Benziger Brothers, 1948.

Truth [1256–1259], vol. II, tr. J.V. McGlynn, S.J., Chicago, Regnery, 1953.

Arendt, H., *Eichmann in Jerusalem: A Report on the Banality of Evil*, New York, Viking Press, 1964.

Love and St. Augustine, Chicago, University of Chicago Press, 1996.

Aristotle, *The Nicomachean Ethics*, tr. D. Ross, revs. J.L. Ackrill and J.O. Urmson, Oxford, Oxford University Press, 1980.

Arminius, J., "A Declaration" [1608], *The Works of James (Jacob) Arminius*, vol. I, tr. James Nichols, London, Longman, Hurst, Rees, Orme, Brown, and Green (1825), 516–706.

Armstrong, K., *A History of God: The 4000–Year Quest of Judaism, Christianity and Islam*, New York, Knopf, 1994.

Auden, W.H., *Selected Poems*, ed. E. Mendelson, New York, Vintage Books, 1979.

Augustine, *The City of God* [413–425/6], tr. H. Bettenson, New York, Penguin Books, 1984.

Confessions [397–400], tr. R.S. Pine-Coffin, New York, Penguin Books, 1961.

The Enchiridion on Faith, Hope, and Love [421], tr. J.F. Shaw, Washington, D.C., Regnery, 1961.

On Christian Doctrine [397, with a fourth book added in 426], tr. D.W. Robertson, New York, Macmillan, 1958.

On Free Choice of the Will [395], tr. A.S. Benjamin and L.H. Hackstaff, Indianapolis, Bobbs-Merrill, 1979.

On the Morals of the Catholic Church [388], *Basic Writings of Saint Augustine*, vol. I, tr. R. Stothert, ed. W.J. Oates, New York, Random House, 1948.

The Trinity [400 –*c.*420], tr. E. Hill, O.P., ed. J.E. Rotelle, O.S.A., Brooklyn, New York, New City Press, 1991.

Baer, H.D., "The Fruit of Charity: Using the Neighbor in *De doctrina christiana*," *Journal of Religious Ethics*, vol. 24, no. I (Spring 1996), 47–64.

Barth, K., *Church Dogmatics*, II/2, tr. G.W. Bromiley *et al.*, Edinburgh, T.&T. Clark, 1957.

Church Dogmatics, III/4, tr. A.T. Mackay *et al.*, Edinburgh, T.& T. Clark, 1961.

The Resurrection of the Dead, New York, Fleming H. Revell Co., 1933.

Bataille, G., *Erotism: Death & Sensuality*, tr. M. Dalwood, San Francisco, City Lights, 1986.

Berlin, I., *Four Essays on Liberty*, Oxford, Oxford University Press, 1982.

Berry, W., *Collected Poems: 1957–1982*, San Francisco, North Point Press, 1984.

Black Elk, *Black Elk Speaks*, as told through J.G. Neihardt, Lincoln, University of Nebraska Press, 1961.

Blake, W., *The Complete Poetry and Prose of William Blake*, ed. D.V. Erdman, New York, Anchor Books, 1988.

Bloom, A., *Love and Friendship*, New York, Simon & Schuster, 1993.

Blum, L.A., *Friendship, Altruism and Morality*, London, Routledge & Kegan Paul, 1980.

Blustein, J., *Care and Commitment: Taking the Personal Point of View*, Oxford, Oxford University Press, 1991.

Boethius, *The Consolation of Philosophy* [524], tr. R. Green, Indianapolis, Bobbs-Merrill, 1962.

Boff, L. and Boff, C., *Salvation and Liberation: In Search of a Balance Between Faith and Politics*, Maryknoll and Melbourne, Orbis/Dove, 1985.

Bolt, R., *A Man for All Seasons*, New York, Vintage Books, 1988.

Bonhoeffer, D., *The Cost of Discipleship*, New York, Simon & Schuster, 1995.

Booth, W.C., *The Company We Keep: An Ethics of Fiction*, Berkeley, University of California Press, 1988.

Bruccoli, M.J., *Some Sort of Epic Grandeur: The Life of F. Scott Fitzgerald*, New York and London, Harcourt Brace Jovanovich, 1981.

Brunner, E., *The Divine Imperative*, tr. O. Wyon, London, Lutterworth Press, 1951.

Buchanan, A., "Justice and Charity," *Ethics*, vol. 97, no. 3 (April 1987), 558–575.

Burke, K., *A Grammar of Motives*, Berkeley, University of California Press, 1969.

Burnaby, J., *Amor Dei: A Study of the Religion of St. Augustine*, London, Hodder & Stoughton, 1938.

Cachin, F., *Gauguin: The Quest for Paradise*, tr. I.M. Paris, New York, Harry N. Abrams, Inc., 1992.

Camus, A., *The Plague*, tr. S. Gilbert, New York, Knopf, 1964.

Casey, J., *Pagan Virtue: An Essay in Ethics*, Oxford, Oxford University Press, 1990.

Cavell, S., *The Claim of Reason: Wittgenstein, Skepticism, Morality, and Tragedy*, Oxford, Clarendon Press, 1979.

Clark, G.R., *The Word "Hesed" in the Hebrew Bible*, Sheffield, JSOT Press, 1993.

"Clement's First Letter," *Readings in Christian Ethics*, ed. J.P. Wogaman and D.M. Strong, Louisville, Westminster John Knox Press, 1996.

Cohen, M., Nagel, T., and Scanlon, T., ed., *War and Moral Responsibility*, Princeton, Princeton University Press, 1974.

Coles, R., *Simone Weil: A Modern Pilgrimage*, Reading, MA, Addison-Wesley, 1987.

The Compact Oxford English Dictionary, vol. 1, Oxford, Oxford University Press, 1984.

Conrad, J., *Heart of Darkness*, Englewood Cliffs, NJ, Prentice-Hall, 1960.

Lord Jim, New York, Penguin Books, 1986.

The Dalai Lama (Tenzin Gyatso), *A Flash of Lightning in the Dark of Night: A Guide to the Bodhisattva's Way of Life*, tr. The Padmakara Translation Group, Boston and London, Shambhala, 1994.

Kindness, Clarity, and Insight, tr. J. Hopkins, Ithaca, Snow Lion, 1984.

Derrida, J., *The Gift of Death*, Chicago and London, University of Chicago Press, 1995.

Dictionary of the Bible, ed. J. Hastings and rev. F.C. Grant and H.H. Rowley, New York, Charles Scribner's Sons, 1963.

Doppelt, G., "Is Rawls's Kantian Liberalism Coherent and Defensible?," *Ethics*, vol. 99, no. 4 (July 1989), 815–851.

Douglas, M., *Purity and Danger*, London, Routledge & Kegan Paul, 1966.

Dupré, L., "Evil – A Religious Mystery: A Plea for a More Inclusive Model of Theodicy," *Faith and Philosophy*, vol. 7, no. 3 (July 1990), 261–280.

Dworkin, R., *Life's Dominion*, New York, Alfred A. Knopf, 1993.

Eareckson, J., *Joni*, New York, Bantam Books, 1978.

Edwards, G.R., *Gay/Lesbian Liberation: A Biblical Perspective*, New York, Pilgrim Press, 1984.

Epictetus, *Discourses*, tr. W.A. Oldfather, Cambridge, Harvard University Press, 1979.

Etzioni, A., *The New Golden Rule*, New York, Basic Books, 1996.

Ferreira, M.J., "Kant's Postulate: The Possibility *or* the Existence of God?," *Kant Studien*, vol. 74 (1983), 75–80.

Feuerbach, L., *Thoughts on Death and Immortality*, tr. J.A. Massey, Berkeley, University of California Press, 1980.

Fitzgerald, F.S., *The Crack-Up*, ed. E. Wilson, New York, New Directions, 1964.

The Romantic Egoists, ed. M.J. Bruccoli, S.F. Smith, and J.P. Kerr, New York, Charles Scribner's Sons, 1974.

Tender Is the Night, New York, Charles Scribner's Sons, 1962.

Foucault, M., *The Archaeology of Knowledge*, tr. A.M. Sheridan Smith, New York, Pantheon Books, 1982.

Ethics: Subjectivity and Truth, vol. I of *The Essential Works of Foucault 1954–1984*, ed. P. Rabinow, New York, The New Press, 1997.

The History of Sexuality, vol. I, tr. R. Hurley, New York, Vintage Books, 1980.

The Order of Things: An Archaeology of the Human Sciences, tr. A. Sheridan, New York, Random House, 1973.

Frei, H., *The Identity of Jesus Christ*, Philadelphia, Fortress Press, 1975.

Freud, S., *Beyond the Pleasure Principle*, tr. and ed. J. Strachey, New York and London, W.W. Norton, 1961.

Civilization and Its Discontents, tr. and ed. J. Strachey, New York and London, W.W. Norton, 1961.

The Ego and the Id, tr. J. Riviere, rev. and ed. J. Strachey, New York and London, W.W. Norton, 1960.

The Future of an Illusion, tr. W.D. Robson-Scott, rev. and ed. J. Strachey, Garden City, N.Y., Anchor Books, 1964.

Group Psychology and the Analysis of the Ego, tr. and ed. J. Strachey, New York and London, W.W. Norton, 1959.

Moses and Monotheism, tr. K. Jones, New York, Vintage Books, 1967.

"The Most Prevalent Form of Degradation in Erotic Life," *Sexuality and the Psychology of Love*, ed. P. Rieff, New York, Collier Books, 1963.

New Introductory Lectures on Psychoanalysis, tr. and ed. J. Strachey, New York and London, W.W. Norton, 1965.

"On Narcissism: An Introduction," *The Standard Edition of the Complete Psychological Works of Sigmund Freud*, vol. XIV, tr. and ed. J. Strachey, London, The Hogarth Press, 1957.

Frye, N., *Fearful Symmetry: A Study of William Blake*, Princeton, Princeton University Press, 1969.

Furnish, V.P., *The Love Command in the New Testament*, Nashville, Abingdon Press, 1972.

Galston, W., *Liberal Purposes: Goods, Virtues, and Diversity in the Liberal State*, Cambridge, Cambridge University Press, 1991.

Gandhi, M.K., *All Men Are Brothers*, New York, Continuum, 1998.

Garrow, D., *Bearing the Cross: Martin Luther King, Jr., and the Southern Christian Leadership Conference*, New York, Vintage Books, 1988.

"*Gaudium Et Spes,*" *The Documents of Vatican II*, ed. W.M. Abbott, S.J., Chicago, Follett Publishing Co., 1966.

Gay, P., *A Godless Jew: Freud, Atheism, and the Making of Psychoanalysis*, New Haven and London, Yale University Press, 1987.

Gewirth, A., *Reason and Morality*, Chicago, University of Chicago Press, 1978.

Gide, A., *Strait is the Gate*, tr. D. Bussy, New York, Vintage Books, 1952.

Gilligan, C., *In a Different Voice*, Cambridge, Harvard University Press, 1982.

Gilman, R., *Decadence: The Strange Life of an Epithet*, New York, Farrar, Straus and Giroux, 1979.

Ginzburg, C., *Ecstasies: Deciphering the Witches' Sabbath*, New York, Pantheon, 1991.

Girard, R., *Violence and the Sacred*, tr. P. Gregory, Baltimore, Johns Hopkins University Press, 1977.

Grant, C., "For the Love of God: Agape," *Journal of Religious Ethics*, vol. 24, no. 1 (Spring 1996), 3–21.

"A Reply to My Critics," *Journal of Religious Ethics*, vol. 24, no. 1 (Spring 1996), 43–46.

A Greek-English Lexicon of the New Testament, Chicago, University of Chicago Press, 1957.

Green, R., "Enough Is Enough!: *Fear and Trembling* Is Not About Ethics," *Journal of Religious Ethics*, vol. 21, no. 2 (Fall 1993), 191–209.

Kierkegaard and Kant: The Hidden Debt, Albany, State University of New York Press, 1992.

Religion and Moral Reason: A New Method for Comparative Study, Oxford, Oxford University Press, 1988.

Greenlee, M.B., "Echoes of the Love Command in the Halls of Justice," *The Journal of Law and Religion*, vol. 12, no.1 (1995–1996), 255–270.

Gudorf, C.E., *Body, Sex, and Pleasure*, Cleveland, The Pilgrim Press, 1994.

Gurdjieff, G.I., "Inner Slavery: An Early Talk of G.I. Gurdjieff," *Parabola*, vol. 15, no. 3 (August 1990), 16–18.

Gustafson, J., *Ethics from a Theocentric Perspective*, vol. I, Chicago, University of Chicago Press, 1981.

Hampshire, S., *Morality and Conflict*, Cambridge, Harvard University Press, 1983.

Hampton, J., "Selflessness and the Loss of Self," *Altruism*, ed. E.F. Paul, F.D. Miller, Jr., and J. Paul, Cambridge, Cambridge University Press, 1993.

Harvey, V.A., *Feuerbach and the Interpretation of Religion*, Cambridge, Cambridge University Press, 1995.

Hauerwas, S., *After Christendom?*, Nashville, Abingdon Press, 1991.

God, Medicine, and Suffering, Grand Rapids, Eerdmans, 1990.

Hauerwas, S., with C. Pinches, *Christians Among the Virtues: Theological Conversations with Ancient and Modern Ethics*, Notre Dame, University of Notre Dame Press, 1997.

Haynes, S., "Not Just Another Apocalyptician," *The New York Times Book Review* (November 3, 1991), 30.

Hays, R., *First Corinthians: Interpretation*, Louisville, John Knox Press, 1997.

The Moral Vision of the New Testament, San Francisco, HarperCollins, 1996.

Hegel, G.W.F., *Lectures on the Philosophy of Religion*, ed. P.C. Hodgson, Berkeley, University of California Press, 1988.

Heidegger, M., *Being and Time*, tr. J. Macquarrie and E. Robinson, New York, Harper and Row, 1962.

Heller, A., *Beyond Justice*, Oxford, Basil Blackwell, 1987.

Hemingway, E., *The Complete Short Stories of Ernest Hemingway*, New York, Charles Scribner's Sons, 1987.

"Ernest Hemingway Reads," New York, HarperCollins, 1965 & 1992.

The Garden of Eden, New York, Charles Scribner's Sons, 1986.

In Our Time, New York, Collier Books, 1986.

A Moveable Feast, New York, Collier Books, 1987.

Selected Letters, 1917–1961, ed. C. Baker, New York, Charles Scribner's Sons, 1981.

The Sun Also Rises, New York, Charles Scribner's Sons, 1954.

Hemingway, M., "Hemingway," *Look Magazine*, September 12, 1961.

Heyd, D., *Supererogation: Its Status in Ethical Theory*, Cambridge, Cambridge University Press, 1982.

Heyward, C., "Lamenting the Loss of Love: A Response to Colin Grant," *Journal of Religious Ethics*, vol. 24, no. 1 (Spring 1996), 23–28.

Hick, J., *Death and Eternal Life*, San Francisco, Harper and Row, 1976.

Evil and the God of Love, New York, Harper and Row, 1978.

Homer, *The Iliad*, tr. R. Fagles, London, Penguin Books, 1990.

Ignatieff, M., *The Needs of Strangers*, New York, Penguin Books, 1984.

Jackson, T.P., "Arminian Edification: Kierkegaard on Grace and Free Will," *The Cambridge Companion to Kierkegaard*, Cambridge, Cambridge University Press, 1998.

"Is God Just?," *Faith and Philosophy*, vol. 12, no. 3 (July 1995), 393–408.

"Liberalism and *Agape*: The Priority of Charity to Democracy and Philosophy," *The Annual of the Society of Christian Ethics* (1993), 47–72.

"Must Job Live Forever?: A Reply to Aquinas on Providence," *The Thomist*, vol. 62, no. 1 (January 1998), 1–39.

"Naturalism, Formalism, and Supernaturalism: Moral Epistemology and Comparative Ethics," forthcoming, *Journal of Religious Ethics*, (Fall 1999).

"The Possibilities of Scepticisms: Philosophy and Theology Without Apology," *Metaphilosophy*, vol. 21, no. 4 (October 1990), 303–321.

The Priority of Love: Christian Charity and Social Justice, forthcoming Princeton University Press.

"Review of D. Keck's *Forgetting Whose We Are* and S. Post's *The Moral Challenge of Alzheimer Disease*," *Studies in Christian Ethics*, vol. 11, no. 1 (1998), 94–99.

"Review of K. Løgstrup's *The Ethical Demand*," *Modern Theology*, vol. 14, no. 3 (July 1998), 459–461.

"Review of S. Silverstein's *The Giving Tree*," *First Things*, No. 49 (January 1995), 43–44.

"The Theory and Practice of Discomfort: Richard Rorty and Pragmatism," *The Thomist*, vol. 51, no. 2 (April 1987), 270–298.

Jaggar, A.M., "Love and Knowledge: Emotion in Feminist Epistemology," *Gender/Body/Knowledge: Feminist Reconstructions of Being and Knowing*, ed. A.M. Jaggar and S.R. Bordo, New Brunswick and London, Rutgers University Press, 1989.

James, H., "The Middle Years," *The Figure in the Carpet and Other Stories*, ed. F. Kermode, New York, Penguin Books, 1986.

John Paul II, Pontiff, *The Splendor of Truth* ("*Veritatis Splendor*"), Washington, D.C., United States Catholic Conference, 1993.

Joyce, J., *A Portrait of the Artist as a Young Man*, New York, Viking Press, 1964.

Kant, I., *Critique Of Pure Reason*, tr. N.K. Smith, New York, Saint Martin's Press, 1965.

Kaufmann, W., *Existentialism, Religion, and Death: Thirteen Essays*, New York, Meridian, 1976.

Keck, D., *Forgetting Whose We Are: Alzheimer's Disease and the Love of God*, Nashville, Abingdon Press, 1996.

Kierkegaard, S., *The Concept of Anxiety*, ed./tr. R. Thomte and A.B. Anderson, Princeton, Princeton University Press, 1980.

The Concept of Irony, tr. L.M. Capel, Bloomington, University of Indiana Press, 1968.

(Johannes Climacus), *Concluding Unscientific Postscript*, tr. D.F. Swenson and W. Lowrie, Princeton, Princeton University Press, 1968.

Eighteen Upbuilding Discourses, ed./tr. H.V. and E.H. Hong, Princeton, Princeton University Press, 1990.

(Johannes de Silentio), *Fear and Trembling*, ed./tr. H.V. and E.H. Hong, Princeton, Princeton University Press, 1983.

For Self-Examination, ed./tr. H.V. and E.H. Hong, Princeton, Princeton University Press, 1990.

Gospel of Sufferings, tr. A.S. Aldworth and W.S. Ferrie, London, James Clarke & Co. 1955.

Journals and Papers, vols. I–IV, ed./tr. H.V. and E.H. Hong, asst. G. Malantschuk, Bloomington, Indiana University Press, 1967–1975.

(Johannes Climacus), *Philosophical Fragments*, tr. D.F. Swenson and rev. H.V. Hong, Princeton, Princeton University Press, 1974.

The Point of View for My Work as an Author, tr. W. Lowrie, New York, Harper and Row, 1962.

(Constantin Constantius), *Repetition*, ed./tr. H.V. and E.H. Hong, Princeton, Princeton University Press, 1983.

(Anti-Climacus), *The Sickness Unto Death*, ed./tr. H.V. and E.H. Hong, Princeton, Princeton University Press, 1983.

Works of Love, tr. H.V. and E.H. Hong, New York, Harper and Row, 1962.

King, M.L., Jr., *Strength to Love*, Philadelphia, Fortress Press, 1981.

Stride Toward Freedom, San Francisco, Harper and Row, 1958.

Why We Can't Wait, New York, Mentor, 1964.

The Words of Martin Luther King, Jr., ed. C.S. King, New York, Newmarket Press, 1987.

Klassen, W., "Love (NT and Early Jewish Literature)," *The Anchor Bible Dictionary*, vol. IV, New York, Doubleday (1992), 381–396.

Love of Enemies: The Way to Peace, Philadelphia, Fortress Press, 1984.

Kott, J., *The Eating of the Gods: An Interpretation of Greek Tragedy*, New York, Random House, 1973.

Kramer, H. and Sprenger, J., *Malleus Maleficarum*, tr. M. Summers, Tiptree, Essex, Arrow Books, 1971.

Kreeft, P., *Love Is Stronger than Death*, San Francisco, Ignatius Press, 1992.

Lacan, J., *The Ethics of Psychoanalysis, 1959–60, The Seminar of Jacques Lacan*, Book VII, ed. J.-A. Miller, tr. D. Porter, New York, W.W. Norton, 1992.

Laing, R.D., "Violence and Love," *Counter-tradition: The Literature of Dissent and Alternatives*, ed. S. Delany, New York, Basic Books, 1971.

Larmore, C., "Pluralism and Reasonable Disagreement," a paper delivered at Yale University, April 8, 1993.

Larrabee, M.J., ed., *An Ethic of Care: Feminist and Interdisciplinary Perspectives*, New

York, Routledge, 1993.

Lasch, C., "Conservatism Against Itself," *First Things*, no. 2 (April 1990), 17–23.

Levenson, J.D., *The Death and Resurrection of the Beloved Son: The Transformation of Child Sacrifice in Judaism and Christianity*, New Haven and London, Yale University Press, 1993.

Lewis, C.S., *The Four Loves*, New York and London, Harcourt Brace Jovanovich, 1960.

"The Weight of Glory," *The Weight of Glory and Other Essays*, Grand Rapids, Eerdmans, 1979.

Lister, R., *The Paintings of William Blake*, Cambridge, Cambridge University Press, 1986.

Little, D., "The Law of Supererogation," *The Love Commandments*: *Essays in Christian Ethics and Moral Philosophy*, ed. E. Santurri and W. Werpehowski, Washington, D.C., Georgetown University Press, 1992.

Løgstrup, K.E., *The Ethical Demand*, Notre Dame, University of Notre Dame Press, 1997.

Lovelace, M.H., "Abomination," *The Interpreter's Dictionary of the Bible*, ed. G.A. Buttrick, vol. I, Nashville, Abingdon Press (1962), 12–13.

Lowrie, W., "Translator's Notes," *Fear and Trembling*, Princeton, Princeton University Press, 1970.

Luker, K., *Abortion and the Politics of Motherhood*, Berkeley and Los Angeles, University of California Press, 1984.

Luther, M., "A Commentary on Saint Paul's Epistle to the Galatians" [1531], *Martin Luther: Selections from His Writings*, ed. J. Dillenberger, Garden City, Anchor Books, 1961.

"The Freedom of a Christian" [1520], *Martin Luther: Selections from His Writings.* ed. J. Dillenberger, Garden City, Anchor Books, 1961.

Lynn, K.S., *Hemingway*, New York, Fawcett Columbine, 1987.

MacIntyre, A., *After Virtue*, Notre Dame, University of Notre Dame Press, 1981.

"Søren Aabye Kierkegaard," *The Encyclopedia of Philosophy*, vol. IV, New York, Macmillan and the Free Press, 1972.

Megill, A., *Prophets of Extremity: Nietzsche, Heidegger, Foucault, and Derrida*, Berkeley, University of California Press, 1985.

Meilaender, G., "*Eritis Sicut Deus:* Moral Theory and the Sin of Pride," *Faith and Philosophy*, vol. 3, no. 4 (October 1986), 397–415.

Friendship: A Study in Theological Ethics, Notre Dame, University of Notre Dame Press, 1981.

The Limits of Love: Some Theological Explorations, University Park and London, The Pennsylvania State University Press, 1987.

Mellow, J.R., *Hemingway: A Life Without Consequences*, Menlo Park, CA, Addison-Wesley, 1992.

Menchú, R., *I, Rigoberta Menchú: An Indian Woman in Guatemala*, tr. A Wright, London and New York, Verso, 1984.

The Metropolitan Museum of Art Guide, ed. K. Howard, New York, 1992.

Miller, J., *The Passion of Michel Foucault*, New York, Simon and Schuster, 1993.

Moore, C.H., *Ancient Beliefs in the Immortality of the Soul*, New York, Longmans, Green, and Co., 1931.

Morris, H., "Nonmoral Guilt," *Responsibility, Character, and the Emotions*, ed. F. Schoeman, Cambridge, Cambridge University Press, 1987.

Morris, L.L., "Abomination," *The New Bible Dictionary*, ed. J.D. Douglas, Grand Rapids, Eerdmans, 1967, 4.

Murdoch, I., *Metaphysics as a Guide to Morals*, New York, The Penguin Press, 1993.

The Sovereignty of Good, London and New York, Routledge, 1970.

Nagel, T., "The Fragmentation of Value," *Moral Dilemmas*, ed. C.W. Gowans, Oxford, Oxford University Press, 1987.

The View From Nowhere, Oxford, Oxford University Press, 1986.

Ness, C., *An Antidote Against Arminianism* [1700], Edmonton, Alberta, Still Waters Revival Books, 1988.

Newland, G., *Compassion: A Tibetan Analysis*, London, Wisdom Publications, 1984.

The New Oxford Annotated Bible, New Revised Standard Version (NRSV), ed. B.M. Metzger and R.E. Murphy, New York, Oxford University Press, 1991.

The New Standard Jewish Encyclopedia, ed. G. Wigoda, New York, Facts on File, 1992.

Niebuhr, R., *Leaves From the Notebook of a Tamed Cynic*, Hamden, CT, The Shoe String Press, 1956.

Nietzsche, F., "The AntiChrist," *The Portable Nietzsche*, ed. and tr. W. Kaufmann, New York, The Viking Press, 1974.

Beyond Good and Evil, in *Basic Writings of Nietzsche*, ed. and tr. W. Kaufmann, New York, Modern Library, 1968.

On the Genealogy of Morals, in *Basic Writings of Nietzsche*.

Noddings, N., *Caring: A Feminine Approach to Ethics and Moral Education*, Berkeley, University of California Press, 1984.

Nordau, M., *Degeneration*, New York, D. Appleton and Co., 1896.

Nussbaum, M.C., "Emotions as Judgments of Value," *The Yale Journal of Criticism*, vol. 5, no.2 (Spring 1992), 201–212.

The Fragility of Goodness: Luck and ethics in Greek tragedy and philosophy, Cambridge, Cambridge University Press, 1986.

Love's Knowledge: Essays on Philosophy and Literature, Oxford, Oxford University Press, 1990.

The Quality of Life, ed. M.C. Nussbaum and A. Sen, Oxford, Clarendon, 1993.

The Therapy of Desire, Princeton, Princeton University Press, 1994.

Nygren, A., *Agape and Eros*, tr. P.S. Watson, New York, Harper and Row, 1969.

O'Donovan, O., *The Problem of Self-Love in St. Augustine*, New Haven and London, Yale University Press, 1980.

Outka, G., *Agape: An Ethical Analysis*, New Haven and London, Yale University Press, 1972.

"Equality and Individuality: Thoughts on Two Themes in Kierkegaard,"

Journal of Religious Ethics, vol. 10, no. 2 (Fall 1982), 171–203.

"Equality and the Fate of Theism in Modern Culture," *The Journal of Religion*, vol. 67, no. 3 (July 1987), 275–288.

"Theocentric Agape and the Self: An Asymmetrical Affirmation in Response to Colin Grant's Either/Or," *Journal of Religious Ethics*, vol. 24, no. 1 (Spring 1996), 35–42.

Pailin, D., "Abraham and Isaac: A Hermeneutical Problem Before Kierkegaard," *Kierkegaard's Fear and Trembling: Critical Appraisals*, ed. R.L. Perkins, University, Alabama, The University of Alabama Press, 1981.

Paoli, A., *Freedom to Be Free*, tr. C. Quinn, Maryknoll, Orbis, 1973.

Paul VI, Pontiff, "Respect for Life in the Womb: Address to the Medical Association of Western Flanders," *On Moral Medicine*, ed. S. Lammars and A. Verhey, Grand Rapids, Eerdmans, 1987.

Plato, *Crito*, in *The Last Days of Socrates*, tr. H. Tredennick, Harmonsworth, Penguin Books, 1969.

Euthydemus, tr. W.R.M. Lamb, Cambridge, Harvard University Press, 1977.

The Republic, tr. A. Bloom, New York, Basic Books, 1991.

Poole, R., *Kierkegaard: The Indirect Communication*, Charlottesville and London, University Press of Virginia, 1993.

Porter, J., "*De Ordine Caritatis*: Charity, Friendship, and Justice in Thomas Aquinas' *Summa Theologiae*," *The Thomist*, vol. 53, no. 2 (April 1989), 197–213.

Post, S.G., *The Moral Challenge of Alzheimer Disease*, Baltimore, Johns Hopkins University Press, 1995.

A Theory of Agape: On the Meaning of Christian Love, London and Toronto, Associated University Presses, 1990.

Pound, E., "A Brief Note," *Henry James: A Collection of Critical Essays*, ed. L. Edel, Englewood Cliffs, NJ, Prentice-Hall, 1963.

Preus, J.S., *Explaining Religion: Criticism and Theory from Bodin to Freud*, New Haven and London, Yale University Press, 1987.

Purvis, S.B., "Mothers, Neighbors, and Strangers: Another Look at Agape," *Journal of Feminist Studies in Religion*, vol.7 (Spring 1991), 19–34.

Quine, W.V.O., "The Ways of Paradox," *The Ways of Paradox and Other Essays*, Cambridge, Harvard University Press, 1977.

Quinn, P., "Agamemnon and Abraham: The Tragic Dilemma of Kierkegaard's Knight of Faith," *The Journal of Literature and Theology*, vol. 4, no. 2 (July 1990), 181–192.

"Moral Obligation, Religious Demand, and Practical Conflict," *Rationality, Religious Belief, and Moral Commitment*, ed. R. Audi and W. Wainwright, Ithaca and London, Cornell University Press, 1986.

"Tragic Dilemmas, Suffering Love, and Christian Life," *Journal of Religious Ethics*, vol. 17 (1989), 151–183.

Rahner, K., *Theological Investigations*, vol. VI, tr. K.-H. and B. Kruger, New York, Seabury, 1977.

Ramsey, P., *Basic Christian Ethics*, New York, Charles Scribner's Sons, 1950.

The Patient as Person, New Haven, Yale University Press, 1970.

War and the Christian Conscience, Durham, NC, Duke University Press, 1961.

Raphael, S.P., *Jewish Views of the Afterlife*, New Jersey, Jason Aronson, 1996.

Ridderbos, H., *Paul: An Outline of His Theology*, tr. J.R. Dewitt, Grand Rapids, Eerdmans, 1975.

Rilke, R.M., *Letters to a Young Poet*, tr. S. Mitchell, New York, Vintage Books, 1986.

Rist, J.M., *Augustine: Ancient Thought Baptized*, Cambridge, Cambridge University Press, 1994.

Eros and Psyche: Studies in Plato, Plotinus, and Origen, Toronto, University of Toronto Press, 1964.

Rolle, R., *The Fire of Love* [1343], tr. C. Wolters, Harmondsworth, Penguin Books, 1972.

Rorty, R., *Achieving Our Country: Leftist Thought in Twentieth-Century America*, Cambridge and London, Harvard University Press, 1998.

Contingency, Irony, and Solidarity, Cambridge, Cambridge University Press, 1989.

"Feminism and Pragmatism," *The Michigan Quarterly Review* (Spring 1991), 231–258.

"Method, Social Science, and Social Hope," *Consequences of Pragmatism*, Minneapolis, University of Minnesota Press, 1982.

"Science as Solidarity,"*Objectivity, Relativism, and Truth: Philosophical Papers*, vol. I, Cambridge, Cambridge University Press, 1991.

"Solidarity or Objectivity," *Objectivity, Relativism, and Truth: Philosophical Papers*, vol. I, Cambridge, Cambridge University Press, 1991.

Rosen, S., *Nihilism: A Philosophical Essay*, New Haven and London, Yale University Press, 1969.

Rumi, J., "Four Poems on the Night," *World Poetry*, tr. J. Moyne and C. Barks, ed. K. Washburn, J.S. Major, and C. Fadiman, New York, W.W. Norton, 1998.

Russell, D.E.H., *The Secret Trauma: Incest in the Lives of Girls and Women*, New York, Basic Books, 1986.

Sade, Marquis de, "To Libertines," *Philosophy in the Bedroom*, tr. R. Seaver and A. Wainhouse, New York, Grove Weidenfeld, 1965.

Sakenfeld, K.D., "Love (OT)," *The Anchor Bible Dictionary*, vol. IV, New York, Doubleday (1992), 375–381.

The Meaning of Hesed in the Hebrew Bible, Missoula, Scholars Press, 1978.

Santurri, E., *Perplexity in the Moral Life*, Charlottesville, University of Virginia Press, 1987.

Scarry, E., *The Body in Pain: The Making and Unmaking of the World*, Oxford, Oxford University Press, 1985.

Schwartz, B., *The Battle for Human Nature: Science, Morality, and Modern Life*, New York, W.W. Norton, 1986.

"Secret of a Wild Child," *NOVA* video, WGBH/Boston Science Unit, BBC-TV, 1994.

Seneca, "*De Constantia*," *Seneca: Moral Essays*, vol. I, tr. J.W. Basore, Cambridge,

Harvard University Press, 1985.

"*De Providentia,*" *Seneca: Moral Essays*, vol. I.

Shakespeare, W., *The Complete Signet Classic Shakespeare*, ed. S. Barnet, New York and London, Harcourt Brace Jovanovich, 1972.

Shklar, J., *The Faces of Injustice*, New Haven and London, Yale University Press, 1990.

"The Liberalism of Fear," *Liberalism and the Moral Life*, ed. N.L. Rosenblum, Cambridge, Cambridge University Press, 1989.

Ordinary Vices, Cambridge, Harvard University Press, 1984.

Singer, I., *The Nature of Love*, vols. I–III, Chicago, University of Chicago Press, 1984–1987.

Singer, P., *Practical Ethics*, Cambridge, Cambridge University Press, 1993.

Rethinking Life and Death: The Collapse of Our Traditional Ethics, Oxford, Oxford University Press, 1995.

Sinott-Armstrong, W., *Moral Dilemmas*, Oxford, Oxford University Press, 1987.

Soble, A., *The Structure of Love*, New Haven and London, Yale University Press, 1990.

Speer, A., *Inside the Third Reich*, tr. R. and C. Winston, New York, Macmillan, 1970.

Speiser, E.A., tr. and comm., *The Anchor Bible: Genesis*, Garden City, New York, Doubleday, 1964.

Spender, S., "Double Shame," *Selected Poems*, New York, Random House, 1964.

Spicq, C., O.P., *Agape in the New Testament*, vol. I., tr. Sister M.A. McNamara, O.P., and Sister M.H. Richter, O.P., St. Louis and London, B. Herder Book Co., 1963.

Theological Lexicon of the New Testament, tr. and ed. J.D. Ernest, Peabody, MA, Hendrickson, 1994.

Spiro, M., *Culture and Human Nature*, Chicago, University of Chicago Press, 1989.

Steiner, G., "Sainte Simone – Simone Weil," *No Passion Spent: Essays 1978–1995*, New Haven and London, Yale University Press, 1996.

Stendahl, *On Love* [1822], tr. P.S. Woolf and C.N.S. Woolf, Mount Vernon, The Peter Pauper Press, n.d.

Stout, J., "Modernity Without Essence," *Soundings*, vol. 74, nos. 3–4 (Fall/ Winter 1991), 525–540.

"Moral Abominations," *Ethics After Babel: The Languages of Morals and Their Discontents*, Boston, Beacon Press, 1988.

Stump, E. and Kretzmann, N., "Eternity," *The Concept of God*, ed. T.V. Morris, Oxford, Oxford University Press, 1987.

Talbot, M., "Attachment Theory: The Ultimate Experiment," *The New York Times Magazine* (May 24, 1998).

Taylor, C., "Cross-Purposes: The Liberal-Communitarian Debate," *Liberalism and the Moral Life*, ed. N.L. Rosenblum, Cambridge, Cambridge University Press, 1989.

Philosophy and the Human Sciences: Philosophical Papers, vol. II, Cambridge,

Cambridge University Press, 1985.

Sources of the Self: The Making of the Modern Identity, Cambridge, Harvard University Press, 1989.

"What Is Human Agency?," *Human Agency and Language: Philosophical Papers*, vol. I, Cambridge, Cambridge University Press, 1985.

Thielicke, H., *Theological Ethics*, vol. I, Grand Rapids, Eerdmans, 1979.

Tilley, T., *The Evils of Theodicy*, Washington, D.C., Georgetown University Press, 1991.

Tinder, G., *Against Fate: An Essay on Personal Dignity*, Notre Dame, University of Notre Dame Press, 1981.

Tipler, F., *The Physics of Immortality: Modern Cosmology, God and the Resurrection of the Dead*, New York, Doubleday, 1994.

Unamuno, M. de, *San Manuel Bueno, Martir*, tr. M.E. Valdes, Madrid, Editorial Castalia, 1973.

Tragic Sense of Life, tr. J.E. Crawford Flitch, New York, Dover Publications, 1954.

Vacek, E.C., S.J., "Love, Christian and Diverse: A Response to Colin Grant," *Journal of Religious Ethics*, vol. 24, no. 1 (Spring 1996), 29–34.

Love, Human and Divine: The Heart of Christian Ethics, Washington, D.C., Georgetown University Press, 1994.

van Heijenoort, J., "Gödel's Theorem," *Encyclopedia of Philosophy*, vol. III, ed. P. Edwards, New York, Macmillan, 1967.

van Inwagen, P., *The Possibility of Resurrection and Other Essays in Christian Apologetics*, Boulder, Colorado, Westview Press, 1998.

Volf, M., *Exclusion and Embrace: A Theological Exploration of Identity, Otherness, and Reconciliation*, Nashville, Abingdon Press, 1996.

von Rad, G., *Genesis: A Commentary*, Philadelphia, The Westminster Press, 1972.

Wallwork, E., "Thou Shalt Love Thy Neighbor as Thyself: The Freudian Critique," *Journal of Religious Ethics*, vol. 10, no. 2 (Fall 1982), 265–319.

Walzer, M., "Emergency Ethics," The Joseph A. Reich, Sr., Distinguished Lecture on War, Morality, and the Military Profession, no. 1, Colorado, United States Air Force Academy (November 21, 1988), 1–21.

Just and Unjust Wars, New York, Basic Books, 1977.

"Political Action: The Problem of Dirty Hands," *Philosophy and Public Affairs*, vol. 2, no. 2 (Winter 1973), 160–180.

Weil, S., *Gravity and Grace*, tr. E. Craufurd, London and New York, Ark Paperbacks, 1987.

"Human Personality," *The Simone Weil Reader*, ed. G.A. Panichas, Mt. Kisco, NY, Moyer Bell Limited, 1977.

Intimations of Christianity Among the Ancient Greeks, London and New York, Ark Paperbacks, 1987.

La Pesanteur et La Grâce, Paris, Librairie Plon, 1948.

Waiting for God, tr. E. Craufurd, New York, Harper and Row, 1951.

Wells, J., *Charles Hodge's Critique of Darwinism*, Lewiston, NY, Edwin Mellen

Press, 1988.

Williams, B., *Ethics and the Limits of Philosophy*, Cambridge, Harvard University Press, 1985.

Moral Luck, Cambridge, Cambridge University Press, 1981.

Wilson, A.N., *Paul: The Mind of the Apostle*, New York, W.W. Norton, 1997.

Wolf, S., "Moral Saints," *The Journal of Philosophy*, vol. 79, no. 8 (August 1982), 419–439.

Wright, D.P., "Molech," *Harper's Bible Dictionary*, ed. P.J. Achtemeier, San Francisco, Harper and Row, 1985.

Wycliffe, J., tr., *The New Testament*, original 1380 edition, London, Pickering, 1848.

Wyschogrod, E., *Spirit in Ashes: Hegel, Heidegger, and Man-made Mass Death*, New Haven and London, Yale University Press, 1985.

Zeitlin, I.M., *Jesus and the Judaism of His Time*, Oxford, Polity Press, 1988.

Index of names

Index of subjects

abomination, the abominable, xi, 22, 35 and n4, 38, 92–128 *passim*, 155, 183, 187, 198, 202
abortion, 77, 93–94, 104
affection, 2 n2, 24, 54, 85 and n133, 190
afterlife, *see* immortality
agape, the agapic, x-xiii, 1, 2 n2, 9, 11 and ns25 and 26, 13, 15, 18 and n33, 19, 20–31, 52, 54–91 *passim*, 96–97, 117, 121, 131, 136, 138, 150, 156, 158–159, 163, 168–170, 172, 177–178, 181, 190, 193, 197 n43, 204–205, 211, 214–220, 224–225, 227, 229, 230
  as a metavalue, 20–21, 28, 205, 211
  strong, xiii, 15 n31, 20–31, 62–64, 78, 82–83, 86, 90, 104–105, 132, 142, 144, 146, 150–151, 157, 158, 163, 165, 168, 170, 174, 176, 202 n2, 205–206, 210–217, 219–220, 227–230
  three interpersonal features, 15–18, 79
  weak, 22–23
the *Akedah*, 185, 192, 197 n45, 222
altruism, 58 and n17, 122, 134, 161, 218, 219, 225
amicitia, x n2
amor, x n2, 65, 69
amor fati, 50, 59 n23, 76, 123, 163
amor sui, 9, 54, 90
anthropodicy/ies, xii, 137, 169–174 *passim*
appraisal (of worth), 61, 64–65, 135, 138 and n24, 151, 176, 212 and n22
aretology, the aretaic, 98–100, 107–108, 214
Argument from Design, 173 and n108, 206
Argument to Design, 173 and n108, 206
Arminianism, 4 n6
askesis, x, xii n4, 230
atonement, the Atonement, 4, 6, 10, 49, 51, 117, 167, 210
atheism, v, 24, 57 n10
autonomy, 22, 87–88, 94, 100, 105, 107, 110, 116 n47, 128, 144, 146, 155, 197, 206, 220
Axiological Optimism, 202–205, 209, 212, 220, 227, 229 n52

Axiological Pessimism, 203–205, 212–213, 222, 229

Babylon, 44
bestowal (of worth), 62, 64–65, 135, 138 and n24, 140, 176
Buddhism, 38 and n7

Calvary, 15, 216
care, 29 and n53, 65, 82 n120, 85, 96, 100–102, 105–108, 110–111, 113, 115, 117, 121, 122, 127, 128, 138, 151, 156, 159, 175, 183, 191 n25, 212, 217
caritas, 11 n25, 55, 61–62, 65, 68 and n62, 71, 156
certainty, certitude, x, xii, 130–133, 136, 152–153, 157, 167, 170, 172, 176, 202, 204, 215
charity, x-xii, 1 n1, 4, 5, 10, 11 and n25, 15–22, 24–31, 55, 62, 64–65, 67–69, 76, 79 n113, 83–84, 88, 116 n47, 117, 119, 121 and n54, 131–132, 140–144, 146–147, 150, 152–155, 158–161, 163, 166–167, 169, 174–176, 178, 180, 185–186, 202, 211, 212 n22, 217–220, 224, 227, 229
  putting charity first, 19, 26, 62, 65, 130, 132, 141–142, 147, 152, 154–155, 157, 159, 163, 166, 170, 174, 176, 205–206, 214, 220
comfort/s, xii, 31, 133, 137, 140, 169, 226
commandment/s, 67, 86–89, 147–148, 177–200 *passim*, 214, 222, 225–226
  the Ten Commandments (the Decalogue), 1–3, 9 n18, 12, 87, 104
  the two love commandments (of Matt. 22–37–40), 3, 8, 9 n21, 12–14, 27–28, 63–64, 88–90, 117, 127, 142, 148 and n57, 158, 166, 177–179, 194, 199, 222, 228
  Jesus's final (love) commandment, 6–7, 11 n25, 13, 55, 88–90, 169, 225, 228
compassion, 2 n2, 25, 31, 38 n7, 44, 51 n49, 53 n52, 63, 66, 144 n48, 152, 157, 163, 167, 216, 229

250

Made in the USA
Lexington, KY
15 August 2013